T.
To my best
friend from
your best friend.
May this bring you
many hours of enjoyment.
Love You,
J.

Happy
Valentine's Day
1988

R. Grinnell

For Tony Smith —

An avid angler on
the Baja scene —

With best wishes,

George Reiger

1 February 1988

PROFILES IN

Illustrated by Roy Grinnell

SALTWATER ANGLING

A History of the Sport – Its People and Places,

Tackle and Techniques

GEORGE REIGER

PRENTICE-HALL, INC.
Englewood Cliffs, N.J.

1973

ENDPAPERS
Broadbill swordfishing,
     Cape Breton, Nova Scotia.
Mike Lerner sights and fights a big one.

Books by George Reiger
ZANE GREY: OUTDOORSMAN
PROFILES IN SALTWATER ANGLING

Profiles in Saltwater Angling by George Reiger

Copyright © 1973 by Prentice-Hall, Inc.
under International and Pan-American copyright conventions.

Printed in the United States of America
Color plates printed in Japan

Prentice-Hall International, Inc., London
Prentice-Hall of Australia, Pty., Ltd., North Sydney
Prentice-Hall of Canada, Ltd., Toronto
Prentice-Hall of India Private Ltd., New Delhi
Prentice-Hall of Japan, Inc., Tokyo

Library of Congress Cataloging in Publication Data
Reiger, George.
Profiles in saltwater angling.
Bibliography
1. Salt-water fishing. I. Title.
SH457.R38   799.1'2   73–8761
ISBN: 0–13–726133–0

FOR MY FATHER

*Whose legacy includes Bimini and Brielle, Catalina
and Key Largo, Acapulco, Wedgeport, and Stuart*

AND FOR MY BROTHERS

*With whom I shared all this that was irreplaceable
and which is no more*

PREFACE

The saltwater angler is not a separate species from the freshwater fisherman. In fact, he's often one and the same man.

But if you enjoy driving to the beach in winter to watch the surf foaming endlessly up the strand; if you'd rather test your plug tackle on bluefish than black bass, or your fly gear on bonefish than brook trout; if you prefer to visit an offshore island to an inland lake for a holiday—then you, my friend, are an ocean angler.

Nothing yet caught in salt water was bred in a hatchery. And there's no way to plan or predict the outcome of any day at sea. Saltwater men rejoice in the incalculable and the fact that the world-record bluefin tuna was caught by an amateur—not by one of the legion of men who have spent fortunes pursuing the prize. And even among that legion there have been few disappointments. For all men who fish the sea have had more than their share of adventures. The ocean in its variety is comparable with life in a pond in the way that a mountain is comparable to a grain of sand.

Saltwater fishing has come a long way since *Field & Stream* felt impelled "to explain sea-coast fishing" in an 1898 editorial. Today, according to the latest U.S. Department of Interior figures, saltwater angling is one of our fastest growing outdoor sports with already over ten million participants. Though half that number fish along the Atlantic coast, a man's residence seems to have little to do with his preference or passion for the sport. Last winter in Minneapolis, I talked with a salesman at the Eddie Bauer sports store who marveled at the amount of saltwater tackle and accessories he sold—nearly as much as the main store in Seattle.

"When it gets to be minus 10°," he said, "everyone packs up for Florida, the Caribbean or Mexico, and they all want to go fishing."

Can you blame them?

Despite this tremendous growth of interest and activity, few saltwater anglers—not even those who have been fishing the sea since childhood—have a clear idea of the origins of their sport. For example, who were the pioneers? How did their tackle compare with ours today? Where were the first great fishing grounds? And how did the customs and standards of the sport develop?

That few anglers know the answers to these questions is all the more surprising when you learn that many pioneers of particular techniques, tackle, or coasts are still alive. Determined to reach as many as I could before the record of what they'd contributed was lost, I began work on this project in the spring of 1970.

Some of the grand old men of the sport I failed to reach in time. Harlan Major and Van Campen Heilner died before I could interview them, though their stories are an important part of the present volume. Others I reached just before they passed away—men like Tommy Gifford and Philip Wylie whose first-person narratives greatly enrich their chapters on the sport. Finally, I chose some younger men to fill in the gaps between *then* and *now* and to provide the reader with some prospectus for the future. The range in their talents and experience, as well as what the profiled anglers have contributed to the sport, varies enormously, but each one fits the pattern of this book the way the different pieces of a puzzle make an overall design.

The profiles are arranged in approximate chronological order and according to the type of saltwater fishing with which that man is most familiar. In all, this volume represents a review of the sport's origins in commercial fishing centuries ago, to its development in the nineteenth century because of the rise of a new leisure class devoted to science as well as sport, and finally to its flowering in this century due to new technologies which have created special areas of interest ranging from surf and bridge fishing to fly casting to the pursuit of thousand-pound gamefish off distant shores.

Many people contributed to this book, but I most especially want to single out George C. Thomas III, for his courtesy and candor, and Francesca LaMonte, whose diplomatic skills match her many qualities as a marine scientist. I would also like to thank all the anglers who took time to talk with me or write to me about their contributions. And I'm well aware that for every man herein profiled, there are literally dozens of others whose lives in angling are as worthy of mention. Finally, special thanks to artist Roy Grinnell for sharing my enthusiasm for the project; to editor Dennis Fawcett for sharing my faith; and my wife, Barbara, for sharing all the nuisance or nasty details involved in compiling such a volume.

Saltwater angling is presently at a crossroads. With more and more people coming into the sport; with more and more competition for available resources from great and growing commercial fleets; and with expanding destruction of essential marine nurseries, the saltwater sports fishermen will have a number of crises to deal with in the years ahead. One can foresee a day when all sea anglers will be required to buy licenses, and when all sea-angling clubs will play a large role in creating legislation affecting the management of marine resources. There are difficult times ahead—but also exciting ones. And it is my small hope that this volume will provide some idea of where we've been and where we are today, so that we can all more effectively contribute to the great sport of ocean angling tomorrow.

George W. Reiger
Locustville, Virginia

CONTENTS

Fishing the George's Banks

Section One

THE BEGINNINGS

ONE

COD, HADDOCK, AND EMPIRE

> Let not the meanness of the word *fish* distaste
> you, for it will afford as good gold as the mines
> of Guiana or Potosi.—Captain John Smith.

After the voyages of Columbus, the most important explorations touching the destiny of the New World were those of Cabot, Verrazano, and Cartier. John Cabot, who was probably a Genoese named Cabotto, sailed for Henry VII from Bristol in 1497. Giovanni da Verrazano was a Florentine who sailed for Francois 1er from Dieppe in 1524. And Jacques Cartier was a Breton sailing from Saint-Malo in 1534. Their reports of America—particularly the forests, furs, and fisheries—spread through France and England, preparing the ground for empire.

While Spanish adventurers searched far inland for cities of gold, their more practical French and English adversaries settled along the northern coasts to tap the riches of the rivers, bays, and the Continental Shelf. Fishing boats from Brittany and Normandy began working present-day Canadian waters as early as 1504—just twelve years after Columbus's first voyage—and the cape called Breton is probably the oldest European name north of the West Indies.

[2]

The English were slow to join this fishery since they had been long accustomed to finding all the cod and haddock they required in the waters around Iceland. But in 1517, the first English vessel joined the French and Portuguese[1] fleets on the Grand Banks. In 1548, Parliament, determined to protect her nascent New World fishery, passed a law prohibiting admirals of warships from making exactions in fish or money from English fishermen "going on service" of fishing off Newfoundland. Later, when the Church of England offered no particular guidance concerning food for fast days, Parliament again acted to prohibit meat in order to encourage the capture and sale of fish.

In 1578, the French had some 150 boats working Canadian waters, while the English still had only 15. But by 1615, the English fleet had grown to 250 vessels.[2] About this same time, Captain John Smith advised his countrymen in *Description of New England*[3] (1616) that "he is a very bad fisher[man] [who] cannot kill in one day with his hook and line one, two, or three hundred cods, which dressed and dried, if they be sold there [America] for ten shilling a hundred, though in England they will give more than twenty."

If a man works but three days in seven he may get more than he can spend unless he will be exceedingly excessive. Now that carpenter, not make this a pretty recreation, though they fish but an hour in a day, to take more than they can eat in a week; or if they will not eat mason, gardener, tailor, smith, sailor, forger, or what other, may they it, because there is so much better choice, yet sell it or [ex]change it with the fishermen or merchants for anything you want; and what sport doth yield a more pleasing content, and less hurt and charge than angling with a hook, and crossing the sweet air from isle to isle, over the silent streams of a calm sea; wherein the most curious may find profit, pleasure and content.[4]

---

[1]No one knows how long the Portuguese have been fishing the Grand Banks. However, there are tantalizing historical hints that suggest Basque and Portuguese fishing boats were visiting the New World long before Columbus's first voyage west.

[2]Taking a page from British history, the Soviet fishing fleets, with government support and guidance, have come to dominate the world's seas in the past two decades. The Russians seem to appreciate the fact that empires are more solidly built on the humble deeds of anonymous men in foul-weather gear than by the courageous rhetoric of generals and presidents.

[3]Among his many contributions, Captain Smith was the first writer to describe the region between the St. Lawrence River and the mid-Atlantic as "New England."

[4]*Captain John Smith's America, Selections from His Writings*, edited by John Lankford, New York, 1967, page 142.

When John Smith first came to America, the striped bass must have been at one of their cyclic peaks (either that, or Smith's imagination was), for listen to this description of the abundance of the fish from Smith's *New England's Trials:*

The Basse is an excellent Fish, both fresh and salte, one hundred wherof salted (at market) have yielded 5 pounds [value.] They are so large, the head of one will give a good eater a dinner, and for daintinesse of diet they excell the Marybones of Beefe. There such multitudes that I have seene stopped into the river close adjoining to my house with a sande [bar] at one tide so many as will loade a ship of 100 tonnes. I myself, at the turning of the tyde have seene such multitudes passe out of a pounde that it seemed to me that one mighte go over their backs drishod.

Another relevant anecdote of the time is told by William Bradford, Pilgrim Father and five-term governor of Plymouth Colony. In his "Briefe Narration," Bradford writes that when the delegation from the congregation at Leyden waited upon King James to beg that they might be permitted to enjoy liberty of conscience under his protection in America, they promised that they would endeavor the advancement of his Majesty's dominions by all due means:

"This," His Majesty said, "was a good and honest motion"; and, asking what profits might arise from the part we intended (for our eye was upon the most northern parts of Virginia), 'twas answered, "Fishing."
To which he replied, with his ordinary asseveration, "So God have my soul, 'tis an honest trade; 'twas the Apostle's own calling!"

And so colonists fanned out from Roanoke to Cape Race to harvest the riches of the sea.
We have no detailed contemporary record of what the early commercial fishery was like, but in 1865, Mr. J. C. Wilcocks of Guernsey published *The Sea Fisherman*, which includes a description of cod fishing off Newfoundland that cannot be so very different from what it was two and a half centuries before:

The Great Bank of Newfoundland is an extensive shoal lying to the south-east of the island, measuring upwards of three hundred and thirty miles in length, and about seventy-five in width, the water varying in depth from sixteen to sixty fathoms.

[4]

The season for the fishery commences about May, and continues till August for exportation, but by the inhabitants is continued into September. Each vessel, as she arrives at the island, takes her station opposite any unoccupied part of the beach which may afford a convenient situation for the curing of the fish. The first proceeding is to unrig and take down the upper masts, &c., of the vessel, and to erect or prepare the stage on shore. This is a covered platform projecting over the water, strongly built, and guarded with piles to prevent injury from the boats. On the stage is a large firm table, on which all the processes to be hereafter described are performed.

Near the shore the fishing is carried on in boats about eighteen feet keel, in the offing by large boats and on the Great Bank itself in schooners with a crew in proportion to the size of the craft.

Sometimes the crew consists of females or boys only, provided they are strong enough to handle the line. Each person manages two, and each line carries two hooks; so that if there are four men in the boat, which is usually the case, there are sixteen baits out. The bait consists of Herrings, Capelin, Squid, Mackerel or Launce. Good hands will take from three to four hundred fish in a day; but it is severe labour, from the weight of the fish and the extreme cold felt in such an exposed situation during easterly winds; in fine weather with the wind between S. and W., the temperature is agreeable.

The boats take their station on the edge of the shoal, and the lines being baited, are thrown out. When a sufficient load has been taken, it is carried to the stage, for if the fish were kept too long unopened, it would be materially injured.

Next we find that the assembly-line concept (or, in this case, "disassembly line") is a few hundred years older than Henry Ford:

Each fish is taken by a man standing on one side of the table, who cuts its throat with a knife. He then pushes it to a second on his right hand called the *header*; this person, taking the fish in his left hand, draws the liver out, which he throws through one hole into a cask under the table, and the intestines through another which is over the sea, into which they drop. He next separates the head, by placing the fish against the edge of the table, which is constructed curved and sharp at this part for the purpose; and pressing on the head with the left hand, he with a violent and sudden wrench, detaches the body, which by the action is pushed to a third man opposite to him, the head falling through an opening in the stage into the water. The man who performs this feat sits in a chair with a stout back to enable him to use the necessary force; and his left hand is guarded with a strong leathern glove to give him a better hold.

[5]

The *splitter* cuts the body open from the neck downwards with rapidity, but with a skill acquired by practice; the value of the body depending on its being done in a particular way. The soundbone is detached by the process, and is suffered to fall also into the sea, unless the sounds[5] and tongues are intended to be saved for use, in which case the requisite number of them and of the heads are thrown aside, and removed, so as to offer no interruption of the main business.

When the barrow into which the split bodies are thrown is full, it is removed to the *salter* at the further end of the stage, who piles the fish in layers, spreading on each as he takes it out, a proper quantity of salt which must be apportioned with accuracy and judgement; a deficiency or excess of it at this part of the process being deterimental to the proper curing.

After further details on the curing of salt-dried cod, the author observes:

The whole coasts of Labrador and Nova Scotia, as well as Newfoundland, are the scene of these fisheries. Twenty thousand British subjects are annually employed, with from two to three hundred schooners on the Labrador stations.

But he ominously adds:

Cod formerly here abounded in such countless numbers that it seemed impossible any diminution in the supply should ever arise; frequent complaints have, however, of late years been heard of the deterioration of this important fishery.[6]

In 1670, America's first free public school system was initiated at Plymouth with proceeds derived from the fishing industry. By the time of the American Revolution, the cod fishery of Massachusetts alone employed more than 4,000 seamen and some 28,000 tons of shipping with an annual worth of more than one million dollars— a considerable sum for those days.

Several statutes had been passed in the seventeenth century in Massachusetts and New Hampshire to protect this most important industry. However, the regulations were designed less to protect the fish in order to guarantee a sustained yield than to control the fisheries'

---

[5]The air bladder which yields a high-quality gelatin (isinglass) used in making glue and jelly and as a thickening agent in cooking.

[6]*The Sea-Fisherman, or Fishing Pilotage*, J. C. Wilcocks, Guernsey, Great Britain, 1865, pages 182–185.

[6]

trade and protect the reputations of the colonies marketing the fish.

For example, one Massachusetts statute of 1668 specified that no cod could be killed or dried for sale in December or January; another that no mackerel could be caught before June 1 except for barter while fresh. While these articles may have inadvertently given the great school fishes some respite during a part of the year, and even protected certain species during their spawning periods, the laws were originally enacted because it was believed that roe-laden fish were inferior items of trade that would ruin the fame and value of salt-fish barrels bearing the seal of Massachusetts.[7]

Cod was still king—with haddock, herring, mackerel, and other school fishes acting the part of his finny retinue. All species were so plentiful that many fishermen believed the seas were not only inexhaustible but that they were carrying on God's work in extracting sufficient tons of these fishes so the world would not be overwhelmed by their numbers! Had you suggested to sailors of the seventeenth century that by the third quarter of the twentieth century, cod stocks would be everywhere depleted, and that the common haddock and herring would be in danger of commercial extermination, they would have thought you mad. It was inconceivable that fishing could ever reduce the vast schools found everywhere in the western Atlantic.

Sturgeon swarmed in all the coastal rivers and were taken in particular abundance from the tributaries of the Chesapeake Bay. Captain John Smith claimed to have taken 52 sturgeon in a net on one occasion and 62 another time. He noted: "We had more Sturgeon, then [sic] could be devoured by Dog or Man." Even as late as 1760,[8] the Reverend Andrew Burnaby observed of the Chesapeake that "sturgeon and shad are in such prodigious numbers that one day, within the space of two miles only, some gentlemen in canoes caught above 600 of the former with hooks which they let down to bottom, and drew up at a venture when they perceived them to rub against a fish; and of the latter above 5,000 have been caught at one single haul of the seine." Despite their bottom-grubbing existence, sturgeon can be wonderful jumpers, and in 1833, Dr. Jerome V. C. Smith reports that sturgeon, six to nine feet in length, were frequently seen leaping during the summertime in Boston harbor. Today, except for a remnant popu-

---

[7]From the testimony of Elihu Root, U. S. Counsel to the *Atlantic Fisheries Arbitration* (JX 238.N69, 1917), page 168.

[8]*Travels Through the Middle Settlements in North America, in the Years of 1759 and 1760, With Observations Upon the State of the Colonies* by Andrew Burnaby, London, 1775; reprinted New York, 1970.

lation in the Hudson River, we do not hear much of sturgeon along the Atlantic seaboard.

Despite extensive damming of their spawning rivers, salmon still ran up many New England streams in the early 1800's. The Connecticut had an especially large run—so large, in fact, that when farmers went to the river to buy shad, they were required to take an equal number of salmon in the bargain.

Catches of herring, menhaden,[9] and mackerel were so great that countless tons were plowed into fields for fertilizer, burned for fuel, or fed to livestock. The cattle at Provincetown, Massachusetts, were fed with fish to the point—according to the *Barnstable Journal* of February 7, 1833—that when they were given a choice between fish or grain, the cattle invariably chose the former:

We have seen the cows at that place boldly enter the surf, in pursuit of the offals thrown from the fish boats on the shore, and when obtained, masticate and swallow every part except the hardest bones. A Provincetown cow will dissect the head of a cod with wonderful celerity. She places one foot upon a part of it, and with her teeth tears off the skin and gristly parts, and in a few moments nothing is left but the bones.

Today, processed menhaden feed millions of broiler chickens every year, but herring, mackerel, and cod are becoming too precious to use for feed, fuel, or fertilizer.

The examples of then and now are legion: Flounders—both winter and summer varieties—are currently one of our most important food and sportfishes.[10] Yet in the early days of this nation's history, flounders were primarily sought as easily acquired bait for lobster traps, being speared in the shallows during low tide or at night with lights.

---

[9]This fish is also known as the "mossbunker" or "pogy." The latter nickname is not to confuse the species with the porgy or scup of the genus *Stenotomus*. Both "scup" and "porgy" derive from the Narragansett Indian name for this fish: *mishcuppauog*. The Indians also called menhaden, *poghaden* (both names meaning "fertilizer")—or "pogy" for short when the colonists adopted the word. Ichthyologist George Brown Goode sought to alleviate this confusion in the nineteenth century by insisting that the porgy be called *scuppaug* and the *menhaden*, just that. Unfortunately, his appeal fell on ears too used to old ways.

[10]In 1965, a survey of 256,000 sport fishermen indicated that summer flounder, also called fluke, was the tenth most frequently caught fish along the mid-Atlantic coast. Unfortunately, since the onslaught of foreign trawler fleets in the late 1960's, this figure has plummeted and countless boat liverymen, bait dealers, and others who once depended on this fish for their livelihoods from Long Island to the Carolinas now pump gas or sell shoes in shopping centers.

COD, HADDOCK, AND EMPIRE

Lobsters themselves were so common that they often served as cod bait when squid or herring were unavailable.

And, except for an occasional harpooning—sometimes as much out of curiosity as commercial interest—the great tunas and swordfish wandered unmolested up and down the Atlantic seaboard. Few people saw any reason to risk their necks pursuing such giant fish when there were many more easily caught, and presumably better eating, fishes to be taken by the bushel inshore with multi-hooked handlines.

Incredibly enough, one of the first Americans we know of to take exception to the rule that saltwater fishing meant commercial fishing was none other than George Washington, father of our country and sleeper in countless beds. Records indicate that early in the last decade of the eighteenth century, President Washington and a party of fellow anglers chartered a boat to take them from Long Island to Sandy Hook, presumably for some bottom bouncing with handlines. The source for this interesting story goes on to suggest: "Undoubtedly party-boat fishing had its early beginnings in the discovery by some commercial fishermen that money could be realized at times by taking out persons to enjoy the sport of angling."[11]

The first American saltwater angler to write about his sport was a far less renown figure than Washington—but still interesting. Jerome V. C. Smith was a medical doctor and amateur naturalist who lived for several years in the early 1800's on a small island in Boston harbor and caught occasional striped bass while fly casting for sea-run brook trout off Poket Point. He even once conjectured that Atlantic mackerel might be fair sport on fly tackle:

We actually wonder that the worshippers at the shrine of honest Izaak Walton, who cannot angle for trout in the ocean, do not turn their attention to mackerel chases in our beautiful harbors.

But saltwater fishing still meant commercial fishing to most people, and few sportsmen thought to try their techniques and tackle in the sea. Some thought that the fish were too strong or that their tackle was too delicate to withstand the corrosive effects of the ocean. But most sportsmen in this period held that the only true angling was cast-

---

[11]"The Recreation Fisheries," by Dr. James R. Westman, *A Biological Survey of the Salt Waters of Long Island*, 1938, Part I, New York State Conservation Department, Supplemental to Twenty-eighth Annual Report, 1938; Albany, N. Y. 1939.

Another saltwater fishing adventure of President Washington's—this time off Portsmouth, N. H., for cod—is described in Charles Goodspeed's *Angling in America*, Boston, 1939, page 337.

ing flies over fresh water for trout or trolling baits for pike and pickerel.

Even the thoughtful Dr. Smith was basically a freshwater man, and he devotes all of his "Practical Essay on Angling" from *Natural History of the Fishes of Massachusetts* (1833)[12] to descriptions of trout and salmon fishing in New England and Canada. Saltwater fishing went begging at the doctor's doorstep because it was still too closely associated with commerce and industry. Angling, after all, had been established as recreation from the ordinary labors of life. And if the leisured classes of Britain in the 150 years since Walton had managed to lace the sport with custom and tradition, the newly rich and independent Americans seemed determined to gild it with ritual. Most American anglers never thought to cast flies over schools of breaking mackerel because the Supreme Angler, Walton, had never done it. Thus, while striped bass, bluefish, weakfish, and a dozen other varieties of gamefish swarmed in their front yards, the merchants of Boston and the bankers of New York packed their fishing tackle for the long and difficult journeys to Sebago Lake or the St. Lawrence River.

It finally took an English aristocrat to persuade American anglers to try the bays and ocean. Perhaps, with quality as a birthright, he had less to prove than the "nouveaux amateurs de sport" of New York and Boston and was therefore able to view American angling opportunities with a fresh eye. Whatever the reason, saltwater angling in America really begins with the writings of Henry William Herbert.

----

[12]Earlier in the 1810's and 1820's, Governor DeWitt Clinton and Dr. Samuel Latham Mitchill assembled information for a "Natural History of the Fishes of New York State" and presented the material to the Literary and Philosophical Society of the City of New York. While there is little reference to saltwater angling in this collection, it was here Governor Clinton suggested that *basse* derives from the Dutch word for *perch*. Hence, the striped bass was known for a number of years as the sea perch, rock perch, or rock fish (which it is still called in the South), and the fish was classified in the *Perca* genus. This collection also occasioned some little controversy when Dr. Mitchill named the striper for himself. He created a new genus *Roccus* (and then later changed it back to *Perca* to conform with Clinton's findings), and Dr. Smith in Massachusetts argued that Mitchill had neither the right to invent a genus nor to name the fish for himself.

"By what authority," writes Smith, "Dr. Mitchill gave his own name to the striped bass, *Perca mitchilli*, we cannot divine: he might with equal propriety have tacked his name to the white shark, or to the bones of the Mastodon, and the last would have savored less of vanity, than affixing his cognomen to a common table fish, known from time immemorial all over Europe."

Of course, Dr. Smith is wrong about the striper being common to Europe. But the controversy surrounding the fish's name still continues. Even within the last decade, we have seen its classification altered from *Roccus saxatilis* to *Morone saxatilis*. So much for the definitiveness of scientific classifications!

TWO

THE OUTSIDER

> As no man is born an artist,
> So no man is born an angler.—Izaak Walton

The angler who first describes a different type of tackle or a new casting technique is frequently assumed to have invented that technique or tackle. Yet he may only have been following in the footsteps of others.

Ernest Hemingway wrote a book about Bimini, and, to the public at large, he's the man most associated with that island's early angling history. But charter skipper Bill Fagen first told Hemingway about Bimini, and Fagen first heard about the fabulous fishing around the island through another charter guide, Charlie Thompson.[1] But just who told Thompson has been forgotten.

---

[1]Captain Charles Thompson led a National Geographic expedition to the Bahamas just after World War I. It culminated with the expedition leader, John Oliver La Gorce, harpooning a huge manta ray some 22 feet wide off Bimini harbor on February 14, 1919. Incidentally, this Charles Thompson is *not* Ernest Hemingway's close hunting and fishing friend of the same name, whose family ran a fishhouse, cigarbox factory, ship's chandlery, icehouse, and hardware store and tackle shop in Key West.

[11]

Yet what does it matter? Just so long as somebody took the time to tell us.

And so it is with the very beginning of saltwater angling in America. We have three names. One, the man who first described our sport and gave it respectability by linking it with the already respectable pastimes of trout and salmon fishing; and the other two, men who taught the former what he knew about fish and fishing.

Henry William Herbert did not write much about saltwater angling, but that he wrote at all is due largely to the interest and efforts of his lawyer, Philo T. Ruggles, and a servant, Charlie Holt.

The story of H. W. Herbert, alias Frank Forester, English remittance man and America's first great outdoor writer, is a book unto itself. And 40 years ago, a biography did appear with the appropriate subtitle "A Tragedy in Exile."[2] Few men who fished or hunted with Herbert knew the reasons for his coming to the United States in 1831. Perhaps even his two closest friends here, Philo Ruggles and Anson Livingston—both of whom later acted as officers for the modest trust established by Herbert's father—never knew the entire story of the young man's precipitous flight from England. Certainly neither they nor anyone else has left us with a clue to the scandal that drove Herbert abroad and which kept him here until his suicide 27 years later.

Henry William Herbert was born in London on April 7, 1807. His father was the Honorable William Herbert, Doctor of Laws, Member of Parliament, and third son of Henry Herbert, Lord Portchester, and first Earl of Carnarvon. His mother was Letitia Emily Dorothea, second daughter of Joshua, Fifth Viscount Allen.

Years later, after a day of trolling for bluefish in New York harbor, or drifting for weakfish in Newark Bay, when young Herbert and his angling colleagues retired to Manhattan's Washington Post Tavern for refreshment, his companions would sometimes wink and smile behind Herbert's back as he compared the outdoor sports of an English aristocrat with those available to the average American. Yet Herbert's claims to intimacy with the British gentry were entirely genuine.

Herbert's father was something of a renegade—although with far more orthodox results than his son. About the time Henry William was born, the father abandoned a successful political career to begin study for the ministry. Of course, this was a less remarkable step in a time

---

[2] *Frank Forester: A Tragedy in Exile*, William Southworth Hunt, Newark, N. J., 1933.

when Church and State were complementary faces of the same Establishment coin. However, Herbert's father pursued his contemplative career as earnestly as he had his political one, and the fact that his family arranged for him upon his ordination to have the lucrative parish of Spofforth in the West Riding district of Yorkshire only made his linguistic and literary pursuits a mite more comfortable. With an annual income equivalent to better than $50,000 (and this at 1814 prices), the Reverend Doctor William Herbert had sufficient funds to dig the ponds and build the greenhouses he needed for his other hobby: botany.

It is a small irony of the Herbert dynasty that a son, bred to prolong the family's immortality, created immortality for the pseudonym "Frank Forester," while the father, educated to politics, achieved his immortality in a book he never saw. William Herbert died before Charles Darwin published *On the Origin of Species*, in which he respectfully cites the Reverend Doctor's achievements in botany. And two plant species, *herberta* and *herbertia*, are named for him.

Young Herbert loved Spofforth, and that was where he spent much of his vacation time from Eton and Cambridge, learning the ways of guns, dogs, and horses. He knew something of fishing, too, but apparently did little before coming to America. It must have been incredibly bitter for both father and son that the son, less than a year after graduating Cambridge with his Bachelor of Arts degree, should have to flee to the cultural backwaters of New York City with the possibility of never seeing home again.[3] Whatever the reason Henry William Herbert left England, he arrived a young man in a young country to play the remarkable role of being that nation's first sporting conscience and historian.

Romantics portray the antebellum South as a land of pastoral moods and idyllic landscapes. The North is rarely considered in storybook retrospects of how pleasant American life must have been before the Civil War. Perhaps it is difficult to imagine much of the Northeast in terms of pastoral settings, for the penalties of industrialism have been every bit as disastrous and far more permanent than the ravages of war.

---

[3]Debt was the ostensible cause of Herbert's exile, but since we know that his father paid off the boy's obligations (amounting to some $7,500) within the first year of his going overseas, the evidence rather suggests that Henry William was guilty of breaking some incredibly rigid social taboo. This idea is reinforced when we consider that his father later established a trust for him while still refusing to let him return home.

[13]

Although men who respect power will insist that New York and New Jersey prevailed over the Carolinas in the War Between the States, a casual comparison of these two regions today gives the thoughtful observer the distinct impression that the South may have won out in the long run. To read Henry William Herbert's descriptions of the wilds of Nassau County, Long Island, or the tranquility of Essex County, New Jersey, makes the sensitive reader who values environment as much as income weep for this region today.

Even Manhattan Island was a not unpleasant setting for men who valued the outdoors. With a bustling population of 200,000 located at the isle's lower end, most New Yorkers thought they had gone about as far as they could go in development of their city. A man with a day off could wander up to the open country of what is now the East 30's and enjoy the good food and wine of Cato Alexander's roadhouse located at a turning in the Boston Post Road.[4] There, on weekends, horse races were held on a mile-long track paralleling the highway.

A little further north, fishermen could cast from shore into the swarming schools of white perch found in the Harlem River throughout the spring and summer,[5] or they could rent boats for trolling at Hell Gate, where striped bass of forty and fifty pounds were regularly taken on natural squid baits, or on tin and pewter facsimiles. If an angler did not have the whole day off, plentiful supplies of squeteague

---

[4]This thoroughfare was later converted to Third Avenue. Many streets in New York City have pleasant associations with outdoor sport, even though it may be difficult for today's reader—used to contemporary Manhattan—to believe them. In Fred Mather's *Men I Have Fished With* (New York, 1897), the author recalls a conversation with President Chester A. Arthur (1830–1886) about the fine woodcock shooting Arthur had before the Civil War in a covert at the present corner of Fifth Avenue and 23rd Street. Another friend of Mather's, Polish immigrant Baron Berthold Fernow, who served as a Major in the Union Army, wrote Mather toward the end of the last century that: "I am now living at 151 West 61st Street ... a place where I used to shoot rabbits when I first came to America, and where I once got lost in the underbrush and strayed off to the northeast, where the Astoria ferry now is." Fred Mather sums up these contrasts between the Manhattan that was and New York City in the 1890's: "As a historian, in a feeble way I record it. As an American and a naturalist, I regret it." (page 318)

[5]As late as the 1880's, the Harlem River was still considered countryside, being far north of the crowded areas of Manhattan Island. In his autobiography, financier Bernard Baruch reminisced about his childhood summers spent in New York, and among other pleasant memories was this one: "For fifty cents we could hire a flat-bottomed boat, ideal for getting up the shallow creeks and salt marshes of the Harlem River, which then were thick with soft-shelled crabs." *Baruch, My Own Story*, New York, 1957, page 45.

[14]

(weakfish)[6] or barb (king whiting) were found in the lower harbor. And sheepshead, for which a bay in Brooklyn was named, was still the preeminent food and game fish of Manhattan Island.

Even party boat fishing in the last century off New York had a flavor and character utterly missing in today's Sheepshead Bay runs to the sea bass and porgy grounds. Here's John J. Brown's description from *The American Angler's Guide* of "sea-basse" and "porgee" outings 130 years ago:

These are both sea fish, and abound in immense quantities in the ocean outside of Sandy Hook, New-York [*sic*], on what are called the Sea-Basse and Porgee Banks. In the summer months, to the pent-up citizen who is obliged to stay in the city during the sweltering heat of July and August—the stranger who would view the beauties of one of the finest harbors in the world—and to the more scientific angler, who, after a season's fishing at the gently gliding stream, or the romantic mountain lake, would like to try the more bracing atmosphere of the ocean—this mode of angling will often afford a day of amusement and gratification.

During the above-mentioned months, steamboats are prepared and fitted up for this species of fishing, and make their trips sometimes daily, returning, often, with well-satisfied amateur ocean anglers, each with their string of fish. In the summer of 1843 [for example], immense quantities were taken—the steamboat often returning with from six to ten thousand porgees, and a porpoise weighing five or six-hundred pounds. In order to enliven the scene on these occasions, a band of music is taken, and cotillion parties are made up on the upper deck. A skilful harpooner sometimes makes one of the party, and gives excitement to the scene by striking and taking a porpoise. The boat touches at Coney Island, giving the passengers an opportunity of a sea bathe and a clam bake; and also at Fort Hamilton, allowing an opportunity to view the fortification of the harbor [pages 214–215, 1849 edition].

---

[6]The origin of the popular name "weakfish" for *Cynoscion regalis* has puzzled more than one generation of saltwater anglers along the mid-Atlantic coast. Supposedly, the name refers to the fish's fragile jaws through which the angler's hook will tear if the fisherman tries to rush his catch. However, John J. Brown, a tackle dealer and outdoor writer of the last century, suggested that "weakfish" was actually a corruption of "wheatfish," referring to the harvest months when this species is in greatest supply. Still another possibility exists in George Brown Goode's premise that since the Dutch called the species *weekvis*, "weakfish" is merely a corrupt form of this word from the days when New York City was still New Amsterdam.

Describing the milieu of mid-nineteenth-century Manhattan, George Bird Grinnell, future editor and owner of *Forest and Stream,* wrote that "New York at that time was not unlike a big country town; people lived simply and without pretense or airs."

In fact, in those days, which now seem so long ago, a very considerable proportion of the men of any class in New York knew most of the other men in their class. All the dry goods merchants knew all the other dry goods merchants; all the businessmen downtown were likely to have their watches cleaned, set, and regulated by some particular man who had been long established in business.[7]

Although Herbert arrived in the New World as an exile, letters of introduction from his father quickly provided him with a number of significant acquaintances. Foremost among them was Anson Livingston, son of Brockholst Livingston of the U. S. Supreme Court, and grandson of William Livingston, first governor of New Jersey under the 1776 Constitution. A mutual respect for antecedents and education, as well as a shared enthusiasm for the outdoors, were the bases for Herbert's and Livingston's camaraderie. In fact, not three months after Herbert's arrival in America in 1831, Livingston had him off on a hunting and fishing expedition to Warwick, New York, in Orange County. Livingston later became "The Commodore" or "A——" in the Frank Forester stories.

Another good friend was Philo Ruggles, a lawyer who later became a judge, and then, with Livingston, a trustee in the peculiar estate created by Herbert's father for his son. Ruggles' first love was fishing, and much of what Herbert knew about the sport, he learned from his counselor. Indeed, Ruggles instilled such respect for fly tackle in Herbert that when the latter first began saltwater angling, he used the fly wherever possible.

Since fly fishing is in current and growing vogue among saltwater anglers, many modern fishermen find it hard to believe that there were anglers who shared this enthusiasm a century and a quarter ago. However, more than a decade before the outbreak of the Civil War, Frank Forester was advising his readers that "with the sole exception of Salmon fishing, this [striped bass fishing] is the finest of the seaboard varieties of piscatorial sport. . . . The fly will take them brilliantly, and

[7]*The Passing of the Great West; Selected Papers of George Bird Grinnell,* edited by John F. Reiger, New York, 1972, page 12.

at the end of three hundred yards of Salmon-line, a twelve-pound Bass will be found quite sufficient to keep even the most skilful angler's hands as full as he can possibly desire."[8]

To his contemporary American readers, Herbert was something of a revolutionary in suggesting that a given fish species might have some value other than food or fertilizer. He raised eyebrows by suggesting that herring were a fine gamefish simply because they could be taken on fly tackle, as he had many times done, using "a gaudy peacock tail fly, in New York harbour, in the vicinity of Fort Diamond."[9] He also called for a more sportsmanlike pursuit of shad, another great fly-taking fish, that was more often netted commercially than fished for with rod and reel:

From personal experience and success, I can assure the fly-fisher that he will find much sport in fishing for the Shad during his upward run in the Spring, with a powerful Trout-rod, a long line, and such flies as he will procure in perfection at Conroy's in Fulton-street, New York.[10]

In addition to upsetting the assumption that saltwater fly fishing is of comparatively recent vintage, a thoughtful reading of Herbert's writings suggests that the story about Julio Buel inventing the spoon lure in 1834—when he dropped a spoon from his lunch box into a Vermont lake and saw it attacked by fish—is more of a pleasant legend than bona fide history. In an essay composed about mid-century for the first edition of *Fishing with Hook and Line*, Henry William Herbert refers to the "common pewter spoon" used by "down-east fishermen"[11] to catch bluefish. If the spoon was invented after Herbert's arrival in

---

[8]*Frank Forester's Fish and Fishing of the United States and British Provinces of North America*, Henry William Herbert, London, 1849, page 391. The text continues: "The fly to be used is any of the large Salmon flies, the larger and gaudier the better. None is more taking than an orange body with peacock and bluejay wings and black hackle legs; but any of the well-known Salmon flies will secure him, as will the scarlet bodied fly with scarlet ibis and silver pheasant wings, which is so killing to the Black Bass of the lakes."

[9]*Ibid.*, page 25. In the third, revised edition of this work (page 178), Herbert added that the best fly for herring has a "scarlet chenil body" and is fished "with a single BB shot attached to the gut an inch or two above the fly, so as to troll with it, as it were, slightly sunken below the surface."

[10]*Ibid.*, Third Edition, page 181.

[11]*Fishing with Hook and Line: A Manual for Amateur Anglers, Containing also Descriptions of Popular Fishes, and Their Habits, Preparation of Baits, etc.*, Frank Forester, page 48.

America and was, therefore, something of a novelty when he began his outdoor writing, you would think that Herbert would have made more of it than this casual reference as just another lure—and "common" at that.

As for the sport of bluefishing itself, listen to this enthusiastic commentary, seasoned with sound angling advice, of 125 years ago. Except for the exchange of motors for sail, and rods for handlines, this description could be of a family outing today.

Sail for him in a large cat-rigged boat, and the fresher the breeze, and the brisker the sea, the better. In large schulls [sic] he swims near the surface, leaping at every living thing which crosses his track of devastation.

When you have the luck to strike a schull, stick to it perseveringly, crossing it tack and tack, as fast as you can go about in the direction of its course; and if the gods of the deep look with benignance on your labors, you shall kill a hundred at the least in a tide.

Thus fish for him: To a stout cotton line of a hundred yards, affix a squid of bright tin, or bone,[12] armed with a good-sized Kirby hook, with a strong gimp hook-link [leader]. Make fast the end of your line to a cleet [sic] in the stern of the boat, then whirl out the squid to the whole length of your line, and play it with both hands alternately. The fish will strike itself, and is hauled in with a regular even pull, never jerked, nor yet slacked for an instant, for if it be, the fish will disengage himself almost certainly.

When you tack your boat, if the water be shoal, haul in your line, else shall you foul it in the sea-weeds.

When you have hooked your fish, raise your squid with the hook uppermost, and a slight shake shall cast him into the bottom of the boat. [Most early jigs were barbless, or nearly so.]

Babylon, Islip, and Quogue, on Long Island, in Fire Island inlet, and Pine inlet, Shrewsbury, Squam-Beach, and Barnegat, in New Jersey, the estuaries of the rivers in Connecticut, and the tideways in Boston harbor, are all favorite grounds for Blue-Fishing.

To conclude: There is not pleasanter summer day's amusement than a merry cruise after the Blue-Fish, no pleasanter close to it than the clam-bake, the chowder, and the broiled Blue-Fish, lubricated with champagne, learnedly *frappe*, and temperately taken, no unpleasant

---

[12]According to John J. Brown's edition (1845) of *The American Angler's Guide*, artificial squids were also made of pearl, ivory, pewter, and lead. Incidentally, Brown's influence on Herbert has never been fully documented. We do know, however, that Herbert was not adverse to lifting material from Brown when it suited his purpose!

medicine. What adds most to the zest of such a day, is the presence of the charming sex, this being one of the few sports of field or flood in which they can femininely, and therefore fittingly, participate. For the rest, you may take Blue-Fish, say the philosophers, of thirty pounds weight, though I doubt it.[13] Of four and five pounds you shall catch him surely; if of eight, rejoice; if often sing paeons [sic],—for that is a triumph.[14]

Although Herbert arrived in New York with a few hundred dollars in his pocket, he quickly spent that on his first Warwick trip and an expedition that fall to Canada. Throughout his life, Herbert spent money as quickly as he earned it, but in the winter of 1831, he first needed to make it to spend. Returning to Manhattan, he took a job teaching Greek and Latin in the Reverend R. Townsend Huddart's Classical Institute located just off Bowling Green. He worked there eight years before his many publishing activities enabled him to quit teaching in order to give full attention to writing.

That he wrote at all is, perhaps, due to another teacher at the Reverend Huddart's school—an immigrant Scot by the name of Andrew D. Patterson. Patterson taught English but added to his meager salary by contributing articles to a variety of newspapers and magazines. The advent of the steam-powered press and new techniques for producing cheaper paper combined to create the world's first publishing boom. For the first time in history, it was less of a problem for an aspirant writer to get something published than for publishers to keep enough material coming to satisfy the appetites of the reading public. Herbert saw the relative ease with which Patterson picked up a dollar here, a few dollars there, and he decided to do the same.

---

[13]In January 1972, the fabled 30-pound barrier was finally broken with a bluefish nearly 32 pounds in weight taken by a sports angler trolling in Hatteras Inlet, North Carolina. Previous records had always been well below 25 pounds.

[14]*Frank Forester's Fish and Fishing*, Third Edition, pages 320–321. Commercial fishermen also used the catboat to good advantage to take blues. In 1845, George Brown Goode was cruising aboard the U. S. Fish Commission yacht *Mollie* at Martha's Vineyard where he made the following observation: "Off Cape Poge we noticed at least 30 cat-boats trailing [the original word for *trolling*] for Bluefish. These boats were about 20 feet in length, sharp-sterned and well-housed over. Each carried three lines, one at the stern and two at the end of large rods projecting over each quarter. When we anchored at dusk in Edgartown harbor, these boats were coming in, dropping alongside of a New York market boat, which lay at the wharf. The bright lantern under the deck awning, the black forms of the fishermen, the busy changing of the little sails, the eager voices of bargaining, gave an impression of brisk trade. The same scene is repeated day after day, from July to October, in scores of New England seaport towns."

[19]

Most of Herbert's efforts were elaborate stories and novels about such historical figures as England's Cromwell and Rome's Catiline. Herbert found the work stimulating as well as remunerative, and in March 1833, he and Patterson founded *The American Monthly Magazine*. Patterson stayed with the effort but a year, and Herbert sold his own interest in the magazine to Park Benjamin the year following Patterson's departure, but the creation of *The American Monthly* served to acquaint Herbert with many more of the personalities and possibilities of American publishing than had he remained merely a freelancer throughout his life. His sales increased tremendously, and although his contemporary, Edgar Allan Poe, once remarked that Herbert "has written more trash than any man living with the exception of Fay,"[15] Herbert nurtured hopes that his American literary fame might provide him with a new reputation in England—one that would eventually enable him to return home.

However, Henry William's everlasting need for money forced him to tap the unprestigious, but lucrative, market for tales of horse racing, hunting, fishing, and other "idle pastimes." He was initially ashamed of these writings and used a pseudonym to hide his real identity, thereby protecting his more "literary" reputation.

William T. Porter, editor of *The American Turf Register*, and his brother George, co-owners of *Spirit of the Times*, were the men who first suggested the name "Frank Forester" to Herbert. The Porter brothers also tried to persuade him that there was nothing wrong or "lowbrow" in writing about something he knew and loved. They stressed that the natural, well-informed style of Herbert's horse racing and hunting tales was far more likely to outlive its author than the stiff pomposities of his novels. Herbert listened dubiously, but he did change his pen name from "Harry Archer" to "Frank Forester" in a story[16] first published in the May/June 1839 issue of *The American Turf Register*, just four months after William Porter bought this magazine from John Stuart Skinner. Six years later when a collection of these *Turf Register* stories was published as *The Warwick Woodlands*, Herbert found to his surprise and satisfaction that his British readers seemed to prefer the sporting writings of Frank Forester to the novels

---

[15]*Frank Forester: A Tragedy in Exile*, page 55. Also, *Henry William Herbert and the American Publishing Scene*, Luke Mathews White, Newark N. J., 1943, page 27. Theodore Sedgwick Fay (1807–1898) was an American diplomat and author of novels with names like *The Countess Ida* (1840) and *Hoboken* (1843.)

[16]The story was entitled "A Week in the Woodlands; or, Scenes on the Road, or in the Field and Round the Fire."

of Henry William Herbert. He therefore publicly "confessed" that they were one and the same man, and thereafter, most of his outdoor writings bore both names.[17]

The year *The Warwick Woodlands* first appeared was also Herbert's first year in a new home. Herbert's young wife had died at 23 years of age in Philadelphia the previous March. He was left with a daughter, Louisa, who died five months after her mother, and a son, William George, who was then three years old. Herbert's father, recently appointed Dean of Manchester, was concerned for his grandson's welfare and had doubtless heard of his son's continual shortage of money. Thus, in December 1844, the dean tactfully suggested that little William George be sent to England for his education and upbringing, while Henry William was to pick a homesite and erect a building of moderate cost against the day that Dean Herbert should visit America. Of course, his son could, in the meantime, occupy the home free of expense.

Henry William happily agreed to his father's proposal and with his friends Livingston and Ruggles acting as trustees, bought and began construction of a house in the spring of 1845 with the $1,500 sent over by his father.[18]

As an alien, Dean Herbert could not own property in New York State. However, the New Jersey state legislature, not many years previous, had removed all such barriers to foreigners in order to enable another exile, Napoleon's brother, Joseph Bonaparte, to settle near Bordentown. Thus, Henry William Herbert picked out a lovely acre and a quarter overlooking the Passaic River just a few minutes row upstream from the village of Newark. Gully Road, an old Indian thoroughfare, bordered the north side of this property and led, after a half hour's stroll, to the town of Belleville. Herbert planted some cedars near the house as it was being constructed, and upon its completion, he christened his new home The Cedars.

From 1845 until his death 13 years later, Herbert led an increasingly solitary life. With his wife and family gone, he saw old friends only occasionally, and in the last years, hardly at all. He was an excellent

---

[17]Publicizing his association with "Forester" may not have been a gesture of pride alone. Outdoor writing was increasingly popular—and lucrative—work, and some people had begun to attribute Forester's writings to lawyer Henry Beck Hirst, who was turning out similar material under the name Harry Harkaway.

[18]Dean Herbert added a curious note to this amount, saying that "had a safe man like Henry Clay been President of the United States," he would have felt like investing more. *Frank Forester: A Tragedy in Exile*, page 71.

[21]

cook and handled most of these domestic chores himself. Charles A. Dana, at the time, editor of the *New York Tribune*, once stopped by for a visit and commented afterward on the outstanding dinner Herbert prepared for him.[19] But in his final decade Herbert had only one regular companion, his handyman or "groom" (as Herbert referred to him), Charlie Holt. It was from Holt that Herbert received his final education in angling.

Holt was a native of Essex County and had spent most of his life fishing and boating on the Passaic River and in Newark Bay. In these early years, the Passaic was still a healthy tidal stream that often saw sizeable striped bass take up station in the lee of Green Island just in front of Herbert's home. Holt provided more than one of Herbert's dinners from the river, and Herbert in turn spent considerable time studying Holt's use of the spear, eel pot, and handline. Seeing Charlie's pleasure and proficiency with these instruments caused Herbert to revise his thinking about what constitutes sport. And while he never ranked commercial angling in the same category with sport fishing, Herbert definitely shows greater tolerance for the former in the writings of his final years. Where once he had considered party or head-boat[20] fishing as merely a kind of work—"not the less so for . . . the fact that hauling in the small, cutting line, hand over hand, and the salt water, are apt to make the fingers exceeding sore, if gloveless; and to use gloves in angling, would be something like donning the upper Benjamin with foxhounds"[21]—he later determined that whatever gave people pleasure and provided recreation should be considered sport. He even recommended (in *Fishing with Hook and Line*, page 37) that in sea bass and porgy angling, an old pair of leather gloves will be useful "to preserve your hands from blistering while drawing up your fish." And "though I eschew large congregations of humanity for sporting purposes, deeming them rather social and convivial in their true character, and holding sociality and conviviality, though excellent things in their way, as utterly averse to the spirit of sportsmanship, have I not found it good sport, at times, to sally out from some sequestered fishing hamlet, in the trim schooner or more humble yawl, and try my fortune with the Cod, the Haddock, and the Halibut."[22]

---

[19]Herbert was fond of appending in the back of his angling books various fish recipes he had created or heard of.

[20]So named because anglers paid the captain individually (per head) rather than chartering the entire boat for the day.

[21]*Frank Forester's Fish and Fishing*, page 417.

[22]*Ibid.*, Third Edition, page 20.

Years after Herbert's death, neighbors remember seeing him and Charlie Holt working together on their garden behind a hedge next to the house. Despite a lack of eyewitnesses, Herbert, also, doubtless sallied forth with Holt on many of the latter's nighttime fishing forays to study the fine arts of eel bobbing and flounder spearing. And though the English gentleman never quite succumbed to the charms of fundamental fishing, always considering them inferior to "the skill exerted in casting and managing the fly, or the spinning-minnow; much less to the playing, killing and basketing the heaviest kind of fish with the lightest running tackle,"[23] Herbert, unlike all others of his sporting contemporaries, came to honor the skills of the experienced waterman and bottom angler. He wrote with admiration of the "watchful observation of minutiae, such as the foulling [sic] of the line, the correct depth of the plummet or sinker, and such like" as well as the "delicacy of hand in feeling, appreciating and humoring the victim, when coquetting and nibbling about the bait."[24]

Herbert saw in the preparation of natural baits some of the same finesse requisite to the tying of flies. Here, for instance, is his description of the proper way to rig up a squid bait for striped bass fishing:

To fasten the squid to your hook, you should use a needle and waxed linen thread. Take off the skin of the squid, and pull out the spine [actually a vestigial internal shell]—then insert the needle through the opening made by the spine, and in this way, fasten your hook so the point will pass through near his eye—commence sewing him on to the hook from his tail, and stitch up to his neck.

This is so troublesome a process that few sportsmen use it; but very large fish are taken in this manner.[25]

Part of Herbert's extensive writing on natural bait fishing was a result of demand. Despite his preference for fly tackle and artificial lures, bottom fishing with handlines remained the Atlantic seaboard's most popular way to catch fish until well after the Civil War. But even in Herbert's day, rods and reels were found in increasing use for such species as striped bass and weakfish, and, perhaps, Herbert included special sections on these "shoal water fishes" to encourage the spread of this more sporting tackle. Then, too, he may have felt a certain sadness in the gradual decline and disappearance of such Manhattan

---

[23]*Ibid.*, page 21.
[24]*Ibid.*, page 21.
[25]*Fishing with Hook and Line: A Manual for Amateur Anglers*, page 27.

mainstays as the king whiting and sheepshead. By suggesting that anglers should catch these worthies on rod and reel, he at least made their departure a more sporting proposition. After once observing that the king whiting, "which was formerly very abundant in the waters of New York and vicinity, is becoming daily less frequent," Herbert says this is all the more a pity because kingfish are "the gamest of all the shoal salt-water fishes":

The angler regards the King-Fish in his basket much as the sportsman looks upon the Woodcock in his bag—as worth a dozen of the more easily captured and less worthy fry.[26]

Curiously, only once in his writings did Herbert speculate on the reasons for the disappearance of these fishes from the New York area. After citing an example of a man and his son who, in six hours of fishing in Jamaica Bay in 1827, took 472 kingfish,[27] Herbert suggests, as others had done, that the kingfish were no longer available in such numbers because of "the persecution of the bluefish."[28] We now know that water temperature changes, pollution, parasites, the dredging and filling of marshlands, and, yes, predators, all contribute to the rise and fall of certain littoral species. But even today, we little discuss the role overfishing may play in reducing some species whose reproductive capabilities are not equal to man's demand.

But if some species were declining, some seemed to appear almost overnight. In *Fishing with Hook and Line*, Herbert comments on the "strange and recent appearance" of the hake in United States waters. Since they were at one time considered to be the dominant offshore species of Ireland, Herbert muses on the possibility that "the hake has followed in the wake of their masters," the Irish immigrants. He says that Bostonians call the new fish "Poor Johns." But considering their

---

[26]*Frank Forester's Fish and Fishing*, Revised Edition, page 210.

[27]See Appendix A.

[28]A contemporary of Herbert's has left us an account of how an invasion of bluefish shaped men's, as well as fishes', lives in Massachusetts. Captain Atwood of Provincetown reported that bluefish "did not come north of Cape Cod so as to affect our fisheries until 1847, when they appeared in vast abundance and drove away from our bay nearly all other species.... When they first appeared ... I was living at Long Point (near Provincetown), in a little village containing some 270 population, engaged in the net-fishery.... The Bluefish affected our fishery so much that the people were obliged to leave the place. Family after family moved away, placing their houses upon floats and towing them across the harbor to Provincetown, until every one left the locality, which is now a desolate, barren, and sandy waste." *Game Fishes of the United States*, S. A. Kilbourne and G. Brown Goode, New York, 1878, page 18.

Irish ancestry, "Poor Pats would be more appropriate" (page 36). Actually, hake were probably always available over the continental shelves of the North Atlantic, but the Irish immigration to the New World created a market for these fishes in New York and Boston, which meant that offshore fishermen, instead of culling out the hake they caught when after cod or haddock, began to bring them into the cities for sale.

Herbert is also one of our first sporting writers to note the cycles of abundance and scarcity of certain school fishes such as the bluefish (see Appendix B):

It is a singularly erratic fish, sometimes swarming on the coasts, and again almost entirely disappearing. It occasionally runs far up rivers, and was taken in the Hudson so high up as the Highlands [Palisades] in great quantities in the year 1841. It appears to have been entirely unknown on the coasts of New York before the year 1818, since which it has been, on the whole, gradually on the increase, while in like proportion its victims, the Weak-fish and King-Fish, appear to be dying out.[29]

Herbert prided himself on not just being a sporting journalist but a natural historian as well. It was such pride that motivated him to revise and supplement, particularly in the growing area of saltwater angling, *Frank Forester's Fish and Fishing* with each new edition. However, he sometimes made mistakes. On page 220 of the 1864 printing (copyrighted 1859, the year after his death), Herbert notes that where formerly blackfish ranged "only from the capes of the Chesapeake to Massachusetts Bay, I have recently learned that this fish . . . is becoming common in Charleston [South Carolina], having, it is believed, escaped from the car of a fishing-boat, and bred there."

Unfortunately, Herbert, who never traveled in the South, did not know that the blackfish his Charleston correspondent, a Mr. King, referred to was actually the sea bass, *Centropristes striatus*, found commonly from Long Island to northern Florida. Popular names have often confused anglers unfamiliar with local species. And since scientific nomenclature was not in any better shape until well into this century, tourist sportsmen have traditionally had to do a little guessing

---

[29]*Frank Forester's Fish and Fishing*, Third Edition, page 218. Old-timers Herbert talked with may not have remembered bluefish before 1818, but this species had undoubtedly known earlier cycles of abundance along the Atlantic coast.

when asking about species in waters new to them. For example, yellow-tail in the Pacific is a kind of jack; yellowtail in the Atlantic is a kind of snapper. Neither should be confused with the yellowtail rockfish or yellowtail flounder, both sometimes called "yellowtail" for short.

Herbert's error was not in imagining that tautog (or as Virginia fishermen call them, "oysterfish," to distinguish the species from "oyster toads" or just plain "toadfish"—see what we mean?!) could not be found off South Carolina—for they will occasionally move that far south in cold winters—but in accepting the name "blackfish" at face value. Similar confusion exists over his secondhand references to "Cavalle" and "Horse Cavalle," also taken from letters with his Charles-ton angling correspondent. These may be Jack crevalle and amberjack, but since the Spanish in Florida called king mackerel "cavalla," we cannot be sure. All these fish range up the Atlantic coast to the Carolinas.

However, one Florida fish Herbert cites he may have known from the fish stalls on Fulton Street. The exquisite flavor of the pompano has always made it a favorite of gourmets, and even a century ago, the fish commanded an average price of $1.50 a pound in the New York markets. Such fish were sometimes carried north from Florida in the summertime in boats having live wells aboard or towing live-fish cars in those prerefrigeration days. Such activity, as Herbert alleges in the case of the Carolina "blackfish," may actually have contributed to the spread of some coastal fishes. Dr. Jerome V. C. Smith claimed tautog were unknown in Boston harbor before the American Revolution. At that time "a subscription was successfully undertaken for bringing several of them alive in cars from Newport, Rhode Island, which were supposedly the first of the species which had ever been to the eastward of the Cape."[30] Since tautog are still uncommon north of Cape Cod, we may presume failure for this experiment. Yet other fish transplants were attempted, and some were reported successful.[31] Thus, we can

---

[30]*Natural History of the Fishes of Massachusetts*, page 254. Smith also tells us that the word tautog is Mohegan Indian for *black*.

This early special interest in blackfish may have derived from something other than the species' notable food and sporting qualities. Seventeenth- and eighteenth-century colonists thought the tautog resembled the fresh water tench (*Tinca tinca*) of Europe. Since the tench was revered for the alleged healing qualities in the slime of its body, early American efforts to get its saltwater equivalent established everywhere along the Atlantic seaboard may stem from this resemblance, as well as its stout fight when hooked and its fine flavor on the table.

[31]The most famous transplantation of an American saltwater game-fish oc-curred in 1886 when fingerling striped bass were successfully introduced to Cali-

understand Herbert's assumption that blackfish had indeed became established in South Carolina via this mode of travel.

Forced into the role of an outsider early in life, Henry William Herbert always felt a certain sympathy for other outsiders—be they fish or men. Perhaps it was this feeling that encouraged him to upgrade the game reputation of the common herring and to disparage the popularity of sea bass and porgy fishing. By mid-century so many steamers were running parties to the offshore banks for bottom fishing from harbors in New York and New Jersey that what was once sport was fast taking on the aspect of an industry. This alone was sufficient to inspire Herbert's contempt.

He therefore took special pleasure in upgrading a nuisance fish like the cunner or bergall (*Tautogolabrus adspersus*) to sea bass status by allotting similar space for both species in his third revision of *Frank Forester's Fish and Fishing*. He also described the pleasures of shark fishing—a sport that anglers of more "respectable" fish cannot comprehend, even to the present day. Herbert calls it "stupendous sport resorted to by persons who have a hankering after excitement," and he directs the novitiate first to a ship chandler for the line he will need, and then to a blacksmith for the proper hook. Then:

When you get to your sharking ground, you launch your small boat, and tie your line to the stern. The hook should be fastened to it by a chain and swivel, and is baited with a good-sized piece of beef or pork.[32] You then row your boat along rapidly until you get a bite. Do not get too far from your vessel, as when you once get a bite, and hook the monster, you must bring him alongside before you attempt to land him, or he may upset you in his wrath.[33]

The story of Henry William Herbert ends abruptly. On February 16, 1858, he married a woman who shortly deserted him, either because of his dangerous temper or because she was disappointed that he was not as rich as she had hoped. Already frayed in imagination, this desertion seems to have broken his will. On May 15, he invited all his friends to a banquet. However, the invitations were sent out only the

fornia. Their Pacific range now reaches from the Columbia River in the north to Los Angeles in the south.

[32]Such recommended bait suggests that Herbert probably never did any shark fishing himself. While slabs of beef and pork will attract sharks, they cannot begin to compare as bait with the less expensive and more readily available fish heads and guts.

[33]*Fishing with Hook and Line*, page 61.

day before the dinner, and just one man showed up—a former student from the Classical Institute, Philip Hone Anthon.

Herbert was in a terribly depressed mood, and the two men stayed up most of the night, with Anthon doing all he could to distract Herbert from his threats to commit suicide. Just about the time Anthon thought he had succeeded, Herbert excused himself, went into the next room, and shot himself in the chest. He returned and stood before the stunned young man, said simply, "I told you I would do it," and fell dead. The Reverend John Shackelford, who had remarried Herbert, refused to read the burial service over his grave near The Cedars, and nearly two decades passed before a tombstone was erected to mark the spot.

There is little of Herbert's history left in the Passaic landscape today. For years The Cedars stood abandoned and allegedly haunted. Only schoolboys sneaked near to break windows, and eventually the house burned down. The village of Newark became a city that absorbed The Cedars and then swallowed the river. The channel between Green Island and Herbert's home that had once yielded many a fine striped bass was filled. The Parsippany Marsh and meadows where Herbert had once gone to shoot snipe and waterfowl were broken into lots and developed. In time, the Passaic River became so rank that herring and shad could no longer spawn there, and after awhile, even the rugged white perch and striped bass gave way before the oil and sludge. When you consider Newark today, it is difficult to believe that fish and game —and a man who called himself Frank Forester—ever lived there.

Yet the legacy of Henry William Herbert survives. His writings were the first to establish guidelines to separate saltwater sports angling from commercial fishing, and he gave ocean anglers pride in their newfound sport. Herbert forever held the Atlantic salmon to be the king of all fishes, but he did so in the name of saltwater sport, not of fresh.

He distinguished gamefish according to their contact with brine, and he once wrote that "those fish which never visit salt-water are unquestionably so much inferior to others of their own family which run periodically to the sea, that they are with great difficulty recognized as belonging to the same order with their roving brethren while of those, none of which are known to leave the fresh-water, but two or three kinds, are worth taking at all; and even these are not to be compared with the migratory, or the pure sea-fish."[34]

---

[34]*Frank Forester's Fish and Fishing*, page 12.

THREE

THE TEACHER

> He was so commanding a presence, so curious
> and inquiring, so responsive and expansive, and
> so generous of himself and his own, that every-
> one said of him: "Here is no musty *savant*, but
> a man, a great man, a man on the heroic scale,
> not to serve whom is avarice and sin!"—
> William James describing Louis Agassiz

In the foreword to *Frank Forester's Fish and Fishing*, Henry William
Herbert expresses gratitude to "Professor Agassiz, who kindly afforded
me every assistance in his power, with free access to his fine library
and unrivalled collection of fishes, from which most of my drawings
are taken."

Herbert met Louis Agassiz on a trip to New England in the early
1850's. Had he met the famous naturalist earlier in his life, or had he
been introduced to the intellectual society of Boston-Cambridge-
Concord when he first arrived in America, his life might have had a
different ending. At least every other man who came under the spell
of the world's first real marine naturalist found his life pleasantly
enlarged. And although Agassiz was not primarily a fisherman, his
enthusiasm and curiosity about the sea and sea fishes forever stamped
the developing American salt water sport fishery with his personality
and perspectives.

[29]

Jean Louis Rodolphe Agassiz was born on May 28, 1807, in the village of Motier-en-Vuly on the shores of Lake Morat, Switzerland. He was the first of five children born into a pastor's family to survive babyhood, and we can, therefore, sympathize with his parents' indulgence of their extraordinary son's activities. At an early age, he was permitted to keep all kinds of wildlife in his bedroom, while a spring pool in the backyard held his ever-changing collection of fishes.[1] In addition, he spent countless hours on the lake with local anglers, asking questions and learning all he could about the fish they caught and the techniques they used to catch them. Before he was eight years of age, he knew the name, classification, and habits of every freshwater fish in Switzerland. Years later, Agassiz's credo for his students included the advice to "study nature; not books," and to never be afraid to say "I don't know."

Agassiz was born into an age of optimism. The word *progress* was not yet spoken in irony, and man's faith in the future was firmly linked to his faith in science. The oceans, in particular, were attracting thoughtful minds. In 1775, Abraham Gottlob, a lecturer at Freiburg Mining Academy, suggested that while the geological formations of the earth held the key to its history, the oceans contained the answer to the origins of life. A student of Gottlob's by the name of Alexander von Humboldt decided to test this theory on an extensive cruise to the South Atlantic and Pacific oceans. His reported observations of currents, coastlines, and briny flora and fauna excited people's imaginations everywhere.

Soon the sea as a macrocosmic laboratory was considered as essential to a young scientist's work as microcosmic dissecting rooms had been to his undergraduate studies. Botanist Karl von Martius and zoologist Johann von Spix followed in von Humboldt's wake in 1821 with a three-year expedition to Brazil that included much coastal cruising and a trip up the Amazon. Charles Darwin was just 22 years old when he sailed in December 1831 on his epic-making cruise aboard the *Beagle*. And at mid-century, a 25-year-old biologist named Thomas Henry

---

[1]At least tradition has it that there was a backyard spring. Professor Franklin W. Hooper, Director of the Brooklyn Institute of Arts and Sciences, in the Centennial Address in 1907 commemorating the birth of Agassiz, held that "the watering trough in the front yard was Agassiz's first aquarium. Into it he peered hour by hour and day by day to watch the movements of the fish, their colors and their habits." Backyard, front yard; spring or trough—Agassiz early exhibited an obsession for fishes.

Huxley returned from his voyage of discovery aboard the *Rattlesnake*.

However, for a schoolboy named Agassiz, the earliest of these events was, at the time, of little moment. When he was 10, Agassiz was sent to a boarding school at Bienne, some 20 miles from home. There his scholastic efforts included a broadening of language capabilities. French was his native tongue, but as a Swiss, Agassiz was also familiar with German and Italian. At Bienne, he soon picked up English, in addition to his regular Greek and Latin studies.

With no clear goal in life but possessing a passion for nature, Agassiz was sent next to a senior secondary school known as the College of Lausanne, where it was expected that he would study for a business career. However, the boy was persuaded by the uncle he lived with, Dr. Mathias Mayor, that medicine and natural history were compatible disciplines, and in 1824, he enrolled in Zurich's medical school at the age of 17.

Once his studies were focused, they picked up momentum. Two years in Zurich were followed by more advanced schooling in Heidelberg and Munich. While at Heidelberg, Agassiz founded a Swiss Club and was soon known as its best fencer. The story goes that German students in another club challenged Agassiz to a match with their best swordsman. Either through a misunderstanding or because he had absolute confidence in his own abilities, Agassiz determined to take on every member of the German fraternity, one after the other. He finished off four opponents and was starting on a fifth when the Germans gave in. This incident in a region of Europe renown for its swordsmanship made him as famous in the community at large, as did his compulsive hiking and fishing activities to a smaller band of fellow students. Among his closest friends were future scientists of nearly equal fame: Karl Schimper, Arnold Guyot, and Alexander Braun.

Braun invited Agassiz home one summer to Karlsruhe, then a serene town dominated by the Duke of Baden's castle, extensive parks, and poplar trees. Braun's letter to his parents introducing Agassiz stated, "I bring to you one who knows every fish which passes under the bridge."[2] The two students spent the holiday collecting specimens, dissecting them, and with the aid of Alexander's artistic sister, Cecile, drawing them.

In November 1827, Braun and Agassiz set off for the University of

[2]*A Scientist of Two Worlds*, Catherine Owens Peare, Philadelphia, 1958, page 24.

Munich to finish their medical studies. Agassiz's primary pleasure in visiting new cities was to make a beeline for the central fish market to see what different species he could find. With his obvious interest in fishes, he soon came to the attention of Professors von Martius and von Spix, just back from their expedition to Brazil. Eager to examine the fishes von Spix had in his collection, Agassiz volunteered to help the older man classify the specimens. At first, this was occasional after-school work, with Agassiz's medical studies dominating his routine. But gradually his greater interest in von Spix's collection caused him to spend increasing amounts of time in the professor's laboratory. When von Spix suddenly died, von Martius asked Agassiz to continue this work of classification and to prepare the results for publication.

This was a rare opportunity for any young scientist. The Martius-Spix expedition was famous throughout Europe, and the scientific community was eagerly awaiting the conclusions of their findings. To be associated as a partner in this enterprise was Agassiz's dream-come-true. However, he was concerned about his youth and lack of accreditation. In the midst of his medical studies and while continuing the work of classifying the South American fishes, Louis Agassiz commuted to the neighboring university town of Erlangen to earn a Doctor of Philosophy degree in 1829, just so he would not diminish the value of the forthcoming publication by being without a title on the cover page!

That summer the study *Brazilian Fishes* appeared in Latin and was dedicated to Georges Cuvier, zoologist, friend of von Humboldt, and creator of the science of paleontology. After Cuvier received his copy of the publication, he wrote Agassiz a letter commending the classification with these words: "The importance and the rarity of the species therein described, as well as the beauty of the figures, will make the work an important one in ichthyology, and nothing could heighten its value more than the accuracy of your descriptions. It will be of the greatest use to me in my *History of Fishes*."[3]

Louis Agassiz was now a young man in a hurry. He received his medical degree on April 3, 1830, when he was not yet 23 years of age, and soon set off for Paris. Although medicine was his apparent career, Agassiz knew in his heart he wanted to be what he called a "traveling naturalist." He lived on the Left Bank with an artist-friend, Joseph Dinkel. That he chose this location with an eye to both his ostensible and desired careers can be read in a letter to his father, where Agassiz

---

[3]*Louis Agassiz, Scientist and Teacher*, James David Teller, Columbus, Ohio, 1947, page 20.

points out that his new quarters are within a 10-minute walk of the medical school, but only 200 steps from the Botanical Gardens.[4]

His correspondence with Georges Cuvier enabled Agassiz to seek out the elderly paleontologist, who in turn introduced him to von Humboldt. On the centennial of von Humboldt's birth in 1869, Louis Agassiz addressed an audience at the Music Hall in Boston, Massachusetts, about his early association with the great oceanographer:

Humboldt had at this time (about 1830) two residences in Paris: his lodging at the Hotel des Princes, where he saw the great world, and his working room in the Rue de la Harpe, where he received with less formality his scientific friends. It is with the latter place I associate him; for there it was my privilege to visit him frequently. . . .

At this period I was twenty-four, he was sixty-two. I had recently taken my degree as Doctor of Medicine, and was struggling not only for a scientific position but for the means of existence also. I have said that he gave me permission to come as often as I pleased to his room, opening to me freely the inestimable advantages which intercourse with such a man gave to a young investigator like myself. But he did far more than this. Occupied and surrounded as he was, he sought me out in my own lodging.

The first visit he paid me in my narrow quarters in the Quartier Latin, where I occupied a small room in the Hotel du Jardin des Plantes, was characteristic of the man. After a cordial greeting, he walked straight to what was then my library, a small book shelf containing a few classics, the meanest editions bought for a trifle along the quays, some works on philosophy and history, chemistry and physics, his own *Views of Nature*, Aristotle's *Zoology*, Linnaeus's *Regne Animal*, and quite a number of manuscript quartos, copies which . . . I had made of works I was too poor to buy, though they cost but a few francs a volume. Most conspicuous of all were twelve volumes of the new German Cyclopedia presented to me by the publisher.

I shall never forget, after his look of mingled interest and surprise at my little collection, his half-sarcastic question as he pounced upon the great Encyclopedia: "Was machen Sie denn mit dieser Eselsbrücke?" —"What are you doing with this ass's bridge?"—the somewhat contemptuous name given in Germany to similar compilations.

"I have not had time," I said, "to study the original sources of learning, and I need a prompt and easy answer to a thousand questions I have as yet no other means of solving."

It was no doubt apparent to him that I was not familiar with the

---

[4]Peare, page 42.

good things of this world, for I shortly afterward received an invitation to meet him at six o'clock in the *Galerie vitrèe* of the Palais Royal, when he led me into one of the restaurants, the tempting windows of which I had occasionally passed by. When we were seated, he half laughingly, half inquiringly, asked me whether I would order the dinner. I declined the invitation, saying that we should fare better if he would take the trouble, and for three hours, which passed like a dream, I had him all to myself. How he examined me, and how much I learned in that short time! How to work, what to do, and what to avoid; how to live; how to distribute my time; what methods of study to pursue—these were the things of which he talked to me on that delightful evening.[5]

Agassiz's stay in Paris also made possible his first visit to the sea. Alexander Braun came on a holiday and persuaded Agassiz and Dinkel to make a short trip to the Norman coast with him. We have no diary or journal record of this momentous sabbatical, but in a brief letter home, Agassiz wrote ecstatically, "At last I have looked upon the sea and its riches!"[6]

In the fall of 1832, incomprehensibly to his French and German friends, Agassiz decided to leave Paris and return to Switzerland. Von Humboldt had just arranged for a sizeable gift from the King of Prussia to help support Agassiz in his research, and he was therefore aggravated and mystified by his young colleague's determination to settle in the no-where town of Neuchâtel. Agassiz tried to explain his decision in a letter to von Humboldt written just before leaving:

It seems to me that in a quiet retired place like Neuchâtel, whatever may be growing up within me will have a more independent and in-dividual development than in this restless Paris, where obstacles or difficulties may not perhaps divert me from a given purpose, but may disturb or delay its accomplishment.[7]

However, another reason for returning to Switzerland, and one aris-ing out of the reason he gave von Humboldt, was Agassiz's hope that his practice as a country doctor would yield sufficient income and leisure to finish the giant study of fossil fishes initiated by Georges Cuvier and then passed on to him for completion when Cuvier died

---

[5]*Louis Agassiz: His Life and Work*, Charles Frederick Holder, New York, 1893, pages 153–154.

[6]Peare, page 46.

[7]Teller, page 23.

of cholera that spring. Agassiz was determined to leave *Recherches sur Les Poissons Fossiles* as a memento to Cuvier; at the same time it would represent his most substantial bid for fame in the science world.

Meanwhile, Dr. Agassiz made the same kind of contributions at Neuchâtel that he was later to make in Boston. Few people had ever heard of the little Swiss town before Agassiz decided that it would become a European scientific headquarters. Within a year of his arrival, Agassiz had founded the Society of Natural Sciences, a Museum of Natural History, produced the first volume of his study of fossil fishes (with a Neuchâtel dateline), and converted the entire community into students of natural history. Merchants took up rock collecting; bankers became butterfly collectors; lawyers saved any odd fish they caught in their seines along the lakefront.

One of the techniques Agassiz used for teaching a student to examine the world with fresh eyes was to leave the student alone with a given specimen for many minutes—even hours. When Agassiz returned, he would ask the student to tell him all he had learned in the interim. When the student started by reciting the fish's name and classification, Agassiz would say, "Wrong, wrong. You have not learned that since I left you; you knew that before you came in. Look at the fish as though you have never seen one before." Then Agassiz would leave the room for an even longer period of time. Sometimes several such sessions— even days—were necessary before the student began to perceive details in the fish's fins, tail, or mouth, and to ask himself how this fish differed from other fishes and why. Forced to concentrate on a single specimen, the student became an observer of all fish, which to Agassiz was the first step in becoming a naturalist.

Another technique consisted of presenting a student with a box full of the jumbled skeletons of half a dozen unrelated fishes and then asking the student to reassemble them. A month or more went into such work, but lessons learned in this manner were not easily forgotten. Agassiz's philosophy of education lay behind such gestures. As he once put it, "Facts are stupid things until brought into connection with some general law."[8] The students most capable of reassembling skeletons were given new fish; these were frequently all of the same genera. As the students worked, they began to see the similarities in this new batch and to comprehend the differences between these and the fish previously assembled. Thus their understanding of what they were about was built on experience, not mere memorization.

---

[8]*Louis Agassiz as a Teacher*, Lane Cooper, Ithaca, N. Y., 1945.

Agassiz's five volumes on fossil fishes (he finished the last one in 1834) has many lessons for the layman. Previous to Agassiz's writing, the only major division of fishes was between the *cartilaginous* and *osseous* types. While most early nineteenth-century natural histories correctly put the sharks and rays into the cartilaginous category, they often mistakenly included true fishes like the eel or sturgeon for no other reasons than eels looked like lampreys, and sturgeon had bottom-hugging habits like a dogfish. Agassiz suggested that a more realistic classification could be made after comparing internal structure, organs, and scales. He drew examples of different scale types and explained that toothlike placoid scales were found on very primitive sharks, skates, and rays; diamond or rhomboid-shaped ganoid scales identify the ancient gars and sturgeons; round, smooth cycloid scales represent other relatively old fish like the salmon; and saw or spine-edged ctenoid scales are found on the more recently evolved sea bass and perch.

Agassiz also adopted Ernst von Baer's theory that the evolution of a species could be seen in the development of a single egg, and he illustrated how a modern fish embryo goes through stages that resemble various ancient forms. In fact, Agassiz made Baer's theory so widely known that even today he's popularly credited with creating it.

Agassiz did not spend all his time at Neuchâtel. He made a couple of trips to Great Britain to examine fossil fish forms foreign to central Europe. In England he learned of his great popularity in America and first conceived the idea of going there. Harvard, Yale, and the Boston Natural History Society were among the many subscribers to his *Research on Fossil Fishes*, and Agassiz was intrigued by the many natural history organizations he heard were multiplying throughout the United States. "Every educated American is a naturalist," he was told, and in the cities as many tradesmen attend science lectures as professionals. Through the assistance of the British geologist Sir Charles Lyell, who had already made an American tour, Agassiz was commissioned to give a lecture series at the Lowell Institute in Boston. With a parting gift of 15,000 francs from the King of Prussia, the Swiss naturalist sailed for the New World in September 1845.

A century ago the Cunard docks were located near the South Ferry that ran between East Boston and Boston proper. When Agassiz arrived, in a daze of fresh impressions, he went straight from the steamer to the ferry and stepped off at Atlantic Avenue into the courtly presence of John A. Lowell, trustee and director of the Institute. In a matter of weeks, Agassiz was convinced he had found a new home.

He was most impressed by the nature of the audiences he spoke to. The rumor that a genuine cross-section of America existed in the lecture hall was true. Since tickets to the Lowell lectures were obtained in drawings, there were as many shopkeepers and street cleaners in his audience as students and fellow scientists. The faith that education was the key to social betterment was part and parcel of nineteenth-century man's faith in science.

Some European colleagues viewed this popular approach to education with alarm—even contempt—but Agassiz loved it. He rented a three-story brick house at water's edge in East Boston from which he went out into the harbor every morning to dredge or seine, bringing back specimens for his house tanks and worktables mere hours before he would give a lecture on the results of that day's outing before a Standing Room Only audience at the Institute. As soon as one lecture series was completed, another subscription was quickly raised. Bostonians would not let him go. As many visitors came to Agassiz's home as went to his lectures, and regardless of what other work he was doing at the time, Agassiz was always eager to show the curious around, commenting on something unique about this fish or that, treating each visitor as though he were a scientific colleague. Soon all kinds of little boats were seen in Boston harbor, their occupants noting sea creatures for the first time as objects of wonder rather than merely something "good to eat" or "not good to eat."

Familiar with European fishes and now confronted by an entirely different spectrum of American species, one of the first observations Agassiz made on behalf of American marine science was to suggest that there were considerably more fish in the world than the 1,000 or so species claimed in natural histories up to that time. While Agassiz found some fishes overclassified—for example, some ichthyologists thought the young Atlantic sea bass or "pin bass" found in the bays and inlets were different from the large "humpback" adult males found offshore—he more often found American naturalists parochial or timid in not recognizing the possibility of species beyond their experience.

When Bostonians heard there was a ray in southern waters that reached a width of 20 feet from wing tip to wing tip, they could only suppose this was a tropical variety of their local skate or stingray. Many naturalists wrote that all catfish were the same; saltwater varieties in the south were merely sea-run hornpout, and stories of huge eels in coral seas with toothy mouths that would put a shark to shame were either false—if the local naturalist's experience with eels went no further than what was found in the New England bays and rivers—or true, if the northern naturalist was familiar with the conger. In neither case did they imagine the moray.

Agassiz's Boston audiences respected his education and experience, and his descriptions of fish and animals in faraway places excited their awe as thoroughly as the advent of cinema did for audiences 50 years later. However, spellbinding was not Agassiz's intention. Basically, he wanted people to examine nature, and where possible, to dispel mythology, comprehending that function derives from form. For example, it was nonsense to claim that eels are the boa constrictors of the sea, as one natural historian put it, "oftentimes overpowering their prey by suddenly coiling round the bodies of fishes, whose bones and flesh are bruised instantly into jelly"[9]—simply because neither the eel's body structure—nor that of its prey—gives this fish the smothering or crushing capabilities of a constricting snake.

It was also absurd to suggest that sturgeon are great predators that rush through the water, seizing and tearing prey nearly their own size. Even a cursory examination of this fish's vacuum-cleaner type mouth would inform any thoughtful naturalist that he was dealing with a scavenger. The examples, and therefore the lessons (and potential lectures) were endless.

Dr. Agassiz was practical about any surplus specimens brought his way. Always short of money and generally overstocked with common varieties of local fishes, he converted many of them into meals when a day's work was done. He once crowned an exhaustive study of a live giant sea turtle by turning the animal into a series of soups, steaks, and pot pies that lasted his household of 20 visiting and resident naturalists for days.

Dr. Alexander Bache, great-grandson of Benjamin Franklin and Superintendent of the U. S. Coast Survey, urged Agassiz to use the local Survey steamer whenever he wanted. By this means, Agassiz was soon out and about Cape Cod, Nantucket Island, Martha's Vineyard, and the Elizabeth Isles—fishing, collecting, dissecting, preserving, studying. He recruited assistants on the basis of willingness, and such was the enthusiasm engendered by this Pied Piper of the Seas that he

---

[9]*Natural History of the Fishes of Massachusetts*, Jerome V. C. Smith, Boston, 1833, page 240.

was soon changing fishmongers into naturalists and commercial fishermen into marine scientists.

He was not always successful. On his first visit to New York City, Agassiz postponed all official presentation of letters until he had made a tour of the Fulton Fish Market, the leading commercial fish center of America. Fish were brought here from up and down the Atlantic seaboard and from the Caribbean islands, and many were kept alive in display aquaria built into the stalls. While most of the fishmongers were intrigued by Agassiz's presence and countless questions, and charmed by his curious accent, one fellow is reported to have remarked: "The more worthless the fish is, the more he likes it. He's daft, I'm thinking."

Agassiz often depended on anglers for his saltwater specimens. And sometimes in that great age of discovery, the specimen was more than of passing laboratory interest. For instance, Mr. A. C. Jackson set the scientific world on its ear in 1852 with a pair of perch he caught in San Salita (Sausalito?) Bay, San Francisco, California. Not only were the fish a new species (which Agassiz acknowledged by naming them after Jackson), they represented a wholly new concept in marine biology; a seaperch that bears its young alive!

Here is Mr. Jackson's story of his catch as reported in "On Extraordinary Fishes from California Constituting a New Family," published by Louis Agassiz in 1853:

I rose early in the morning for the purpose of taking a mess of fish for breakfast, pulled to the usual place, baited with crabs, and commenced fishing, the wind blowing too strong for profitable angling; nevertheless on the first and second casts I fastened the two fishes, male and female, that I write about, and such were their liveliness and strength, that they endangered my slight trout rod.

I, however, succeeded in bagging both, though in half an hour's subsequent work I got not even a nibble from either this or any other species of fish. I determined to change the bait, to put upon my hook a portion of the fish already caught, and cut for that purpose into the largest of the two fish caught. I intended to take a piece from the thin part of the belly, when what was my surprise to see coming from the opening thus made, *a small live fish.*

This I at first supposed to be prey which this fish had swallowed, but on further opening the fish, I was vastly astonished to find next to the back of the fish and slightly attached to it, *a long very light violet bag, so clear and so transparent, that I could already distinguish through it*

[39]

*the shape, color and formation of a multitude of small fish (all fac-
similes of each other) with which it was well filled.* I took it on board
(we were occupying a small vessel which we had purchased for survey-
ing purposes,) and when I opened the bag, I took therefrom *eighteen*
more of the young fish, precisely like in size, shape, and color, the first
I had accidentally extracted.

Agassiz designated a new family for these viviparous seaperch and
called it *Holconoti* or *Embiotocoidae*. The first specimens Jackson sent
from California, Agassiz titled *Embiotoca Jacksoni*, which still stands
as the scientific name. However, most West Coast anglers more commonly know the fish as the blackperch, and at that, most of them are
unaware that these remarkable spiny-rayed sea fishes are unusual in
their live-bearing characteristics.

Agassiz's lectures took him to Philadelphia (where he first met Spencer Fullerton Baird, America's leading native-born naturalist)[10]; Washington, D. C. (where he visited the recently-founded Smithsonian Institution); and Charleston, South Carolina (where he met English novelist
William Makepeace Thackeray, also on a tour of American cities). In
the winter of 1850, Agassiz traveled south to the Florida Keys with
Dr. Bache and there studied the reefs and reef fishes. So widespread was
Agassiz's fame that in 1854 when he needed only 500 subscribers to
launch a 10-volume study of the natural history of the United States
(at $12 a volume), he received over 2,500 orders in the first few weeks
of publicity.

"Amazing, amazing!" Agassiz wrote his family in Europe. "There is
not a class of learned men here distinct from the other cultivated members of the community. On the contrary, so general is the desire for

---

[10]Spencer F. Baird, future U. S. Fish Commissioner and founder of the marine
research facility at Wood's Hole, Massachusetts, was just 24 years of age when he
met Agassiz. Although he was already a recognized fisheries and wildlife expert
whom even John James Audubon sought out for positive identification of a species,
young Baird clearly regarded Agassiz as the senior statesman of their profession.
Baird volunteered to collect specimens for Agassiz, and after several other meetings,
Agassiz in turn proposed they publish a cooperative monograph on American
fishes. Baird immediately began to fulfill his end of the bargain, but Agassiz never
got around to doing his share. Years after both men's deaths, David Starr Jordan
edited and published the six sketches that Baird had done.

Agassiz was frankly jealous of his reputation as America's leading naturalist,
and as Baird grew older and wiser, his awe of Agassiz changed to an attitude of
cautious respect. However, toward the end of their lives, a great opportunity for
joint effort was once again missed when Agassiz asked Baird to lecture at his
summer school on Penikese Island in Buzzards Bay. Baird thanked Agassiz but
said he was tied to fisheries research in Maine and unable to get away.

knowledge, that I expect to see my books read by operatives [laborers], by fishermen, by farmers, quite as extensively as by the students in our colleges, or by the learned professions."[11]

His enthusiasm for America was so great that he became a United States citizen in January 1865.

Gradually, Agassiz began to attract wealthy patrons who not only freed him from the pesky worries of rent, travel expenses, and equipment costs, but provided him with considerable sums to do precisely the kinds of things he had always dreamed of doing. Thomas Cary presented Agassiz with a summer cottage and laboratory on the northeast shore of Nahant, a rocky peninsula just north of Boston, where Agassiz spent afternoons with fellow naturalist, Dr. Joseph B. Holder, collecting fishes from Lynn Bay. Francis C. Gray left $50,000 in his will for the purchase of specimens for a museum of comparative zoology to be established at Harvard College. Agassiz took on the task of acquiring money for the building and, through personal persuasion and influence, wrangled $100,000 from the Massachusetts legislature and raised $71,000 in private donations. This biological facility is still one of the nation's finest. Classification of the many collections bought for the museum took years and was carried on by countless volunteers, among them, Dr. Holder's son and future founder of the Catalina Tuna Club, Charles Frederick.

Perhaps the most wonderful conversion of a monetary gift to the natural history education of the New World occurred when millionaire John Anderson offered Agassiz little Penikese Island in the Elizabeth Chain south of Cape Cod, plus $50,000 to operate a summer school of natural history.

Dr. Agassiz was tired that spring of 1873. Within recent years he had made a number of long sea voyages, including one to Brazil and another, completed only the year before, around Cape Horn to San Francisco. On the latter trip he had personally collected 265 barrels and countless cases of specimens, all of which needed sorting and organization. But the urge to teach was too strong. He accepted Anderson's gift and set about recruiting the best possible staff and processing the applications of hundreds of eager students.

Today that list of the 44 selected students (16 women and 28 men)[12]

---

[11]Peare, page 136.

[12]In his autobiography, *The Days of a Man* (Yonkers-on-Hudson, N.Y., 1922, page 108). David Starr Jordan recalls that there were "thirty-five men and fifteen women" in the summer school. Apparently some students came and went during

reads like a Who's Who of American natural history. Foremost among future marine scientists was a young man by the name of David Starr Jordan who coauthored the popular *American Food & Game Fishes* in 1902 with Barton Warren Evermann,[13] and he wrote the even more important two-volume *Guide to the Study of Fishes* in 1905.

As Jordan later commented in his *Science Sketches*, "none of us will ever forget his first sight of Agassiz. We had come down from New Bedford in a little tug-boat in the early morning, and Agassiz met us at the landing-place on the island. He was standing almost alone on the little wharf, and his great face beamed with pleasure.... He greeted us with great warmth as we landed. He looked into our faces to justify himself in making choice of us among the many whom he might have chosen."

Then in typical Agassiz fashion, barely giving the students time to put down their luggage, he hurried them off across the island, collecting shells and seaweeds on one shore and asking for a geological explanation of another. This was the start of a summer that was to become legend in the history of American academe and which was to influence teaching methods in science for generations to come.

That winter Agassiz's energy ran out. Suffering from heartache and general fatigue, he spent much of his time in bed. One day, after a lecture in Fitchburg, Massachusetts, Agassiz returned to Cambridge, made out his will, and died soon after on December 14, 1873, at age 62.

The story goes that when he went to his lawyer to have his will prepared, the attorney asked him how he was to be identified in the preamble: as a doctor, naturalist, author, zoologist, what? Without hesitation, Agassiz said: "I'm a teacher."[14]

"The school of all schools in America which has had the greatest influence on American scientific teaching was held in an old barn on an uninhabited island some eighteen miles from the shore. It lasted barely three months, and in effect it had but one teacher. The school at

---

the summer, for the list of those who eventually finished the course included only the 16/28 figures cited in the text above.

[13]Evermann had been head of the U. S. Fish Commission's expedition to Puerto Rico in 1899.

[14]*Louis Agassiz: Pied Piper of Science*, Aylesa Foree, New York, 1958, page 236. Same anecdote is found in *Louis Agassiz as a Teacher*, page 1.

Penikese existed in the personal presence of Agassiz; and when he died, it vanished."[15] Thus recalled David Starr Jordan.

But the spirit of Agassiz lives on. He organized and added to our knowledge of the oceans. He turned fishermen into students, and students into teachers. He built bridges between men of leisure and men of science so that in the century since his death few men of wealth have undertaken a major angling expedition without recruiting men of science to share their experiences. The ghost of Agassiz sailed south during a collecting trip to Mexican waters in the 1930's aboard Willets J. Hole's *Samona*. His spirit was with staff members of the American Museum of Natural History who accompanied Michael Lerner on his angling expeditions to the South Pacific and South America. And Agassiz was aboard the *Argosy* with Alfred C. Glassell, Jr., when he and a team of Yale scientists fished off the Seychelles in the Indian Ocean in 1956.

The spirit of Agassiz is part of any angler who wants to know more about the fish he pursues and who wonders about the wriggling catch in his net or on the gaff—wondering how its life and man's are linked.

---

[15]*Science Sketches*, David Starr Jordan, Chicago, 1887, pages 242–243.

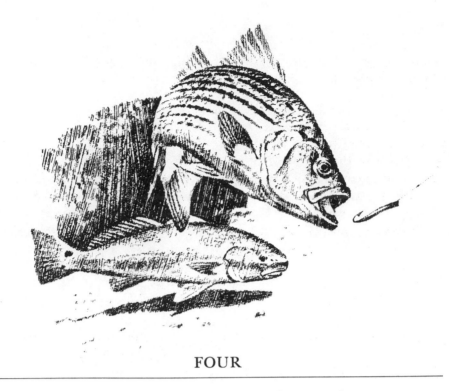

FOUR

ANGLING NORTH AND SOUTH
A CENTURY AGO

> The next best thing to fishing is to sit and read about it.—Anon.

Regional differences in saltwater angling along the Atlantic coast have never been set according to the lines drawn by Mason and Dixon. If any surveys have been made, they have been made by the fishes themselves. For one angler, the North ends when you stop catching weakfish, and the South begins when you start taking spotted sea trout. Another fisherman says it is where the winter range of the codfish overlaps the summer range of the king mackerel.

As a consequence, saltwater angling has had few regional reporters. Henry William Herbert, for example, was based near New York City, but he tried to cover species and techniques from Massachusetts to Florida. Most outdoor writers since his time have attempted to do the same. An interesting exception was a wealthy planter by the name of William Elliott (1788–1863) from Beaufort, South Carolina. Although educated at Harvard, widely traveled, and politically a Unionist, Elliott preferred to describe only the fish and fishing available in his native

[44]

state. Not only did he feel he knew this region better than any other, but he thought no littoral species the equal of a Carolina bass—channel bass, that is:

[When I describe] that beautiful sea-fish, the bass . . . , I do not mean the sea-bass of New York (our blackfish . . .), nor yet the striped bass taken among the rocks at Newport (our rockfish . . . [which] in very fine condition is taken at the South in the fresh-water rivers),[1] but *the bass, —Corvina ocellata*,[2]—weighing thirty or forty pounds,—three feet and upwards in length,—elegantly shaped,—brilliant with silvery and golden hues, and distinguished by one or more dark black spots upon the tail.

Originally writing for sporting journals under names borrowed from Walton—"Piscator" and "Venator"—Elliott decided to collect the best of his writings and add a few new selections under one cover. *Carolina Sports by Land and Water, Including Incidents of Devil-Fishing &c.* was published in Charleston in 1846. While the book devotes half its space to upland game sports, the leading half of the volume concerns Elliott's fondness for "transparent waters stocked with a variety of sea-fish." In a letter to the editor of a "Sporting Magazine," he calls himself a "hereditary sportsman" whose grandfather first conceived the Elliott family's passion for spear and line fishing along the Carolina shore. And "perceiving the relish with which some of your contributors talk of their capture of perch and trout of two pounds weight, and other fish of that caliber, I am tempted to give you an account of the sport enjoyed by my grandfather; and which bears the same relation to your lauded trout fishing, as a Bengal tiger hunt to a match at snipes."[3] William Elliott then describes "the established [summer] diversion of the planters in the vicinity of Port Royal Sound [who] make Bay Point their place of rendezvous, and, well-provided with lances and harpoons, sally forth in search of [Devil-fish] at or about high water when they enter the inlet to feed upon the shrimps and small fish that abound along the shores."[4]

---

[1]Some of the best striped bass fishing in the world today is found in South Carolina's vast Santee-Cooper freshwater reservoir and in the brackish Savannah River.

[2]Classified today as *Sciaenops ocellata*.

[3]*Carolina Sports By Land and Water*, p. 8.

[4]*Ibid.*, page 49. Elliott's first encounter with a manta ray was from a small dory, and the huge fish carried him some 20 miles up the coast before it could

[45]

While spear and harpoon fishing are often scorned by rod-and-reel anglers today, these activities have many times prepared the way for the more refined fishing that followed. Tarpon were harpooned for years before anyone thought to bait them with a hook. And this is equally true of tuna and broadbill swordfish. In addition, the hazards and difficulties of "devil-fishing" were felt more keenly a century and a quarter ago than they would be today. Elliott and his colleagues worked out of small oar- or sail-powered dories with primitive ropes and irons. More importantly, the men's fear of this "Vampire of the Ocean" did much to spice the chase with excitement. No wonder Elliott felt a certain contempt for men who were thrilled by a two-pound brook trout.

Spearing manta rays was a social custom among young bloods from the coastal plantations. Drum fishing was also a social sport, but it frequently included the presence of ladies. In the spring the black drum arrived in such vociferous numbers that their grunting or drumming could be heard in boats anchored in the channels around Hilton Head and Parris Island. When one fish was hooked, fishermen in other boats would characteristically pull anchor and row nearer to take advantage of the school. Fortunately, the fish were generally so abundant that no arguments broke out as to who was invading whose fishing territory. Today, such behavior might earn an intruding angler a sinker slung his way, or a few rude remarks at the very least. Perhaps, because ladies were along, usually as spectators to the struggle of these sturdy fish on handlines, there was more camaraderie and flirtation than temper tantrums.

Another social sport, but one that Elliott clearly feels is best experienced in small groups or alone, was channel bass fishing. He thought these fish more wary and certainly more handsome than black drum, and, perhaps, he sought to dignify their capture through solitude. In any event, in his chapter on channel bass, Elliott gives us our first written account of beach surf fishing:

The mention of Egg Bank reminds me that there is another mode of taking bass, which, to say the truth, I have not pursued much of late. This bank lies, or more properly speaking did lie, south of the public lot at Bay Point—distant half a mile. Covering several acres in extent and

be subdued. This battle made headlines and pictures in the London *Illustrated News* and turned Elliott into something of a celebrity in the South. His writings were admired generally, and especially by Henry David Thoreau who, in his journal for February 21, 1861, termed Elliott "a regular sportsman."

[46]

lifting its head a few feet above [the] high water mark, it served as the secure roosting-place of the curlews [probably willets], sea-gulls, and other aquatic birds; and here, too, in the spring, they deposited their eggs.

But the hurricanes which periodically sweep along our coasts have so obliterated it, that its existence as an egg bank will become, in a few years, a matter of tradition. It is now covered at half flood—and its site is marked in stormy weather by the waves, that rushing together from opposite quarters, meet at its summit, and jutting upwards into the air, fall in a sheet of foam.

When the bank stood above water, it formed a barrier against the sea; and while the surf beat on the outer side, the inner was protected so that a boat could land in security. I used to push over from Bay Point at early flood, land on the inner side of the bank, and, leaving a few oarsmen to take charge of the boat, walk over to the seaside of the bank with a servant or two to carry bait and lines—and, wading out into the surf waist-deep, toss my line into the breakers in quest of bass.[5]

Artificial reef projects are currently in vogue up and down the Atlantic seaboard. Used cars, worn-out tires, and even old ships have been sunk to create havens for sportfish. However, this practice is certainly not new, and reef building as a form of fish cultivation was doubtless practiced by earlier civilizations.

Early in nineteenth-century America, the sea islands of the Carolina coast were cleared of trees and brush so that cotton could be planted on them. Even fallen trees at the water's edge were cleared away. Tidal action had once encrusted the upper branches of these fallen trees with barnacles and other shellfish. Sheepshead had then sought the tree tops as a refuge from their enemies and fed on the marine growth they found there. When coastal planters discovered they were eliminating this favorite food fish, they still continued to clear their islands, but they replaced the once fallen trees with more carefully composed reefs:

Logs of pine or oak are cut and framed into a sort of hut without a roof. It is floored and built up five or six feet high; then floated to the place desired and sunk in eight feet [of] water by casting stones or live-oak timber within. As soon as the barnacles are formed, which will happen in a few weeks, the fish will begin to resort to the ground.

It is sometimes requisite to do more before you can succeed to your wishes. The greatest enemies of this fish are the sharks and porpoises, which pursue them incessantly and destroy them unless they can find

---

[5]*Ibid.*, pages 72–73.

secure hiding-places to which to retreat. Two of these pens, near each other, will furnish this protection; and when that course is not adopted, piles driven near each other, quite surrounding the pen, will have the same effect.

Your work complete, build a light staging [dock] by driving down four upright posts at the distance of fifteen feet from the pen; and then take your station on it, provided with a light, flexible and strong cane reed of twenty feet length with fourteen feet of line attached, a strong hook, and a light lead.

Instead of dropping your line directly down, and poising [sic] it occasionally from bottom, I prefer to throw the line out beyond the perpendicular and let the lead lie on the bottom. The sheepshead is a shy fish and takes the bait more confidently if it lies on the bottom. When he bites, you perceive your rod dipping for the water,—give a short, quick jerk, and then play him at your leisure. If the fish is large and your jerk too violent, the rod will snap at the fulcrum,—the grasp of your left hand. It has happened that at one of these artificial grounds, I have taken sixteen sheepshead at one fishing.

Since some of the best sheepshead fishing in the Carolinas was during the winter months when shrimp baits were in short supply, Elliott gives his readers some interesting advice regarding the use of oysters and mussels as substitute baits. He tells us to cook half our oysters and leave the rest raw. Then using two hooks, bait one with a firm cooked oyster and the other with a softer, hard-to-hook raw one. Sheepshead prefer raw oysters and will come from quite some distance once they smell them. Your chance is slim of hooking a sheepshead while he's stripping a raw oyster from the hook, but the cooked "back-up" oyster is there to take him on the second try. If you use only cooked oysters, you won't attract nearly as many fish. However, once sheepshead are on the feed in the vicinity of your cooked bait, you'll have an excellent chance of getting your fish.

Charleston was never a large or particularly cosmopolitan city, but it did have an excellent medical school—Agassiz lectured there in the winter of 1851—and there were several natural history societies in town and vicinity. One day while channel bass fishing in 1840, a servant of Elliott's caught a fish new to the area,[6] and Elliott decided to send it

---

[6]Probably, a grouper or jewfish. Elliott describes the fish as resembling "the fresh-water perch,—known by the name of 'wide-mouthed perch' [large-mouth bass]. ... Its hue was a greenish-black on the back, subsiding into a faint yellow on the belly; its mouth was unfurnished with teeth, but had slender spikes instead, with which it could hold its prey; its eyes were large and prominent; its tail was large

[48]

up to Beaufort to one of the natural history societies for identification. What happened is an amusing anecdote of amateur marine scientists at work. After waiting through the afternoon for his servant, Jeoffrey, to return with the learned men's conclusions, the slave finally reappeared with a letter saying: "The scientific gentlemen who had examined [the fish] could make nothing of it, except when brought on table—when they had enjoyed it exceedingly."

Elliott later reconstructed the scene in this way:

Dr. Pogonias presides; and a few leaves [pages] of the books of reference that are spread upon the table have been turned when the first incision, to test the internal structure, was made. The knife glides without effort through the tender fiber,—the coats [skin] are lined with luscious looking fat,—and, on further investigation, two fresh sheepshead . . . , fresh and bright and intact, are disclosed on which he had made his morning lunch!

A momentary frown passes over the brow of one of the panel, as if he rebuked in spirit the extravagant epicurism of the defunct. The books are closed. A new direction has evidently been given to their thoughts.

"I wonder," says Dr. P., "whether the copper banks are anywhere nigh? Really, if I wasn't afraid of being poisoned by eating an unknown fish, I should indeed venture to try a little of it."

Whereupon he ordered Jeoffrey to cut off a little slice of twenty pounds and transfer it to his kitchen. The contagion spread—the steel gleamed on every side—and in the twinkling of an eye, the fish was dismembered and divided like another Poland![7]

Most distressing of all to William Elliott was the fact that his "scientific" friends did not even save the skeleton for the local museum!

The chief consequence of the American Civil War for saltwater sportsmen was that it delayed the angling exploration of much of the southern coast. Some regions, such as the Florida panhandle, have

---

at its insertion, and the paddle [caudal] rays small in proportion to the size of the fish. It resembled, in fine, an inhabitant of the fresh water, rather than the sea; was manifestly a heavy and dull swimmer; and it struck me as matter of surprise that a fish thus formed could escape for a day being destroyed by the sharks. I could only solve the difficulty by supposing that he was born and bred among these [Bay Point] Rocks—the crevices of which had sheltered him from their attacks." *Ibid.*, pages 78–79.

[7]*Ibid.*, page 80.

remained relatively unknown to sport fishermen until well into this century.

Otherwise, as far as thousands of anglers and naturalists were concerned, the discoveries of Agassiz and Baird still took precedence over the political struggles of Davis and Lincoln. In fact, during the very darkest days of the war in 1864, a most important volume of sport-fishing first appeared: *The American Angler's Book* by Thaddeus Norris. Combining fishing lore, recreation, and natural history, this book became so popular that another edition was called for even before the war was over. It is a milestone publication in that it is the first American fishing book to include detailed chapters on fundamental aspects of the sport such as tying knots, rod making, and fly tying. Reflecting the bond between sportsmen and naturalists, there is also a section on how to raise fish in captivity.

Although Norris preferred freshwater fishing to salt, he is more tolerant of ocean angling than he might have been a quarter century earlier, for "since the publication of ... *Frank Forester's Fish and Fishing*, sporting fish have decreased in some parts of the country where they were once abundant."[8] Because the streams and rivers in and near major cities such as Boston, New York, and Philadelphia were dying, Norris suggests that angling urbanites should consider the shore as well as the mountains for vacations. Trout and salmon fishermen should take their sporting tackle to salt water and make "honest anglers" of bay and surf handliners.

Norris's saltwater fishing section is not long (just 26 pages of the 692 total), but he gives a modern reader a brief glimpse of what it was like to angle in the once fertile waters of Barnegat Bay:

The topography of our coast shows long stretches of low sandy beach, which beat back the waves of the Atlantic, from Sandy Hook to Cape Florida. Inside of these are interminable sounds, creeks and quiet bays, abundantly stocked with Bluefish, Weakfish, Blackfish, Rockfish, Sheepshead, Barb, Croakers, Pigfish, Porgies, Sea-Bass, etc.

Here the angler may listen to the waves beating against the ocean side of the barrier, and see the white breakers; and at times may even feel the salt spray which flies over the narrow strip of sand sprinkling his face, as he sits in his boat and makes havoc amongst the fins.

Along our seaboard there are places of summer resort, where hotels and boarding-houses are kept for the accommodation of those who come

---

[8]*The American Angler's Book*, Memorial Edition, Thaddeus Norris, 1877, page viii.

to shoot and to fish: the visitors frequently bringing their families to enjoy the bathing and invigorating sea air. To almost any of these let one who is fond of fishing repair between the middle of July and first of September. Let him provide himself with a stout rod, good flax line, large hooks, a felt hat, a red flannel shirt, and a few "store clothes" for Sunday and dress occasions, and he will have fishing to his heart's content—big ones, and plenty of them. If he takes the advice of old fogies, or the man who furnishes his boat and bait, he will fish with a hand-line. If he follows the instinct of the true angler, he will fish with rod and reel, and as a consequence his enjoyment of the sport will be enhanced.

Of all places within easy distance of our city,[9] commend me to Long Beach,[10] where the accommodations are good (barring the butter), mosquitoes few (if the wind is not off land), and the landlord one of the most obliging and appreciative men in the world as to the requirements of the angler or shooter. And moreover where Sammy Shourds[11] is always on hand, Sammy can find soft crabs where no other man can; besides he knows all the fishing-grounds, and when the tides suit at each; when to go on the flats for Weakfish, when in the cove for Barb, when in the channel for Sheepshead, when to the flat, sedgy islands for Rockfish, and when to squid for Bluefish. Here, according to the adjudication of the aforesaid Sammy, a friend and myself caught with our rods in three mornings (fishing four hours at each time), over five hundred pounds of Weakfish and Barb, and touched up the Rockfish in the afternoons at the islands.[12]

Five hundred pounds of weakfish and barb (king whiting) is impressive fishing. But it also tells us that although nineteenth-century sportsmen differed from their commercial colleagues in the kind of tackle they used, their ideas of what constituted angling success (namely, a boatload of fish) were all too often identical.

Spencer Fullerton Baird was familiar with angling on the Jersey shore, and in the summer of 1854, he explored sport fishing possibilities from Cape May to Long Island. His report to the Smithsonian is an

---

[9]Philadelphia. Although Norris (1811–1877) was born in Warrenton, Virginia, his family moved north soon after his birth, and he considered himself a Pennsylvanian throughout his life.

[10]Long Beach is the barrier island between Beach Haven and Barnegat inlets.

[11]Shourds (also spelled Shourdes) is an old Jersey Shore name. Doubtless a "cousin" of Sammy's, Harry V. Shourdes (1861–1920) of Tuckerton was one of the Atlantic coast's premier decoy carvers.

[12]Norris, pages 277–278.

interesting blend of science, travel, and anecdote. He tells us that "some of the best sport I ever witnessed with [weak]fish was had by using the eye of those already caught as bait." Or, astonishing to a modern angler increasingly denied the pleasure of angling for porgies by the vast trawler fleets that intercept them before they reach the inlets and bays, Baird describes porgies so numerous that "they became very troublesome by their great numbers and the destruction of bait caused by their incessant nibbling."

Because of his work as assistant secretary for the Smithsonian Institution, most of Baird's angling activities before the war were confined to the Potomac and nearby Chesapeake waters. This was not such a hardship a century ago:

The rock [striped bass] takes a bait readily; and, from the vigor of its actions, affords fine sport with the rod and reel; the fly especially adapted to the capture of this species. . . .

The rockfish is more abundant in Chesapeake bay and its tributaries than anywhere else to the northward. Here they occur all the year round, and are taken in great numbers. During their migration, they feed voraciously upon the herring bound on the same errand up the fresh-water streams. These they ascend to a great height, in the Susquehanna, before the dams were built, reaching the forks at Northumberland, and possibly beyond. The falls of the Potomac offer serious impediments to their passage much above the city of Washington. Arrested in this way, they accumulate in considerable numbers, and afford great sport to the citizens of the place during spring and early summer. The late Mr. Webster[13] was frequently to be seen patiently exercising that skill which made him eminent among the celebrated fishermen of the day.

Owing to its abundance, the rock is the chief staple of the Washington fish-market, where it is to be seen throughout most of the year. It is usually sold at moderate price, and it is no uncommon thing to have the opportunity of purchasing one of 30 or 40 pounds for 75 cents.[14]

---

[13]Secretary of State Daniel Webster (1782–1852) is credited by John J. Brown in *The American Angler's Guide* (page 205) with taking a nine-pound codfish on a fly rod along the coast near Marshfield, Massachusetts! Congressman Robert Barnwell Roosevelt (1829–1906), patrician conservationist, later New York Commissioner of Fisheries, and uncle of President Theodore Roosevelt, was also fond of fly fishing for Potomac stripers, although he did his angling there after the Civil War.

[14]*Ninth Annual Report* of the Board of Regents of the Smithsonian Institution showing the operations, expenditures, and condition of the Institution up to January 1, 1855. Washington, D. C., page 321.

Several early outdoor writers have left documentation showing that rods and reels were used for this-or-that species in such-and-such a year, but too few have left us with a sufficient memory of what it was like to fly cast on the Potomac or cast from the rocks of Rhode Island a century or more ago. A delightful exception was Genio C. Scott.

We know very little about this man. Charles Goodspeed[15] tells us that Scott was born in Livonia, New York, in 1809, worked as a publisher of fashion plates, and died in New York City in 1879. The first edition of his *Fishing in American Waters* appeared in 1869, and it was later expanded to include more southern coastal fishes and even a section on the Pacific salmon in 1875. Finally we know that Scott wrote for *Forest and Stream* and that George Brown Goode (second U. S. Fish Commissioner after Spencer F. Baird) cites Scott as a "useful" source of fundamental facts about sport fishing. But not even his obituary in the *New York Times* (December 20) can tell us what his middle initial "C." stands for.[16]

This is sad, for we are naturally curious about the man who gave us one of our earliest descriptions of the New England "bassing clubs"; who felt that the striped bass, not the Atlantic salmon, is "the fish of fishes *par excellence*"[17]; and who sealed his preference for salt water

---

[15]*Angling in America, Its Early History and Literature*, Charles Eliot Goodspeed, Boston, 1939, page 227.

[16]We do have one other important reference to Scott. In *American Game Fishes: Their Habits, Habitat and Peculiarities: How, When, and Where to Angle for Them*, edited by George O. Shields in 1892, Francis Endicott, in his chapter on "The Striped Bass" writes: "I have many times fished with an old friend— that thorough angler and excellent writer, Genio C. Scott—on the south side of Long Island for trout, at Rockaway Inlet for Sheepshead; but the one day that we had, off Staten Island, fishing for striped bass, when I sat, as it were, at the feet of Gamaliel, gathering in heaps of fish-lore and occasional fishes, will ever have a place in my memory as one of perfect enjoyment" (page 145).

[17]Scott added: "Casting menhaden bait for striped bass from the rocky shores of bays, estuaries, and islands along the Atlantic coast constitutes the highest branch of American angling. It is indeed questionable—when considering all the elements which contribute toward the sum total of sport in angling—whether this method of striped bass fishing is not superior to fly-fishing for salmon, and if so, it outranks any angling in the world. The method is eminently American, and characteristic of the modern angler by its energy of style, and the exercise and activity necessary to success." *Fishing in American Waters*, Genio C. Scott, New York, 1869, page 64. Another angling writer to describe the striped bass as "one of the finest game and food fishes in the world" was Theodore Gordon, America's most famous fly fisherman. Writing in 1913, Gordon says that "on the same tackle [the striper] makes longer runs and fights as well as the Atlantic salmon. Large striped bass were at one time fished for at the Falls of the Potomac with large flies. I have killed them [myself] with Bumble-puppy flies." *The Complete Fly*

over fresh with a gold-embossed Spanish mackerel[18] on his book's cover, rather than another leaping brook trout or pike.

Many anglers today believe that surf fishing had its start just before World War II, and that the sport really got going in the late 1940's when a wave of veterans came home, converted jeeps and Model A Fords into beach buggies, and did nothing but fish for awhile to forget the war. Certainly the tremendous increase in surf fishing in the 1940's can be called a major rediscovery of the sport. But the first flowering of shore and beach fishing occurred in the 1840's, not the 1940's, and even Genio Scott was not around for the first cast.[19]

Fisherman, the Notes and Letters of Theodore Gordon, edited by John D. Mc-Donald, New York, 1947, page 331. Bob Boyle, author of *The Hudson River—a Natural and Unnatural History*, adds in personal correspondence dated February 18, 1973, "I suspect Gordon did the latter in the sloughs of Haverstraw on the Hudson, across the river from where I live."

In the 1890's, a distinguished sports writer, Dr. Leroy Milton Yale, coined a phrase describing the striper as "the salmon of the surf." But such self-conscious and competitive comparisons between striped bass and salmon generally ended about the turn of the century with the rise of the tarpon as America's most prestigious gamefish.

[18]In addition to a streamlined shape which makes the Spanish mackerel an attractive design element, this species (*Scomberomorus maculatus*) underwent a veritable population explosion in the New York Bight following the Civil War. Thus, it was well known to many potential buyers of Scott's book on angling.

In an essay on "The Fishes of New York Market" published in 1854, Theodore Gill says this fish is of slight commercial importance. Yet within two decades, more than 300,000 pounds were annually being sold through Manhattan markets. Just after the war, Genio Scott wrote, "My experience in trolling for Spanish mackerel off the inlets of Fire Island has convinced me that the fish is as numerous as the bluefish, more so than the striped bass at certain seasons, and a little further seaward than either of those fishes. Every year the shoals become more numerous and more are taken."

Yet by the turn of the century, except for rare stragglers, the fish were gone from off the New York coast. As with most phenomena of the sea, no one knows precisely why vast schools of Spanish mackerel ever moved so far north in the first place—and why they later disappeared. But as the resource diminished, commercial fishermen sold other fishes as "Spanish mackerel," and in 1878 George Brown Goode reported "large quantities" of Atlantic bonito (*Sarda sarda*) so sold. Thus the fisheries historian is more frustrated than most, for he never knows for sure whether the popular name he's looking at in an old ledger is actually the fish described or some more euphemistic title the wholesaler dreamed up to help sell the catch to a trusting buyer.

[19]According to Julian T. Crandall, President of Ashaway Line and Twine Manufacturing Company, his great grandfather, Captain Lester Crandall, was making handlines for members of the Cuttyhunk Club as early as 1832. Handlines then gave way to rods and reels in the early 1840's when Captain Crandall began to import Irish linen from which he made a finer diameter twisted line for better storage and casting qualities than the tarred cotton used for handlines.

Let's go back 100 years and join Scott on a tour of the clubs along the north shore of Long Island Sound. We find surf fishing an elegant pastime for men in ties and jackets casting from specially-built piers with "gillies" to ladle out the chum and gaff the fish. That is a long way from today's solitary cussing after occasional splashes of cold water down the front of your waders. A century ago, the day was capped with a silver-service supper in the clubhouse—not a cup of lukewarm coffee in the back of a friend's pickup camper. I am not sure which sport is "better." Our contemporary way of doing things adds an element of humility and makes the experience of our first night-caught, surf-run bass a highly personal, nearly religious experience. But then I remember at least one occasion when having a "gillie" on hand to manage the gaffing would have saved a big fish, and more than a few times when a well-cooked, waiter-served dinner would have gone a long way toward mitigating weariness at the end of a long afternoon of slinging lures at the horizon.

But let's follow Scott and a visiting doctor from Great Britain as they talk and tour and fish among the islands of southern New England. Note that the theatrical dialogue,[20] an awkward device by contemporary standards, serves the purpose of instructing the reader in the tackle and procedures for this kind of angling:

Scott: Well, Doctor, having arrived at West Island, which is owned by an association of gentlemen who have formed themselves into a club for the incomparable enjoyment of angling for striped bass, they will, of course, assign us stands to fish from tomorrow. It is the practice here for all members to draw at night for the choice of stands to fish from the next day.

Doctor: A gentleman just handed me a card containing a number with "outside the Hopper" marked on it.

Scott: The members have given us their best stand! That is typical courtesy in all the bassing clubs.[21] On the morrow we will try to do honor to their estimate of us.

---

[20]I have taken the liberty of editing the dialogue to make it more comprehensible and less redundant for the modern reader. Purists are encouraged to look up the original text.

[21]According to A. Foster Higgens' account of "Striped Bass Fishing" in *The Out-of-Door Library: Angling* (1897), such courtesy began even as the fishermen were leaving the little steamer that ran passengers to the island, for the boat's whistle would toot out the number of visitors aboard so that by the time the men reached their quarters, their beds would be made and drinks would be waiting. Furthermore, any angler who forgot to bring tackle found that "tender of rods, reels, lines, will speedily be made, until he is more amply equipped" (page 132).

(The pleasurable anticipations of the morrow's exploits caused us to awake early, and I sounded the doctor before daylight.)

Scott: Hallo, Doctor! Mosier, our gaffer, rapped and said it was four o'clock.

Doctor: Well, sir, I have been up an hour, and down in the court trying to joint my rod, but I didn't have sufficient light.

Scott: Wait till we get to the Hopper Rocks to joint your rod. We'll be ready by the time Mosier gets the fish chummed in. Mosier calls up bass here just as a farmer brings his chickens to feed. But there is no use to make a cast before sunrise.

[*Later at the stand*]

Mosier: I've throwed in the chum of six fish,[22] but them scups and cachocket[23] comes up and takes it for all the world as if they was game! And I hain't seen nothin of no bass yet.

Scott: Doctor, in fastening the hook to your line, cast two half hitches with the end of your line over the shank, just below the head; then turn up the end of the line, and cast a half hitch over it and the shank, and turn the hook round in the tie thus formed to see that it revolves easily—cut off any superfluous end of line. See how Mosier chops up the chum, and where he throws it. Just where he throws the chum, cast your baited hook. . . .[24]

Scott: Your reel overruns? You should keep your thumb on the reel, and check it as the bait drops on the water. Mosier, bait my hook. I have on a medium-sized hook with a headed shank, and I am going after the fish missed by the doctor.

Mosier: Mr. Scott, jist cast along there in Snecker's Gap, for they are reether sassy there on the young flood.

Scott: Well, Mosier, here goes for a 40-pounder! [*Almost immediately, he hooks one.*]

Mosier: There! I told you so. I knew that feller wanted breakfast, and I guess he's got enough to last him!

Doctor: Mr. Mosier, as I have at last succeeded in getting my line unsnarled, shall I cast now?

Mosier: Not quite yet, I guess, for there's no knowing where that critter will lead Mr. Scott.

---

[22]Menhaden were the usual chum and bait. It has been frequently claimed that lobster tails were the chief bait used in the New England striped bass clubs. However, bait choices were pretty well divided between menhaden fillets, lobster tails, and small eels—with menhaden preferred for chum. Indeed, Robert B. Roosevelt complains about lobster bait as "deficient in tenacity, and has to be tied on like menhaden" (*Superior Fishing*, New York, 1865, page 154).

[23]Porgies and cunners.

[24]One advantage to stand fishing was that the bait did not have to be cast far to be over fish, and consequently sinkers were unnecessary.

Doctor: Mr. Mosier, do you think that fish will ever be landed? He has run nearly all the line off the reel already.

Mosier: I can't say. There's no counting on them chaps till they're landed if you're fishing with a pole. But if I had on my handline, I'd make him come humming, and show no quarter!

Scott: Mosier, keep my line away from the rocks with your gaff, for he seems bent on rounding the Hopper Rock, and its corners may cut or chafe and part my line.

There! He has tacked again. Be ready to gaff him if I get him near enough, before he makes another run.

Mosier: I see his mate akeeping alongside him all the time. She's 'bout as big as the hooked one. I mean to gaff that one first. How like tarnation the feller fights, and tries to whip out the hook with his tail! That shows he's getting tired. When they curl themselves up on the top of the water so you can't budge 'em, you had better be careful not to hold so hard as to let 'em break the line with their tail, nor cut it off with their back fin; nor so loose as to let him git slack to unhook. There! See him straighten out! He has made his last fight, and got shipped! His mate has gone. 'Twas no use for her to stay any longer, for she knows he's dead. Now, with the heave and haul of the tide, there is more danger of breaking the line and losing him that if he was alive. But here he comes, and here goes the gaff. [*He strikes.*] A 40-pounder at least!

Scott: Well done, Mosier! Struck just in time, for the hook has let go.

Mosier: Jist so. I hain't no confidence in them hooks with the barb curling out so that you can not git it into the flesh. The Kinsey point and Sproat bend, or the O'Shaughnessy with the Kinsey point, are the best.

Doctor: Well, my preconceived notions of bass fishing have all been cast wide. When you first hooked the bass, I thought I could take a seat and be a quiet looker-on at the play; but I have been so excited by alternate hopes, fears, doubts, and surprises, that I want you to pardon me for getting into your way several times. The truth is, it astonishes me to see the fish on *terra firma*. I thought him lost a dozen times! And I cannot now fully realize how it is possible to play successfully so large a fish, and one so game, in such boisterous water, with such slender tackle. I am really afraid to try to make a cast, for I expect if I get a strike, I shall either break my rod, or the fish will part my line.

Mosier: Doctor, you jist make a cast out into the Rifle Pit, and do it right away. For I see by their whirls that they're hungry.

Scott: See that your thumb-stalls are well on, and that your line is clear. Now reel up so that your bait is within two feet of the tip of your rod. And when you cast, hold your thumb gently on the reel-line,

[57]

and as the bait touches the water, press your thumb on the line to check the reel at one, and prevent the reel from over-running.

Doctor: Well, here goes for a second trial.

Scott: Very fair cast. Far enough for bass at this stage of tide.

[*The Doctor hooks a fish.*]

Doctor: I shall not be able to save him! I know I can not, for he runs and pulls so like a reindeer that I cannot check him. There! My thumb-stall is loose, and I feel that my reel is not tight. He's gone! I knew I couldn't save him!

Scott: Don't be so excited, Doctor. Keep cool, and reel in your slack line. He's only studying a new dodge or making a new tack.

Mosier: I seen him! He's a scrouger!

Scott: There, Doctor, he is now laying his course for Newport. Reel as fast as you can, and, if necessary, run back to prevent him from getting slack line.

[*The fight continues for 15 minutes.*]

He has fought until he's finished. Gingerly, Doctor. Reel with the incoming surf, and slacken with the ebb. [*Mosier strikes with the gaff.*] There!

Mosier: He is a game one, and will weigh over 20 pounds. They're always hifalorum in them Rifle Pits![25]—Gentlemen, the breakfast horns have been blowin' a good while.

Doctor: I'm wilted! These rocks are rough to run about on and play a fish. I had long heard that striped bass were game, but all that I ever heard or read did not prepare me for such encounters as I have seen and realized this morning! I am not now surprised that Americans consider this the head of game fishes. The accessories of fishing for it, the scenes where it is taken, together with the *modus operandi* of its

---

[25]Such lively sport was not just a figment of Scott's imagination. Francis Endicott describes a three-month catch of striped bass made from especially built iron piers at Newport by Thomas Winans and his nephew, Thomas Whistler. They caught 124 bass weighing 2,921 pounds, for an average of 23 pounds per bass. The largest fish weighed 60 pounds, and "there were but nineteen 'minnows' taken in the season, that weighed six pounds or under." (*American Game Fishes: Their Habits, Habitat, and Pecularities: How, When, and Where to Angle for Them*, edited by George O. Shields, Chicago and New York, 1892, page 147.)

Winans's stand at Brenton Reef was later bought by a Mr. Davis for a considerable sum of money, and was ranked by A. Foster Higgins as the best stand in all of New England. In second place came the rocks at Narragansett, once known as "Anthony's" in honor of John Anthony, an innkeeper "Yankee born and bred, honest, faithful, willing, and acquainted with all the habits, devices, and iniquities of [striped] bass and bluefish." (From Robert B. Roosevelt's *Superior Fishing*, page 151.) Besides Newport, West Island, Cuttyhunk, and Pasque Island, stand fishing and striper clubs developed at Point Judith, Squibnocket, Block Island, and Montauk Point, Long Island.

[58]

capture by artistic means, render the sport the most exciting that I know of under the head of angling!

[The story then continues as a straight narrative told by Scott.]

"As the breakfast-table is the morning's trysting-place for the members of the club, where they recount their exploits over their tea and coffee, with broiled bluefish, striped bass and scopogue, or with broiled chicken and beefsteak, the tender of congratulations to my friend for his success, and the stories of successful takes by some, and of parting tackle with others, acted as charming opiates to witch away the time. And when we rose from the table we saw our yacht hove-to, and the sails flapping an invitation for us to step aboard. With great reluctance and regret we parted from the members of the West Island Club, and the most attractive five-acre island in America.

"The sail to Cuttyhunk was remarkably interesting, presenting views of the picturesque landscape, alternating with villas and foliage on the Massachusetts shore, and the group of Elizabeth Island and Martha's Vineyard, with No Man's Land peering above the waves far out in the ocean. We arrived before lunch time, and, having examined the trout preserve, the black bass and white perch ponds, and taken each a couple of striped bass from that incomparable stand, 'Bass Rock,' we adjourned to dinner, where we were regaled with choice viands, wines, and the recital of angling exploits by the members of the club,[26] who are justly celebrated as amateur experts with rod and reel.

"After dinner we shook hands as an *au revoir pas adieu*, and ran over to Pugne [*sic*] Island[27] to drop in upon John Anderson, Esquire, and learn from him what charms he could see in his little island of a hundred acres to induce a millionaire of his industrious proclivities and habits—without a knowledge or taste for field-sports or yachting— to shut himself out thus from the enjoyments of the greatest and most social city in the Union—his birth-place, where he has, by enterprise, accumulated a fortune, and possesses one of the finest residences in the metropolis. He informed us that the charming climate, with the constant feast to his eyes in scenery made up of the mainland and the islands, with the ever-changing aspects of the sea, filled his soul with rapture and made his cup of happiness full to over-flowing. With a

---

[26]The Cuttyhunk Fishing Association was formally incorporated in 1865. It was dissolved in 1907 because of the relative scarcity of stripers compared with former days.

[27]Either a misprint or an antique spelling for Penikese—the same island Anderson turned over to Louis Agassiz for his summer school.

promise to visit him before taking final leave of Vineyard Sound, we steered for Pasque Island, only six miles distant.

"Here we found a club-house with appointments calculated to render not only the members of the club and their families comfortable, but all such guests as members of the association think proper to extend invitations to. The island includes more than a thousand acres, which the club has divided into two farms, erected commodious buildings, including club-house, ice-house, stabling, etc. The club has also vegetable and flower gardens, sail-boats, and row-boats, and the river, which sets back a mile into the island, is stocked with a hundred-thousand menhaden as bait for the use of the club.[28] This is the *ne plus ultra* of a place for angling. It also contains a large pond well stocked with black bass, besides several perch ponds; the latter is not regarded as a very valuable accessory to any piece of real estate, for perch fishing is not considered sport in America. I mean the common yellow perch with barred sides; but the white perch, like those of Cuttyhunk, offer good sport to ladies and children, and are a very good pan-fish, ranging in size from three ounces to three pounds.

"We remained at Pasque Island several days, most of the time angling for striped bass, but occasionally, on a dark day, spending it in a cruise after swordfish, which we took with the harpoon. Other days we rowed a little boat out a hundred rods from shore, when we put down killick and still-baited for squeteague, weighing from five to fifteen pounds each. Then, again, if the bluefish came in such shoals as to turn our strait into a state of commotion resembling soap-suds, we rigged to the end of our bass-line about two feet of piano wire, on which we wound a hook with copper wire. Then we anchored on the edge of the tide, and cast out a hook baited without much care, and the moment afterward we were saluted by a jerk and a somersault a yard clear of the surface, and a short, vigorous fight to bring the bluefish to gaff. An hour of energetic sport, and twenty bluefish of from eight to twelve pounds each generally satisfied us; and though the fish challenged us

---

[28]Before the advent of wholesalers devoted to its distribution and before refrigeration to ensure its preservation, fresh bait was often difficult to obtain. Robert B. Roosevelt, writing about the New England striper clubs in 1865, warns that "there is often great difficulty in obtaining bait, particularly during a storm, which is the time that it is most needed, as the fish bite best in rough weather, and on going from the cities it is well to pack a few hundred menhaden in a box with ice and sawdust, and this insures a supply for some days ahead." *Superior Fishing*, page 149. Obviously, a tidal river stocked with live menhaden made the Pasque Island Club one of the most desirable in New England.

by menacing leaps to continue the contest, we preferred to retire—however ignominious it might appear to them—and recuperate for another time.

"It was hard to part from those charming scenes and the healthful recreation. The doctor decided to return home to England, arrange his business, come back, and spend his life at Pasque Island. But how to leave those captivating aquatic scenes, ranging from simple loveliness to grandeur, and sometimes rising to sublimity? What scene can be more refreshing and exaulting than an expansive view of the mighty waves, dotted here and there with such beautiful islands as those in the Vineyard Sound?

"The Elizabeth Islands offer the condiments of existence to season the dry hurry-scurry and commonplaceism of the business world on the main lands of America. And they will, before many years, be numbered with the watering-places of the world *par excellence*. While aquatic birds skim the waves, and the gulls are screaming, dipping, and darting over a shoal of bluefish or menhaden, vessels outward and homeward bound are always passing, for it includes in its range of view the packets and steamers for England, and the steam and sailing crafts between New York and Boston.

"We have here the foreground and perspective worthy the pencil of Claude de Lorraine, while the background is formed by the granite shores of Massachusetts, with its improvements so varied and important as to give surety of an intelligent and industrious population. Who would not delight to angle here?"[29]

A rhetorical question, of course. But the saltwater angler's answer was already being confused by attractive alternatives. Florida had been introduced to many Yankees during the Civil War, and with that conflict now ended, and with business booming in the mills and plants at home, wealthy sportsmen from New York and Boston varied their summers at Cuttyhunk and West End Island with cruises to southern waters. Spanish names like Boca Grande and Punta Rossa began to crop up in the lexicon of saltwater angling. And rumors of a marvelous new gamefish—the savanilla or Silver King—sailed north to tempt men of leisure from their newly established allegiance to the striped bass.

---

[29]*Fishing in American Waters*, New York, 1869, pages 69–77.

FIVE

THE SILVER KING

Grant me, oh Lord, a grand 'écai,
So great and grand that even I
May have no need
To lie. . . .—Louis Babcock's version of
the Angler's Prayer

The reputation of Florida as a fisherman's mecca actually goes back
before the Civil War. Coastal schooners and packet steamers trading
between northern ports and such southern destinations as Havana,
New Orleans, and Tampico, Mexico, frequently slipped into one or
another of the uncharted inlets found along both coasts of the
Florida peninsula. There, while waiting for a storm to pass or while
foraging ashore for firewood and water, a member of the crew would
fish. The numbers he caught—and the many he could not even land—
amazed the mariners. Descriptions of Florida as an angler's paradise,
as well as a cornucopia of sea fare, returned north with the homeward-
bound sailors.

Novels, as well as published diaries, of men's adventures in this
sub-tropical land further fed the imaginations of sportsmen-naturalists
who had never been there. In 1852, a Georgian by the name of F. R.

Goulding[1] wrote a book describing Florida as a place where bear, deer, and turkey hunting was as effortless as walking a few feet from your campsite, and where limitless sheepshead and sea trout fishing was merely a matter of finding salt water for your baited hook. In Goulding's account, even the ospreys help people catch fish!

The Young Marooners[2] *on the Florida Coast* went through three printings the first year out and was shortly issued by six different publishing houses in Great Britain alone. The book's theme of survival in the wilderness was as exciting 100 years ago as it is today. And Florida as a wilderness was even more exotic to mid-nineteenth-century sportsmen than Africa or South America is to us today. Goulding's armchair adventures were further enhanced by no mention of heat, humidity, or mosquitoes.

After the Civil War, many sporting expeditions to Florida were undertaken. In the winter of 1873–1874, the most important of these, an expedition sponsored by the weekly newspaper *Forest and Stream,* was sent to explore the "sporting attributes" of Lake Okeechobee. The following winter and into the spring of 1875, a similar expedition, again commissioned by *Forest and Stream*, was sent to report on the south Florida coast along the Gulf of Mexico. The newspaper's owner, Charles Hallock, then published *Camp Life in Florida*, composed entirely of observations made during these two expeditions. Hallock's chief fisheries expert was S. C. Clarke, who contributed the angling world's first description of a gamefish that, in just another decade, would provide the foundation for an entirely new saltwater sport fishery and the springboard for the development of big-game angling to come.

The tarpum [*sic*] I have not seen. It . . . is rare,[3] and is described to belong to the mackerel family,[4] growing to the weight of 80 to 100 pounds. A surface fish, very active and strong, with brilliant silvery

---

[1]Born near Midway, Georgia, on September 28, 1810, Goulding was a minister most of his life. In addition to young people's books, he compiled a *Confederate Soldier's Hymn Book* in 1863. He died August 21, 1881, and is buried in the little churchyard at Roswell, Georgia.

[2]There is double entendre here. In addition to its usual connotation, coastal Southerners of the last century described any hunting or fishing trip to an offshore barrier island as "marooning."

[3]Or so he thought—probably because he had not seen one.

[4]The tarpon is a member of the family *Elopidae*, which includes the ladyfish and machete. It is more of a herring than a mackerel, albeit a herring that may reach 300 pounds in weight!

[63]

scales the size of a dollar. It is rarely taken with hook and line, as it generally carries away the tackle, however strong.

It goes in schools, and leaps from the water when struck, either with hook or spear. The only successful way of killing the tarpum, I am told, is to strike it with a harpoon, to which is attached by a strong line a small empty cask; the fish, by struggling with this buoy, exhausts itself so that it may be approached in a boat and killed with a lance. . . .

Not having access to any works on ichthyology, I am unable to give the scientific names of these fishes. They are mentioned under the above name by Captain Romans, who wrote a *Concise Natural History of Florida* about 1773. New York anglers, who kill 30- or 40-pound striped bass with the rod, would find . . . tarpum foemen worthy of their steel.[5]

Dr. James Alexander Henshall, the noted black bass authority, claimed in 1908 that he took his first tarpon on sporting tackle in 1878. Using a salmon fly rod and "large gaudy flies," he caught small tarpon "running from ten to forty pounds."[6] However, writing before the turn of the century, Henshall had other memories of his first encounter with "tarpum." The fly-caught fish range only up to 10 pounds, and nowhere is there a suggestion by the doctor that hundred-weight tarpon could even be landed on rod and reel.[7] On a visit to Horr's Island near Marco in the fall of 1881, he finds men engaged in an activity that seems entirely reasonable considering the size of their quarry:

The boat being poled quietly along the fringe of mangrove bushes at the edge of the channels, the man standing in the bow with the grains[8] ready, at length spies a great tarpum some six feet long, like a giant fish of burnished silver, poised motionless in the shade.

When within striking distance, he hurls the grains by its long handle with a skillful and dexterous thrust and unerring aim born of long experience, which strikes home with an enormous thud, when the

---

[5]*Camp Life in Florida: A Handbook for Sportsmen and Settlers*, compiled by Charles Hallock, New York, 1876, pages 63–64.

[6]"But even at these weights they demanded the best skill of the angler, inasmuch as they were hooked in the mouth, and only occasionally could one be landed." *Favorite Fish and Fishing*, James A. Henshall, New York, 1908, page 123.

[7]Henshall never did get with the tarpon craze. In his *Bass, Pike, Perch and Other Game Fishes of America*, first published in 1903, he still seems to be denying the existence of this gamefish—as though, by not writing about tarpon, he hopes they'll go away and leave his beloved black bass alone. In his considerable saltwater section, Henshall cites everything from striped bass to Bermuda chub, pinfish, and turbot (ocean tally)—but no tarpon!

[8]A stout, two-pronged spear.

monster tears away with a tremendous spurt, leaps clear of the surface, and, falling back, makes the water fairly boil and seethe in his desperate efforts to escape.

But the barbed grains hold fast, and the long stout line is as tense as a bow-string. The great fish tows the boat around like a cockleshell until his fierce struggles and grand leaps begin to tell on him, and at length he is towed ashore completely exhausted. Sometimes the boat is capsized or swamped by an unusually large and powerful fish, but . . . these "Conchs"[9] are almost amphibious, and seldom lose their fish, even under the most adverse circumstances.[10]

Another early description of the fish is found in Dr. G. Brown Goode's *American Fishes*, published in 1887. After commenting on the value of tarpon scales as a tourist item (they sold for 10 to 25 cents apiece) and estimating that fewer than 100 specimens are landed per year by any means anywhere in America, Goode reports the findings of one of Dr. Spencer Fullerton Baird's associates, a Mr. Stearns:

The tarpum will take a baited hook, but it is difficult to handle and seldom landed. The Pensacola seine fishermen dread it while dragging their seines, for they have known of persons having been killed or severely injured by its leaping against them from the seine in which it was inclosed. Even when it does not jump over the cork-line of a seine, it is quite likely to break through the netting before landed.[11]

Although Goode cites Dr. C. J. Kenworthy of Jacksonville, Florida (who used the pseudonym "Al Fresco" when contributing articles to sporting periodicals) as the man most responsible for making the tarpon a gamefish, Kenworthy's experience with tarpon was principally at the end of a handline. Credit for the first tarpon caught on rod and reel generally goes to a Mr. W. H. Wood of New York City. Perhaps, more importantly, credit for publicizing this "new game species" goes to America's leading sporting periodical of the time, *Forest and Stream*.

In the April 23, 1885, issue of this journal, Mr. Wood reports that he caught his first tarpon in Tarpon Bay, Florida, on March 25. It was five feet, nine inches long, and weighed 93 pounds. It took 26½ minutes to land. Wood caught another, smaller fish that day, and then three more at the mouth of the Caloosahatchee River on March 31. A Mr.

---

[9]Native Floridians—usually in the Keys—who make their living from the sea.

[10]*Camping and Cruising in Florida*, Cincinnati, 1884, pages 191–192. This book is a compilation of Henshall's Florida sketches originally published in *Forest and Stream* and the *American Field*.

[11]*American Fishes*, G. Brown Goode, Boston, 1903 edition, page 407.

John Smith of Fisherman's Key near Punta Gorda was his guide on both occasions.

Records are sometimes established, it seems, less to be broken than disputed, and Wood's claim quickly created controversy in the angling press. Mr. S. C. Clarke, who contributed our first description of the "tarpum," wrote *Forest and Stream* to say that a Mr. S. H. Jones of Philadelphia had actually taken the first tarpon, weighing 174 pounds, about 1878 in the Indian River on Florida's east coast. Not to be outdone, A. W. Dimock claimed that he was battling big tarpon on rod and reel as early as February 1882—"three years before the recognition of the tarpon as a gamefish."[12] Of course, there was Dr. Henshall's claim to fame with catches of baby tarpon on salmon tackle in the fall of 1878, and still other, less qualified claims followed.

But since the capture of Mr. Wood's 93-pounder was widely acclaimed by *Forest and Stream*, and since the affidavits of Clarke, Henshall, and others were generally disregarded, the fame—whatever it's worth—of having caught the first tarpon on rod and reel belongs to Mr. Wood. After all, his catch was what created interest in tarpon angling as a sport.

Word of his success crossed the Atlantic, and the *London Observer* on August 26, 1886, included the following item in their sporting section:

Here, at last, there is a rival to the black bass of North America, to the *Silurus glanis* [a giant catfish] of the Danube, to our own European salmon, and possibly even to the sturgeon, were that monster capable of taking a hook and holding it in its leech-like sucker of a mouth. Sportsmen may go to Florida for the tarpon, as they now go to the Arctic Zone for the reindeer, walrus, and musk-ox.[13]

The "silver rush" was on!

In the decades ahead, British anglers would make a considerable contribution to the development of sport fishing along our southern coasts. By the time *The English Angler in Florida* appeared in 1898, tarpon fishing was a significant tourist enterprise. The author, Rowland Ward, speaks of the "hundreds of citizens" who migrate south every winter for this sport. And he advises his British readers that

---

[12]*The Book of the Tarpon*, A. W. Dimock, New York, 1911, pages 14–15.

[13]Amusingly, this notice upset American outdoor writer Robert Grant when it reached our shores—not for what it said about the tarpon but for its implication that the Atlantic salmon was somehow the sole property of Europe!

London is just nine days from Punta Gorda, Florida, including a lay-over in New York City to be properly outfitted with tackle at Edward Vom Hofe's, "a practical tarpon fisherman himself, and a well-known frequenter of the Florida waters."

Even earlier, in 1891, *Camp-Fires of the Everglades, or Wild Sports in the South*, originally published in New York in 1860, was reprinted in Edinburgh—only this time the book included a chapter and accompanying illustration on tarpon fishing. The author, Charles E. Whitehead (1829–1903), was president of the New York, Pennsylvania and Rock Island Railroad, and he liked to boast that he had fished or hunted in every state of the Union. However, there were so many amazing details in his narrative of outdoor life along the Florida coast that one British reviewer expressed doubt as to the book's accuracy. Yet the reviewer also admitted he had never heard of a place called the Everglades!

In 1902, Englishman J. Turner-Turner, published *The Giant Fish of Florida*, which gives an excellent account of angling at Boca Grande at the turn of the century. Although the only accommodation near the cut was a gigantic houseboat called the Hughes' Floating Hotel, Turner-Turner recommends that anglers bring their ladies along, for "the gentler sex seems to have taken to tarpon fishing to an extent quite unforeseen when first men introduced the sport."

The author also suggests that his readers try night fishing:

Tarpon fishing by night is exciting work, somewhat too exciting for many people. The fish, however, bite with far more certainty than by day, particularly when the moon is shining. There is an element of danger about this nightfishing. . . . It is impossible to know how far one is drifting towards the open sea, and on all sides one hears the plunges of mighty fish, which are far more likely to land in the boat than during the day. A great tarpon may seize the bait and get round behind the angler to his utter confusion. Even if the shore is reached in time, there is considerable difficulty and excitement in landing a tarpon on a dark night.[14]

---

[14]*The Giant Fish of Florida*, J. Turner-Turner, London, 1902. Still another English angler helped publicize the sport early in this century by taking with him to Mexico and Florida an Ottamar Anchutz camera with a Goerz lens capable of being stopped down to 1/1,000 of a second. Even with the relatively slow films of that day, the pictures taken by E. G. S.-Churchill in 1905 for his *Tarpon Fishing in Mexico and Florida* are sensational. Some 27 half-tones are scattered throughout the text and include some wonderfully clear shots of leaping tarpon with the town of Tampico or the old lighthouse at Boca Grande in the background. In

Mr. Turner-Turner makes other perceptive observations on angling the Florida passes 75 years ago:

Tarpon fishing is a social gathering, and not by any means a solitary sport. Whether the undoubted charm of this distinction lies in the inherent gregariousness, often undiscovered, in the angler's bosom, or rather perhaps in the rare pleasure of seeing one's friends in all manner of difficulties, it is quite certain that tarpon fishing would be far less popular under other conditions. As it is, where the fish are seen on the move, there must everyone go, and twenty or thirty boats will soon be clustered with no more than twenty yards between each.

An element of excitement is also imported by the continual apparition of great fish leaping high in the air, falling into boats and jeopardizing life and limb, for it is a poor choice whether you will have 150 pounds of lively fish dropped on the top of your skull, or whether you will rather have it fall in the side, with the risk of being knocked overboard to the sharks.[15]

Turner-Turner closes this descriptive section with an interesting prediction:

In thus discounting the skill at present necessary to the killing of tarpon, I do not overlook the fact that this state of things will not in all probability continue indefinitely, since there are already signs that the tarpon may become both scarcer and better educated as the sport gains more adherents; nor is it other than probable that we do not yet know the best methods of catching this splendid fish.[16]

The baits and techniques used to take tarpon at the turn of the century *were* primitive by modern standards. For starters, many anglers believed that large hooks and wire leaders were necessary for any and all saltwater fishing. Shiny stiff wire not only turned away countless leader-shy tarpon,[17] it made contests with the frequent shark inter-

---

addition, the author includes a special "wallet" on the inside back cover with 16 stereoscopic views of fighting fish that probably sold as many copies of the book as the text and other photos combined. S.-Churchill's photography was a sophisticated precursor to the Dimock brothers' great work 10 years later.

[15] *The Giant Fish of Florida*, page 47.

[16] *Ibid.*, page 48.

[17] W. N. Holdeman, writing in 1891, disagrees with this judgment. "When I began fishing," he says, "I used a snood [leader] made of piano-wire, and landed several Tarpon with it, which is contradictory to the statement of some authorities that the Tarpon will instantly detect the wire and spit it out." However, Holdeman gave up wire, not because he was not catching enough tarpon but because

lopers inevitable, or, at least, cost a great deal of valuable line that otherwise the shark could have nipped off at the hook. Only gradually did rawhide or fiber snells come to replace wire.

The first baits used were whole or half mullets with the hook so carefully hidden that the barb more often caught the bait again than the tarpon! The first fishing grounds were deep holes well inside the inlets where the bait was cast and allowed to sit on bottom by the hour. A dozen yards of line were stripped from the reel and coiled loosely by the fisherman while the rod lay athwart the gunwales near at hand. Then the angler waited. He slept, read, talked with his companions, and in some cases played cards or chess beneath an awning or umbrella to ward off the sun and occasional showers.

Surprisingly many tarpon were caught this way. However, countless more rays, sharks, jewfish, sawfish, and gafftopsail catfish were landed or lost, sometimes after major combat. Unwanted species would be all the more certain to appear when the boatman chummed. And since most boatmen, following the instructions of their northern clients who had learned the effectiveness of chumming for striped bass, did in fact season the waters around the boat with small bits of mullet, odds were always in favor of a shark or ray when the line finally started to move out.

But even here there were lessons the better boatmen learned to save their customer's time and adrenalin. A jerky runoff of line, a few inches at a time, meant catfish were after the bait. A slow, steady pull usually indicated a stingray. A rapid rush, pause, then rush again often meant a shark was swallowing the mullet; while a short, slow run—a pause—then another slow run—pause—alerted the angler to be ready for the leap of a tarpon when his line at last came taut. However, jewfish regularly confounded such neat formulae of fish behavior by imitating any or all of the above.

By the turn of the century, tarpon anglers had discovered that their time in Florida could be more profitably spent fishing tide changes at the inlets—either drifting or trolling whole mullets or mullet strips— and then returning to their yachts or hotels to rest up for still another

---

sharks were costing him too many hooks *and* wire leaders. As he put it, "the expense of wire snoods is by no means insignificant." He successfully tried cotton leaders and additionally reported that "to prevent the fraying contingent upon playing a fish for an hour or two, some fishermen incase their snoods with rubber tubing [although] I am not aware how successful this has proved." *American Game Fishes: Their Habits, Habitat, and Peculiarities: How, When, and Where to Angle for Them*, page 119.

effort after the sun went down. They learned to fish when the fish were likely to feed, not when they felt like fishing. And although rolling tarpon in an inlet are frequently impossible to tease into taking a baited hook, a fisherman's chances there were usually far better than sitting over a mosquito-infested hole on some windless creek. Besides, the occasional king mackerel, snook, and jack crevalle that took mullet baits lobbed to rolling tarpon were more exciting sport than the stingrays and catfish caught on bottom.

While sophistication in tarpon angling was a long time coming, the international fame of the sport marks the beginning of the development of specialized saltwater tackle capable of handling all the larger seafishes. The Vom Hofe brothers, Julius and Edward, produced fishing reels at their Brooklyn, New York, factory as early as 1857. But it was not until the 1880's that they began to respond to the particular demands of saltwater anglers from Cape Cod to Cape Sable. They improved and enlarged an earlier reel made for the New England angling clubs, and in E. M. Vom Hofe's catalog of the 1890's called this their striped bass *or* tarpon reel, made of the "finest quality rubber and German silver, full steel pivot with German silver bands, S-shaped balance handle to screw off, sliding oil cap, [and] tension click drag." Built in the tradition of the Kentucky craftsmen[18] who pioneered revolving spool multiplying reels, the Vom Hofe products were of such precision and dependability that the only significant differences between them and the light and medium ocean reels made today are in their greater bulk and lack of an internal drag system. Pressure was put on the line by an angler's "thumb stall," or, more generally, the leather "check" or brake attached to one of the reel pillars. Since there was also no free-spool lever, anglers had to be especially wary of bruised or broken knuckles when a fast fish took off.

The rods that went with these reels were veritable baseball bats by contemporary standards. The butts, including rustproof, corrosive-resistant German silver reel fittings, cost about four dollars apiece in

---

[18]A Kentucky watchmaker by the name of George Snyder made the first multiplying bait-casting reel in 1810. The Meek brothers (Jonathan and Benjamin), also Kentucky watchmakers, improved Snyder's basic design in the 1830's with a sliding button click, drag springs, and other refinements. Then about this same time, John W. Hardman, still another Kentucky watchmaker, produced the first quadruple multiplying reel with a 4:1 gear ratio, rather than the 3:1 and $3\frac{1}{2}$:1 ratios popularized by Snyder. The advantage, of course, was more line recovered per crank of the handle. In fresh water, this meant faster line retrieves; in saltwater angling this meant greater control over a fish rushing the boat or in pumping up a deep-sounding gamester.

[70]

the 1890's. Their six-foot tips were made of greenheart, split cane, or plain bamboo (with the latter the most common), and cost between 5 and 20 pre-1900 dollars. Most tips included double line guides, back to back, so to speak, under the theory that when the rod warped one way under the strain of many fish and much use, the angler could turn it over and warp it back. Naturally, when this theory was put into practice, it resulted in a lot of broken tips!

The tip of the rod was quite long and stiff, and in tarpon angling, this stiffness did serve to drive a hook into the tarpon's uncompromising mouth. The tip ring was also often fitted with a moveable agate collar, which eliminated the possibility of the line grooving and then breaking on soft-edged metal. (However, agate is prone to fracture, and today we settle this problem with special alloys or roller guides.)

Ultimately, line quality determines success or failure in fishing, and here again technology had responded to angling demands. The Ashaway Line and Twine Company goes back to 1824 when Captain Lester Crandall gave up his schooner and his fishing activities on the Grand Banks to go into the line business full-time, supplying his former colleagues with the tarred cotton he manufactured so well. Setting up a line walk and a waterwheel to turn his spindles on the banks of the Ashawog River in Ashaway, Rhode Island, he first supplied the New England striped bass clubs with twisted lines made from Irish linen in 1842. The original Cuttyhunk 9-thread was a 50 lea[19] line that tested at two pounds per thread when dry. After the turn of the century when angling regulations were being established by many clubs, the dry test was found to be an inadequate gauge of breaking strength which varied with atmospheric conditions and the moisture content of the line itself. Since thoroughly wet linen is 20 percent to 30 percent stronger than dry linen, a more realistic test was evolved to determine the line's breaking strength during the time a fish is actually challeng-

---

[19]A technical term designating a system for numbering linen yarn by the weight in grams of 300 yards. In describing some of the difficulties in maintaining quality control over line in the early days, Julian T. Crandall (in correspondence with the author dated February 22, 1972) writes: "As you know, linen is a plant fiber and the spinners had to boil off the natural flax fiber after it was spun to remove the gum Nature had used in its growth to hold the fiber together. The percent of natural gum varied some, so it was almost impossible for the spinner to tell beforehand just how much fiber to use to end up with a 50 lea. A #–1 lea is 300 yards of linen thread that weighs 7000 grams, a #–2 lea: 3500 grams, a 50 lea: 140 grams, and a 100 lea: 70 grams. Therefore, some batches of linen would end up 49 to 51 lea. If one batch came through 49, the line would test more than a batch made of 51 lea, et cetera."

[71]

ing the line's capacity. Ashaway and other line manufacturers developed a standard of testing line after it had been soaked in 72° F. water for 30 minutes. Cuttyhunk linen then moved from a rough two pounds to a firm three pounds per thread breaking strength. Hence, light tackle 6- and 9-thread lines are officially measured at 18 and 27 pounds breaking strength respectively. The heaviest thread lines were 54 and 72, but 24-thread (72-pound test) had become the standard for tarpon fishing by the turn of the century.

While tackle for this great gamefish was developing, man's knowledge of the tarpon's breeding and migration patterns was also growing. Most important, Florida anglers had discovered that the winter tourist season was not the best time to fish for tarpon. The winter and spring months were far more productive in places like Tampico, Mexico, and Port Aransas, Texas. Summers can be stifling on the Florida Gulf Coast, and while dedicated tarpon men and women showed up summer after summer at Boca Grande, Naples, and Marco, Henry Morrison Flagler's East Coast Railway[20] drew increased numbers of tourist-anglers away from the Gulf Coast and funneled them to Palm Beach, Miami, and the Keys. By 1910, the tarpon shared the Atlantic limelight with sailfish, king mackerel, barracuda, and other fishes that were successfully being taken with tackle originally developed for the Silver King. However, the tarpon's decline as the premier gamefish of salt water might have been less precipitous but for the activities of a group of California sportsmen. New problems for tackle manufacturers and challenges for anglers were suddenly recognized when the first bluefin tuna were caught at Catalina in 1898.

---

[20]Organized in 1886, it was extended to Miami a decade later, and then on to Key West in January, 1912.

[72]

Landing a Broadbill Off Catalina

R. Günnell

Section Two

OFFSHORE
AND DISTANT SEAS

SIX

BLUE BUTTONS, BLUE SEAS

And I think, as I angle for fish,
  In the hope that my hooks will attach 'em,
It's delightfully easy to fish—
  But harder than blazes to catch 'em.
  —"Fishin' Off Long P'int"
    by Wallace Irwin, 1904

As with tarpon fishing, big-game angling[1] has an official birth date and founding father. On June 1, 1898, Charles Frederick Holder of Pasadena, California, landed a 183-pound bluefin tuna on rod and reel off Catalina Island.

That Holder did not actually catch the first tuna on rod and reel is as immaterial as the possibility that W. H. Wood's rod-and-reel tarpon was not the first. Both catches were responsible for bringing the world's attention to their respective categories of saltwater sport, and other claims are as inconsequential as those on behalf of the Phoenician, Chinese, or Viking sailors who may have visited the New World before Columbus. As far as history is concerned, an undeveloped event is something that never happened.

Still it is fun to conjecture, and what is intriguing about the story

---

[1]Although tarpon reach big-game sizes, they generally are not included in this category of offshore, blue-water fish.

of this first tuna is the refusal of the executive branch of the big-game angling fraternity to consider any other hero but Mr. Holder. Many respected elders of the sport have treated the possibility of another "first" fish as though it was a potential scandal—a little like having a traitor in the family.

In *Men, Fish and Tackle* (1936), reel manufacturer Joseph A. Coxe talks with Ralph Bandini (and the reader) about the early days at Catalina and the first tuna caught on rod and reel. In an aside ostensibly meant to protect the Founding Father, but which rather results in a slight to Holder's memory, Coxe says:

Incidentally, the man who took that first fish never got the credit for it. But there's no use bringing that up. Everybody concerned is dead and gone, and there's nothing gained by digging into the dead past.[2]

What's curious about all this is Holder's own admission that he did not catch the first tuna on sporting tackle. In *The Log of a Sea Angler* (1906), he tells us, "I did not take the first tuna, but I caught the first large one." He gives more particular credit in other texts, but the historian is still not sure who did what in the way of pioneer work, because different names are mentioned. In *An Isle of Summer* (1901), Holder tells us that attempts to land bluefin tuna on rod and reel go back to the mid-1890's: "Gradually others became interested and in 1896 Col. C. P. Morehouse . . . landed the first tuna with rod and reel." Then in *The Game Fishes of the World* (1913), he tells us that "tunas had been taken before [my 183-pound catch], notably by Mr. W. Greer Campbell, but not very large ones."

The closest we have to a neutral observer in this confusion is Horace Annesley Vachell, one of the original officers of the Catalina Tuna Club and an acquaintance of Holder, Morehouse, and Campbell. He provided an article entitled "Tuna Fishing in the Pacific" for the November 1898 issue of the *Pall Mall* magazine, in which he reports the first tuna as "killed with rod, reel, and tarpon line by Mr. Morehouse of Pasadena in 1896."

In the years since the turn of the century, Colonel Morehouse's fame in angling annals has been preserved with the 251-pound tuna he caught the year following Holder's first big fish. Morehouse's tuna still represents the Tuna Club record, and the Morehouse Cup, which was to have been presented by the colonel to the man who caught a larger

---

[2]*Men, Fish and Tackle*, Ralph Bandini, Bronson, Mich., 1936, page 9.

fish, has never been nor will likely be claimed, considering the deteriorated condition of Catalina tuna angling today.

However, the fame of Greer Campbell, one of the original officers of the Tuna Club and second vice-president, was quite literally lost for many years when lists of Blue Button winners[3] in the club yearbooks did not carry his name. He was only rediscovered in 1948 when club historian Arthur N. Macrate put him back on the honor roll. The early records of the club, along with the first clubhouse, were destroyed by a fire in 1915.[4] Still one wonders why Campbell and two other mystery figures, W. M. Rockwell and J. G. Chapman, were absent for so long when everyone else was speedily resuscitated.

Part of the murkiness surrounding the history of the early Catalina efforts to catch tuna on sporting tackle may be traced to a certain embarrassment felt by some members of the newly found club for the methods used by Charles Holder to gain recognition for their organization. While the press had generated most of the interest in the first tarpon catches on rod and reel without any particular guidance from the anglers concerned, Mr. Holder became the Tuna Club's—and his own—best press agent.

The *Pasadena Daily News* of June 2, 1898, based its story of his catch on information provided by Holder, which included such flourishes as "for three hours and forty-five minutes [the angler] played the big fellow with pertinacious skill," and "the Professor[5] [has] eclipsed

---

[3] A bluefin tuna swimming from right to left on a blue field became the club's emblem and the design of the lapel pin awarded to any man who caught a tuna of more than 100 pounds on tackle specified by the club. In later years other designs and other color combinations suitable to a variety of gamefishes and a variety of tackle were created by the club, but the Blue Button was always the most prestigious. Or, as the editors of *Field & Stream* called it early in this century, "the world's greatest angling insignia."

[4] Joe Coxe generally takes the credit for rebuilding the clubhouse: "I went over there the morning after the big Avalon fire and found the clubhouse just a few charred pilings. Nobody thought there was any use in rebuilding—but I did! I had a tough job raising the money—but I raised it. Then, when I was ready to ship the materials over, I found that the freight across the channel would cost more than we could afford. So, I hired a barge, and loaded it with everything needed, right down to nails. Then I had it towed across by a tugboat, and unloaded on the beach, right where we were going to build. The whole thing cost me less than the cartage at Avalon would have cost! Then, with the stuff on the ground, I stayed right there, watching every plank and nail that went into the building. The old clubhouse burned down in November. The next June we opened a bigger and better house!" *Men, Fish and Tackle*, pages 75–76.

[5] C. F. Holder held an honorary Doctor of Laws. He rarely used the title, partly because his father had been a "real" doctor—that is, an M.D. In his writings,

all previous achievements in the line of angling." That same day, the *Los Angeles Daily Times* reported the catch and announced that an Avalon composer, C. A. Clark, has "named his latest musical composition 'The Tuna Twostep!'" The June 3 issue of the *Pasadena Daily News* retells the story and advises its readers to "keep close to Pasadenians if you want to catch big fish at Catalina."

On June 15, a preliminary meeting of the Catalina Tuna Club was held, and in reporting this event, the *Pasadena Daily News* again exults over the capture of the big fish and adds: "If anyone doubts that Dr. Holder caught a fish of 183 lbs., there is a photograph in the *News* office." Finally, this little note from the *Los Angeles Daily Times:*

Professor Holder claims that five pounds should be added to his 183-lb. Tuna, the largest ever caught on the Island, for shrinkage and loss of blood, making the correct weight, according to the present code of weighing, 188 lbs. At a meeting of the Club, held at the Hotel Metropole on August 22, 1898, a reference was made to the *188-lb.* Tuna caught by him, "which is still the record fish."

Holder's motive for publicity was not entirely self-glorification. He had fished from Massachusetts to Florida, but felt that nowhere was there such a pleasant blend of temperate climate and sporting variety as off the coast of southern California. He therefore wanted to share his discovery with the rest of the angling world.[6]

More importantly, Holder felt that by publicizing his rod-and-reel tuna catch he would shame many handliners into giving up their more primitive equipment to become sportsmen. United, Holder and his new allies would then work to restrict the disastrous effects of commercial netting. By organizing a club of anglers who sought tuna with rods and reels, Holder hoped to discourage, if not eliminate through legislation, the capture of any gamefish by other than sporting means.

The original constitution of the Catalina Tuna Club states that the organization is:

. . . hereby formed and composed of gentlemen and ladies[7] who have by their skill and perseverance succeeded in taking with rod and reel in

---

only the British edition of *The Game Fishes of the World* carries a reference to the title after Holder's byline.

[6]Wise fishermen are less inclined to such generosity today.

[7]Later, in July 1901, when the club was incorporated under California law, membership was confined to "gentleman anglers" only.

the waters of this State, and with a line not stronger than a 24-thread, one leaping tuna[8] of not less than 100 pounds weight.

By the end of July 1898 there were 24 members who had achieved this distinction, and Holder determined to direct their sporting perspectives and skills into all areas of marine angling. Three years later, the preamble to the 1901 constitution reflects this broader view when it states simply: "The object of this Club is the protection of the game fishes of the state of California."[9]

Holder came to his role as sport-fishing spokesman for the state of California because of a family tragedy. On April 9, 1885, his first and only child died at five months of age. In order to help his wife forget the loss, Holder decided to take her from familiar surroundings in New York and Boston and explore the new country of California. They arrived, stayed awhile, and liked the area so well they established their new home there.

Although Charles Holder was only 34 when he arrived, the fame of his family and his own accomplishments quickly enabled him to find a place in the rather exclusive community of Pasadena. Before coming West, Holder had served as assistant curator for New York City's American Museum of Natural History, being first appointed to this post at age 21. He had also been elected to a number of distinguished science academies and was widely known for his recently published *Elements of Zoology*.

In California he furthered his writing interests and became quite a booster of Los Angeles County as editor of the *Los Angeles Tribune*. He shortly left this newspaper, however, to found and edit his own *California Illustrated* magazine. Holder was one of the area's first trained natural historians, and he later contributed his sizeable zoological collection to the museum of the Pasadena Academy of Sciences.

---

[8]A curious characteristic of the tunas of Catalina was their habit of jumping —usually when feeding on flying fish. Atlantic bluefin rarely jump—at least within sight of men—and many of the early anglers of southern California were Easterners who traveled all the way West merely to catch this "leaping variety" of the bluefin tuna.

[9]One of the notable achievements of the club occurred when Governor Pardee, a friend of the association, came into office. In 1913, he signed a bill recognizing Catalina as an oceanic "spawning ground," effectively eliminating all commercial netting within three miles of the island's shores (Holder's *The Game Fishes of the World*, page 110). More generally, the club's influence made California the first state to set up a system for the collection and analysis of sea fishing statistics—a system supported by saltwater fishing licenses.

Yet undoubtedly, his most popular claim to fame is as founder of Pasadena's Tournament of Roses.

Probably one of the reasons C. F. Holder took so readily to California was because, for the first time in his life, he was able to slip from beneath the shadow of his father's fame. In academic and social circles back East, he was known principally as the son of Dr. J. B. Holder. While his father's influence had been benign, it was still important to Charles Frederick to develop his own reputation.

Most of young Holder's exposure to the sea had been a result of his father's interest in the subject. In 1856, when C. F. was still a little boy, a giant tuna weighing 1,000 pounds was taken off his hometown of Lynn, Massachusetts. Ten feet long, six feet in girth, it had been harpooned and finally killed by three men in a dory. Since in those days tuna were sought less for food than for oil (a large fish produced roughly 24 gallons), Dr. Holder purchased the great fish, had it mounted, and presented it to the Lynn Historical Society rather than see it reduced to so much candlepower. Dr. Holder was the society's president, but in those days before deductible donations, the fish was a considerable gift. In later years, his son noted with pride that "this was the first tuna ever seen in a scientific institution in America."[10]

From then on, and including nearly six years of residence in the Florida Keys, young Charles was his father's regular companion and assistant on fishing and collecting trips. In retrospect, even Charles's appearance at the Museum of Natural History at age 21 is less remarkable when we consider that his father was one of the founders of that institution with Professor Albert S. Bickmore in 1869 and then served as its assistant director and curator of zoology from 1871 to his death in 1888.

In 1902, Charles Holder wrote a genealogy of *The Holders of Holderness*, beginning with their Danish forebears, proceeding through the life of Christopher Holder—pioneer Quaker minister and author of the first Declaration of Faith in Friends—and other illustrious antecedents in Boston and Lynn, and ending with a biography of his father. Charles's memories of his father are instructive, both in what they tell us about Dr. Joseph Bassett Holder's life, and in those elements of his father's life the influenced the son:

[Dr. Holder] was a man of high cultivation, of artistic tastes, with a strong leaning for scientific pursuits. A birthright Friend, he was

---

[10]*Big Game Fishes of the United States*, Charles Frederick Holder, New York, 1903, page 53.

educated at the Friends' School at Providence, and later studied medicine at Harvard. He early became a friend of Louis Agassiz, then living at Nahant, and [I] often visited the home of the great Swiss naturalist with him. The two men [Agassiz and Dr. Holder] dredged the bay and collected together, and the friendship materially influenced Dr. Holder's later career.

While at Harvard he was demonstrator of anatomy for Oliver Wendell Holmes, and was present at the first application of ether. . . . He made the first list of plants and birds of Essex County; was the founder and president of one of, if not the first, Natural History societies of Lynn; and was interested in collecting data relevant to [the] history of the county and town. He was [also] an artist of more than ordinary talent. . . .

In 1859 Louis Agassiz and Spencer Baird, of the Smithsonian, induced him to go to the Florida Reef to study its growth and development in the interests of science. This he did, also becoming surgeon-in-charge of the Engineer Department [at Key West]. He sent North valuable collections and data to Agassiz and the Smithsonian, the Museum of Comparative Zoology at Cambridge, College of the City of New York, etc. One of the important discoveries he made related to the growth of corals. It was believed that coral grew very slowly, but by keeping specimens under observation and in a sea aquarium[11], he found that branch corals grew five or six inches a year, and meandrina were also fast growers, a small head doubling its size in a year, thus upsetting all preconceived ideas about the extreme slowness of the growth of corals.

On the breaking out of the war [between the states], Dr. Holder entered the army and became health officer and surgeon of the military prison at Fort Jefferson, remaining at Tortugas seven years, fighting yellow fever during the Civil War and saving hundreds of lives at the risk of his own. . . .

Dr. Holder was a frequent contributor to the magazines of the day . . . [also, with] many articles and papers in scientific publications. He was a patron of the Metropolitan Museum of Art, Fellow of the New York Academy of Sciences, member and one of the founders of the Ornithological Union, member of the Society of Naturalists of the Eastern United States, the Geographical Society, member of the Harvard Club and others.[12]

---

[11]Charles Holder built and maintained this sea aquarium for his father. It consisted primarily of a screen across a break in the wall about the old moat at Fort Jefferson, Dry Tortugas, so that the tides could pass through but not undesired fish.

[12]*The Holders of Holderness*, Charles Frederick Holder, Pasadena, Calif., 1902, pages 226–230.

It is therefore easy to understand the burden that Charles Frederick felt as Dr. Holder's son and only child, and why an independent start in California was just what the doctor ordered.[13]

Although Holder lived in Pasadena, his favorite bit of California was Santa Catalina Island. In fact, one of the main attributes of Pasadena, as far as Holder was concerned, was that you could see the peaks of Catalina and San Clemente islands—some 30 and 50 miles away respectively—from the downtown area.[14]

Holder first visited Catalina in 1886, arriving in the midst of one of those yellowtail free-for-alls for which the Channel Islands were once famous:

Men and boys were standing on the beach catching yellowtails with cod hand-lines. As fast as they could cast, they had strikes. The fish ranged from 20 to 35 pounds in weight, and every few minutes there would be wailing and gnashing of teeth as a yellowtail would break the ropes they were fishing with.[15]

The Atlantic equivalent of one of these fabled yellowtail drives is a Florida "jack beat" in which crevalle by the hundreds push mullet up against a shore or seawall and lash the water to foam in their feeding frenzy. Catalina records show that in the days before commercial netting, some of these yellowtail runs were so vast they churned the surface of Avalon harbor and the shoreline for half a mile on either side.

An amusing anecdote from Holder's time concerns a clergyman who was holding his Sunday service in a tent chapel at the edge of the beach in Avalon.[16] Suddenly, and despite the loud singing of a hymn, his congregation heard what sounded like an erratic surf on the shore. A parishioner in the back put down his hymnal and sneaked out for a look. He was soon back, whispered something in a companion's ear, and the two of them slipped out together. Meanwhile the commotion in the bay had turned to the roar of breaking water. Other parishioners began to sneak away. The minister, standing on a small podium at the front of the congregation, was visibly agitated. He looked fiercely

---

[13]The 1902 edition of *Who's Who* tells its readers that Charles F. Holder was in California "for his health."

[14]Smog and a generally dustier atmosphere make this a rare sight today.

[15]*The Channel Islands of California*, Charles Frederick Holder, Chicago, 1910, page 336.

[16]When the island was first being developed, most of the workers lived in tents along the harbor front.

at the remainder of his flock and sang louder to drown out the background noises of tumbling water and the whoops of men fishing on the beach. Finally, when there was just a handful of people left, the preacher could stand it no longer, threw down his hymnal, and dashed down the aisle. As he raced for his own tent and tackle, he yelled to the crowd already strung out along the beach with whirling handlines and flapping fish around them: "Hold up, brethren, let's start fair!"

After his first visit to Catalina, Holder sought out the Lick family of San Francisco, who owned the island and operated it as a sheep ranch. He hoped to buy it for a retreat and to develop its fishing potential in the same way West End and Cuttyhunk islands off New England had been developed. We do not know precisely why he never fulfilled this plan, but we do know that Holder later stated the family wanted between $1 and $3 per acre for the 55,000-acre island, and he apparently counted on paying less. Considering the value of that island today, even the $3-per-acre price is staggering![17]

About 1889 or 1890, Holder returned to the island with "an old black-bass rod that had a record of $4\frac{1}{2}$ and $5\frac{1}{2}$-pound black bass in the St. Lawrence River," determined to take a yellowtail. The only guide on Catalina in those days was José Felice Presiado, alias Mexican Joe, who at one time not long previous had been the island's only resident. When Holder showed him the tackle he hoped to use on yellowtail, Mexican Joe laughed heartily at anyone crazy enough to fish without a handline. But Joe took the "loco gringo" fishing anyway. Unfortunately, and as Joe predicted, the fragile outfit did not last out the first fish.

This story has a happy ending, though, for nearly 20 years later, the two men tried light tackle again. Holder had by this time taken countless yellowtail on a variety of rod, reel, and line combinations— including 17- and 20-pound fish on his 8-ounce split cane fly rod[18]— but he wanted to try the new 3/6 tackle developed in 1908 by Tuna Club member Thomas McD. Potter.[19] In the years since their first

---

[17]The Banning family purchased the island in 1892 from a George Shatto representing an English syndicate, which had presumably bought it from the Licks. Early in 1919, the Bannings sold it to the Wrigley family (of chewing gum fame) who still own most of it to this day.

[18]In *The Game Fishes of the World*, Holder claims he "could have landed a fifty pounder, but it is too hard work" (pages 9–10). While he encouraged the use of light tackle whenever and wherever possible Holder seasoned this encouragement with common sense. For example, he would doubtless have viewed the taking of marlin on fly tackle as a grotesque stunt.

[19]The name "Three/Six" is said to describe Potter's original specifications for

encounter, and primarily due to Holder's sponsorship, Mexican Joe had become the dean of Catalina boatmen and had long since given up handlines—in fact, refusing even to take handlines aboard his boat. But he still laughed heartily, Holder recalled, when the angler carelessly broke his new rod on a yellowtail after first managing to land several.

In 1888, Holder wrote the booklet *All About Pasadena and Its Vicinity,* in which he described the area's climate, flora, and outdoor recreation. It is interesting to contrast his summary of Catalina angling opportunities that year with all he knew of the sport just a few years later. At this early date, there is no mention of bluefin tuna, of course. But there is also no description of yellowtail fishing, perhaps because Holder objected so strenuously to seeing these fine fish taken on handlines. But he was doubtless embarrassed after the turn of the century by his suggestion that "greater sport" was to be had in harpooning white sea bass (*Cynoscion nobilis*) than in trying to catch them on hook and line:

The salt-water fishing [of Southern California] compares favorably with that of the East. The gamy barracuda takes the place of the bluefish, while the Spanish mackerel[20] and several varieties of this tribe constitute good sport. Boats for fishing may be had at San Pedro, but the fisherman will do better to make Santa Catalina his headquarters.

Here in June and July the barracuda run in schools, and some days are caught by thousands; again [other days], they will not take the hook. In these months, the sea bass, a magnificent fish much resembling a salmon, fill the bays, swimming at the surface and occasionally taking the hook but affording greater sport with the harpoon. They attain a length of three or four feet, and run to seventy pounds weight.

A large variety of fish are caught, including a small sea bass, much resembling a black bass and quite as gamy. It must be confessed that none of these denizens of the sea have the flavor of the game fishes of the East, due in all probability to the high temperature of the water.[21]

this tackle: a 6-ounce rod, 6-feet long, and 6-thread line. However, there may have been another "6"—rather than rod length—in mind when this combination was first developed. The original circular for Three-Six Tackle says that the club of anglers using the equipment is "limited to six members, [with] six-ounce rods, [and] six-strand lines." The *Los Angeles Examiner* of March 15, 1908, also speaks of a new fishing club with "six charter members, six ounce rods and six thread lines." (The original members were Potter, Holder, L. P. Streeter, E. H. Brewster, Gilmour Sharp, and T. S. Manning.)

[20]Not the Atlantic Spanish mackerel but the Monterey variety or "mackerel jack," *Scomberomorus concolor.*

[21]*All About Pasadena and Its Vicinity,* pages 86–87. The comment about water

The giant California black sea bass (*Stereolepis gigas*), which reaches weights up to 600 pounds, was the first large gamefish to be taken in the Pacific on rod and reel. In fact, its capture doubtless led ambitious anglers like Charles Holder to hope to take big bluefin tuna with the same tackle.

The big sea bass were once quite common in the waters around Catalina,[22] but "hawser" handlines were the only known way to catch them before the 1890's. In fact, this was the one fish for which Holder condoned the use of a handline. In the early 1890's, he took a number of these creatures on handlines ranging from 100 to 347 pounds in weight. This was exciting stuff from a little skiff crowded with an angler and guide trying to land a fish sometimes weighing more than both people put together. But it still was not rod-and-reel fishing.

Finally, in 1894, Charles Holder went out in one boat with General Charles Viete in another to see what could be done with standard tarpon tackle and a little luck. Holder's theory was that the big fish must be fought from an anchored position, believing this was the best if not the only way to prevent the fish from running into the kelp or under a ledge. So doing, he promptly broke four rods on four fish. Having gone through all the sporting tackle aboard, he resorted to a handline and caught two big sea bass—one weighing 248 pounds— while waiting for the general to conclude his day.

Meanwhile, General Viete had cast loose his mooring immediately after hooking his first bass. He was towed off and fought his fish for two hours before it finally took refuge in a kelp bed some distance from where it had been hooked. Still determined to win the battle, the general tightened up his line and tied it to the rod. Then he lashed the rod to an oil drum and left it floating while he went off for lunch and reinforcements. He returned some hours later with a grapnel and succeeded in tearing away the kelp without breaking the line. Then, after another half hour of furious combat, he finally gaffed the 227-pound fish.

In following years, other anglers caught giant sea bass on rod and reel,[23] but never with quite the thoroughness of the general's first vic-

---

temperature affecting flavor is curious, for most contemporary · fishermen/cooks tend to attribute their catch's flavor to what the fish eats and what kind of water (chemically speaking, that is) it swims through.

[22]Today overfishing, and particularly spearfishing, make the giant sea bass rather uncommon—at least in the large, old-age sizes that once seemed so abundant.

[23]Holder never did succeed in taking one on rod and reel; nor did he manage to catch a striped marlin or broadbill swordfish—two other future favorites with club members.

tory. However, by using such tactics as strumming the line to keep the fish moving, by pouring small amounts of fish oil overboard to calm the waters immediately around the boat, and by working the fish hard at the very outset of the struggle, the average time that it took to land one of these monsters was greatly reduced. For example, in 1898, the year of Holder's tuna record, Mr. Frank V. Rider[24] landed a 327-pounder on tarpon tackle in the astonishing time of just 55 minutes.

Holder later described the outfit used for this type of fishing:

His rod and reel were designed especially for leaping tuna and black sea-bass; the silent reel was equipped with heavy, patent, anti-over-running brake and leather thumb brake, and held perhaps six hundred feet of 21-thread linen line. The rod was a split bamboo, seven feet in length, with a long butt and single joint mounted with agate guides. A six- or seven-foot bronze wire leader[25] was attached to the line, the hook being the Van Vleck pattern—a singularly-shaped silvered hook in high favour among tarpon experts.[26]

This was the same primitive tackle Holder used to take his first large tuna. Today, ball-bearing reels with internal braking systems, balanced rods, flawless lines, specially designed harnesses, fighting chairs with foot rests and removable backs, highly maneuverable fishing boats, and flying gaffs all make the taking of tuna six times the size of Holder's largest a reality. But at the turn of the century, such heavy sport bordered on heroism. Fitch Dewey, for instance, lost a "mighty tuna" on July 12, 1898, after he dislocated his right arm during the contest. *The Land of Sunshine* magazine in December 1900 described a five-hour battle with a 180-pound tuna by Herbert S. Earlscliffe who "dropped senseless in the boat as it came to gaff." Countless broken knuckles and battered hands were a result of every tuna season, and a section of the Hotel Metropole porch, where the Tuna Club had their first headquarters, was known as the Tuna Hospital, where the walking wounded gathered to console one another. Perhaps, most dramatically, Article I of the 1898 Rules concerning records stipulates that:

---

[24]Formerly of New York but, like Holder, a convert to Pasadena living, Frank Rider was the Tuna Club's first secretary-treasurer.

[25]At the turn of the century, wire leaders were generally made of heavy piano or phosphor-bronze wire in two or three link sections joined by brass swivels. This was to give the otherwise impossible stiff wire flexibility.

[26]*Life in the Open: Sport with Rod, Gun, Horse and Hound in Southern California*, Charles Frederick Holder, New York, 1906, page 254.

Should it happen that by reason of absence *or exhaustion* [italics added], neither record nor signature [in the book] can be made; any three members of the Club shall have the right and are hereby directed to record the catch and affix the said signature.

After these real and potential hazards, the story of Holder's first big tuna seems almost anticlimatic. After all, the only remarkable thing about that struggle was that at one point the boat capsized, whereupon Holder and his guide, Jim Gardner, climbed back in, and while Gardner bailed and continued to back oars against the fish's pull, Holder carried on the fight. In addition, the tuna towed the two men an estimated 14 miles in something approaching four hours, and yet, Holder guessed, the fish was finally gaffed not 100 feet from where it had first been hooked.

Still that was just another good fish fight. Here is the one I like best about bluefin tuna fishing in the days of yore at Catalina. And it all begins *after* three men load one 95-pound fish into one small skiff.

My boatman, Jim Gardner, of Avalon,[27] gaffed [the tuna], hauled it in, and we were about to give way to exuberance befitting the occasion, when the tuna, as near as I can recall, doubled up, opened out, shot up into the air, and fell upon the rail. As we were standing, we lost our balance, and the next I knew, I was treading water. The boat went down out of sight, then came up bow first, shooting into the air, spilling the oars, gaffs, lines and everything else, into the sea, nearly a mile from shore. I was inclined to take it as a joke, as we had a launch not four hundred yards away; but my companion suddenly announced that he could not swim, and throwing his arms about the bow of the boat, she rolled over in a menacing fashion. Jim and I got him in, but the boat still rolled, being light and shallow; so we tipped her over, bottom up, helped the non-swimmer onto the bottom, where, by remaining perfectly quiet and lying flat, he was safe. I then looked for the launch, and noticed that in the excitement I had dropped my rod, a valuable piece of angling machinery.

The launch had not moved, and we saw the engine would not work; so I decided to leave my companion, as the boat would not hold more than one, and swim to the launch. Gardner was a professional swimmer, and I was fairly at home in the water, having had many capsizing

---

[27]Originally from Liverpool, England, Gardner visited Catalina one day and decided to stay. He became one of Holder's favorite guides and Holder later gave him the mounted 183-pound "first big one" as a momento of that epochmaking fight.

[86]

experiences in Florida; but I was handicapped by a heavy, impossible suit of corduroy, leggings and heavy shoes.

The sea was perfectly calm, and I soon distanced Gardner who, I thought, had not been very active about arranging the boat for my companion, nor did he seem to make much headway for a professional. But it was not exactly the time for criticism, and I took it easily, and was perhaps fifty feet ahead of Gardner, when I saw the launch had started and was coming for us, the men waving and shouting encouragement.

How far we swam I do not know, but my armor of corduroy was deadly and I felt relieved to see the launch coming. She had almost reached us, and I was slowing up, when my boatman's wife, who was aboard, raised her voice in a scream that made the welkin ring.[28] It suggested sharks to my somewhat excited imagination, especially as she cried, "Jim's drowning." I stopped swimming and turned for a second, treading water, but could see nothing, as my eye-glasses had tipped; when I straightened them, Jim was indeed gone, and way back, seemingly on the horizon, was my angling companion, lying placidly on the bottom of the boat.

I started to swim back, but had not gone five feet, I confess with the fear of sharks in my heart, when Jim's head shot out of water just long enough to grin at me, then went down. As he came up again, I shouted, "What's the matter?" that grin having put sharks out of my mind.

"I've got your tuna, sir," and down he went again, to immediately reappear.

I could not believe the evidence of my eyes, and could only laugh as he went down up to his eyes, then pulled himself up to the surface. But he had my tuna, had never released his hold on the gaff in all that exciting turmoil, and had held it with his left hand, helping to turn the boat with his right, and when I suggested that we swim, to give the other angler a fair chance, he said nothing but bore on after me; and when he disappeared the tuna had merely rushed ahead, tried to sound, and had dragged Jim down a foot or two, a clever, and too suggestive imitation of a man being jerked down by a shark.

The launch was now alongside, and Jim threw his legs about the propeller, while I was lashed to the shrouds, as the two men could not for the moment haul me in, the corduroy seemed to weigh a ton; then I was taken aboard.

Jim's entire thought was for the tuna; so I leaned over the stern, the head appeared, when I thrust my hand down into its big mouth, and

---

[28]Although portrayed as something of a hysteric in this account, Mrs. Gardner was actually an experienced sailor and anglerette, who in 1900 caught unaided a 136-pound bluefin tuna.

[87]

securing a grip on its gill rakers, gave the word. Heave-o-ohoy! came the chanty. The men hauled on my legs, and I pulled the tuna, and in a few seconds dropped it into the cockpit, when we cheered as anglers will; then Jim was hauled in by a rope which had been tossed him by his wife.

All this time we had kept an eye on the angler on the bottom of the boat, and now steamed for him. He was lying so quiet that one might have fancied he was asleep; but he denied the imputation. The sea was covered with wreckage, and Captain Harry Doss, one of the boatmen of Avalon, who had seen the catastrophe, came out from the shore and picked it up. A rope was tossed to my companion, Mr. Dennison of Philadelphia, who fastened it about his waist and was hauled aboard. The boat was righted, and with the first tuna of the season we turned toward Avalon, four miles distant, to claim the Tuna Club prize for the event in rods, etc., which of course went to Jim Gardner.

This is enough for the average fish story, in fact, it is as much as the ordinary listener who has his limitations will believe, yet as there *were* three or four disinterested witnesses I will go on. As soon as the launch got under way, I noticed Jim grasping for something, then he cried to the engineer to stop, and stood up, and in his trousers was the hook which caught the tuna; in some way, either during the capsize, or the swim, it had been flung out, and had hooked onto the gaffer. Jim saw that the line led overboard, and to make a very long story short, he hauled in six hundred feet of line, and at the end, up came my rod and reel which had gone to the bottom and slowly unreeled to the end. I have not claimed a Carnegie hero medal for my boatman, but all anglers will appreciate the cleverness and nerve of this man in saving his patron's fish under what, to put it mildly, were adverse circumstances.

Besides organizing the Catalina Tuna Club and acting as its chief mentor until his death in 1915, Holder sparked considerable interest in saltwater angling through numerous books and articles on the subject. In addition to his own writing, he encouraged fellow California immigrant Dr. David Starr Jordan, President of Stanford University, to contribute popular articles on fish and fishing. In 1909, the two friends co-authored the book from which the foregoing excerpt was taken.[29]

For fishermen who sometimes wonder whether angling in California,

---

[29]*Fish Stories, Alleged and Experienced, with a Little History Natural and Unnatural*, Charles Frederick Holder and David Starr Jordan, New York, 1909, pages 254–257.

along the Florida reefs, or on the Texas coast could have been any better 75 years or more ago than it is today, the answer found in the writings of such trained observers of the sea as Jordan and Holder is a resounding *yes*. Holder's reminiscences of the Florida Keys are especially agonizing to fishermen familiar with what is happening to that area today. His descriptions of snook and cobia fishing—long before the rest of the angling world were aware of such critters—are exciting, but it is the incredible abundance and variety of the reef that he seems to take for granted that so impresses the contemporary angling reader. Today, only a very few hard-to-find ledges and seamounts produce fishing such as Holder had wherever he fished bottom corrugated by coral.

In *The Log of a Sea Angler*, Holder tells of a winter holiday he took with three other men—all local Conchs (natives)—on Garden Key well before the turn of the century. Their experiences with sawfish and sharks, pelicans and flamingos, manta rays and sea turtles, all make for delightful reading. Their adventures are crowned one day when they capture a sailfish that wanders in over the reef. Mostly, however, Holder fishes with a sturdy 10-ounce greenheart rod and Vom Hofe reel for hogfish, snappers, grouper, barracuda, jacks, and his own "first place" favorite "for game and fighting qualities": the spadefish. His bait consists of the once abundant crawfish or Florida spiny lobster, and the day's action is never long because the angler has all he wants shortly after starting. As Holder warns: "Fishing here even with a rod[30] was liable to drift into slaughter."[31]

Such excellent and varied fishing is almost gone from the shallow reefs of Florida, and only deep-jigging or bottom-fishing expeditions to remote places like Cay Sol can approximate the kind of angling Holder knew a century ago.

As early as the first annual meeting (so-called despite the fact that the club had just been founded weeks before), held on August 11, 1898, a report was read indicating that catches of tuna by club members "had attracted attention all over the East and even in Europe." This early international recognition of the club was due in large part to Charles Holder's newspaper efforts and personal correspondence with friends in all parts of the country and abroad. As a member of the world science community, his tales of big fish on what was then con-

---

[30]His companions adhered to handlines.
[31]*The Log of a Sea Angler*, Charles Frederick Holder, Boston, 1906, page 20.

sidered to be flimsy tackle were more acceptable than had they come from just any source. Equally important, his many contacts made possible a rapid dissemination of the Tuna Club's activities and accomplishments. As Holder himself was fond of recalling:

Nearly every notable catch of the sixty-six men of the Tuna Club [this was written in 1909], who have taken this fish under the rules (over one hundred pounds in weight), was telegraphed everywhere by the Associated Press, after the fashion of a battle; and a friend, who it chanced was in Paris at the time I made a lucky catch of a very large fish at Santa Catalina, informed me that he read the account the next morning in the French press. The American press in New York had the occurrence illustrated by some occult means the following day, and I had the pleasure of seeing myself pictured calmly treading water and playing a tuna, which was leaping forty or fifty feet in air.[32]

Holder was especially flattered by the number of clubs that appeared suddenly from coast to coast in imitation of the Tuna Club. At least one of them, the Aransas Pass Tarpon Club founded in Texas in 1907, was closely patterned after the Catalina Club because its founding fathers were Tuna Club members. The Tuna Club's first historian, L. P. Streeter, was the Tarpon Club's first president, and A. W. Hooper, also a TC member, was second vice-president. Characteristically, the new club's motto was: "To encourage the use of light tackle for a higher standard of sport."

Another club to share affiliation with the Tuna Club, and which closely followed activities at Catalina with an eye to its own development, was the British Sea Angler's Society of London, England.

Great Britain had lagged behind America in development of its saltwater sport fishery, but this was not because the English lacked interest. It was more a matter of indifferent sport fishing opportunities in the waters around the British Isles. Ocean rod-and-reel fishing in America was established by the New England striper clubs in the 1840's and given enormous impetus by the advent of Florida tarpon angling in the 1880's. In England, the nearest cousin of the striped bass, *Morone labrax*, never grows as large nor as plentiful as the American bass, and there is nothing in Britain to compare with the tarpon. Even England's secondary sportfishes, the pollock and whiting, are not on a par with the American equivalents, bluefish and squeteague. As a result, and as was seen in previous chapters, English sea

[32]*Fish Stories*, page 253.

[90]

anglers started coming to the United States for their sport in the middle of the last century.

The English long had an interest in sea fishing, and their literature on the sport actually goes back before America's. A Mr. Richard Brookes published the *Art of Angling: Rock and Sea Fishing* in 1801. However, this volume, as with most else published in Great Britain before 1890, describes multihooked handlines and the like as appropriate sporting tackle. Not until 1887, with the appearance of John Bickerdyke's[33] *Angling in Salt-water*, did a British writer evince a preference for rod fishing in the sea over handlines. Unfortunately, Hudson's popular *Sea-fishing for Amateurs*, published the same year, tended to cancel out Bickerdyke's contribution by favoring handlines over rods and condemning the use of artificial lures as "impractical."[34] Really not until 1891, with the publication of Frederick G. Aflalo's *Sea-fishing on the English Coast*, did British ocean anglers find a literary spokesman to rank with America's Forester and Scott. Aflalo's leadership was further confirmed when he organized the British Sea Angler's Society at the end of the century.

Holder was a rather worshipful Anglophile, and he was always most proud of his club's association with the British Sea Anglers. Perhaps the high point in his devotion to all things English occurred not many years before his death when he attended a London meeting of the B.S.A.S. as their special guest of honor.

In a reciprocal visit in 1908, Frederick Aflalo fished at Catalina Island. In *Sunset Playgrounds*, published the next year, Aflalo tells of his wanderings through the United States and Canada, and in particular he leaves us a delightful account of the coast and conditions of angling off Southern California 65 years ago.[35] However, there was one feature of the Tuna Club's activity that even diplomatic courtesy could not keep him from citing because it distressed him so much:

The inordinate thirst for "buttons" does much to spoil the true spirit of sport. It may be suggested that, having carried away no honours myself, I am jealous of others. This, in a sense, is justified by the fact that I never claimed the bronze button of the club, to which the very

---

[33]His real name was C. H. Cook.

[34]Frank Hudson's publication has been revised more than a dozen times since 1887, and its more recent editions now feature chapters on artificial lures and "rod-fishing as the most sportsmanlike method of all sea-fishing styles."

[35]Aflalo published a number of books and many articles about sports and travel in out-of-the-way places around the world. Yet this young wanderer died just three years after Holder, at the age of 48.

first fish I caught, a 33½ lbs. yellowtail on light tackle, entitled me. Had it weighed but twenty-four ounces more I could have claimed a silver button, and that also would have remained in the island. I do not, however, urge for more than it is worth a purely personal objection to the competitive element in fishing, for I know that in these days such old-fashioned argument is like trying to stop the tides. All the same, it would be refreshing if a little of this button-hunger were to abate, for, if the truth must be told, it is all but intolerable to those not educated to such weird ideals. Dear old ladies jostle their grandchildren on the quay, all on the warpath for buttons. Gentle females, so I am told, toss through sleepless nights on their pillows because they have failed to qualify.[36] Proud *decorés* stroll languidly into dinner at the Metropole long after the rest of the company is seated, and from the expression on their faces you might think they heard a ghostly orchestra playing "See the Conquering Hero comes!" Almost everyone wears a button of some sort; indeed, it is as difficult to evade the stamp of skill (or at any rate, of success) as Mark Twain found with the ribbon of the Legion of Honour. Genial evening conversation on fishing round the comfortable fire in the hall is interlarded with such personalities as "By the way, when I won that gold button . . ." or, "Say, tell us about that silver-button yellowtail of yours. . . ."

The air reeks of rivalry. The secretary, or some other official, of the club is everlastingly at his desk dispensing decorations or taking evidence from claimants. And the spirit of sport, as Walton knew it, as Holder still knows it, [un]folds its wings and flies sadly away into the starry night.[37]

Perhaps such vanities among lesser members was inevitable in a fraternity that included and was to include such illustrious personalities as Grover Cleveland, Theodore Roosevelt, Gifford Pinchot, Winston Churchill, Herbert Hoover, and General George S. Patton, Jr.—the latter joining the club in its early days and earning buttons at all ranks from lieutenant on up.

And if the competitive thinking that went into the Tuna Club's button program is today mirrored in the countless state and provincial Chamber of Commerce plaques, cups, and tournaments that make one-upmanship rather than recreation the name of the angling game along some coasts, the statistics on fish weights, lengths, etc., that also go into these contests have provided marine science with a vast index of information on growth and migration patterns for many species of game-

---

[36]An exaggeration since women were not allowed to compete for buttons.
[37]*Sunset Playgrounds*, Frederick G. Aflalo, London, 1909, pages 106–107.

[92]

fish. In addition, the international view of angling that Holder encouraged, and his insistence that the oceans were a common ground for the world's sportsmen, even while they may remain a barrier for politicians, indirectly led to the formation of the International Game Fish Association forty years after his Tuna Club began. Many thousands of anglers speaking different languages, but all using the same sporting tackle, today contribute to an organization that girdles the globe. The reasoning behind the IGFA is simple: If the pelagic game-fishes are international in outlook, why not the men who fish for them?

Charles Frederick Holder would have been pleased.

SEVEN

KITES, CLEMENTE, AND A NAVIGATOR NAMED GEORGE

Two California anglers made a weekend trip to San Clemente Island. Sunday late, they started in. The navigator told his companion to follow the North Star while he got some rest. Four hours later he came back on deck and found the boat heading due west.

"What happened to the North Star?" he exclaimed.

"Oh, we passed that one about an hour ago."

In the summer of 1913, Tuna Club member William C. Boschen became the first man in angling history to catch a broadbill swordfish on hook and line. The fish weighed 358 pounds and was taken off Catalina Island on a special kite-trolled bait rigged by his boatman. The next year off San Clemente, Boschen caught his first striped marlin. According to Zane Grey, "It weighed over three hundred pounds, leaped clear into the air sixty-three times, and gave a spectacular and magnificent surface fight that simply beggared description." The same boatman was with Boschen again.

While men of leisure pioneered big-game angling, there has been insufficient honor paid to the chartermen who helped develop the techniques and tackle that made this fishing possible.[1]

---

[1]An exception to this rule is found in the writings of Charles Holder, who noted in *Big Game Fishes of the United States* that "there are two essentials in tuna fishing: a cool, intelligent and practical gaffer, and perfect tackle."

Although William Boschen is remembered for having created the first internal star drag reel, which was later built by Julius Vom Hofe and called the B-Ocean,[2] one wonders how much of the credit for this development should go to his regular guide, George Farnsworth. Certainly Boschen thought highly of Farnsworth, for when Boschen died,[3] the famous angler willed his former guide $10,000, with the request that his ashes be spread on the sea between San Pedro and Santa Catalina in the area where he had taken his first broadbill swordfish. Farnsworth did so and never told where—it was his and Boschen's secret.

Known variously as chartermen, guides, or, particularly at Catalina, as gaffers, these men made (and still make) the difference between an exasperating outing or a world record, between a fruitless day at sea or a new experience in fishing. The best of them are energetic, inventive, and always confident. Such a man was the legendary "Tuna George" Farnsworth.

The newly founded Tuna Club was fortunate in enlisting the talents of this resourceful boatman. Saltwater history owes him not only many world records but some fresh thinking in tackle design and techniques of boat handling that are still used today on all major deep-sea grounds. Farnsworth also gave us the kite.

---

[2]"Vom Hofe wanted to call it the Boschen reel, but Boschen didn't want that, so they compromised on the name B-Ocean. I have seen many of them so named." From personal correspondence with George C. Thomas III, dated December 29, 1970. Specifically the reel held 1,500 feet of 24-thread line, and George Thomas testifies that "Boschen and Farnsworth together with someone at Abercrombie & Fitch in New York, developed the star drag reel" (from correspondence dated July 6, 1972).

[3]It has long been legend that during a standing battle with a swordfish—Boschen considered it unsporting to fight any fish sitting down or wearing a harness—the great angler's rod butt slipped from the belt cup he was wearing and so seriously injured the man that, despite one or more operations to save him, he died several months thereafter. The story is untrue, but it is characteristic of myths to accrue to men who do not need them to hold a place in history.

William Boschen was remarkable in many respects. He was the strongest of the early club members at Catalina; he had only one eye; and he landed more broadbill swordfish than anyone else in his lifetime. He caught his first blue button tuna on July 8, 1911. The fish weighed 113¼ pounds and was caught with George Chase Farnsworth as his guide. The two men became inseparable angling partners, and at the end they kept to themselves the secret that Boschen was dying of cancer.

"When he left the Island that year [1918], both he and Farnsworth knew it would be his last trip. The band always played 'La Golindrina' when the steamer pulled away from the dock, and I noted that George always 'clammed up' whenever that song was played. I truly believe that Boschen was Farnsworth's favorite person" (from personal correspondence with George C. Thomas III dated January 15, 1971).

[95]

The inventions of any culture are not always the best means of determining the progressiveness of that culture. The Romans were no more imaginative than their Greek and Egyptian predecessors. They merely developed the arch for building purposes because they *needed* the arch for the type of work they wanted to do. An appraisal of the great beehive tombs of Mycenae informs the thoughtful observer that the Greeks never designed an arched building—not because they were less inventive than the Romans—but because they did not need the arch in their style of architecture.

And so it is in angling. Harlan Major, the man who carried the concept of kite fishing from the Pacific to the Atlantic, made much of the possibility that Malayan fishermen used kites two millennia before the birth of Christ to get their baited lines well offshore. Thus he claimed no particular novelty for George Farnsworth's development of the kite at Catalina.

The point is that Farnsworth never heard of the "Procto-Malayan era," and he wasn't interested in getting his line well offshore. He developed kite fishing without any knowledge of prior use by other cultures simply because kites were *needed* in Catalina's nascent tuna sport fishery.

George Clifford Thomas, Jr., writes in *Game Fish of the Pacific, Southern California and Mexico* that, "in the summer of 1911, Captain George Farnsworth of the Avalon fishing fleet mystified everyone on the Island by bringing in great numbers of tuna while others caught none. Nearly every day saw the tuna flag (the banner indicating that fish had been taken) flying at the masthead of his cruiser, *Mable*. Naturally he was harassed with questions on shore, and followed and spied upon at sea, but he swore his anglers to secrecy, and by clever ruses outwitted pursuers. He wanted to perfect his idea."

All kinds of devices were being used to outwit the suspicious tuna. Sea sleds and outrigger poles were experimented with to see if they could keep a bait clear of the boat's wake. Success was limited. Some boatmen even spread the wings of their flying fish with wires to make them seem more natural skipping from wave to wave. Success for this technique was even more limited.

George C. Thomas III, in personal correspondence, writes: "When our bluefin started schooling (breezing, we called it), they would not take a trolled bait. Having flown kites as a kid in Northern California, [Farnsworth] conceived the idea of using a kite to keep the bait out of the wake of the boat. He told me that he got the idea in bed one night

[96]

—about 1904 or '05—made up a kite, took a dozen flying fish out by himself, and worked the schools. With no hook in the bait, he lost the twelve flying fish in short order, and knew that he had the answer.

"He was a most secretive man, and told no one. The tuna left Catalina waters for several years, and when they returned, circa 1909, he really gave his kite method a workout. It worked. He told me that in 1911 he brought in quite a few fish while the other boats landed none.

"He went to Pete Reyes, who owned the tackle store in Avalon, and told him to order a gross of kites (paper ones, I guess), and said that he would buy all that Pete had left at the end of the week. On July 4th, he came into Avalon with his kite flying, and an American flag on the line just above the bait. The secret was out! All of Reyes's kites were sold in short order. George said that he went out, shut off [his engine], and watched kites falling into the water. And knowing him, I'm sure he doubled up with laughter!

"Anyway, he was the first to develop the kite method of hooking bluefin. He told me that he had quite a time keeping his secret, and used many ruses to keep it. He had a demountable double ladder and a black canvas drop, which he would put over the side of his boat (the *Mabel F.*). Then he would run into a bunch of commercial albacore boats and come out the other side with his ladder up and the canvas down. Of course he was spied on, but managed to elude his followers. One of his anglers, who shall remain nameless, gave the secret away the previous winter at Aransas Pass to the tarpon fishermen. Rumor has it that this angler had taken a few too many, but I do know that George never spoke to him again."

Even after the secret of the kite was out, Farnsworth was regularly followed by other boatmen in the hope he would lead them to tuna. One day, just to tantalize one of his shadows, Farnsworth put up a kite as usual, then fastened a bucket to his angler's line. The fishermen "hooked" the pail and then went through all the motions of playing a big fish while a passenger aboard jumped about and patted the angler on the back encouragingly.

The tagalong boat could not resist the bait. It abandoned discretion and came up nearby to see what kind of fish Farnsworth and his party had on. After a final flourish of histrionics with the "fish" at boatside, Farnsworth reached out with the gaff—and brought in the bucket. There were many laughs and a few frowns in the clubhouse that night.

Still the followers persisted. They became so much of a nuisance that when World War I came along, Farnsworth contemplated painting his

[97]

boat a camouflage design like our Navy destroyers to see if that would help. What he did do, finally, was to study convoy and submarine evasion tactics and try them out on his trackers. Tradition has it that after awhile he became so good at this that his boat sometimes "vanished" even as you watched her.

Catalina tuna were different from tuna in other seas. They seemed to associate the turbulence and reverberations of any motorboat with trouble, and they sounded if an engine's noise approached too near. In the Atlantic, trolling for bluefin often *requires* you to have your line in the sudsiest part of the wake if you want action. But after motorboats were introduced to Catalina—most fishing done before the turn of the century was done from rowboat or sailboat—anglers had trouble getting the tuna to strike. The sport fishery might have had an early death except for Farnsworth's inspired kite "outrigger."

George C. Thomas, Jr., was the first of the Thomas family to fish with Farnsworth. In 1920 he trolled Catalina waters for 30 days with other guides and landed but a single 63-pound tuna on heavy tackle. While the largest fish to that point in his life and a battler that fought Thomas longer than he had ever imagined a fish (or he himself) could last, the gaffer snorted and called it "a little snoot."

Joe Coxe, who was then president of the Tuna Club, had engaged Farnsworth for a month's fishing in 1921. When Coxe suddenly had to return East on business for the first two weeks of his charter, he gave Thomas, by this time a new associate member of the Tuna Club, a note to Farnsworth, telling him that Thomas was taking over the first two weeks of the charter. This is the way George C. Thomas III continues the story:

They had never met, my father was a novice, and, when he handed the letter to Farnsworth, George looked him in the eye and said words to the effect that he didn't know that he cared to fish with him. After a few moments of silence, George finally said, "Well, Mr. Thomas, I'll take you out tomorrow, and then I'll let you know the answer." He took my father out into the rough water,[4] my Dad kept his mouth shut, was not seasick, and Farnsworth agreed to fish with him. That was the beginning of a long association, and I, as the kid, filled in when my father couldn't go. In the beginning, I am sure that he resented me.

In 1930, father and son Thomas collaborated on *Game Fish of the*

---

[4]The elder Thomas in *Game Fish of the Pacific* (page 57) notes that the outing was "over fifty miles from Avalon and return."

Pacific, Southern California and Mexico, one of the few publications that has left us with some impression of the remarkable Mr. Farnsworth. Let's go fishing now with the father, who, writing in the third person, describes those first days of angling following his acceptance by the guide:

Today *Gray Gull*[5] was being gone over; rods and lines were to be tested at the Tuna Club. Tomorrow would see the real start of the fishing. A quick, alert assistant secretary politely and skilfully went over the tackle, the rod being stamped "TC," the box holding the line initialed, and the line's breaking strain noted thereon.

The new associate sidled into the reading room where, after kindly salutation and introductions, he was made at home. He suddenly found that after it was understood he would fish with Farnsworth he became of some value, and apparently, he was a nonentity no more. He appreciated that he was expected to "produce."

For three days *Gray Gull* searched the seas. She did not linger near the east end and, as the westerly appeared, seek shelter with kite aloft in the doldrums of the island lee. Not she! She flew her kite after locating tuna; blind trolling did not appeal.

In the late afternoons and evenings the new fisherman had time to study the records and the names of the gold medals in the prize cases, to hear talk of tuna, of broadbill and of marlin. No tuna were being taken, but reports from the waters southward gave promise.

The fourth day dawned a flat calm. If anything, a light easterly obtained. The water was leaden. As usual, *Gray Gull* darted away alone at high speed. This time going north of west along the island shore and away from reported fish. Long Point was passed. Bird Rock and Isthmus came into view and the course westward was continued, whereas on the first days the ocean had been "checkerboarded" near home, but no kite flown. In due time the west end was reached. *Gray Gull* slowed down. She was the only boat in sight. Not a catspaw rippled the water, but far off shore a flock of birds wheeled, circled and screamed; perhaps hovering close to the surface, oft times anxious over one place; at others, searching here and there until again they came together and repeated their hovering.

Somehow, the birds excited the angler. He remembered other birds and other fish, for example near Block Island, with bluefish years before.

"There's your school of tuna," said Farnsworth, "let's get ready."

---

[5]This boat was the product of Boschen's legacy to George Farnsworth. Designed and built by Farnsworth, George C. Thomas III describes *Gray Gull* as "a true fishing machine."

With quick, trembling fingers, the novice passed the double line through the guides and tip, and the boatman very calmly and, to the angler, very slowly, attached the end of the "double" to the short piano-wire leader, and next placed on the hooks a flying fish carefully selected from the generous supply. In truth, "Tuna George" seemed hard to satisfy, rejecting several fish baits before finding one to his satisfaction.

Gray Gull lay still, gently rising and falling to the easy swell, but the sea was calm. How could one fly a kite? The boatman let in the clutch and slowly went past the tuna. Looking them over, yet saying nothing. The fisherman was impatient—anxious. Would his guide do anything? How could he get the kite working without the wind?

The boat left the tuna which could be seen surfacing without feeding. Apparently, the fish lay resting almost lazily, the dorsals moving, slowly advancing, the school shimmering and the water vibrating around them.

"Small fish," said Farnsworth, "let's find bigger ones," and he deliberately left the tuna and continued his former course.

It was a let-down. Disappointment gripped, yet the novice retained his desire to appeal or demand a try for the fish.

Somehow, intuitively he realized that the silent, forceful guide knew his business and was selecting the wise course. Nevertheless, the reaction from expectancy and hope to blank nothingness, over an ocean devoid of fish, and to a zone without birds, was exasperating.

The boat stopped, the guide methodically prepared his kite, while the faintest suspicion of a barely perceptible breeze stirred the water. At the same time to windward a bird appeared miraculously from nowhere, and almost instantly was joined by a second—by a dozen—by scores, with others continuing to arrive everywhere.

In a moment the scene changed to one of action; the birds screamed and circled and hovered as before. The angler's hope revived, but he could see nothing else to indicate the presence of fish. Yes! Suddenly a thrill shot through him. The waves under the birds boiled, foamed and burst, and one—two—six—a dozen big, dark fork-tail forms leaped upward or rose and slashed on the surface and disappeared. The birds wheeled, flying wildly in all directions—here, there, away and back again. Then, with apparently a preconcerted action, all concentrated, and beneath them the sea swirled with the rush of the big tuna.

"Hundred pounders—watch your tip—take off the drag," came to the now fearfully excited angler, as the guide, holding the kite with one hand, steered and advanced his throttle with the other, while *Gray Gull* bounded forward, tearing in a wide circle, partly away from fish and birds. The line, thumbed to prevent over-running and back-lashing, rushed out, and the kite, held by a short length attached to the 24-thread of the angler not far above the leader, rose slowly and flutteringly, while the flying-fish bait, supported by kite and given life by the strain of the fast moving line, now stopped from running off the reel and so held by the drag, approached the tuna. . . .

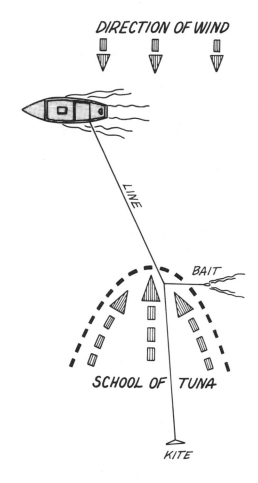

"Make him jump! Make him jump," came advice. The slow heave of the rod made the flying-fish skip forward above the water in jumps of six to ten feet. The angler watched the bait and tried to see the kite, and at the same time looked for tuna. He knew that his kite was falling as the boat turned in its arc slightly from the wind, and he realized it was a question of calculation of height of kite, upheld by wind and boat speed, judged against distance and direction to be covered without forgetting the movement of tuna. The kite was coming down fast. The bait was nearing the tuna splashes. *Gray Gull* tore on.

"Make it jump! Look out for him!" This time the words came as a quick, sharp command. Behind his bait a black form raged, tearing

[101]

with incredible speed and parting the flat surface like a plowshare. It hurtled through the air and crashed in foam and spray just behind the bait. Another fish, with unbelievable velocity, threw itself free and jumped beyond the line, descending on the water with a whacking splash.

The kite was close to the waves now, but the bait still jumped forward as if on wings. Then everything seemed to happen at once! Another huge, leaping tuna flung ahead of its fighting, struggling fellows, rose in a clean curve and hit the bait squarely between its gaping jaws. The angler struck on instinct, the intuition born of other strikes in other waters on quickly moving quarry, little realizing that the skill of the master had kept his line tight long enough to secure the rise before the kite fell. The reel roared, the line ripped from the spool, literally flew through the guides; the rod bent with the heavy drag. The tuna, in his first mad, headlong rush, sped away, outward and downward, with appalling force and paralyzing rapidity. *Gray Gull* wheeled and turned; foam flew as she rounded yawing in almost her own length, following the direction of the fish by the knowledge of the steersman gained from the moving line.

The angler, from the start of the 600-foot run, could do nothing until the boat swept swiftly past the top of the belly of the line, when it was possible to recover some, and yet necessary to exert properly applied power to do so. The boat stopped. The angler secured more line and then came the dogged fight, the slow reeling, pumping foot by foot, inch by inch, from a foe which never yields. The tuna may be forced and turned by a superior strength, but he never gives up. He dies dead game.

Words from the guide: "Don't make that loop with your tip before you stop. All the way down. Go slowly and reel on a tight line."

Meanwhile, aiding the angler, *Gray Gull* backs toward the fish, which fights wickedly and forcefully, and jerks savagely. Although unreasoned, the fisherman senses that the game is yielding; but the moments fly, and sometimes the tuna gains. The left hand finds it hard to stand the strain when the right turns the reel handle; the right hand is cramped, the novice is fighting hard, but not skilfully.

More encouragement as the man at the rod labors on. "Hold him on the outer circle as he heads away. That's right, now pump as he turns toward you."

The double line appears; somehow it moves through the tip, hesitates, then creeps along the rod guides. At last, it is on the reel, and tired fingers find better holding while, wonder of wonders! there is a long, monster fish turning slowly, just out of reach. He is silver and green. He approaches in spirals—he is very near. But oh, what a strain! The arms crack, yet hold. The leader swivel retreats, advances

[102]

and at last slowly approaches the boatman's outstretched hand. It wavers, the fish tries to take line as he swings outward. He turns back. The wire is seized, and there is a swish, a slight thud, then a huge splash, and "Tuna George" has gaffed a new man's first sizeable fish.

"Take off your drag. Watch him!"—Splash—thrash—water flies everywhere! The men are wringing wet. Farnsworth is doing something with a rope looped at the end. Then he shifts his gaff and, to the tired man's delight, the huge head with open jaws and quivering, silvery side, green upper body and black back with the trembling, orange yellow finlets of a big tuna come up over the edge. Another quick, heaving pull, and the fish flops over into the cockpit. He is conquered. Oh, the joy of it! The wonderment! The beautiful thing he is!

Then fearfully comes the thought of his weight. Is he a "button" fish of one hundred pounds?

After securing him, head and tail by two ropes, the boatman slaps and prods the prize thoughtfully, appraises him and remarks, "about a hundred; the leader's missed, let's get some more."

Some hours later the *Gray Gull* slipped into Avalon Bay with seven tuna, averaging close to one hundred pounds, safely aboard; the largest of these was well over the Blue Button limit.

Farnsworth was not only competent, he was downright prescient. On the first day of the fishing season in July 1924, he took the two George Thomases out Avalon Bay on their new cruiser, *Fairplay*. As they met the swell of open sea, the guide turned to his patrons and announced: "We're going to steer southeast by south for two hours and forty minutes; the tuna'll be there, and they'll be big fish, over 150 pounds."

George C. Thomas III was highly skeptical of such a pronouncement. It was equivalent to a man standing at home plate and pointing the way of a homerun to be hit on the next pitched ball:

It was like saying that a particular patch of kelp which *Fairplay* should pass would harbor dolphin, or some other equally difficult forecast. He longed to ask the boatman how he knew where the tuna might be. With other fishermen he simply had cruised until game was sighted, and did not believe it possible to tell where it would be found unless one already had seen the school. Farnsworth had not been on the water for two weeks, and no tuna had been reported for almost as long a time. He remained quiet, however, and watched the course and the clock above the wheel with much interest.

When the allotted time lacked but a minute or two of completion, "Tuna George" stopped the boat.

"There are the fish!" was all that he said.

[103]

Both anglers climbed atop the jitney and looked. The ocean was as calm as Avalon Bay, but of tuna there was no sign. There were no ripples to mar the flat surface. There was nothing to indicate schooling fish below. They turned to the boatman with questioning glances. Doubt assailed the mind of the younger man; too often he had seen the tell-tale indications of surfacing fish not to know them when he saw them. He believed that there were no fish there.

"Where are they, George?" he asked. "I can't see them."

"Those fish are down just now," replied the boatman. "I know you can't see them, but they're there just the same; big ones, nearly two hundred pounders, and they'll be up on top in about twenty minutes; then we'll go after them. Let's run out a bit further; maybe we'll see some other schools."

Fairplay resumed her course and the anglers kept watch. They felt that their boatman was trying to fool them into believing that he had proved his prophecy. In their misguided ignorance, they thought that they could see fish as well as anyone else. Had they not spent four years in hunting tuna?

At the end of ten minutes *Fairplay* turned back. As she approached the spot where the fish were alleged to be, she slackened her speed. What caused that dark patch of water just ahead of the boat? Tuna? It must be. It was! Farnsworth pulled the clutch and the three men watched those giant fish as they plowed through the swells and pushed wavelets with fins and noses.[6]

From that school George Thomas III took a 163-pounder, the largest he had caught to that time and the second largest tuna of the season:

Many times since that day has Farnsworth demonstrated to the anglers his uncanny ability to find and see tuna. How he does it can only be surmised, since he will tell no one his secret. Often when he would point out schools which the others could not see, they would ask him what signs to look for, but he seemed unable to explain or to show them the indications. Constant familiarity with these fish must have given him an intuition which is lacking in others.[7]

It was more than intuition. As Melville's Captain Ahab studied the worldwide movement of the great whales, Captain Farnsworth studied the migration of the tunas. He kept logbooks of every outing, noting when and where he took fish, the conditions of the sea, color of the water, and other indications. He went to all the other boatmen in the

[6]*Gamefish of the Pacific*, pages 69–71.
[7]*Ibid.*, page 73.

evening and tried to find precisely where they had taken their fish that day. In addition, he consulted every available record and description of tuna fishing.

He came up with some interesting conclusions, such as the fact that the leaders of the migratory bands of tuna are always three weeks ahead of the main body, yet the schools follow exactly the same path taken by the leaders. The main body of migrating fish then breaks into at least five separate smaller schools when it reaches Catalina waters. One group travels just east of the island, another west, and still another goes coastwise further north. Then, north of the Santa Cruz Islands, the five separate schools combine as one on a perfect time schedule. Farnsworth also noted that the fish sound and rise to feed on a similar time schedule, and this is what always enabled him to be at the right place at the right time.

Furthermore, tuna, like many pelagic wanderers, have cycles of abundance and scarcity. Farnsworth believed the "big cycle" for tuna occurs every 53 years, but that there are smaller, regular cycles within this basic pattern.

George Farnsworth planned to put all these observations and lore into a book he would write one day, but like many another would-be writer, he died before this was done. A pity and our loss.

"Tuna George" was an apt nickname for Farnsworth. One day the *Fairplay* discovered a school of fish near San Clemente. With no breeze, the angler did not see how Farnsworth would fly his kite—particularly during the difficult maneuvering involved in presenting the bait. But without a word, the guide rigged up and started the boat full tilt for the tuna, letting the speed of the boat carry the kite into the air, but with the bait running in the wake. Farnsworth charged the school of tuna, and for a minute his angler thought he was committing some weird act of desperation. Bait close up in the wake? And cutting the boat right through the school? Surely every one of the fish would stampede and sound!

Farnsworth ordered the angler to jump the bait. Halfheartedly, the fisherman did. Splash! Crash! A strike.

By noon, using this highly unorthodox method for Catalina grounds, George Thomas, Jr., had taken six tuna, most of them over 100 pounds. Another Avalon boat had run out during this time to share in the sport. Not carefully observing what Farnsworth was doing, the other boat went fishless all morning long.

Thomas and Farnsworth called time out for lunch and sat eating, watching and studying the nearby tuna. Rested, the angler went back to work and caught five more big fish that afternoon—a new Tuna Club record, and one made on a listless day.

In December 1970, I started writing George C. Thomas III, now living on the island of Hawaii, to ask him about Farnsworth's life and fishing skills. Following are more excerpts from Thomas's fascinating correspondence:

George's family came to Catalina Island about 1900. His father was the engineer who surveyed the road from Avalon to the Isthmus. George was born in [Stafford Springs], Connecticut [in 1883]. While very young his parents moved to Northern California, and then came to Avalon, where he became interested in fishing.

He told me that he caught his first bluefin tuna (100 plus pounds) in the late Nineties, and, having no gaff, ran his arm down the fish's throat and grabbed the outside of the gill cover. Needless to say, he was really cut up!

George Farnsworth was a perfectionist, a loner, and, in some ways, a very selfish man. He did not like people as such, and he was a truly hard man to know. I really believe that I knew him as well as anyone, and I do know that he was fond of me. In the early years with him, the early Twenties, he always referred to me as "the Kid." On the boat he was a hard taskmaster, almost a Captain Bligh. With no outriggers, I sat in the fishing chair all day long, holding the rod: with the kite, making the bait jump; for marlin, with the reel on free-spool. Unless we were in fish, his sole words were, "Good morning," "here's your lunch," and "see you tomorrow." It had to be done his way.

He had great loyalty to his friends, and at times, particularly after a snort or two, could be most charming. He drank but little, perhaps I should say seldom, but occasionally he would get a good "glow," let the bars down, and be great fun. He did have a sense of humor, not always, and never while fishing. I really believe that he was rather shy, and covered this shyness by trying to act tough.

Farnsworth was the finest seaman and fishing guide I ever knew. His navigation was astounding—I nearly believe that he was part sea gull. He found many of the offshore banks long before they were on the chart. He knew when seals came up with a rock cod, that they had gone to a bank below. Many times he and I fished the Cortez Bank, some fifty miles southwest of San Clemente Island. In those days we would have to run some four and a half hours to the bank, and George, despite wind and current, always hit it on the nose. I remember one day that he stopped the boat and began taking soundings with a light-tackle [30-pound test] rod. I asked him what the heck he was doing. He answered, "Somebody moved my marker; it's no longer there."

[106]

"What marker?" I asked. He became very mysterious, and said, "The marker to my bank." What bank? "Oh, I found a bank just 48 feet down, just about where we are now, but my marker's gone." In time he found it, and it is now on the chart—eight fathoms, some mile and three-quarters off Ben Weston Point on Catalina. If you look at a chart of the Island you will see the Farnsworth Bank—named by him for his father.

Another story, which I still find hard to believe, is the time he told me that I always steered to starboard. I disagreed, and we used to kid about it. One day, a year or so later, he and I were coming down from Santa Cruz Island to the west end of Catalina. It was exceptionally clear, and about twelve miles from the west end, George said that he was tired and asked me to take the wheel. I did, and ran the *Aerial* to about a mile or so from Catalina. George looked at me and said, "Where is Ship Rock?" I answered that it should be inside the end of the Island. He told me to turn the boat to port, 90° from our course. I did, and after about two hundred yards, Ship Rock came out from behind the west end. George looked at me and said, "When I gave you the wheel, Ship Rock was barely showing outside the point. You steer to starboard. You always have, and you always will."

When his appendix burst in 1937, he was a very sick man and, in his delirium, he thought that I was lost at sea. He tried to insist on going out to look for me. He told the doctor and the restraining nurses that I always steered to starboard, and that only he knew how much!

There is a story about him that was well known in Avalon. One foggy, very foggy day, one of the other skippers bet him that he couldn't run out from Avalon, stay out of sight of Catalina, circumnavigate the island, and come straight back into Avalon. He won his bet.

Still another example of his particularity and pride in navigation came about after the repeal of prohibition. We used to have a bottle of beer with our lunch. I knew him far better by then and was allowed to sit up at the wheel holding the rod there. We always parked our beer bottles above the instrument panel, next to the compass. The year that beer came out in metal cans, not thinking, I put the can where the bottles used to sit. Without a word George grabbed the can and threw it over the side. When I asked him why, he reminded me that it would affect the compass and said that, by tossing the can overboard, I would never forget it, but that if he had simply asked me to move the can, I would probably have put it up there again. Needless to say, the lesson sank in.

Boatmen have to understand not only navigation but the ways of fishes, tackle, engines, and, of course, the fine art of gaffing. This was

[107]

an important feature of an early boatman's job. Since he was alone with the angler, and therefore responsible for the landing of all fish, early guides were appropriately called gaffers. When these men grew old and could no longer stand in a rolling boat, or when they could no longer see the flocks of birds diving in the distance, they lost their clients but hung around the docks anyway to keep in touch with gossip afloat. They were then known kindly as "old gaffers," and the term slipped into our vernacular to describe any aging man of action.

George Farnsworth was as effective a gaffer as he was anything else in fishing. The George Thomases could not recall a time when he needed more than a single swipe to secure a tuna. He was also familiar enough with most other Catalina species so that he was able, like many good boatmen, to identify unexpected fish merely by the characteristics of its strike and struggle.

But on one occasion George Farnsworth missed. Here's the story as told by the elder Thomas:

The *Aerial*, with angler aboard, had been scouting the sea for signs of broadbill. Many floating patches of kelp were noticed as they drifted along, and when the angler happened to look under one of these closely meshed masses, he believed he discerned flashes of blue. He immediately thought of dolphin, and, as he had never been fortunate enough to capture one of these prizes, he suggested to Farnsworth that they troll a feather jig past the kelp to try to raise one of them. The boatman agreed, and the line was put out.

Sure enough, the line had no more than started to circle the floating island when there was a terrific strike, and a gleaming, flashing blaze of color hurled itself shimmering into the air. In a few short minutes the quarry was brought to gaff, the first dolphin that the angler had ever hooked.

"Don't miss him, George, I want to have him mounted," said the angler, as with perfect confidence he brought the leader to the boatman's hand. . . . Three quick passes with the gaff, when "Tuna George" generally needed but one, and the dolphin was impaled. As the gleaming sides of the golden-hued form appeared above the gunwhale [sic] preparatory to being lifted inboard there were a few quick motions, the fish slipped off the gaff and off the hook, and fled to the depths. His speed and agility were astonishing.[8]

This was in the summer of 1929, one of the last great marlin years off Catalina, during which over 200 of these spearfish were landed.

---

[8]*Gamefish of the Pacific*, pages 172–73.

It was also one of the last years of generally good fishing for the Tuna Club.

When C. F. Holder first visited Catalina in 1886, he "saw men catching fishes from the beach which tipped the scales from twenty-five to forty pounds, caught with short handlines and crude weights." But thirty years later, development of the island and commercial fishing had reduced the now legendary inshore shoals of white sea bass and yellowtail to occasional small schools.

Even remote San Clemente Island, 36 miles across the channel from Catalina, had become less productive, and some folks conjectured that the San Clemente monster might have something to do with this.

Few interesting areas of the sea do not have at least one old moss-backed monster of whatever species is most sought after, to make life more exciting for old-timers and novitiate anglers alike. Tahiti has a giant 20-foot marlin with an underjaw longer than its upperjaw; Madagascar has a sailfish fully 25 feet long. Even the Florida Keys has an ancient jewfish[9] called the "Brunose-Wampus-Cat," with enough old hooks, lines, and leaders in his mouth to open a tackle shop when the critter's finally caught—or so they say.

The Catalina area also had its monster, but not a variation on a game species. And what's startling about this creature is the large number of extremely sober souls who took oaths to having seen it. Even more significant, some members of the Tuna Club were annoyed when they saw it, feeling that whatever they might say thereafter on any subject touching credulity would be viewed with suspicion.

Among those associated with the club who saw the San Clemente monster were Ralph Bandini, Joseph A. Coxe, George C. Thomas III, and George Farnsworth. Coxe saw the creature several times—once quite close, just under the boat. When Dr. David Starr Jordan suggested that what people were seeing was a sea elephant, Coxe replied, "I've seen plenty of them [sea elephants]—have been out to their rookery on Guadalupe Island. . . . If that was a sea elephant—then I'm a Martian!"[10]

Here is Thomas's account of his sighting:

Around 1924 or 1925, we were going to Clemente—George Farnsworth and I—on the old *Fairplay*. We took a course to the east end of Clemente. The sea was calm and glassy. I imagine it was in July. We

---

[9]Charles Holder believed this name was a corruption of "Junefish"—the month of greatest activity and abundance for these giant groupers.

[10]*Men, Fish and Tackle*, Ralph Bandini, Bronson, Mich., 1936, page 74.

were looking for tuna. I would say we were about 8 miles off the coast of Clemente. I happened to look to starboard. Two miles away I saw this shape in the water. First, I thought it was the sail of a Japanese albacore boat. It was, well, just a big black form. Then I thought to myself: it can't be a sail, there's no wind. I put the glasses on it and still couldn't tell what it was.

I said to George: "What the hell's that?"

He said: "The Clemente Monster."

We went towards it. We got to within ¾ of a mile. Then it went down. It didn't impress me particularly at the time. It was just another marine animal so far as I was concerned. But since then I have thought this thing over a thousand times. You know, after a number of years, it's possible to start exaggerating.

The remarkable thing about each sighting of the Clemente Monster was that eye-witness descriptions never vary. Unlike other famous sea monsters that differ in appearance according to the personality and perspective of the observer, the Clemente creature was always the same.[11] Here is Ralph Bandini's logbook account dated September 16, 1916:

Left Mosquito at 7:00. Overcast, no wind, light roll coming down coast. Worked up toward Long Point and about a mile and a half off shore. I was sitting on top the cabin, and Roy [my boatman] was below doing something. Rod lashed to chair. Off White Rock saw something big and black out of the corner of my eye and to seaward. Turned, and there it was—the Clemente Monster! Nearly fell off cabin. Yelled to Roy to head for it and clapped my glasses on it. It's hard to describe just what I saw. The thing lifted out of the water about 20 feet I should say and looked to be 8 or 10 feet thick. A sort of huge barrel, or tree trunk, with a kind of lizard-like head. On each side the head, which I gathered was lowered, as I didn't see any mouth, there were two huge eyes. They must have been sixteen or eighteen inches across and were round and bulging. Dead and expressionless. The head was turning slowly. I got the impression of coarse reddish hair, or bristles, on the columnar part that was in sight. It was about ¼ of a mile off when I sighted it and I think my glasses being 7-power should have brought it up to within perhaps 200 yards of us.

It is only an hour ago that we saw this thing and I am writing this carefully and while all details are fresh in my mind. Roy stuck his head

---

[11]Not having been sighted since the end of World War II, some people believe the Clemente Monster was a casualty of that conflict, probably destroyed by an American ship or plane that mistook the creature for a Japanese submarine!

through the hatch and let out a sort of little squawk when he saw it. We both knew what it was because we had both heard of it and talked to people who had seen it and I saw it once a long way off. The description given by others checked with the thing I was looking at. All of them had described it as a thick body surmounted by a reptilian head and with God awful eyes. Certain the eyes I was looking at were God awful enough. I never want to look at anything like them again!

The head was turning, sort of pivoting. It appeared to see us and stopped, staring at us for perhaps a minute, perhaps more. Then it started to sink. There was no convulsive movement or anything like that. It just sank down slowly and deliberately much as a whale's flukes sink when it up-ends and sounds. When it disappeared there wasn't any discernible ripple or swirl. It just went under. Looking back and taking stock of things I remember another thing: The little roll coming down the coast *broke* against it! That gives some hint of the size of it.

We've been lying to for the last hour hoping that it would come up again. Roy and I have been trying to figure out what in the name of God the thing is. Certainly it's no known living creature. The thing looked very much like the models I have seen of brontosaurs (I hope I'm spelling that right!) that I've seen in museums. Roy is plain scared and I don't mind saying I'm not so happy as I might be. As I write this I am sitting on the cockpit bench and I find myself glancing overside all the time. Still, I wish it would come up and let me have another look at it. I don't know how long it was up but would guess at about two minutes. Roy says five, but I don't think so. I know we didn't seem to get appreciably nearer to it.

After it was all over I realized I had a kodak [camera] on board! But I don't suppose it would have shown anything but something black sticking up out of the water. One thing, visibility was good. The island behind us stood out in clear detail and the horizon edge was sharp. So there was no haze to distort what we saw. I don't know what the thing is—and don't think anybody else does. But I know now that there is something out there that is unknown and unclassified. Probably it is something that has come down out of prehistoric times. I am certain the thing is warm blooded and has to surface to breathe. There were no signs of gills that I could see. Roy's impressions of it coincide with mine—except that he says it was fifty feet high! That's nonsense! I think it lifted up 20 ft.—but it might have been less. It might have been 6 ft. thick and not 10. But the neck, or body, or whatever it was we saw was apparently perfectly round—and the head was flattened and reptilian. And nobody can laugh away those eyes.

Later: We got the horse laugh in camp tonight but the fact remains that we saw something that isn't! I've wracked my brains to see if I've overlooked anything but if I have I can't think of it. Incidentally we caught one marlin—about 175 lbs. Put up a nice fight with about 30 jumps. Somehow or another, though, my mind isn't on fishing today! What in the hell was that thing?!

Some people who never saw the San Clemente monster not only believed in it but blamed it for the falling off of fine fishing around that island. However, the elder Thomas (who believed the monster existed) knew that the disappearance of the gamefishes around San Clemente was caused by circumstances a little less ethereal. On a visit in 1921 to George Michaelis's camp on the island,[12] he commented:

In the past, many marlin had been taken by Clemente's shores, and yellowtail had been abundant, but the fact that fish had been slaughtered in great quantity by net-boats, coupled with the live-bait industry, had changed the old angler's paradise. Yellowtail were practically eliminated. Tuna were very scarce, and when schools did appear, the round haul net-boats not only decimated and frightened them, but made it difficult for rods to work them.

Fewer fish for more fishermen led to tackle refinement. Transparent gut leaders and tiny hooks in live baits replaced traditional wire leaders and large hooks in dead baits in an effort to outwit the increasingly wary California yellowtail.

But still Catalina angling continued to wane. Glowing reports from other seas suggested to even the most tradition-oriented members of the Tuna Club that the southern limit of their territory might have to be extended if the club itself was not to die.

---

[12]In the letter dated January 15, 1971, George C. Thomas II writes: "As to the Camp at Mosquito Harbor on San Clemente Island, the Tuna Club originally had a place about two miles east of there at the Fish Hook. It was managed by a man named Al Shade. This was just after World War I, and that camp was washed out in a northeaster one winter. The camp was moved to Mosquito and put under the direction of George Michaelis, who was one of the old-time Avalon boatmen. I knew Michaelis very well, and my dad and I stayed there many times. There used to be great yellowtail fishing there, and, in the early twenties, lots of marlin and 100-pound tuna. It was a wonderful place.

The Clemente Camp was under lease to the Tuna Club from the U. S. Government, which still owns San Clemente Island. The camp accommodated about 16 people, and non-club members could stay there if room was available.

The two Georges [Farnsworth and Michaelis] were great friends, and, for some reason, always called each other 'Bill.' Farnsworth told me that they often used to fight—just for the heck of it. They were both powerful men, and, although good friends, really slugged it out. I believe that these battles generally ended up in a draw, although I never saw one."

Several members made trips to Mexican waters, and George Farnsworth acted as guide on at least three of these expeditions, including the first. On October 26, 1908, with Farnsworth at the helm, the *Comfort*, owned by C. G. Conn, with L. G. Murphy (the rod manufacturer) and Gilmour Sharp along as guests, sailed from San Diego. She traveled nearly 3,000 miles in a little over two months and went as far south as Concepción Bay. Fishing was fantastic, with many new game species such as *cabrillo* and *turel* discovered and some world records broken. Many years later, the George Thomases made a similar trip with Farnsworth and encountered equally excellent fishing. In one day, for example, they caught and released nine large marlin.

But it was finally decided that waters south of the 32nd parallel were, after all, Mexican, and while the Tuna Club's membership was international in scope, it would be false to the concept of the club's founding fathers, as well as unfair to their remarkable records, to seek buttons beyond the limits proscribed in the original charter. Hence, while most members continued to show great loyalty in their association, the club itself as a hub of angling activity and innovation began to fade. New York, Boston, and Philadelphia members talked with pride of the early days, but they more often went to Florida to fish.

Charles Holder had been a New Englander who founded big-game angling in the Pacific. Now the sport was returning to many of the zones along the eastern seaboard where his father and Louis Agassiz had first instilled in him a curiosity about all creatures within the sea.

George Farnsworth lingered at Catalina as long as there were any of his old charter friends to take fishing. In 1938, six years after the elder Thomas's death, George C. Thomas III took Farnsworth to Liverpool, Nova Scotia, where Thomas participated as a member of the U. S. (Sharp Cup) Tuna Team:

Before the matches I was fortunate in landing a 715-pounder. George [Farnsworth] was with me, and it really thrilled him to see tuna of that size. He was not, of course, permitted to go out on the team boats during the actual matches, but he did manage to get an available charter boat and use his kites with marked success. The fish, for Nova Scotia, were small, around 100 pounds, but I do know that he hooked more bluefin than any of the competing team boats.

Immediately after the Japanese attack on Pearl Harbor in 1941, the Navy closed all ports to sport fishing. However, the government did allow the closely supervised commercial fleets to continue their activities. George C. Thomas III's boat, *Aerial*, would have been of no use as a sport fisherman, so Thomas "sold" the boat to Farnsworth for ten dollars with the understanding that after the war Farnsworth would "resell" the boat to Thomas for the same amount. Farnsworth kept his word, but four years of commercial activity during the war crippled his interest in sport fishing. Probably he discovered he could make more money commercial fishing for albacore than chartering out of Catalina. Possibly, too, since he managed to do all his commercial fishing by himself, its solitude may have been more appealing to a man who preferred doing things alone anyway.

After the war, he bought a surplus 63-foot Coast Guard cutter, the *Sea Rider*, and roamed far and wide with the albacore fleet—often staying out more than a week at a time. George Thomas and other friends persuaded him to take on a deckhand, pointing out that something unforeseen could occur and possibly leave him helpless.

Early in 1952, it did. While far out at sea, George Farnsworth suffered a massive cerebral hemorrhage. His right side was completely paralyzed, and he could move only with the greatest difficulty. Thanks to the presence of a mate, the *Sea Rider* made it back to San Pedro.

Since this boat was docked in Los Angeles harbor and was a documented vessel, Farnsworth, as her captain, was entitled to government hospitalization. He spent his remaining years in and out of several different Navy and Merchant Marine hospitals. George Thomas, the "Kid," watched over Farnsworth to the end and only moved to Hawaii after the older man died in San Francisco in 1959.

Before he died, Farnsworth asked George Thomas to scatter his ashes at sea as Farnsworth had done for Boschen. Thomas then asked a close friend to accompany him on the trip, and they found a place far offshore with no other boats in sight.

"I asked my friend to give the Invocation," Thomas writes, "to say a small prayer. I shut off the engine and said that I was ready. In a stentorian voice, he began, 'Oh Heavenly Father, we hereby commit to the deep the mortal remains of George—George——' Then in a stage whisper to me,—'What the hell was his middle name?' 'Chase,' I whispered back, and we ended the rite. I am sure that old George looked down and laughed at us, and said, 'You really loused that up!' And then he laughed again."

Men who share the sea share experiences unknown to most landsmen. Such sharing makes for close friends. Even so, the friendship of the three Georges—Farnsworth and the two Thomases—was exceptional.

[114]

EIGHT

A BOY NAMED PEARL

> You can't tell: Maybe a fish goes home and lies
> about the size of the bait that got away!—Anon.

One afternoon in August 1914, a brash young man arrived in Avalon, sought out the Tuna Club's official taxidermist, Charles Browning Parker,[1] and began to describe exactly how he wanted his first Blue Button tuna mounted. Parker looked the fellow up and down in amazement and then suggested he go out and catch one first. The presumptuous angler finally did—five years later. Yet despite this slow start, Zane Grey went on to become the most celebrated blue-water fisherman of his generation.

There were really two Zane Greys: the Western writer known to countless millions of readers round the world, and the pioneer angler known to a much smaller audience of frequently jealous fishermen.

Many of Zane Grey's contemporaries were jealous of his fame and

---

[1]Parker (1867–1924) first went to Catalina as a representative of the Smithsonian Institution. Like many another visitor, he was delighted by what he found and decided to stay.

leisure, and there were those in tackle shops and marinas from New York to Los Angeles who disparaged his reputation and ridiculed his achievements while ZG himself was away fishing distant oceans they would never see. On his return he found he had to answer absurd charges, such as he had been shooting his world's records ("I have," he replied. "With a camera.")—or that his biggest catches were a result of teamwork between a number of hired anglers fishing impossibly heavy rods and lines ("Certainly," said ZG, "and we use trained whales to round up only the very best trophies.")

Zane Grey was a legend in his time, and like most legends, he was regularly pursued by the malicious gossip of lesser men.

Even today, there are those who envy Zane Grey. However, now it is because he fished places like Catalina and the Florida Keys in the 1910's, Nova Scotia and Panama in the 1920's, and Tahiti and Australia in the 1930's. He fished coasts that will never again be as primitive nor as productive, and he caught fish in sizes and abundance that are rarely seen anymore. Zane Grey's descriptions of shoals of breaking tuna as far as the eye could reach may someday rank with nineteenth-century descriptions of the limitless herds of buffalo on the Western plains. Commercial fishing is rapidly doing for the pelagic fishes what commercial hunting did to the bison a century ago. And Zane Grey's sea world has already become a part of the "vanishing wilderness" he tried to preserve—and did so in part—through the seven books he wrote and the four films he made on ocean angling.

Zane Grey's far-ranging outdoor life and his conservation activities were by-products of a considerable income that derived entirely from a prolific pen. Indeed, some of his fans imagine that Zane Grey *invented* the frontier novel, if not all the legends of the Wild West. Yet what Grey did do was to inherit and refine a genre of literature that was popular long before he was born but had never been fully exploited. Grey led the way of great escape for millions of Americans who, in imagination or fact, had reached the limits of their continent and now sought to retain the romance and mystery that had inspired their pioneering forebears.

James Fenimore Cooper (1789–1851) was the father of frontier fiction, and Thomas Mayne Reid (1818–1883) was one of its early exponents. Reid thrilled a generation of Easterners beginning in 1850 with romantic accounts of his exploits on the Great Plains. Joseph Holt Ingraham (1809–1860) and his son, Prentiss (1843–1904), also contributed their share of frontier adventures, although they focused on the wild regions that once were Kentucky and Missouri. The year the older Ingraham died, the dime novel appeared, and Prentiss eventually outdid his dad in writing volume—and violence—with this popular predecessor to the paperback. Then there was Edward Zane Carroll Judson (1823–1886), alias Ned Buntline, who thrilled a huge audience of readers through the post-Civil War period with innumerable adventures about Wild Bill Hickok, Wyatt Earp, and other "historical figures."[2] Zane Grey's fiction was merely a larger, more passionately felt, edition of these earlier efforts.

Zane Grey was actually christened Pearl (Zane) Gray,[3] named for the color Queen Victoria had made popular at the time of his birth in 1872.[4] "Pearl gray" was the official mourning color honoring the tenth anniversary of the Prince Consort's death. Like the boy named Sue, he grew up hating his first name, and he fought countless battles with schoolmates to assure them of his masculinity.

However, his mother's family was descended from the Virginia Zanes, an adventurous lot offering young Pearl several illustrious ancestors. Most outstanding was Ebenezer Zane, the boy's great-grandfather, who had left Hardy County, Virginia (now part of West Virginia), not long before the American Revolution to move west and

---

[2]Judson's influence on ZG's life and work has never been properly assessed. For starters, the name *Zane* was shared by both men—a fact that would not have been lost on ZG, who was always fascinated by Zane family history. Furthermore, Judson's father had written a book entitled *The Sages and Heroes of the American Revolution*, with which Grey was familiar through research for his own first book, *Betty Zane*. Finally, that Judson was an Easterner who made his fortune by writing fiction based on his Western travels, and that he owned a favorite house, "The Eagle's Nest," in the Catskills not unlike Grey's home on the Delaware, will all make for interesting homework by an enterprising student someday when universities come to view these two major figures of popular American literature a little less snobbishly than they do today.

A footnote to a fishing history that might have been is that Judson (an avid angler) and Henry William Herbert were introduced to each other at a dinner party. However, the two men quarreled over some snide comment Judson made about the courage of English seamen. But for that, Ned Buntline and Frank Forester might have been fishing companions!

[3]ZG later changed the spelling of his last name *Gray* to *Grey*. This latter spelling offered less of a reminder of the hated christian name/surname combination given him by his mother.

[4]Zane Grey felt he was late getting started as a famous author (he was 40 by the time *Riders of the Purple Sage* was published in 1912), and he hoped to make people believe he was more precocious than he was. Therefore, he gave *Who's Who* his birth year as 1875. After his death, his widow had the true year inscribed on his tombstone in Lackawaxen, Pennsylvania. However, the 1875 date is still erroneously cited by most modern encyclopedias and dictionaries.

settle an outpost on the Ohio River. At the outbreak of the war, he was made a colonel in the American militia, and he and his men—many of them kinsmen—built a stockade and called it Fort Henry in honor of Patrick Henry. When a sizeable British and Indian force attacked the fort later in the war, Colonel Zane's young sister, Betty, saved the day by carrying powder from the arsenal to the stockade through a hail of shot and arrows. Thus preserved, the fort became the hub of Wheeling, West Virginia.

General Washington personally commended the Zane clan for their outstanding defense of this strategic post, and, after the war, Congress voted Colonel Zane 10,000 acres of land in the Ohio Valley for "services rendered." The colonel then led other settlers west as a means of establishing and maintaining claims over his new property, and he left us a pioneer highway, Zane's Trace, in the process. He also founded the town of Zanesville, Ohio, where Pearl Gray was born 75 years later.

In an incomplete autobiography begun the last year of his life, Zane Grey reminisced about his youth in Zanesville, remembering school as something that bored him, and fishing as something for which he lived. In fact, according to this personal history, the most important event in his early life was the day he saw his first live fish from the roadside as he was riding in a coach to visit his aunt in Brownsville. He was only six at the time, but he recalls that the coachman identified the fish as "just a chub," but young Gray decided that a chub must be the most wonderful creature in the world.

As it turned out, his younger brother, Romer Carl—more familiarly known to readers of ZG's fishing adventures as RC or Reddy—caught the first fish between them: a monster sucker some 18 inches long. This first large fish landed by the fraternal team of ZG and RC was, perhaps, an omen: Although RC never really cared for oceanic angling the way older brother Zane did (RC suffered from almost constant *mal de mer* during his first years at sea), RC went along on many of the offshore trips and frequently succeeded in one-upping his more famous brother by landing larger fish. Most outstanding, he held the world record for broadbill swordfish for a number of years after taking it away from ZG by a mere six pounds.[5] This was especially frustrating to ZG because he thought of himself as one of the pioneers of broadbill swordfishing and always held the species in the highest regard. While

---

[5]ZG's record had been 582 pounds; RC's was 588. Zane Grey later encouraged Romer Carl to write his own book on ocean angling called *Adventures of a Deep-Sea Angler*. The volume was published in 1930 and helped give RC a modest fan club of his own.

he did not begrudge RC a broadbill swordfish, and while he even went to considerable lengths to help him land his first one, the world's record was something else again! Meanwhile, seasick RC could have cared less.

The Gray boys' father, Lewis M. Gray, was a preacher-turned-dentist —and a severe disciplinarian. He expected perfect obedience from his children, and, as is often true in such cases, his rigidity inspired rebellion. Dr. Gray did not want his boys to "waste time" fishing; as a result, his boys fell in love with fishing. Dr. Gray especially forbade young Pearl from becoming acquainted with a vagrant known as Old Muddy Miser who spent all his days fishing along the Muskingum River; young Pearl could hardly wait to meet the tramp!

Every youthful angler has someone older or a little more experienced in the ways of angling to introduce him to the sport and guide him through his first wonderful, but sometimes awkward, days afield. For some of us, this guide is an older brother, an uncle, or merely a more knowledgeable friend. A few of us are even lucky enough to have one of the grand old philosophers of the sport as our mentor. Muddy Miser seems to have been a congenial blend of all these archetypes.

When young Pearl confessed that his father disapproved of him wasting time by fishing, the old man replied:

You can waste time in worse ways. There is something fascinating about the study of fish. And to be out in the open, to know the sunshine and the rain and the beauty that is all around you—that is a wonderful thing for anyone. . . . You must make fishing a study, a labor of love, no matter what your vocation will be. You must make time for your fishing. Whatever you do, you will do it all the better for the time and thought you give to fishing.[6]

The interpretation of the true worth of fishing became an integral part of ZG's own feelings about the sport. No matter how compulsive he was later to become about the pursuit of trophy fish, Zane Grey's real records in angling are his written descriptions of the smell and motion of the sea, the wonderful sight of graceful birds and splashing fish—all the qualities that go into any trip offshore.

ZG collected fish and he studied them. He also landed some of the biggest fish of certain species ever caught by man. But today his first 1,000-plus-pound blue marlin has been forgotten, along with his world records: 111-pound yellowtail, 63-pound dolphin, 450-pound striped

---

[6]*Zane Grey: A Biography*, Frank Gruber, New York, 1969, pages 15 and 20.

marlin, 758-pound bluefin tuna, and 1,036-pound tiger shark. However, the fact that the Pacific sailfish, *Istiophorus greyi*, is named for him carries an immortality of its own which he would have been proud of.[7]

After angling, baseball was young Pearl's favorite diversion. He was so good at it—primarily as a double-threat pitcher and hitter—he was offered athletic scholarships to the University of Michigan, Chicago Wesleyan, Vanderbilt, and the University of Pennsylvania. He preferred the latter because Penn played a tougher schedule against top schools like Harvard, Yale, and Princeton. And Pearl's father liked Penn because it had an excellent dental school. While Pearl was not too enthusiastic about dentistry, he was delighted to go anywhere that would support him through four more years of baseball—with side trips to fish.

In 1896, Pearl Gray finished his schooling and went off to New York City. He rented space at 117 West 21st Street,[8] changed the spelling of his family name, and put out his shingle: "Dr. P. Zane Grey, D.D.S." However, he quickly decided that dentistry was not his life's work. In fact, he suddenly discovered he hated it! He was not sure what he wanted to do, but he knew it was not pulling teeth and molding dentures. With the spare time he had, he took trips to the Delaware near the village of Lackawaxen to fish with older brother Ellsworth (also known as Cedar), and younger brother RC. He also joined the recently formed Camp-Fire Club of America that boasted such future famous members as Theodore Roosevelt, Gifford Pinchot, and Ernest Thompson Seton. Another club member, George O. Shields, publisher of *Recreation* magazine,[9] encouraged ZG to try his hand at writing up

---

[7]Recent ichthyological research may be threatening even this modest bit of immortality. Most marine biologists now believe the Pacific and Atlantic sailfishes are actually one and the same fish to be classified as *Istiophorus platypterus*.

[8]Researchers, including myself as editor for Prentice-Hall's *Zane Grey: Outdoorsman*, once located ZG's first office at 100 West 74th Street. While he did later practice there, the fact that the building is called the Graystone Apartments perhaps colored our choice! However, according to the New York City Directory for 1899, the 21st Street number was actually his first business address.

[9]We tend to remember writers and politicians—people who put their names on documents—when we consider history. And the history of the conservation movement is no different. We know the names Seton and Roosevelt, but we have forgotten George O. Shields. Yet in his capacity as editor and publisher for the important outdoor journal *Recreation*, he did much to fuel conservation activities. His magazine initiated the League of American Sportsmen, and Shields himself coined the phrase "game hog" to describe greedy hunters and fishermen. In addition, while Dr. William T. Hornaday is generally credited with founding the

some of his angling adventures, and Zane Grey's first byline appeared in the May 1902 issue of that publication.

As a newly published author, Zane Grey was rather taken with himself and full of dreams concerning his future fame and fortune. The trouble was, he *knew* he was going to be a great writer but he did not know precisely what direction this greatness would take!

That same year Owen Wister published *The Virginian*. This was a new kind of Western that gave a respectable luster to an old genre. Since American history already interested ZG through the activities of his maternal great-grandfather, and since *The Virginian* became an instant success that gave its author fame and fortune overnight, Zane Grey decided he, too, would be a writer of frontier fiction.

Through Shields and another writing friend, Alvah James, Grey met his first Western hero, "Colonel" Charles Jesse "Buffalo'" Jones. Jones had come east to show movies about his travels and ranch in the Grand Canyon and Kaibab Forest country of Arizona in order to raise funds for his favorite charity: the American bison. Jones's sobriquet, "Buffalo," had been given him because of the considerable time and energy he had devoted to saving these creatures from extinction.

Jones and Grey got along well together, and the older man invited the apprentice outdoor writer on his next expedition west. When the trip was over, Grey returned with enough story material gathered on the trail and around the campfire at night to make a dozen novels. But success was still a while away. He had to go through several lean years of rejections and rewritten manuscripts before his material began to sell. Finally, with *The Last of the Plainsmen* (a story about Jones) in 1908, *The Last Trail* in 1909, and *The Heritage of the Desert* in 1910, he was on his way.

As Zane Grey refined his talent, he developed a distinctive style that turned heroes and heroines into characters of epic proportions. While Owen Wister prepared the reading public for any work that in some way documented the lost frontier, Zane Grey's fiction provided the fabulous sequels America craved. And his novels continued to do so for the next 30 years of ZG's writing career.[10]

Camp-Fire Club in 1897, it was Shields who devoted full time and energy from the beginning until 1903 to make the organization a going concern. Finally, Shields contributed many excellent angling features to a variety of publications, and edited the important *American Game Fishes: Their Habits, Habitat, and Peculiarities* in 1892. For most of his writing, however, he sought anonymity in the pen name "Coquina."

[10]And they still do. Although ZG died in 1939, he was so prolific that his

Curiously, it took Grey nearly a year to market his most famous Western title, chiefly because editors were worried that the book might offend Mormon readers. Robert H. Davis, editor of *Munsey's Magazine,* was personally enthusiastic about the novel, but was fearful that if he handled its serialization, a political issue could be made out of some of its references to Mormons, which in turn might cripple the efforts of his publisher, Frank A. Munsey,[11] to get Teddy Roosevelt reelected President on the Bull Moose Party ticket.

After a great deal of doubt and delay, Harper & Brothers finally accepted the hardback edition, and *Field & Stream* magazine purchased the serial rights, and almost overnight, *Riders of the Purple Sage* became a tremendous best seller and its author, a household name. At last Zane Grey had the success he dreamed of when he started writing 10 years earlier. And he was two whole years younger than Owen Wister when Wister made his big splash!

Over the next quarter century, with such titles as *Desert Gold, Wildfire,* and *The U.P. Trail,* Zane Grey novels were rarely off the best-seller lists, and his success inspired a host of imitators. Among the best known were Frederick Schiller Faust who, because of anti-German feeling in America during World War I, changed his literary name to Max Brand[12]; Ernest Haycox; Alan LeMay; and Frederick Glidden, alias Luke Short. However, none was ever as successful as Zane Grey, who by 1925 was making better than half a million dollars a year from his Westerns—and doing the kinds of things with this income that most fishermen only dream about.

Of course, Zane Grey's saltwater angling career began long before 1925. Even before the first flush of success provided by *Riders of the Purple Sage,* Grey had sampled school tuna fishing off the Long Island and Jersey coasts and tarpon fishing in Mexico. The latter experience was a by-product of a second trip west to Arizona, after which he went south by train to Mexico City and Tampico, then returned north to New York by steamer. The expedition resulted in a story for *Shields'*

---

publisher did not get around to producing the last of his novels until 1963. Even more remarkable, ZG's titles still sell better than one million copies a year in North America, and Zane Grey continues to be one of our most popular authors abroad.

[11]Munsey was one of a number of energetic publishers at the turn of the century with a modest, but influential, stable of magazines. Today, the only one of his periodicals to survive is *Argosy.*

[12]Faust also left us the popular Dr. Kildare series. He died as a war correspondent in 1944.

Magazine, another one of George O. Shields's publications, and three articles for *Field & Stream.*

Grey's relationship with *Field & Stream* goes back to some of his very earliest writing efforts. The second story ZG ever wrote, "Camping Out," appeared in the February 1903 issue of that magazine. When *Field & Stream* later became the official organ of the Camp-Fire Club,[13] it was appropriate Grey continue submitting most of his fishing material to this magazine, and eventually more than 30 articles on angling appeared under his byline in its pages.

The publisher, Eltinge F. Warner, took Zane Grey fishing on occasional business trips ZG made to the city after he moved full-time to Lackawaxen, Pennsylvania. They sometimes persuaded Bob Davis of Munsey's to join them (despite Davis's predisposition to seasickness), and on September 21, 1912, the three men landed a porpoise on regulation tarpon tackle after first harpooning it off Seabright, New Jersey. Intended only as a once-in-a-lifetime stunt, Warner, Davis, and Grey nevertheless banded together to form the world's first Porpoise Club and announced the design of a Porpoise Button by way of teasing members of the Tuna Club at Avalon.[14]

Soon ZG was traveling regularly to other regions for fishing. Halfway along on a second trip to Tampico with RC, the two brothers were advised to return home because of a yellow fever epidemic in Mexico. They disembarked at Nassau and ended up in the Florida Keys. The latter's beauty and abundance so impressed Zane Grey that soon he was a regular winter visitor to the Long Key Fishing Camp (founded in 1906), while he made his summer headquarters from 1914 to 1927 at Catalina.

As has already been noted, ZG had a little difficulty in getting his first Blue Button tuna at Catalina. However, his initial lack of success was probably as much due to a series of indifferent tuna seasons during World War I as to ZG's inexperience. Once the Blue Button fish returned in quantity, he landed more than his share of trophies. An interesting footnote to ZG's first successful season is his confession that his boatman, Captain O. I. Danielson, located fish only after

---

[13]This association was advertised on the covers of all *Field & Stream* magazines between November 1910 and September 1916. In October 1916, the magazine adopted its present size (from the 9 × 6½ inches it had measured before), changed the overall design of the cover, and dropped the Camp-Fire Club logo.

[14]The porpoise was mounted by John Murgatroyd of New York and for some years thereafter hung in the offices of *Field & Stream.*

following a more resourceful skipper. Although the skipper's name is not mentioned, the area to which he led Captain Dan and ZG lay off the northwest coast of Catalina—one of George Farnsworth's favorite grounds.

By 1918, Zane Grey's fame and financial success were gradually separating him from many former friends. Some of this was the inevitable result of a wandering life plus the fact that ZG now moved in more expensive circles than many of his former colleagues could afford. Zane Grey was not a snob, but some of his acquaintances chose to interpret the fact that they rarely saw him anymore in this light.

Of particular distress to ZG was the discovery that some of his freshwater angling companions were aggravated by his new allegiance to the ocean. Bob Davis who, as ZG once observed, "did not love the sweet, soft scent that breathes from off the sea," was especially contemptuous of ZG's tales of giant fishes. He wrote Grey after the latter's first good season on tuna: "If you went out with a mosquito-net to catch a mess of minnows, your story would read like Roman gladiators seining the Tigris for whales!"

Will Dilg, with whom Zane Grey was to found the Izaak Walton League in 1922,[15] was another freshwater fan. He responded to ZG's telegram that he had at last landed a Blue Button fish with a nine-page prose poem on the qualities of black bass and black bass angling!

Zane Grey grinned and bore it, but his battles with big tuna and broadbill swordfish continued to pull him apart from freshwater friends content with 10-inch trout, who doubted that fish 10 times that size could be caught on essentially the same tackle.

The problem of credibility became even more acute after ZG went to more remote corners of the Pacific for his big-game fishing. After all, he had had many reliable witnesses at Catalina to attest to the size and strength of the fishes he caught there. But what could he do for witnesses in the Galápagos or Tahiti? His continuing interest in photography and film work was a partial answer.

ZG had developed a keen camera eye early in his outdoor career. We have many photos by him of fishing and canoeing trips along the Delaware at the turn of the century. He also used a camera to document his trips west with Buffalo Jones so that people would believe mountain lions really could be lassoed and captured alive. And Jones

---

[15]Dilg provided the motivation and money-raising skills that got the Izaak Walton League started; ZG provided some of the money and later contributed a number of free articles to the *Izaak Walton Monthly*.

himself was an able cinematographer who doubtless stimulated ZG's interest in this relatively new technique.

With this background, it is not surprising that ZG got in on the ground floor of a new industry that grew out of motion pictures. In 1912, a young producer named Jesse L. Lasky persuaded a young play director, Cecil B. De Mille, to film a successful Broadway show, *The Squaw Man*, in the New Jersey Palisades. When fall came and the film was still not done, De Mille and the star, Dustin Farnum, decided to go to Arizona—where there was always supposed to be sunshine—to finish the job. However, when their train reached Flagstaff in a raging snowstorm, the two decided to push on to Los Angeles. They rented a barn next to an orange grove in the farming country of Hollywood and finished the movie. From an investment of a few thousand dollars, all the participants became rich and famous.

When another film producer, William K. Fox, contacted ZG in New York about the movie rights to *Riders of the Purple Sage*, ZG held out until he had also sold *The Light of Western Stars* in a combination package. Furthermore, when Jesse Lasky contacted Grey in 1918 about rights to *Desert Gold*, the negotiations were even more rigorous—and fruitful for Zane Grey. He held out for the unheard of price of $25,000 for a seven-year *lease*. At the end of that time, ZG could sell the property all over again to anyone who met his new demands. No wonder 98 Western movies were made from fewer than 50 Zane Grey titles!

Lasky and some business friends founded a studio they called Paramount, which early attracted ZG's attention. He enjoyed being a spectator to film work and felt that writers could learn a great deal from watching movies being put together. This new interest, new business associations, and, of course, the convenience of Catalina offshore, finally persuaded ZG to pull stakes in Lackawaxen[16] and move full-time to Los Angeles—except for regular angling side trips to other parts of the world. He bought a home in Altadena, a lodge in Arizona (for hunting and up-country movie work), and a hillside house in Catalina overlooking the Tuna Club. He then settled down to enjoy the good life which, until the day he died, consisted of getting up early

---

[16]Grey sold off most of his 1,000 acres along the Delaware, but retained his home and five acres at the confluence of the Lackawaxen and Delaware rivers. When the Depression later cleaned out his friend, Alvah James, he turned the Lackawaxen property over to him. In 1972, the Pennsylvania Fish Commission bought most of this land for a campground and boat launching facility, but Alvah James's daughter, Helen, still lives in the old house, now the Zane Grey Inn and Museum.

every morning, writing on a lapboard in a Morris chair for several hours, and then joining his family and friends for the rest of the day's activities—a ride in the country, a visit to Paramount Studios, or a day offshore for tuna, marlin, or broadbill swordfish.

Marlin (or marlin swordfish as they were generally called in the sporting press through the first two decades of this century) and broadbill swordfish started out their piscatorial careers as substitutes for the more glamorous bluefin tuna. Zane Grey caught a number of striped marlin and landed his first broadbill swordfish in 1917—all before he caught his first Blue Button tuna.

Yet gradually an appreciation for the difficulty of hooking the broadbill and a respect for the fighting spirit of all the "swordfishes" began to seep through the ranks of Tuna Club anglers. An attractive blue-and-gold oval button was designed in 1909 to celebrate the capture of a marlin on heavy tackle, and a circular gold-and-white button was created in 1913 to commemorate the heavy tackle capture of a broadbill swordfish. However, by 1920, still only eight anglers could claim one of the gold-and-white buttons: among them, W. C. Boschen, Keith Spalding, H. R. Johnston,[17] Dustin Farnum[18]—and Zane Grey.

Boschen and Grey were the two club fishermen most obsessed by broadbill. ZG started his offshore career with feelings of adulation for the older, more experienced Boschen. But by 1917 when Boschen brought in a world-record swordfish of 463 pounds, ZG was frankly jealous and falsely sympathetic in his published observation that since Boschen's hook had penetrated the fish's heart during the fight,[19] the struggle had been "unfortunately" short-lived and one-sided.

[17]ZG erroneously refers to this man as "Johnson" in his accounting of the first five swordfish button winners. Lieutenant Hugo R. Johnston caught the largest broadbill for the 1916 season: a 362-pounder.

[18]A number of early Hollywood personalities were associated with the Tuna Club. In addition to Dustin Farnum, there was his brother, actor William Farnum; comedians Stan Laurel and Charlie Chaplin; and producers Mack Sennett and Cecil B. De Mille. They all fished at Avalon and all went away with at least one button for some species or other to their credit.

[19]Two classmates of Grey from the University of Pennsylvania were also members of the Tuna Club. Dr. J. Auburn "Lone Angler" Wiborn—his nickname derived from his preference to fish offshore completely by himself—was a dentist like Grey; and a Dr. Riggin, who enjoyed the fraternity of the clubhouse more than fishing, was a medical doctor with a special interest in anatomy. Riggin dissected many specimens brought to the docks at Avalon, and it was from him that ZG learned the "secret" of Boschen's quick-catch world record. However, George Farnsworth, who was Boschen's guide the day Boschen took the record broadbill,

This reversal of sentiment doubtless stemmed from Boschen's rejection of Grey's overtures of friendship. Boschen and his regular boatman, George Farnsworth, kept entirely to themselves and showed not a little contempt for a Johnny-come-lately member who seemed all too eager to convert every day, every acquaintanceship—no matter how casual—into publicity for himself.

But this was not the whole story of ZG's would-be friendship with Boschen. Grey sincerely felt that there was a special majesty in the broadbill swordfish not to be found in any other species of gamefish. And he correctly sensed that Boschen shared this view. With Boschen's help, he reasoned, the two men could switch Catalina's primary allegiance from tuna to swordfish. Doubtless, in his pursuit of this goal, Grey was trying to initiate a program for which he would get most of the credit. He *did* feel like a Johnny-come-lately at the Tuna Club, and he hoped to start something that would distinguish him from the other members—show them and the entire angling world that he was more than just another fisherman. The fact that Boschen realized this was part of ZG's motivation was one of the reasons he shied away from Zane Grey's proffered friendship.

Ernest Hemingway also sensed this same ulterior motive in Zane Grey two decades later when Grey offered to sponsor a round-the-world fishing competition between himself and Hemingway. Grey's star was fading and Hemingway's was just beginning to give off heat and light, and Hemingway saw no value in linking his future to a dying fire.

Vanity riddled big-game angling society in the early decades. The fraternity of fishermen was much smaller then, and a novitiate's hopes and reputation lay as much in the hands of a few influential elders as it did in his own skill and luck.[20] But intrigue aside, Zane Grey's commitment to ocean angling was sincere. He did not fish merely to make social or business contacts. In fact, he rarely fished with anyone but his family and close friends. And he organized his life in California so as to be offshore as often as he could. And whenever he was at sea,

---

later denied that the swordfish had been hooked in the heart. Unfortunately, my research has not been able to turn up whether Farnsworth was present at the fish's autopsy or not. But there is the fact that Boschen's broadbill was taken on a kite-flown bait, and kite-caught fish seldom swallow the hook.

[20]As big-game angling has become more of an everyman's sport, especially since the advent of smaller boats for offshore work, much of this has changed. However, still today, some of the older tournament committees are tight little islands of influence, and no ordinary industrialist-angler or outdoor-writer receives an invitation to attend these patrician competitions.

he searched especially long and hard for broadbill "finning out."[21]

Zane Grey suffered all the frustrations of any devoted swordfish angler. He kept tally one season and found that in 93 days of angling, he sighted 140 broadbill, baited 94 of them, had 11 strikes, hooked 7 fish and finally landed 4 of them. Such remarkably *good* luck made him the envy of every gold-and-white button seeker in the club!

ZG was a resourceful angler, and his frequent fishing excursions offered many opportunities for experimentation. He decided that kite fishing was inappropriate for broadbill, and that large baits were generally more successful—he figured because they were more readily seen —than small ones. In addition, and by accident, he found that a bait swung up to a cruising swordfish and then dropped back to him even before the strike was frequently picked up as it sank.

He learned the value of teasers in marlin fishing, and he was one of the first anglers to introduce wooden teasers for sailfishing in the Florida Keys to avoid the necessity of constantly replacing bait teasers destroyed by barracuda.[22] But ZG just as quickly learned that teasers were of little value in broadbill swordfishing. In fact, since they were more of a tangling hazard than a help, Grey was one of the few early anglers to concentrate on swordfish to the exclusion of all other angling activity. He rigged only one rod and several baits (keeping the spares on ice) in advance, and kept everything out of the boat's cockpit which was not absolutely essential to the fight. Then he cruised, looking for the fish, rather than trolling blindly with the hope that something else would be caught while waiting for a swordfish to surface. Superstitiously, ZG felt that his odds of seeing a broadbill automatically increased when he was hooked to another, less desirable, fish!

Finally, he installed a sturdy mast in his boat with a platform about two-thirds the way up. He used this crow's nest for two purposes: to spot cruising broadbill and to present his bait from a height so that there would be less trailing line and leader to spook the fish. From the mast, Grey's line ran far astern before touching the water, and the boat

---

[21]This expression describes the sight of cruising broadbill, their dorsal fin and the upper lobe of their tail fin cutting the surface. It is also the name of angling writer Kip Farrington's Easthampton, Long Island, home.

[22]Pflueger tackle later carried a "Zane Grey" teaser, along with a series of Zane Grey hooks; Hardy tackle named rods, reels, and hooks after ZG; and Coxe, a reel. In the 1930's, Ashaway line used his name in various promotional campaigns, and most recently (1972) Everol, the Italian tackle company, has produced a Zane Grey reel.

[128]

itself maneuvered at a much greater distance from the fish. Despite
the drawbacks of a system that has an angler climbing down from a
considerable height with a fresh-hooked fish on—and sometimes in
rough weather—Grey claimed almost 100 percent effectiveness in getting strikes from any broadbill that gave him a chance to present
the bait.

Such innovative systems and concentration paid off. In 10 years of
angling aboard his 52-foot cruiser, *The Gladiator* (named for his
quarry *Xiphias gladius*), Zane Grey landed 24 swordfish while RC
caught 18. Today, with still fewer than 500 anglers worldwide who
have caught even one broadbill swordfish, the *Gladiator*'s record
stands as a monument to Grey's skill and tenacity.

However, ZG permitted his obsession with swordfish and his boast-
fulness to lead to a grave indiscretion—an indiscretion that eventually
cost him many friends, his reputation, and changed his personal life
forever.

Grey caught the largest broadbill swordfish of the 1920 season. It
weighed 418 pounds which, although 45 pounds smaller than Boschen's
world record, was still an outstanding catch. Grey quickly became a
nuisance around the club house as he recounted, over and over again,
the minutest detail of his fight. He was boyish, and sometimes even
charming in his enthusiasm. But in the egotistic way of a child, he
never considered that others might not be as enthusiastic about his
trophy catches as he was. He described how he had rowed all the winter
before to keep in shape for just such a battle. He told about how he
had soaked his hands in saltwater to toughen them against the challenge
of a record fish. He bragged about how *his* big swordfish had been
hooked in the mouth and not in the heart. And he lived over and over
again all the blood, sweat, and tears that went into the battle up to
the gaffing and final flourish at boatside. It got so bad that most Tuna
Club members tried to avoid him, ducking down behind newspapers
when he entered a room, or excusing themselves to run an errand in
town when he sat down on the arms of their chairs.

The following summer, 1921, Mrs. Keith Spalding, who never
weighed more than 100 pounds in her life but was one of the finest
anglerettes ever associated with the Tuna Club, landed a 426-pound
broadbill.[23] That evening nearly every TC member lined up in the
vestibule of the clubhouse to call Zane Grey's home on the hill.

---

[23]Zane Grey wasn't the only Tuna Club member plagued by Mrs. Spalding's

They gave him the business—asking how far did he think Mrs. Spalding had rowed the winter before; suggesting that ZG should use Jergen's Lotion rather than saltwater on his hands; pointing out that Mrs. Spalding's fish had been hooked even farther from the heart than his had, and so forth.

Zane Grey blew his cool. He declared that Mrs. Spalding could not have landed such a big fish by herself. She must have had help.

That kind of angry comment was exactly what some club members had been waiting for. Ray R. Thomas,[24] vice-president of the club that year, notified Grey that he must apologize to the club in writing or resign. Zane Grey did both.

Despite his unpopularity with some of the Old Guard, Grey's resignation was a loss for the club as well as himself. The Tuna Club had benefited from ZG's innovative energy and devotion to the sport, and no one ever quite filled the void he left. As for ZG, losing the club was losing more than several old friends and a base camp; it represented a loss of reason and restraint in much of his angling writing thereafter.

Zane Grey was hurt and angry, and perhaps he wanted to show the angling world that the Tuna Club needed him more than he needed it. In 1927, when *Tales of Swordfish and Tuna* was published, Grey used two of its chapters to attack the Tuna Club's heavy tackle standard and its introduction of "airplane wire" or cable leaders in big-game fishing. Grey claimed that cable leaders were more likely to get wrapped around and cut into fish than single-strand wire.[25] That this was some-

---

proficiency. After several seasons of effort, Jimmy Jump managed to take a 101-pound bluefin tuna on regulation Light Tackle. Shortly thereafter Mrs. Spalding brought one in on the prescribed 9-thread line weighing 103 pounds! Mrs. S. was one of the outstanding lady anglers of all times. Only nine Tuna Club members (including her husband) ever won as many as five buttons for trophy fish. Had she been permitted to join the club, she would have been the tenth.

[24]No relation to the George Thomases, Ray Thomas is best remembered for his experiments with balloons rather than kites for tuna fishing. The experiments were unsuccessful.

[25]The original leader for broadbill swordfishing was light chain. This was soon found impractical because of the frequency with which it twisted and broke under the strain of a big fish. Bronze couplings made in Germany were introduced to give the stiff wire substitutes greater flexibility. Although more durable than chain, even these couplings tended to pull apart on big fish.

Finally, Tuna Clubber Andy R. Martin (one of the nine members entitled to five buttons, and a big-game angler who always regarded gaffs as ugly and unnecessary tools—no matter how large the fish) conceived the idea of using airplane strut wire in broadbill swordfishing. In its original form, the leader was made by taking ⅛-inch Roebling cable, consisting of three strands, and unlaying it with a

thing of a hasty charge can be seen by the fact that Grey himself experimented with cable in later years, and finally settled on braided wire exclusively for his big marlin and broadbill fishing.

But his assertion that 24-thread (72-pound test) was too light a line for really big fish was—and still is—a moot point. ZG observed that other distinguished angling clubs from the Medway in Nova Scotia to the Palm Beach and Long Key clubs in Florida all accepted 39-thread as their heavy tackle standard. Why not Catalina?

ZG maintained that while you would catch a few big broadbill on 24-thread (as he himself had done), you would break off or kill without landing many, many more. This was both unproductive and inhumane angling. Some anglers today agree with Grey. There is a considerable school of thought that insists tackle should be suited to the size of the fish being pursued. And when a man with as much broadbill swordfish experience as Zane Grey suggests that 36- or 39-thread lines are better suited to broadbill swordfishing than 24-thread, these 100-plus-pound test lines should at least be given a fair evaluation by swordfish anglers.

The strength of Grey's argument rested partially on the fact that most of his readers knew ZG was not a meat fisherman. On the contrary, he, more than anyone else, had carried the members of the Long Key Fishing Club out of the handline age into the dawn of rods and reels, and finally into the discovery of Light (6/9) Tackle. Grey argued that nothing caught off the South Florida coast—except an

---

drill. Each one of the single strands then became a leader. Such leaders were undeniably springy and coilsome, and in 1926 Martin himself lost the end of one finger to such a cable while landing a fish off Cabo San Lucas, Baja California. He was also the angler who caught the cable-tangled swordfish in less than six minutes that ZG refers to in his book. Martin himself was not proud of this catch, and he took all the damning photographs of the disfigured fish that appear in *Tales of Swordfish and Tuna*. But no one at the Tuna Club, least of all Martin himself, regarded this capture as anything but a freak. As George C. Thomas III, who was aboard the *Erna III* when the fish was brought in, observed: "This was the only Broadbill that I ever saw so mutilated, and, of course, similar wire is now in use everywhere." That ZG was willing and eager to make a mountain out of such a molehill confirmed most Tuna Clubbers' feelings that they were fortunate to be rid of Zane Grey's membership.

A footnote to Martin's dislike of gaffs comes from George Thomas III: "I fished for many years with Martin—he was a fine sportsman, [who] believe it or not, took several Broadbill without using a gaff. He fought one for 13 hours, 23 minutes, while I was with him. It was hooked in the middle of the pectoral fin, and, when he finally brought it to the boat after an all-night battle, tried to persuade me not to use a gaff. A matter of pride, I guess. I gaffed it anyway!" (letter dated July 6, 1972).

occasional and relatively rare blue marlin—merited heavier tackle. He also stressed that since "heavy tackle means a big catch and light tackle the reverse," and since "tons of good food and game fish are brought in only to be thrown to the sharks," there were moral as well as aesthetic reasons for fishing with light tackle.

Writing in 1919, Grey commended James Jordan as the only Long Key boatman who encouraged light tackle use, and he condemned the other skippers for their greed and vanity that led to the piling up of dead fish at the dock merely to impress the uninitiated. ZG correctly predicted that this pride and competition among chartermen would one day, as much as any other single factor, give big-game angling an undeserved reputation for destruction and waste.

But by 1927, Zane Grey's points of view were riddled with inconsistencies, and his arguments favoring heavy tackle for heavy fish are marred by anger and bitterness. He used much of the chapter discussing heavy tackle as a means to publicly attack the Tuna Club. He complained about anonymous and abusive letters he had received, and he suggested that such correspondence had come from club members. He said that when, after five years of effort, his brother RC caught his first broadbill swordfish, a malicious rumor was started in the Tuna Club that eventually "went all over the world" to the effect that the two brothers had taken turns in fighting the fish. Grey closes his "Heavy Tackle for Heavy Fish" chapter with the statement that such lies are the chief drawback to the great sport of big-game sea fishing.

While ZG's resignation from the club six years before had been handled discreetly as something that involved the big-game fishing fraternity—and that fraternity alone—ZG's published sarcasm and bitterness aroused the interest of the general public. They did not know of the incident involving Mrs. Spalding's broadbill, and when they heard later that ZG had resigned from the Tuna Club, they assumed it was over the club's refusal to let him fish 36-thread line on swordfish. ZG was still embarrassed by the Spalding affair, and he encouraged his public to believe that his resignation resulted from such a "man-to-man" disagreement as heavy versus light tackle. In fact, he grew so attached to this legend that he himself began to pass it around as gospel.

His argument with the Tuna Club seemed to aggravate what had always been a temperamental, not to say cantankerous, nature. ZG was soon at odds with nearly every authority in big-game angling—basically because he felt he should be *the* authority in big-game angling. Many of the disputes were over legitimate and interesting differences of opinion. But no longer able to write polite or even restrained correspondence, ZG's pen flowed with venom.

In 1924, Grey had gone to Nova Scotia and caught the then world-record bluefin tuna of 758 pounds. Not being content with this achievement, he gratuitously attacked one of the pioneers in this region, Englishman L. Mitchell-Henry. Mitchell-Henry was every bit as vain as Grey, and their titanic struggle in the American and British angling press over whom should rightly be crowned the authority among tuna anglers was not resolved—at least to Mitchell-Henry's satisfaction—until 1934 when the latter, with a new world record of 851 pounds to his credit, published *Tunny Fishing—At Home and Abroad*.

Meanwhile, Grey had been to still more exotic grounds. In 1926, he was invited by the New Zealand government to fish the Bay of Islands where, among other records, he caught the first broadbill swordfish ever taken in New Zealand waters. He also introduced trolling with teasers and big-game tackle that had the reel seated on the rod, not slung below it as was frequently seen in saltwater angling throughout the British Empire before 1930. However, not merely content with showing the superiority of American equipment and techniques through superior catches, Grey used the front page of the *Auckland Herald* to say "American tackle and method are so much the better that comparison is misleading." Grey also attacked the local use of treble hooks and harpoons (rather than gaffs) as "unsportsman-like in the extreme." Such tactlessness naturally angered some of his hosts, and ZG's next trip to New Zealand was as a private citizen, not as a guest of the government.

In 1928, Zane Grey made his first trip to Tahiti. He returned again in 1930 and caught a huge blue marlin that weighed 1,040 pounds even after some 200 pounds (ZG's estimate) were taken by sharks at boatside. Zane Grey was understandably proud of this fish—it was the first over 1,000 pounds ever to be taken on rod and reel.

But once before he had paid a penalty for his boasting, and now, after the crowning achievement of his angling career, he again set himself up for a fall. He went into all the glorious details of his epic struggle for the benefit of readers of the November 1930 issue of *Outdoor Life*, and he fought the battle again the following year in his book *Tales of Tahitian Waters*. But he unwisely ignored the competitiveness of his big-game angling rivals, and the naïveté and contradictions of his purple prose left him vulnerable.

Many barbs were thrown but none with as much ruthlessness and

[133]

humor as Mr. Mitchell-Henry's, published in the April 18, 1931 edition of Great Britain's *The Fishing Gazette*.[26] It starts off with a summary and reply to many old accusations and ends with a satiric commentary on the capture of ZG's thousand-pounder:

Mitchell-Henry Replies to Zane Grey

Read any of Mr. Grey's books or articles on big-game fishing describing his captures, and what do you find? Cases of fish hooked by someone else, of broken rods, of rod and line being changed at the beginning or end of a fight, of two or three assistants taking turns to fight the fish, and of cases where the fish has been gaffed by more than the one person allowed under our [British Tunny] Club Rules, all of which are brazenly published amid agonizing details of the exhaustion of Mr. Grey, while everyone of these things, plus the use of engines permitted by them, tends to minimize the strain on the angler by teamwork and engine-power employed in the desire to *kill fish for records*. By way of example of the methods employed by Mr. Grey, I cannot do better than to quote from his own account of the taking of his latest so-called record 1,040 lb. swordfish—a record no club worthy the name would admit. He writes as follows: *"Suddenly I heard a sounding, vicious thump of water. Peter's feet went up in the air. His reel screeched. Quick as thought I leaned over to press my gloved hand on the whizzing spool of line, just in time to save the reel from overrunning."*

(From this it is clear that the fish took Peter's bait, and Grey saved the situation in the first rush.)[27]

"Peter fell out of the chair at the same instant I leaped up to straddle his rod." (So much for . . . Club Rule No. 1.)

"Still I kept working like a windmill in a cyclone to get up the slack. 'Water! Somebody pour water on this reel! Quick!' The white line melted, smoked, burned off the reel. I smelled the scorching. It burned through my gloves." (This will surely tickle big-game anglers.) "John was swift to plunge a bucket overboard and douse reel, rod and me with water; that too saved us. 'After him, Pete,' I called, piercingly. The engines roared, and the launch danced around in the direction of the tight line. Full speed,' I added. Then we had our race; it was far too long for me. A thousand yards from us—over a half a mile—he

---

[26]Now defunct and not to be confused with America's commercial fisheries journal of the same name.

[27]Mitchell-Henry's commentary is interspersed throughout ZG's narrative within parentheses.

came up. . . . 'Slow up,' I sang out. We were bagging the line. Then I turned on the wheel drag and began to pump and reel as never before in all my life; it took all my strength to release the drag, for when a weight is pulling hard it releases with extreme difficulty. No more risks like that." (A most dangerous fault of most reels.) " 'Too much— Peter,' I panted, 'we must get him closer! Go to it! So we ran down upon him, and I worked as before, desperately, holding on to my nerve, and when I got 500 yds. back again on the reel I was completely winded, and the hot sweat poured off my naked arms and breast." (All this from reeling in 500 yds of *slack* line!) " 'Get my shirt—harness.' Warily I let go with one hand, and then with the other, as John and Jimmy helped me on with my shirt and then with my leather harness." (Up to now we have the assistance of Peter, John and Jimmy.) "I saw the line rising. 'Keep him on the starboard quarter, Peter; run up on him. Now Bob, your chance for pictures.' " (To the above, Bob has now been added.) "I missed seeing two leaps, but the uproar from Bob and the others was enough for me." (Some noisy party!) "This was the first time my natives had been flabbergasted, they were as carried away as Bob and John. Many an anxious glance did I cast towards Cappy's boat, two or three miles distant. Why did he not come? The peril was too great for us to be alone at the mercy of that beautiful brute."

(It certainly was most inconsiderate of [Captain Laurie] Mitchell to leave his pupil alone attached to a fish "over half a mile away," with only Peter, John, Jimmy and Bob!) "They held Jimmy back, and a second later I plunged my rod over the side into the water, so suddenly that the weight of it and the reel nearly carried me overboard. 'Hold me—or it's—all day,' I panted, 'let go my line, Peter.' They had to haul me back into the boat. I shook all over as one with palsy, so violently that Peter had to get the rod in the rod socket of the chair. An instant later came the strong electric pull of the line. The revulsion of feeling was so great that it propelled me instantaneously back into my former state of hard, cold, calculating and critical judgement and iron determination." (Big-game anglers take note.)

It then started to rain and Mr. Grey called for a raincoat, and when the shower ceased he "had them remove the rubber coat, which hampered me."

Some friendly sharks then turned up to assist in killing this fish, and the rest of the account consists of a description of disturbing them at their meal by hitting them "On the nose, Bob. Split his nose, that's the weak spot on a shark." "More sharks appeared under Bob, and I was scared so stiff I could not move."

Then Mitchell turned up in his launch, and when he saw the dead fish announced his pleasure in these words: "I'm glad. Now we're sitting on the top of the world again."

The fish was then towed ashore and the weight recorded as 1,040 pounds.

"Every drop of blood had been drained from his body, and this, with at least 200 lbs. of flesh the sharks took, would have fetched his true and natural weight to 1,250 lbs."

So writes Mr. Grey, and thusly he got this moribund fish to the gaff and claims another record!

Summing up this account, what do we find?

The rod was not in Mr. Grey's hands when the fish took the bait, but was being held by one of his assistants, who didn't even strike but promptly "fell out of the chair. The bag in the line, coupled with his momentum had set it" (the hook).

Since it hooked itself, why he fell out of the chair, unless it was from fright, I cannot imagine. Anyhow, "at the same instant I leaped up to straddle his rod." From then on Mr. Grey held on to the rod, and this angler of "long years of experience, skill and endurance" nearly fell overboard from the weight of the rod and reel and had to be hauled back into the boat shaking so with palsy "that Peter had to help me get the rod in the rod socket of the chair," and nearly passed out from exhaustion from reeling in the slack line! Throughout the entire 'fight' there is no suggestion that there was at any time any strain on the line or angler, *due to the fish.*

Mr. Grey attacks our big-game rules because they allow the size of the line to be unlimited, yet in the same article gives this as his reason for resigning from the Tuna Club. . . .

"I want to say that from reading the letters and articles of the Editors of their [British] *magazines, I gather that they are all serious, conscientious and sportsmanlike gentlemen. I am positive that they have not the remotest idea that some of their rules are wrong and that their fishing is not what it should be, as far as British waters are concerned I believe they will find out eventually."*

This kindly condescension to the well-meaning but utter ignorance of the writers of "the letters and articles of these anglers and of the Editors of their magazines," and expression of hope that we will "see the light" some day, is as encouraging to us as anglers, as it must be to the Editors of our magazines referred to.

"Talk is cheap, it's deeds that count," being an Americanism, should particularly appeal to Mr. Grey.

If our would-be teachers desire to prove otherwise let them come over and do so; they will have a new experience, but as Mr. Grey states that he will never again attempt to tell others how to fish, it may

[136]

be that he recognizes the certain outcome, and that discretion is the better part. . . .

Yours truly,
L. Mitchell-Henry.

Zane Grey's stature as a big-game angler never quite recovered from such parodies. Increasingly, he fished alone. Captain Laurie Mitchell, who had been his almost constant angling companion since their first meeting in 1924, was an English remittance man who depended on Grey's largesse as well as friendship. By 1931, Mitchell's remittances were no longer coming from England, and ZG took him on as an employee, as well as companion, for $450 a month plus expenses. But in Tahiti a dispute cropped up over something Mitchell allegedly said, and ZG fired him. Captain Mitchell sued for breach of contract under a French law that gave him, as a former employee, the possibility of attaching all ZG's Tahitian possessions—which included the half-million dollar yacht *Fisherman II*. A lengthy legal battle was avoided only after ZG agreed to keep Mitchell on as an employee—but at a reduced salary. Needless to say, they never fished together again.

About this same time, Zane Grey abandoned his plans to make a fishing odyssey around the world. For one thing, the *Fisherman II*, a huge sail and motor boat manufactured by Krupp for Kaiser Wilhelm II, had proved far more expensive and far less seaworthy than ZG expected. Another and larger reason was that the Depression had finally caught up with Grey, and while still well off, ZG realized that the extreme luxury of his pre-1930 life was no longer compatible with post-1930 economics. When Grey discovered that *Fisherman II* was costing some $5,000 a month to keep, and that he still owed more than $300,000 in outfitting bills, he abandoned his plans for a worldwide fishathon. Disappointed, Grey returned to Altadena to put his finances in order.

By 1936, he was sufficiently recovered to mount an expedition to Australia. He rounded up some of the old crew members from New Zealand and Tahiti days and directed them to meet him in Sydney. The fishing was good, and Grey caught a 840-pound "white death" shark and a world-record 1,036-pound tiger shark. But somehow the fire was gone. His Australian fans lauded him, but on the homefront Grey had trouble persuading his publisher to accept a book of his latest adventures. When *An American Angler in Australia* finally appeared, it lacked the beauty and collector appeal of ZG's other angling

[137]

books. There were no line drawings; no colorful endpapers. The spartan format was partially a result of the new economics of publishing. But part of it, too, was the feeling of ZG's editor that Grey was no longer the premier personality of outdoor sport in America. The book had a mediocre sale.

Since his reception in Australia had been so much more satisfying than his homecoming in the United States, Zane Grey returned there in 1938 and, convinced that Cairns would one day produce 1,000-pound marlin greater than the one he took at Tahiti, he was planning still another trip Down Under when he died at his Altadena house on October 23, 1939.[28]

More than 30 years after his death, more than 30 years after all the jealousy and recrimination have been forgotten, we realize that Zane Grey's legacy to the sport of big-game angling was, after all, enormous. Grey traveled widely and introduced to many lands the techniques and tackle that had shaped the sport in America. But even more important, throughout most of his career, he was a popular figure with a popular following, and he made big-game angling comprehensible and exciting for millions of fans, the majority of whom would never themselves troll for marlin or lean into a leaping swordfish.

His passion for the sport found expression in books and articles that will forever carry the freshness of a new day at sea. His Western stories involved epic heroes in epic settings. Strangely, wonderfully, his books of sea fishing reflect this same monumental quality. He was our greatest storyteller at the dawn of big-game angling history.

---

[28]He had been exercising on his porch in a fighting chair with a rod and reel rigged to springs and weights the day before. He didn't row anymore, or soak his hands in salt water. But he wanted to be fit when and if the next world record's marlin struck.

NINE

THE ENTREPRENEUR

To catch a fish is not all of fishing.—Anon.

A seaplane flight to Catalina takes less than half an hour. Yet you are traveling back decades in time.

You fly from the city of Long Beach through a palpable smog in which it is difficult to distinguish below where the grimy shoreline enters the murky sea. Thirty minutes later, you coast down onto a crystalline harbor where rocks and ledges on bottom are clearly discernible dozens of feet beneath the surface.

At the Pleasure Pier you may sign up for tours that were popular in Charles Holder's day. The glass-bottom boat rides are still there, along with the seal colony cruise. Or you may merely want to wander along Avalon's waterfront, soaking up the sun and the breeze and the sensation of summers past. At one end of the harbor is a huge theater called the Casino. Built in 1928 for $2 million, it hosted Jan Garber, Benny Goodman, and other big-band musicians in the 1930's and 1940's. It now mainly hosts relics from those golden years. Some old-timers say

[139]

the place is haunted, and that on quiet summer evenings after the crowds have returned to the mainland, you can hear faint echoes of the music of long-ago drifting across the water.

Other old-time residents of Catalina recall the crack of a bat and the roar of an appreciative crowd. For after William Wrigley, Jr., purchased the island in 1919 for some $3 million, he brought his baseball team, the Chicago Cubs, there every year for their spring training.

But the Cubs, along with Garber and Goodman, are gone now. They have been replaced by reminiscence. The Wrigley family still owns 75.7 of the island's 76 square miles, and they prefer to keep things as they always were. The trouble is, nothing ever remains the same, and as the visitor wanders along Casino Way, he will pass another island institution that was once part of a larger world, but now exists more in history and legend than the present.

The Catalina Tuna Club sits out over the harbor on its pier legs; restful, dignified—and often empty. There are members today, of course, but relatively few of them come to fish the exhausted island waters. Instead, the active anglers fly to Baja California, Panama, or Venezuela for their sport, and when they do visit Catalina, the club-house is more often used as an entertainment base than a fishing head-quarters.

The club was created for tuna fishing, but the bluefin tuna are about all gone now. The great schools have been thinned by vast fleets of purse seiners, and the few small fish that still visit the waters around Catalina and Clemente islands are so boat-shy as to be, for all practical purposes, unfishable. There is no kite large enough or kite-line long enough to get baits out to tuna having recently escaped the closing circle of a giant net.

The tuna's little cousin, the albacore, is now the most popular mackerel species pursued by the active members of the Tuna Club. And while albacore are less susceptible to nets and long-lines than tuna, they have still been greatly reduced from their former abundance by the destruction of California's sardine schools and their own sus-ceptibility to live-bait fishing—a technique the Japanese pioneered with devastating effect and which still puts more albacore in cans than any other method. Today, Tuna Club members run great distances off-shore to find albacore. The boats then parallel the racing schools long enough to take a few before the anglers have to break away for the

[140]

long run back to port before nightfall. Some of the fish weigh over 30 pounds—but that is still a reduction in size from the 100-pound minimum for bluefin tuna that built the Tuna Club at the turn of the century. Yet, except for marlin and an occasional broadbill, albacore buttons are about the only ones given out these days. The giant sea bass have all been speared out of existence; the white sea bass and yellowtail have all been netted out. Even the barracuda—mostly sought as family sport or broadbill bait in Boschen's and Zane Grey's day—have nearly all gone to the crushed-ice displays of local supermarkets. Catalina has many ghosts, and among them are the shadows of countless fish that once swarmed in her pristine waters.

Philip T. Clock is a member of the Catalina Tuna Club, the Southern California Tuna Club, and several other sport fishing organizations. In addition, he is the young president of the Sevenstrand Tackle Company.[1] Phil is therefore eminently qualified to talk about present and future trends in Pacific angling.

I met him at his office in Westminster, California, but I had hardly sat down, when he urged me up and off on a tour of his plant. As we wandered through the many large rooms devoted to specialized tackle manufacturing tasks, I was impressed by the large and growing number of people in the production end of the business and the fact that so many of them are women. I found dozens of women tying leaders and wrapping line guides in Sevenstrand's plant, and was told that they are there because they have more patience and greater finesse for such work than men.

This scene contrasts markedly with the Coxe, Murphy, and Vom Hofe operations half a century ago, where 10 or 12 men turned out custom-ordered rods, reels, and leaders for a few hundred regular customers. Ironically, some of these early workmen—many of them highly skilled immigrants from Germany, Austria, and Italy—developed the machinery that took much of the perspiration out of rod-and-reel manufacture and eventually made it possible for females to take over so many jobs at the refining or finishing stages. But while German- and Italian-American manpower helped build the fishing industry years

---

[1]Phil was born October 31, 1935. His company manufactures lures, leaders, and the distinguished line of Fenwick rods. Although catering to both fresh and saltwater angling needs, Sevenstrand is exceptional among major tackle companies in having so much of its operation devoted to saltwater.

[141]

ago, it is clear that ladypower of Japanese, Mexican, and Cuban ancestry are doing much of the handicraft today.

When we got back to the main reception area, I barely had time to grab my camera and tape recorder before Phil herded me out the front door to his car.

"Let's hurry," he said, "We have a plane to catch, and we still have to pick up George Clark."

George H. Clark is one of the grand old men of angling in southern California. In 1925, after he discovered that the Catalina Tuna Club was too steep in its annual dues and too remote in its location for his modest Long Beach-based budget, he founded the Southern California Tuna Club "composed of anglers who love the open sea, the thrill of the strike and a fair fight." Although he later joined the Catalina Tuna Club when he began to earn more money, his first allegiance lay with his Long Beach associates. And down through the years he has guided the mainland club to the point that in size and vigor, if not in prestige and tradition, it all but eclipses the Catalina fraternity. I wanted to find out more about the founding and development of the Southern California Tuna Club, and Phil had kindly arranged for me to meet Clark.

We pulled up in front of his home in Seal Beach and were greeted warmly by George and his wife, Ruth. We were just beginning a tour of the house to look at some old angling mementos, when Phil glanced at his watch and began to tug both George and myself toward the door.

"Have to hurry! Got a plane to catch!"

As Phil drove, George filled me in on precisely how the club he had founded came about.

"I was raised in California and used to come down to the coast quite a lot as a young man to fish the surf for spot fin and corbina. These latter we used to get up to five and six pounds,[2] and we always had a lot of fun camping on the beach. Long about 1920 or '21, I made my first visit to Catalina. I knew some of the fellows there, and I was especially good friends with one of the members who was a college classmate from Pomona, George Pillsbury.[3] And, of course, I came over because I loved fishing.

[2]George Clark still holds the Southern California Tuna Club record for corbina, with a 5½-pounder caught in 1939.

[3]George E. Pillsbury, Jr., was an unparalleled billfisherman rated by George Farnsworth as "the best broadbill fisherman we have ever had." He won one of the first Gold Buttons when that award came into existence in 1909, and from 1913 to 1930 he concentrated entirely on billfish. Like Zane Grey's friend "Lone Angler" Wiborn, Pillsbury often made solitary trips to sea where he hooked,

"Percy West was general manager of the Catalina Club in those days, and I discussed with him my interest in joining. I was just a green-foot kid at the time, and he said, 'I don't think you'll like this club, George, it's pretty expensive.' He told me that the initiation fee was $100 and that I'd have to spend a lot of additional money on buttons, special tackle, and so on. Well, in those days, $100 looked like a horse and buggy to me, and I decided that unless a fellow's got a lot of money and a boat to get back and forth on, why he doesn't have much advantage in belonging to the Catalina Tuna Club.

"So I came back here and got together with a couple of other fellows and we talked about it. But nothing much came of our talk until 1925 when I became a tackle dealer in a sporting goods store.[4] Then I discovered there were a whole lot of other people who liked to fish and liked to discuss fishing and who would like to form a local club. A Long Beach Tuna Club had already started up and folded in the meantime, so one day I took a bunch of the guys who met in my sporting goods store down to the old pier at Long Beach and talked with the man who had started up that club.

" 'Yeah, it's a real good idea,' he told us, 'but the funny thing is you'll have it going great guns for about a year or two, and then everybody loses interest, and the organization falls by the wayside. I'll give you the medallions and some of the old literature we have here, just to show people to get them thinking about a club. They'll get all excited, of course, but it won't last.'

"And I told that fellow in front of the rest: 'Well, sir, I'm going to try to get a tuna club started, and once it's started it will last as long as I'm alive, because it will always have at least one member: me! I want to be in a fishing club that gives out buttons for real angling achievements, and I want to win one of those buttons, wear it, and be proud of it. And I know there're a lot of others who think as I do.'

"So I got a constitution drawn up with a list of angling regulations, and I posted them in my store, and I'd sign up fishermen when they came in to buy tackle. When I had 20 people signed up at $10 apiece, I figured we had a club. We made our own buttons, got our own trophies, had regular meetings, and talked about the fun we had fishing. And we sure had fun!"

---

played, and boated completely by himself a great many marlin. This feat alone should entitle him to the angler's hall of fame!

[4]Clark was in charge of the tackle department of Buffum's store in Long Beach, California.

"Your club seems to have lasted more than a year or two," I said.

"Yes, sir, it sure did. Here's our latest publication," said George, brandishing the most recent edition of the Southern California Tuna Club's Year Book.

"You were initially less expensive than the Catalina operation. What other advantages did you have that made the Southern California Tuna Club more attractive—and successful—in the long run?"

"Well, accessibility, of course. We met in Long Beach, which was a lot more convenient for most local anglers than meeting on an off-shore island. But it was how we banded together to share the few boats available to us that really brought the club together. The fellows in the Catalina Club were pretty well fixed, and nearly all of them had boats. And if you had a boat, the best fishing in the country at that time was right around Catalina. But most of us in the Southern California Tuna Club had to chip in to charter a boat, or a group of us would share expenses with someone who owned a boat—more often than not, a dinky little tub that could barely accommodate a couple of fishermen—and we'd all go over to Catalina to fish."

"How well received were you by the Catalina club members?" I asked. "Was there much rivalry?"

"Oh, no—no rivalry." said Clark. "In fact, as we grew in size, a number of their members joined our club, and vice-versa. For instance, I myself became a member of the Catalina Club in 1930, and other dual club members were Bill De Mille,[5] Jimmy Jump,[6] George Pillsbury, Tom Potter,[7] George Thomas III,[8] L. P. Streeter,[9] and many, many more. In fact, it got to the point where some of our members felt there shouldn't be any Southern California Tuna Club—that we should merge with the Catalina Club. But I wasn't about to let that happen. Although we shared a lot of the same rules, our pins and trophies were different, and I didn't want to abandon the pride that had been built into winning one of the Southern Cal awards. For another thing, our organization was open to any angler who lived in

---

[5]William C. De Mille holds both the 3/6 albacore and the light-tackle dolphin records for the Southern California Tuna Club. His brother, movie mogul Cecil B. De Mille, is remembered by anglers for the De Mille Medal, presented to the Catalina Tuna Club member who catches the largest black sea bass of the season.

[6]J. W. Jump holds the marlin and broadbill light tackle records for the Southern California Tuna Club; [7]Thomas McD. Potter, the heavy-tackle black sea bass record; [8]George C. Thomas III, the light-tackle yellowtail record; and [9]Lafayette P. Streeter, the light-tackle albacore record.

[144]

Southern California, and he didn't have to have a whole lot of money to be a member. He just had to like fishing!"

"I'm surprised your two clubs are so compatible. There's pretty fierce competition today among some of the clubs in Florida."

"Well," said Phil Clock with a smile, "you know Californians are more civilized than Floridians! But the real difference is our over-lapping membership and the fact that we don't have the variety and numbers of fish here anymore that we once had—certainly not like what south Florida has. There's just not that much to be competitive about! And while I regret the loss of our fishing, frankly, I think there's too much competition associated with fishing as it is. I prefer days offshore when you're not worried about accumulating points for yourself or your team and are simply fishing."

We turned onto a side road leading to the airfield, and for the first time, I appreciated why Phil had been so anxious about getting to the airport on time. Our plane was a Grumman Goose with barely room for the three of us, my equipment, and another passenger. And when we left, there were three hopefuls waiting at the ticket counter for the next flight to be rolled out.

As we lifted over the ocean, George sat and stared silently out of his porthole window at the sea below. Then he turned to me and spoke above the roar of the engines: "Sometimes you can see whales and even fish from up here. In fact, that's how the commercial broadbill fishermen are locating their catches these days. They used to go out in boats and just cruise around until they found a fish, and they were lucky to harpoon a fish a day. Now, using spotter planes, some of these guys are taking 20 and 30 swordfish in a single day! It's phenomenal— and devastating."

"Have you ever caught a broadbill?"

"No, never have."

"How about marlin?"

"Oh, Lord, yes."

"What was your most memorable day on marlin?" I asked.

"Oh, that might be hard to say." George Clark thought a moment. "Well, there was the afternoon George Pillsbury called me from San Diego and asked me to join him. Since I didn't have a heavy-tackle marlin—one over 200 pounds—he thought this might be my big chance. Marlin were being spotted everywhere, and one of the other club members had landed a 240-pound fish that afternoon. So I packed in a hurry and joined George in San Diego. We tried to get flying fish for bait but couldn't locate them anywhere. We finally had to settle for a bucket of sardines. They weren't especially big sardines, but they were nice and fresh—caught just the day before.

"Next morning we ran out of San Diego Harbor, and we weren't 10 miles off Point Loma, when the entire ocean started showing marlin. I'll never see anything like that again if I live another lifetime! The ocean was full of marlin, full of seals, and full of bait! The marlin were balling the bait, circling the schools and keeping them bunched up. Then every so often, the marlin would go rushing in and slashing up the bait. The seals would go right in with them, and they never bothered one another. They all just milled around, picking up the dead and dying fish, and then they'd ball up the survivors and start all over again.

"And fish were jumping everywhere! I tried to count the number of marlin I could see in the air at any one time, but it was impossible. I started counting in one quarter of the compass: one, two, three, like that—and before I'd made a 360° turn, I had counted over 100 marlin out of the water. I never saw anything like it!

"All we had to do was jab our hook through the nose of a dead sardine and let it run out behind the boat. The bait wouldn't get 30 feet before we had a marlin gobble it up—the action was that fast! I caught two and George Pillsbury caught two, and since we were keeping the fish for record, we soon had four marlin piled into the back of George's little double-ender with barely room for ourselves. We couldn't even fish, much less bring any more into the boat! So we just cruised around and watched marlin jumping and feeding, and when we ran in, that's all you could see behind the boat, was the ocean with fish jumping everywhere!

"Pillsbury got a button for one of his marlin on 3/6 tackle, but neither of my marlin was quite large enough to qualify under heavy-tackle rules. But that didn't seem to matter. I guess it was the greatest fishing experience I ever had."

George Clark had one other anecdote to share with us before landing, and this concerned the great angling writer Van Campen Heilner:

"Heilner had won a Gold Button from the Catalina Tuna Club back in 1921, and he was always proud of it. But about 1933 or 1934 when he was out here for the club's annual banquet, he suddenly discovered that he had lost his Gold Button. Well, he was desperate.

[146]

He called the club and found that there were none in stock, and there didn't seem to be any place he could borrow one. Gold buttons aren't all that common, you know. Yet Heilner couldn't imagine showing up for the biggest angling shindig of the year without his Gold Button!

"Well, I heard he had lost his button and was looking high and low for one, and I had one to give him. I was never entitled to wear a Gold Button, but one of the early club members had passed away not long before and left me his. It was something I held on to in the hopes that someday I'd be entitled to it. But when I heard Heilner needed one and was looking everywhere, I gave him the one I'd been saving. I just told him that someday if I caught a winning fish, I'd get another. Well, he was as pleased as could be and said that 'my' button would doubtless bring him even greater luck. Well, it did. But the luck that went with that button sure left me, for to this day, I've never caught a Gold Button fish!"

The seaplane water-skied to a stop past Cabrillo Peninsula, turned about, and taxied into the Pleasure Pier to let us out. Phil confirmed our flight in three hours time, and we strolled along the waterfront on Crescent Avenue on our way to the Tuna Club. It was December and the island was peaceful, without the tourist crowds you find there even on weekdays in the summertime.

Ray Caswell, Percy West's successor as general manager, met us at the front door of the club. Then for an hour he acted as our guide, leading us from room to room, where every photograph, every artifact, was haloed by angling history. The Catalina Tuna Club is the world's finest big-game fishing museum. Here are collected the souvenirs of half a century of ocean angling from mounted specimens of some of the first saltwater gamefish ever caught on rod and reel down to the memory of Winston Churchill's visit following World War II. Churchill flew in on a plane, immediately went fishing with Ben R. Meyer aboard Monty Foster's *Sunbeam II*, caught a marlin, and returned to the dock —all within 90 minutes time! He drank a scotch and soda at the Bait Box (the club bar) and flew out that same afternoon. *Veni, vidi, vici.* Some club members who worked considerably harder for their first marlin still can't believe it!

After the tour, George, Phil, Ray, and I adjourned to the Bait Box where we sat and talked of by-gone days. I had discovered that George Clark has been particularly close to Harlan Watkins Major, one of saltwater angling's first historians and a superb tackle technician, whose *Salt Water Fishing Tackle* (first printed in 1939) quickly went through

[147]

several editions and is now a collector's item of angling literature. Yet I was surprised to learn from Clark that this famous fisherman was a relative latecomer to saltwater sport:

"The first time I met Harlan Major was when I was a youngster up at Bakersfield working on a ranch. He was working in the sales department of the Ford Company in town,[10] and after I found he was interested in hunting, I invited him out to the ranch on weekends, and we'd chase coyotes around the countryside in one of the cars he got from the company. But then he lost his job."

"For using the company's cars to chase coyotes?"

"No, not that. One day he found that his head man up at Kernville —married fellow—was fooling around with another woman. Well, Harlan was an honest man and genuinely shocked by that kind of thing, and he came back and told his supervisors about it. But the upshot was that his supervisor fired Harlan!

"Major was from the East originally,[11] and here he was, a relative stranger in California, with no money and no way to make any. I went into town one day to get a wagon wheel fixed. While I was waiting, I visited the Old Southern Bar, where I found Harlan sitting at the counter, crying in his beer. After I heard his story, I said, 'Well, if you haven't got anything better to do, pack up your grip and come out to the ranch until you find some work.' So he did, and he stayed with us until we both joined the Army and went off to Mexico. He went into the infantry and I joined the cavalry.[12] When we came back

---

[10]Harlan Major was an acquaintance of Edsel Ford (1893–1943) who helped him get his first job after finishing high school. Harlan showed himself to be clever as well as industrious, and he was soon sent to Nashville, Tennessee, to see if he could improve car sales in that part of the country. In a single year, Harlan more than doubled sales through a stunt that received national publicity and became so popular that postcards and posters were made up to commemorate the event. On August 5, 1911, and with a huge crowd looking on and with considerable money riding in wagers, Harlan Major drove a Model T Ford up the steps of the Capitol, through the Capitol building, and down the back steps on the other side. (The night before this event, while a friend entertained the building's custodian, Harlan made a "test climb" with his car first to be sure it could be done!) For years, Ford distributors throughout the south remembered "Harlan Major Day" in Tennessee.

[11]"Born in Detroit and raised everywhere" was how Harlan Major described himself on the dust jacket of one of his books.

[12]The Mexican Revolution broke out in October 1910, spread widely, and with considerable confusion as to whom was running what, where, and with what authority and for what cause. Early in 1916, bandit or revolutionary hero (depending on your point of view) Francisco "Pancho" Villa executed 15 U. S. citizens

from that adventure, Harlan went off somewhere and started up his own business. I can't recall what it was, but he was doing right well until he went in over his head and lost it all. We had been keeping in casual touch, and he knew I was living in Long Beach at the time. So he called me one day and asked if I'd pick him up in Downey. When I got there, and without saying a word, he tossed his suitcase into the back seat of my car, and we returned to Long Beach.

"He slept on my davenport until I managed to get him a job in the oil fields. But that didn't last long. Harlan was assigned to building derricks, and one of the first days on the job, he was working on the ground floor when some fellow, working on top, dropped a hatchet. Well, the thing fell and passed right in front of Harlan's nose and split the plank between his feet. Harlan looked up. He looked back down. Then he got his coat and walked off the job. He came back to me and announced he was all through building derricks.

"About that time we were organizing the Southern California Tuna Club. We had offices in a little building in Long Beach, and the building had a spare room where Harlan could stay. And that's when Harlan first became interested in saltwater fishing and began to make lures and leaders and things."[13]

---

living in Mexico and then crossed the border into New Mexico, attacking the frontier town of Columbia and killing 17 more.

The U. S. government responded by sending General John Pershing on a punitive expedition that lasted until January 1917. But Pershing's army never did catch up with Villa. George Clark and Harlan Major were members of this American force. When the United States entered World War I in April of that year, Major reenlisted in Sacramento, California, and joined the Rainbow Division. He was first made an engineer, but when he found that title was merely an euphemism for road building, he protested and ultimately became a sergeant in the tank corps. Driving French Renault versions of these newfangled war machines, Harlan Major was once reported "missing in action" (he spent the night in a haystack behind German lines) and another time was wounded by the strafing of a German aircraft while shaving near his vehicle. Fortunately, the many notebooks he always kept in different pockets to take down his observations on everything from wild flowers to captured German weapons absorbed much of the impact and shrapnel, and Harlan Major was out of the hospital not long after Armistice in November 1918.

[13]In 1952, Harlan Major published *Fishing Behind the Eight Ball,* in which he lists those fishermen to whom he owed a special debt of thanks for having encouraged and guided him during his saltwater angling apprenticeship. First and foremost was Thomas McD. Potter (to whom he dedicated *Salt Water Fishing Tackle*), followed by such names as L. P. Streeter ("one of the original nine-thread fishermen"), Colonel Grant E. Dolge ("who showed us the circling method of lifting several hundred pounds of dead [giant sea] bass with a line testing only

"Was Major always a skilled craftsman," I interrupted, "or was this something he developed after he began to fish?"

"No, Harlan always had a talent for working with wood and metal, and he made beautifully balanced rods and lures right from the beginning. He supplied our club members with everything they needed, and then he sold the surplus on the outside. He moved up to Seventh Street where he opened a shop with his own lathes and in no time at all was running the biggest tackle business in Southern California. Everything Harlan ever touched succeeded wonderfully. But it always built up and up until suddenly—*Blewy*—he'd be broke again. And that's what happened to his tackle business. He was the West Coast representative for a number of East Coast firms that made rods, reels, and linen line. And, of course, he was making barrels of his own lures, as well as specialty items like kites and fighting chairs. But then he suffered a severe appendicitis and had to go into the hospital and wasn't able to keep up with all his investments. He had bought a lot of land on speculation, and what with the hospital bills and his being away from the tackle shop, it set up a chain reaction of misfortune. One investment after another foreclosed. When he finally got out of the hospital, he tried to put the pieces back together again, but finally cashed in the remaining chips and went to New York in May of 1929."

From then on, Harlan Major's saltwater angling career can be pieced together from newspaper articles and commentary in his various books. His connections with the Catalina and Southern California tuna clubs were sufficient calling cards to provide introductions to some of the most prominent members—both anglers and guides—of the East Coast fraternity of fishermen. He popularized kite fishing in the Atlantic, and he caught one of the first sailfish in Florida ever taken on 3/6 tackle. Charter skipper Tommy Gifford (who "had faith in what I was trying to do") was his guide.

New York became the base of operations for Harlan Major's rejuvenated tackle business. Like any convert to a new sport, Major was a zealot. He conceived the notion of doing something for the ordinary sea fisherman of New York City. He knew and loved Montauk Point

---

26 pounds"), Jimmy Jump, Harry Adams, George Thomas III ("who headed the younger group"), and George Clark.

Of Clark, Major wrote: "I had ranched with him, wore an Army uniform with him without ever winning an argument, and when he switched to fishing he continued to argue louder and faster. The odd part of it was that a lot of it made sense. He argued twenty-eight lone fishermen into forming the Southern California Tuna Club and it has expanded and gone places ever since" (page 15).

[150]

on the tip of Long Island, and he recognized it as one of the great fishing spots of the Atlantic seaboard. Of course, other men before him had recognized Montauk's greatness, and in 1927 Oliver Cromwell Grinnell made it famous among big-game anglers by catching the first broadbill swordfish ever caught on rod and reel in Atlantic waters. Within two years, Grinnell had taken four more swordfish, and Otto Scheer, William Bonnell, and Charles L. Lehmann had added their own broadbill catches to Montauk's fame. Soon the Atlantic coast's best and most ambitious guides—men like Wally Baker, Owen Duffy, Bill Fagen, Tommy Gifford, Herman Gray, Bill Hatch, Howard Lance, John Sweeting, and Charlie Thompson—were mooring their boats at the Montauk Yacht Club and running their charters to the wonderful fishing grounds available close offshore. In those days, Montauk was a quiet little fishing village, and all this sudden summer activity bewildered some of the locals. But the Yacht Club, at any rate, was thrilled by a precipitous rise in applicants for membership!

Montauk was remote from the city and, generally speaking, only the wealthy could afford the time and money to get there. As Major once described it: "Montauk was the playground of Rolls Royce riders." But in 1933, Major determined to change that. He saw saltwater angling as the sport of Everyman—not just the rich—and he figured that Montauk's abundance could cater to all tastes from rowboat fishermen seeking tautog and flounders, to headboat anglers after cod and pollock, to surf fishermen casting for stripers and blues, to big-game anglers after broadbill and marlin. Montauk had something for everybody. It was just a question of making it economical for the average angler to come from the city to fish, and of persuading the party-boat men that it would be worth their while to dock there.

Needless to say, Major's desire to democratize Long Island's finest fishing grounds was not welcome in all quarters. Carl Fisher, the man who built the Indianapolis Speedway and who had helped develop Miami, Florida, owned much of Montauk at the time, and when Major went to him to see about renting one of Fisher's docks in Fort Pond (now Montauk Harbor), Fisher called him "the damndest lunatic I ever listened to!" and kicked him out.

However, with the help of George Le Boutillier, vice-president of the Pennsylvania and Long Island railroads, Harlan Major persuaded the other railway executives that a special fishermen's train running nonstop on weekends from Manhattan's Pennsylvania Station to Montauk Point could and would make money. The railroad went to Fisher,

[151]

leased his dock, and that first season ran four such excursion trains the 234-mile round trip to Fort Pond.

Once the anglers got there, they found conditions rather primitive. Many of the boats were nothing more sporty than crusty old beam trawlers, and the nearest toilet was half a mile from the dock. But the fishing was outstanding, and the anglers came back for more. Perhaps, most important, the railroad made money on the deal and was now convinced that fishermen were worth catering to.

However, resistance to Major's plan was still not over. Old-time Long Island residents did not like an outsider coming in and bringing a lot of city strangers and new ideas. The local charter fishermen (recently recruited from the ranks of commercial handliners and draggers) were particularly stubborn about changing their ways to suit a sporting clientele. They met every one of Major's arguments with the frustrating logic that since his ancestors were not Eastern Long Islanders he could not possibly know anything about fishing! Major finally recruited some reformed rum runners—men the Long Islanders could respect—and had them work out the details of the more sophisticated fishery the area needed if it was going to survive a full season of "Fishermen's Specials."

The next summer of 1934, the Long Island Railroad carried 35,610 anglers round trip to Montauk for just $1.50 per person. One way, the journey took only two hours—the trains take longer today!—and thousands of other fishermen rode out in old jalopies and trucks or hitchhiked. The railroad built its own docks near the rail terminal, and they soon accommodated some 62 party boats. A special police force was assigned to keep order among the anglers as they raced from the train to their favorite fishing positions on the boats, but after the police were twice trammeled in the rush, the railway withdrew the cops and let each angler fend for himself. Wonderfully, there was not a single accident or mishap that first season, and for more than 20 years the Fisherman's Special was one of the most successful runs on the Long Island Railroad.

Even Carl Fisher admitted the scheme had merit. One Sunday morning while Major was down at the docks watching a 17-coach train disgorge its mob of eager anglers, Carl Fisher's limousine pulled alongside him, and the old man leaned out to apologize: "Major," he said, "you're *not* a damned lunatic."

There were still other diplomatic achievements for this entrepreneur of saltwater angling. In 1935, Harlan Major became the first American outdoor correspondent to go to Chile to investigate the reports of giant swordfish being caught by two men working for British mining operations there. In 1934, George Garey, a Vermonter and the resident engineer for the Anglo-Chilean Champion Nitrate Company, became the first man in history to catch two broadbill swordfish in a single day—twins nearly 490 pounds apiece. That same year, Englishman W. E. S. Tuker, who ran the railroad for the same company, broke the previous broadbill swordfish world record[14] with an 837½-pounder caught off Tocopilla.

In addition to the tackle business, Harlan Major wrote fishing columns for a string of newspapers and contributed free-lance articles to a variety of outdoor magazines. He went to the Grace Line, which sailed ships from New York and Boston through the Caribbean and on down the Pacific coast of South America after crossing through the Panama Canal, and persuaded the company to underwrite an angling expedition, which he assured them would result in a great deal of publicity for angling in South America via the Grace Line. Using many of the same arguments he had employed successfully with Pennsylvania Railroad executives the year before, Major pointed out that a big-game fishery in Peru and Chile could lead to the creation of a long-distance commuter service from New York and Boston for wealthy American anglers similar, but on a grander scale, to the one he had established with the railroad on Long Island. The Grace Line, Major observed, could make far more money hauling fishermen than guano!

Company executives agreed to give him a chance, and Harlan Major did his best. Despite poor weather and several fish losses, Major landed a 410-pound broadbill (which the natives called "Chiquita" because it seemed so small), and a 674-pounder, which would have beaten White-Wickham's record two years earlier.

In addition, Major filled newspaper columns with information about Chilean saltwater angling—such items as the observation that South American swordfish preferred cold water to temperate; that they fed on nothing but huge squid; that all big broadbill are females; and, of course, that the only way to get there is aboard a luxurious Grace Line freighter.

Despite all these efforts, the anticipated commuter service from New

---

[14]H. White-Wickham held it with a 673-pound broadbill taken in New Zealand the year after Zane Grey caught the first swordfish there in 1926. One of the reasons ZG went back to New Zealand was to see whether he could best White-Wickham's record, but he never caught another broadbill there.

York to Tocopilla never materialized due to the approach of World War II. However, Major's efforts did pioneer the way for the Kip Farringtons, Mike Lerners, and Lou Marrons who followed. There's a very definite chain of events from Tuker's and Garey's earliest efforts, through Major's expedition and resulting publicity, to the Lerner and Farrington visits which resulted in a refinement of local skills and know-how, finally to the year 1953, when Lou Marron caught a 1,182-pound broadbill off Iquique, Chile. That world-record swordfish still stands, and it will likely remain so long as commercial long-line interests dominate billfishing on the high seas. But Marron's record just did not happen. His 1,000-plus-pound fish was the fulfillment of a personal dream. It was also the fulfillment of two decades of experimentation and perseverance by many great anglers in Chilean waters. The development of any sport fishery is always a cumulative effort.

After his success with the Pennsylvania Railroad and the Grace Line, the next corporation angling-writer Harlan Major approached was Pan American Airways. Pan Am had recently inaugurated "clipper ship" service across the Pacific, stopping at such unknown islands as Midway, Wake, and Guam. Primarily military outposts, these fueling stops for the big Pan Am clippers were at best endured by most travelers flying from Hawaii to Hong Kong. Harlan Major suggested that if a big-game sport fishery could be developed in the islands, many affluent anglers would make Midway, not Manila, their destination.

At first the airline executives were skeptical. But Major unrolled Pacific charts showing where marlin had been seen around the islands. He insisted that marlin could always be caught where they had been seen—that is, if presented with the right combination of bait and tackle. The company finally agreed to his trip, but Major was told he better catch a marlin! He shrugged and assured them that the fish was practically in the boat and already on its way to the dock for weighing in.

Much to his relief—mixed with some envy—as Major was preparing to take off for Guam from Honolulu on April 10, 1937, he learned that a Lieutenant (j.g.) Henry Wygant had just taken a 100-pound marlin off Guam while trolling a Japanese feather lure. Annoyed that he would not be the first man to land a marlin at Guam, Harlan Major was nonetheless relieved that his claim for billfish in the islands had now been established as fact. At least Wygant's catch had taken some of the pressure off his own visit.

However, when Major landed at Sumay (Apra Harbor), he quickly learned that the natives regarded Wygant's catch as a freak, and that, as the local Pan American official put it, Major still had ample opportunity to prove his theory that there were marlin (that is, more than one) in Guam waters.

So Harlan Major fished. And he fished. And he caught yellowfin tuna and dolphin, wahoo and great numbers of barracuda. But he never saw hide nor scale of a marlin. He was having trouble getting fresh bait suitable to marlin fishing (bonito, mullet, or small barracuda), and the weather with high winds was no help. In addition, the surface sea temperature was considerably higher than Major had anticipated (86° F.), and this especially caused him anxiety. Finally, there were the peculiarities of the local fish themselves. One afternoon after a fishless day offshore, Major returned to port and discovered that the crew of a Navy tug anchored in the harbor had caught a 91-pound yellowfin tuna on a hook baited with a fried egg, with the hook and line merely left dangling over the side as a joke!

That evening our "professional fisherman" and all his special paraphernalia came in for considerable ribbing from the local Navy establishment. At the high point of his persecution, Harlan Major was reminded of his predicted marlin amidst many smiles and much laughter. Perhaps in desperation—or perhaps, after a month of study, he felt he knew what he was talking about—Harlan Major made a dramatic Babe Ruth pointing-over-the-outfield-wall type statement: "Gentlemen, you do have marlin in these waters, and they are right here on the west coast, just about on the edge of the rough water that sweeps down from Point Ritidian."

The gauntlet was down.

Next morning while Major and his crew were running to Point Ritidian, they had their first marlin follow a bait. In the excitement, an inexperienced helmsman abandoned the wheel and the boat turned: The kite supporting the bait fluttered to the surface. The bait sank lifelessly in front of the marlin's snout, and the fish fled.

Major decided that he better employ outrigger devices like those Tommy Gifford was making popular in Florida if he was going to have any success using unskilled assistants. Such permanent outriggers would not only make it easier for amateurs to troll a billfish bait, they would make a fishing boat more readily maneuverable in the choppy seas where Major knew the marlin were. An outrigger-equipped boat could turn and turn again over rough-water edges with relative facility, while a kite-equipped boat had to exercise care to keep the

[155]

kite from falling. Furthermore, since he was developing Guam's sport fishery for the tourists to come, Major decided that two skipping baits trolled at the same time would be more attractive to the charter business than a single kite bait.

Next afternoon, after a morning's work to jury rig a pair of outriggers made of local bamboo, Harlan Major took his boat offshore to Ritidian Point and caught the second marlin ever landed in Guam waters—this one caught on a small barracuda bait especially rigged for the job. Major dismissed the importance of his catch by referring to the fish as "orthodox" in its strike and fight. But that evening at the Officers Club, he was bursting with pride. When people asked him why he had taken so long to raise a marlin, he politely but smilingly explained that since he was a guest of Pan American Airways and the United States Navy, he had wanted them to show all they knew about the local fishery before he decided to show them what he knew. The first 3½ weeks of his stay had been merely a "get acquainted" period.

"But why haven't the natives ever seen marlin out here before?" people asked.

"Because the fish are all in the rough water between Haputo and Ritidian points, and the natives don't take their small boats and canoes out there. It's elementary," he concluded and went to bed.

(On August 21, 1969, Greg D. Perez caught the world-record Pacific blue marlin off Ritidian Point, Guam. The fish was 14 feet, 8 inches long, and weighed 1,153 pounds. Had Harlan Major still been alive to hear of this catch, he probably would have nodded knowingly, smiled, and said, "Elementary.")

Perhaps his own military experience, and certainly his contact with the Navy in the Pacific, made Harlan Major sensitive to the off-duty needs of servicemen when World War II broke out. He was not concerned about G.I.'s in rear areas or those on the homefront; he knew from experience they could fend for themselves. But he was distressed to think of soldiers sitting on a recently captured island surrounded by fabulous fishing opportunities without even a handline in sight.

Using every contact he had and exploiting every conceivable avenue of publicity, Harlan Major organized a vast campaign to ship fishing tackle to troops overseas. Setting up a clearing house in New York City and enlisting the aid of innumerable volunteers, Major's workers sifted through miles of discarded line and countless boxes of old hooks and discarded lures to make up more than 200,000 usable angling kits. When an appeal for lead sinkers went out, the Typographers Associa-

[156]

tion of New York offered their burned type metal and brought over 500 pounds of lead for starters. *Field & Stream, Outdoor Life, Sports Afield,* and *Outdoors* all ran feature articles on Major's operation and needs, and these were followed by other stories in the *New Yorker, Mechanix Illustrated, Yachting, Motor Boating, American,* and *Colliers.* National newspaper syndicates were equally helpful. Finally, Armond Van Pelt, New York manager of the *Sporting Goods Dealer,* sent out appeals to all tackle manufacturers for unfinished or rejected equipment. Soon half-ton lots of fishing supplies were arriving daily at Major's home and office. With such skilled assistants as tournament caster Fred Evers and guide "Sharky" Bill Young, and with the co-operation of the United Service Organizations, Major was soon providing servicemen in every part of the world with lures made from the head of one manufacturer hinged to the body of another and fitted with hooks from two other sources.

And such contrivances caught fish! One of the most marvelous fishing stories to come out of the war originated in Australia where a G.I., dissatisfied with handline casting from the beach, swam out to a tiny rock islet sticking above the water a few hundred yards offshore. On one of his first casts he hooked a mako shark! After a considerable struggle, during which the soldier was dragged more than once from his precarious perch, the shark was subdued and the G.I. swam back to the beach with his 200-pound prize under one arm. He was greeted by a cheering section from his unit, and they promptly set to work butchering the fish for the next morning's breakfast. "Delicious" was the one-word conclusion to the soldier's letter home.

A marine who was in the thick of fighting in the South Pacific was so touched by a gift of tackle that in a letter home he dedicated "the next Jap" to Harlan Major.

A submarine sailor asked for tackle, and he had such fun with it in his off-duty hours that his buddies soon wanted tackle, too. Word spread through the squadron, and in no time at all, Harlan Major and his volunteers were dealing with Vice Admiral Charles P. Lockwood, who wanted tackle distributed to every sailor in his command: Submarine Force Pacific.

There will never be a way to measure the value of the contributions of "Harlan Major and His Fishermen" (as one U.S. Navy citation referred to them), but Major always regarded this "military duty" as his finest hour. He was once asked what his greatest satisfaction was in the program, and he replied: "That we helped a few servicemen understand the true meaning of R & R [Rest and Recreation], and that in the process, we created a few more anglers."

A pleasant irony of Harlan Major's life is that while he did all he could to promote *sport* fishing *during* a war, soon *after* the war he taught a group of people all about *survival* angling.

A Norwegian explorer named Thor Heyerdahl believed that the islands of Polynesia had been peopled by a western migration from South America, not by an eastern migration from Asia as other anthropologists had theorized. To prove his point, Heyerdahl was going to Peru to build a balsa raft some 15 by 30 feet and then drift across the Pacific until, he hoped, he landed on one of the islands of Polynesia. He planned to take a small crew with him to share the adventure, and he needed food for the indefinite time they would be at sea.

Heyerdahl believed that the early raftsmen had caught fish to sustain them on their journey centuries ago, and he planned to do the same. The trouble was that there was no tackle available in recently occupied Norway, and Heyerdahl, through the auspices of the Norwegian Embassy in Washington, D. C., turned to the United States for both the equipment and some basic instruction in how to use it. Although Heyerdahl was the son of a seafaring nation, he did not know much about fishing.

Captain B. A. Rorholt, Norwegian Naval Attaché in Washington, called upon Halvor Mustad of the famous Norwegian fish hook manufacturing family, who happened to be in New York City at the time, and asked his advice. Mustad was aware of Major's activities on behalf of sport fishing during the war and, more important, he knew of his reputation as a Pacific angling expert. Without hesitation, Mustad asked Major for help.

Writing in 1950, Harlan Major summed up his contribution this way: "It was a tough assignment but I checked [the raft's expected] course, made a lot of guesses about what methods and equipment would keep their belts tight, and then rigged the tackle for them."[15]

There was a great deal of responsibility involved, for the prestige of nations as well as the lives of men were at stake. When the first radio message was transmitted round the world that Heyerdahl's raft, the *Kon Tiki*, had safely grounded on Raroia atoll in the Tuamotu group of French Polynesian islands, Captain Rorholt called Harlan Major to tell him the good news.

---

[15]*Norwegian Holiday*, Harlan Major, New York, 1950, page vii.

When their excitement settled down, the captain asked Major if he and his wife, Claire, had ever been to Norway. No, they replied. "Why not?" asked the captain, and before Major could think of a good answer, he and his wife found themselves planning a trip.

The Majors made two visits to Norway, and each one resulted in a history and general information guide to that Scandinavian land. And naturally Harlan Major spent part of each trip learning about local fisheries.

Mrs. Major observed recently that her husband's chief interests in fishing were usually peripheral ones by most anglers' standards. And so it was in Norway. Major never actually fished Norwegian waters. But he filled his notebooks with observations on their laws separating commercial and sportfishing interests; diagrams of how Atlantic salmon maneuver around and over the various traps placed in their way; lists of offshore banks and ledges where giant tuna were found[16]; and drawings of unfamiliar tackle and other European equipment new to him. He found that Norway was full of sport fishing potential—but he felt that at age 60 he was just a little old to once again assume the role of pioneer.

Harlan Major died on September 15, 1968, shortly after his 79th birthday. Although he came to saltwater angling relatively late in life, he accomplished more on behalf of the sport in the 25 years he was actively associated with it than entire centuries of ordinary fishermen. Being a latecomer to saltwater angling enabled him to be more open-minded about the things he saw and heard about. He was a technician but with the spirit of an Agassiz. Instead of doing things the way they had always been done, he experimented with new ideas and techniques, and he proved that any fisherman's "luck" can be improved with study and a compilation of such data as water temperature changes and the stomach contents of the fish he catches.

He was one of the great carriers of West Coast ideas to the East, and we can only guess at California's influence in general, and Harlan Major's in particular, on the ultimate design of such standard saltwater equipment as the fighting chair, rod gimbals and rod holders, the shoulder harness, the flying gaff, outriggers and gin poles.

His angling articles were rarely egocentric accounts of his own piscatorial conquests on the high seas. Rather, they are informative re-

---

[16]Major predicted that Norway would one day be a world center for giant tuna angling. "The fish are there now," he wrote, "waiting to break some tackle for the big-game fisherman." *Ibid.*, page 137.

ports on his or other people's latest angling experiments. Long before the term "territorial imperative" became popular among naturalists, Harlan Major described how certain species of fish will aggressively attack not just a bait but darn near anything unusual that is introduced to their particular area of the reef or kelp bed.[17] Knowledge of such behavior and the ability to exploit it, he suggested, puts more fish in the fish box.

He studied the color of lures and how colors change as lures are worked at different depths. He was intrigued by the success of flashing spoons or "dodgers" used in front of baits in the Pacific Northwest, and he tried to interest fishermen along the Atlantic coast in trying such devices.

Finally, Harlan Major was the kind of man who always met the challenges of pessimism and doubt. Perhaps, like an explorer of another age, he was merely innocent of the hazards ahead. Whatever the origin, his faith enabled him to pick up the pieces of at least three different starts in life and ultimately go on to make one of the largest and most meaningful contributions to the history of saltwater angling.

---

[17]In an article entitled "The Human Side of the Fish" for the May 1934 issue of *Motor Boating* magazine.

Although Henry Eliot Howard's *Territory in Bird Life* was published in 1920, the concept of the territorial needs of wildlife has only become popular in the past two decades. Certainly Major's article is one of its first descriptions in fishes.

TEN

TODAY AND TOMORROW IN
SOUTHERN CALIFORNIA

> The great American nation ... very seldom at-
> tempts to put back anything that it has taken
> from Nature's shelves. It grabs all it can and
> moves on. But the moving on is nearly finished
> and the grabbing must stop.—Rudyard Kipling,
> writing in 1889

The sun had sunk behind the Catalina hills, casting the bay before us
in shadow. The mast of a boat far out on a mooring still reflected the
afternoon light, but all the rest of the harbor was in deep shade. With
the sun gone, the December air became chilly on the porch of the Tuna
Club where Phil Clock and I were listening to George Clark and Ray
Caswell reminisce. Their conversation flowed pleasantly from anecdotes
concerning a Catalina visit by angling writer Kip Farrington to the
time charter man Tommy Gifford came to the island. Ray Caswell
was speaking:

"Maury Webster invited him out for a couple of weeks to fish especially with Ellis Arkush.[1] Someone had told Tommy that the fish

---

[1]Ellis J. Arkush, one-time president of the Tuna Club and holder of four
buttons, was characterized by George Farnsworth as "a marvelous angler but just
a shade overanxious on the strike." One year Arkush won the Swaffield "Hard
Luck" Trophy given to that angler who fishes the "greatest number of hours during
season with the least result." Arkush went an incredible 66 successive days without
even a strike to be overanxious about!

out here were tame, and that there was nothing to finding and hooking them. Besides that, Pacific marlin wouldn't give you much of a fight. Tommy figured his job was going to be a snap—a boatman's holiday.

"Well, he found out different. He was real eager to get Ellis a fish, but nothing he tried seemed to work. Tommy even went up to the golf course and brought back the hollow metal shaft of a broken club to take out the backbone of his mackerel baits with so they'd swim more naturally through the water.

"Finally, on the last day Gifford was here, he got Ellis a marlin. And after Tommy's many experiments, the fish was still hooked on a conventionally rigged flying-fish bait. That evening Tommy came in here and admitted to the rest of us: 'You know, these Catalina marlin are pretty good gamefish after all!' "

"Did Tommy try tuna fishing while he was out here?" I asked.

"Oh, no," Ray replied. "We hardly saw a tuna between 1948 and 1970, and then the last large fish we caught were all yellowfin. The big bluefin have just never come back."

Clark: George Thomas, Charlie Jones, and Jonah Jones went up off Santa Barbara Island back in 1937 to catch the last big bluefin.[2]
Caswell: George Thomas all his life had been trying for the Diamond Button.[3] While his father was alive, he always lost out to his dad by a few pounds. So one year after George's father passed away, he took one of the members from Wisconsin out fishing. You know, one of those members who comes in maybe once or twice a year to whom the resident regulars want to show a good time.

Anyway, they went offshore together and George caught a 100-pounder and was so pleased with it. He figured he had at last broken his Diamond Button jinx. But within minutes this Wisconsin fellow hooked a 125-pound fish that beat George out of the button again that year![4]

---

[2]In correspondence with George C. Thomas III, dated July 17, 1972, Thomas writes: "The big tuna left Catalina waters until 1936. . . . That summer Farnsworth and I found fish at Santa Barbara Island. We caught 19, the largest going 96 pounds. . . . In 1937, Farnsworth landed in the hospital with a burst appendix, and I did not fish much. That was the year that Charlie Jones got his 140½-pounder, and Jonah Jones (not related) his Blue Button."

[3]The Diamond Button was established by Ray R. Thomas for the largest tuna of the season—100 pounds or over. The award is a Tuna Club Blue Button set with diamonds, which passes from the former winner to each new winner. Naturally the scarcity of big tuna in Catalina waters makes this pin both highly prized and likely to remain for many years in the possession of its most recent recipient.

[4]"[The big bluefin tuna] left [Catalina] until 1948, when Captain Leslie Thuet

GWR: Has the club ever considered pushing the territorial limit on tuna south to Baja California where there's a better chance of catching hundred-weight fish?

Clock: It already has been expanded. My brother, Ralph, and I made three trips down to Guadalupe Island in 1967 and had fabulous fishing. The last trip we caught over 100 yellowfin tuna weighing from 50 pounds on up. The biggest weighed 113 pounds three days after capture on the scales in San Diego. We released most of the fish, keeping only those we knew wouldn't live and a bunch more caught in the last few hours of fishing that wouldn't spoil on the run back to the States. We also tagged 17 of the released fish. We ran out of tags or we would have done more. Incredibly, 5 of those 17 tags were recovered within nine months by American purse seinermen working further south— which gives you some idea of the commercial pressure on this species. Anyway, we had such spectacular luck that after we reported the trip, the club here had a vote and decided to maintain the 32nd parallel as our southernmost limit for all fish *but* tuna, and for them it's now 28°30′.

GWR: How far south does that carry you?

Caswell: Just south of Guadalupe Island—250 miles due south of San Diego.

GWR: Any desire to go further south? To Cabo San Lucas, for instance?

Clock: Some talk, but not much chance. A few members resist on the basis of their boat's inability to run any further. Others say we're invalidating all the earlier members' records by reaching so far afield. And there are a few who don't like the fact that we're catching 'California records' in Mexican waters.

GWR: What are the northern and westernmost limits for the Catalina Club?

Caswell: Point Conception in the north. No limit offshore.

GWR: Why not offshore?

Caswell: In the old days, if you had a boat that could run as far as Clemente, you were doing pretty good. There just didn't seem to be any point in an offshore limit.

Clark: I redid the boundaries for the Southern Cal Tuna Club a few years ago, and our members accepted them as the 31st parallel on the south, Point Conception on the north, 50 miles west of Point Concep-

---

and I found some 100-pounders off Catalina's East End from his boat *Angler II*. I got two, the largest being 102 lbs., and then turned the rod over to my good friend, J. Howard Hales of Park Falls, Wisconsin, who got the 125-pounder. He was an associate member of the club, and that was his 'button fish,' as well as the Diamond Button. Ah, me!" From correspondence with George C. Thomas III, July 17, 1972.

tion, and then due south to the 31st parallel for the western border. So Southern Cal does have an offshore limit.

GWR: How far beyond Catalina is 50 miles west of Point Conception? Ten, twenty miles?

Clock: Oh, no. A hundred anyway.

GWR: Is this sufficient to fish albacore?

Clock: So far it is. But every season you find fishermen running further and further offshore. Pretty soon we'll have to open the rules to include Oregon! That's where the action is today.

GWR: Are there any release or fish-tagging programs sponsored by the clubs out here? Phil, you mentioned releasing tuna at Guadalupe. Was that in conjunction with a club program?

Clock: No. But within the last several years, both clubs have begun encouraging the release of fish. We give out release pins and certificates and encourage you to fly a release flag when you put a fish back.

GWR: Isn't that rather late by most sportfishing club standards? I recall receiving my first release button from the Stuart [Florida] Sailfish Club back in 1947, and it was old-hat then.

Clock: Well, the Catalina Tuna Club is not exactly a revolutionary organization, you know. It took a lifetime to come around to recognizing dacron line.

GWR: Are there release buttons for all major gamefish: tuna, marlin, and so on?

Caswell: Yes.

GWR: Broadbill?

Caswell: Oh, no, I don't know of anyone who releases broadbill. [George Clark and Ray laugh at the suggestion.]

Clock: But that does raise an interesting question: How do we find out the movements of swordfish unless we set up some kind of tagging program for them? Thus far, all we know about broadbill is what we can deduce from a few adults caught here, and some young caught there. Here's one of the world's great gamefishes being attacked wholesale with long-line and harpoon, and we're still in the dark about much of its natural history.

The other men's laughter followed by Phil's commentary indicated something of a generation gap, even among anglers. Ray and George, who were both angling before Phil and I were born, look back upon all the excitement that broadbill swordfishing has provided the club in years past. Phil, on the other hand, expresses concern for the future of this great gamefish. He, and many other young anglers, are asking: Are we not dealing with life in the seas in the same take-now, learn-later way that characterized our destruction of terrestrial game a cen-

[164]

tury ago? For some older anglers, this kind of question appears naïve. Yet for all young anglers, it must be answered if we are to have salt-water game fishing 5, 10, and 20 years hence.

That evening after returning from Catalina, Phil invited me to his home for dinner. After a fine meal prepared by his wife, Gayle, and while she was putting their three children to bed, Phil and I had a chance to talk at greater length about fishing in the Pacific.

Clock: I'm glad you had a chance to meet George Clark and compare the club he founded with the one at Catalina. Both clubs are proud of their histories, and as George pointed out, many of their old-timers are interchangeable. But there's a difference between the two organizations, and that difference lies in the fact that Southern Cal is a far more active club. Its tournaments and father-son trips to Mexico, trap shoots, boys-and-girls fishing rodeos, regular weekly luncheons, trips to Lake Mead, and ladies' cocktail parties are, for the most part, not duplicated by the Catalina Club. Most important of all, Southern Cal has had the foresight to bring in younger members to help run the club. Catalina has resisted this kind of thing, and there they sit with a beautiful view of Avalon harbor, talking about the old days, and doing very little with their organization. The Catalina Club is fading because they don't have anything that holds them together—except memories. And memories don't have much appeal to young people who are still building dreams of their own.

GWR: Does the limit to the Catalina Club's membership make a difference? Catalina is a lot smaller than Southern Cal, isn't it?

Clock: Catalina is limited to 200 members and Southern Cal is 300. But size is not the determining factor. The Balboa Angling Club is another active organization out here with a huge membership and small dues. But they're a vigorous club not because they're big or inexpensive. Balboa is alive because they have members who are willing to work hard on behalf of the organization. It's their state of mind that counts—not the number of bodies in the club, or the total dues taken in.

GWR: When did you first become a member of the Catalina Club?

Clock: When I was 21. That's when you're allowed to join. My father has been a member since 1951, and as youngsters, my brother Ralph[5] and I used to use the club when we stayed over there.

---

[5]Phil is the oldest of three sons. The other two are Ralph, president of Clock Construction Company, and Edwin. The Clock family originally came to California from Iowa in 1910 when grandfather Clock established a law practice in Los Angeles County. Phil's father, Henry H. Clock, is also a lawyer, and his youngest son, Edwin, is keeping the family tradition alive as a student at Stanford Law School.

[165]

GWR: Did you actually stay in the club?

Clock: Oh, no. Kids are permitted to go up the outside fire escape to the second floor to take showers. But that's all. Oh, we were also allowed on the front porch. But no one under 21 was allowed on the first floor inside.

GWR: How about women?

Clock: A few members' wives protested some years ago and now they have a 'separate but equal' area with showers, TV, and phone. But they still can't be members.

GWR: If the rules of the Catalina Tuna Club don't exactly encourage young people and women to fish, how did you get your first sea fishing experience?

Clock: George Clark was my earliest mentor. He frequently took groups of us kids down to the beach to fish.

GWR: Pier or surf fishing?

Clock: Surf, mostly. We'd catch corbina, spotfin, yellowfin, and the like. Occasionally we'd get sharks or something else that would run out all our line and break off. But, generally speaking, there's not much variety and very little size in our surf fishing. Not like the Atlantic anyway. And, of course, like much else in the way of California recreation, even the surf fishing isn't what it used to be.

GWR: At one time during our trip today you spoke of yellowtail and barracuda being about all fished out along the South California coast. This may be an exceptional experience, but the last time I fished the kelp beds off Mission Bay and La Jolla back in 1965 we had wonderful luck and could have loaded the boat with both 'cuda and yellowtail, if we'd wanted to.

Clock: Yes, they continue to show up at certain points along the coast, and the newspapers frequently report good fishing for them. But let me give you a better example of what's happening to southern California saltwater angling. Sevenstrand sells a blue nine-inch leader that's used almost exclusively in barracuda fishing. We used to sell a million and a quarter of these leaders a year. We're now down to less than 200,000. That kind of statistic tells me far better than any local Chamber of Commerce announcement that barracuda fishing just isn't what it used to be.

GWR: What's the future going to be then for the average angler who can't get down to Mexico and Panama?

Clock: Unless California makes a real effort to clean up coastal pollution, and unless it puts real limitations on commercial fishing, the average ocean angler will be restricted to bottom fish: rock cod and inshore halibut. Yet these species are important commercial fish, and with the increased sportfishing pressure, one day they may also be in trouble.

And this is something that really burns me up! The State of California has a sportfishing limit of three halibut a day. Yet you'll be quietly fishing in some cove working on your second or third fish when in comes a commercial dragger that swings back and forth around you and pulls up hundreds of pounds of halibut to sack and sell. When the trawler is through, you'll be lucky to find another fish in that cove! It seems increasingly that sport fishermen merely subsidize commercial fishing. You'll hear people say that commercial fishermen only *harvest* our fisheries surpluses. What surplus?! By whose standards?! And as for the word *harvest*, a man harvests what he sows. And commercial fishermen have neither the means nor much interest in putting back seed stock for next year's "harvest."

GWR: Are there any indications that if the State of California puts teeth into protective legislation, the fishing out here will make a comeback?

Clock: Certainly. The kelp or calico bass is an example. It's a great little gamefish, protected with stiff fines for anyone taking more than the daily limit, or anyone keeping a fish under eight inches. Dock attendants and boat operators have been particularly good about enforcing these regulations. As a result, the calico bass has made a wonderful comeback in the last few years. And, of course, another big reason for its return is that calico bass have been classified as a sportfish and cannot be taken or *sold* commercially.

GWR: Could such restrictions bring back the tuna?

Clock: The quota system has already improved our tuna sport fishery. The first year in my memory when we had a decent yellowfin run was 1967—the year following the institution of a quota system by the Eastern Pacific Yellowfin Tuna Association, an international organization. But you'll still never see tuna, or albacore either, running up the channel between here and Catalina until we do something about our coastal pollution. Few tuna come up this way anymore, although good numbers of them are caught 10 to 30 miles south of the Coronado Islands. And few albacore on their northern migrations are found any further east than the channel between San Clemente and Catalina. Mostly they run below what we call the "213," which is a high spot on the ocean floor some 80 miles south of San Diego; then they're found outside the "60," another high spot west of San Diego. The albacore stay outside these two points, swing further outside the Cortez[6] as they come north, and then only move back inshore as they approach Morro Bay north of Point Conception. In the old days, they'd come right up through the Channel Islands. Now there's something chem-

[6]A reef 105 nautical miles west of Long Beach, California.

ically different about the water that's keeping them farther offshore.

GWR: Any research being done to find out what's happening?

Clock: None that I know of. Money for fisheries research is like research money anywhere: It's spent to serve industry. And the canners are the major corporations of the fishing world. Most contemporary tuna and albacore studies I've seen are concerned with discovering ways to put more fish in the freezer, not with ways to bring tuna and albacore populations up to former levels.

GWR: Hasn't the disappearance of forage fish around the Channel Islands had something to do with the disappearance of larger gamefish?

Clock: Absolutely. The sardines and the California mackerel are nearly gone. Just the anchovies are left. The marlin are still around because they've managed to make the switch to anchovies as a major part of their diet. Here again, we can determine a trend in California angling by tackle sales. We used to sell a lot of marlin lures to local anglers, but this market has declined as the local fish have lost interest in larger baits. It's very frustrating to see marlin around the boat and not be able to tempt them with anything you have aboard—unless you just happen to have a supply of lively anchovies.

GWR: Are broadbill swordfish migratory and feeding patterns changing, too?

Clock: Swordfish get so much of their food down deep, they haven't been affected by the disappearance of the mackerel and sardines. However, foreign fleets are dragging the bottom for hake and other bottom fish on both coasts right up to our 12-mile fisheries limit, and I believe this reduction in forage fish will eventually have a drastic effect on the abundance of broadbill. I don't think rod-and-reel fishing has made terrific inroads. George Clark wasn't exaggerating about the effectiveness of this new spotter-plane system the commercial swordfish men are using out here. It's not unusual for these fellows to bring in 1,000 fish a season, and we have hundreds of other boat owners with dollar signs in their eyes who now want to cash in on this kind of thing. That's why the Southern Cal Tuna Club has written regulations to eliminate members who are inclined to do a little free-lance (pardon my pun) commercial swordfishing.[7] We thought for awhile that we'd be safe out here in California from commercial swordfish overkill.

---

[7]Under a section entitled "Boat Regulations," the Southern California Tuna Club specifies:

1) Fish taken on a boat equipped with a pulpit shall be disqualified [some exceptions noted].

2) Fish taken by a SCTC member upon a boat which, on the day of the catch, is equipped with equipment for harpooning shall be disqualified.

3) Any member equipping his own boat with equipment for harpooning shall be considered a commercial fisherman.

[168]

Long-lining—which makes such terrible inroads on your billfish populations in the Atlantic—doesn't work out here because of our vast and aggressive shark populations. Various agencies—including, of all people, the California Fish and Game Department—have experimented with long-lining from time to time, but it never works. There were always too many sharks to eat the bait before the broadbill got to it. But now along comes this spotter plane operation, brought in from the East Coast, and it's really made a dent in the number of swordfish you're likely to see during a summer's fishing.

GWR: With so many sharks here, is there any sport fishery for them comparable to the one that's been developed at Montauk, New York, for instance?

Clock: Currently there's no interest. Every so often a thresher shark is caught—a friend of mine took a 325-pounder not many years back—and that kind of gee-whiz catch makes the local papers. But it doesn't start a fishery. Long Beach decided to have an International Sea Festival sometime ago, and the city solicited prizes. I offered a $1,000 cash prize for the largest shark caught on hook and line during the festival —handline even—just so long as it wasn't harpooned. I was curious to see what the biggest one would be, and, of course, there'd be a demand for durable leaders, which wouldn't hurt the local sales of Sevenstrand wire. But the city turned my offer down, saying it preferred the area remain known as a bathing and sailing resort, and not become a shark fishing mecca. And that about sums up local feeling. There are so many swimmers, surfers, and sailors, they'd just as soon not think about sharks.

GWR: Your company manufactures Konahead and Knucklehead lures. Did these originally come from Hawaii?

Clock: Yes. And there's an amusing anecdote associated with the first one I ever saw long before I got into the tackle business. My father, Ralph, and I were over at Catalina on the *Tick Tock* [the family boat] in 1954 when we heard that Dr. Mulford Smith—one of the club members—had a new "secret" lure especially flown over from Hawaii. Of course, we joked a lot about this extravagance until Smith began to catch more fish than the rest of us. We asked Smith a few pointed questions about the lure, but he was always pretty evasive. Naturally, this made us doubly curious! Then one afternoon he brought in an especially nice marlin while the rest of us went fishless, and Ralph and I determined to see what one of these mystery lures looked like. Mulford's boat was moored about 60 feet from ours, and after he had gone ashore that evening, Ralph and I swam over and sneaked aboard. We took a long look at one of the lures and were on the verge of producing our own imitation model when they became commercially available.

[169]

The manufacturing operation was eventually moved to California, and after I got into the tackle business, we bought all the trademarks and patents.

GWR: What other contribution has Hawaii made to Southern California angling?

Clock: Well, mostly there's been a kind of exchange program between California and Hawaii over the past two decades. For instance, Hawaiians used to fish, by and large, with heavy lures for billfish and tuna. Now they're going more and more to live or fresh-dead baits. This is the West Coast influence. At the same time in California, we're finding better ways to attract these fish with artificial lures—a concept introduced from Hawaii. Aboard the *Tick Tock*, we now troll lures for marlin and carry live bait for when we spot a fish finning out. Twenty years ago, we just trolled dead baits all the time. We simply didn't believe artificial lures could take the big billfish.

GWR: Do you think the live-bait techniques Californians have developed for marlin fishing can be used back East?

Clock: Definitely. But to date—with the exception of south Florida—there just doesn't seem to be much interest. I know a fellow in Maryland, for example, who has a 42-foot Hatteras with a lovely live-bait well aboard which I tried to get him to use when I was last back there. But he said no, that space was for storing his mops and buckets! That kind of inertia seems to be commonplace along the Atlantic seaboard. Frankly, I don't feel you fellows have been as adventurous over the years as we have in trying new ideas. And the pity is, I think you've shortchanged yourselves in the long run. There's a special thrill to live-bait fishing for marlin—hunting them and then hooking them from a near-stationary boat—that you don't get merely cruising around offshore, hour after hour, dragging a pair of soggy mullets.

GWR: How do you locate the marlin?

Clock: The usual ways: watch for birds, water color changes, know particular banks. Many times we simply run out looking for marlin without putting a line over before we see one.

GWR: Have you ever tried chumming for them?

Clock: Yes, but that's not been very successful. The best method seems to be first to find a fish, then cruise slowly up to it and either let out a live bait in your boat's wake and swing it in front of the fish, or get as close as you can to the marlin and toss a live one in front of him. You don't often frighten the fish, and it's exciting to watch them chase and gobble the bait. However, if they're still reluctant to bite, there's an interesting trick George Clark taught me back in 1958 off San Diego when there were still sardines available. At that time the procedure was to troll a pair of dead flying fish and keep your live

[170]

sardines handy until you spotted a marlin. Well, that afternoon a *bunch* of marlin came up and started following along in our wake. But they wouldn't take either the flying fish on the outriggers or the live sardines we put out on flat lines. We even tossed out live sardines without a hook in them, but the marlin still ignored them. We were all pretty stoked by the sight of so many beautiful fish practically within reach—and *frustrated* by our inability to get them to bite. Finally, George came up with a trick that dated back to his experience with live-bait fishermen 40 years ago: He popped an eye out of each of a number of sardines he threw over, causing the fish to swim around on the surface with one side of their heads out of water. Well, this "crippled" behavior caused an instant sensation with our marlin friends. Their stripes practically pulsed with color! They gobbled up those injured sardines as fast as they went over, and we had no trouble after that in getting hook-ups when we threw in baits with hooks in them.

GWR: Great. Any more stories with tips like that?

Clock: Well, in 1957, my brother Ralph and I car-topped an 11-foot boat with a 7½-horsepower outboard down to Mexico to use for our marlin fishing. We caught fish every day of the week we were there, but on the next-to-last day, we hooked a fish that we stayed with almost nine hours. In a very small boat, it's easy to stay on top of a big fish, so we never had more than 50 yards of line out, and the fish was always down—25 or 30 feet below the surface—swimming along and towing us.

GWR: What size fish was this?

Clock: Maybe 180 pounds. Anyway, that night he finally broke off, and we found ourselves some 40 miles up and off the coast from our camp. The engine wasn't running very well, and it was at least a five-hour trip back to the beach. Ralph and I had a long time to think and talk about what had happened that day, and we decided that we had stayed too close to the fish. Ever since then, we've fought all our fish as hard as we can, never easing up on them for an instant. If a fish merely wants to stay with us rather than fight, we make him fight. We'll run line out and then work it back in, all the time making the fish fight the line or the rod, or both. When we have the line in, and the fish still isn't whipped, we sit tight and let him pull the line from the reel and start all over again. This works well with tuna, too, because they generally run from the boat when you run toward them. Since this accomplishes the same goal as moving away from the marlin—namely, making the fish work and tire—it's just as effective.

Since that day in Mexico I've always made the fish fight the equipment, and I've never had any trouble with marlin up to 180 pounds on 20-pound line. And now, over the years, we've developed a fairly

[171]

reliable standard predicting that any angler who plays a big gamefish more than two hours probably won't land that fish. And if he plays it more than four hours, there's a 99 percent chance that he won't catch it. The lighter the tackle, the more true this becomes. A 150-pound fish—even on 12-pound line—shouldn't take more than three hours to land. If it lasts longer than that, either the equipment or the angler will fail before the fish fails.

GWR: Do you have any other suggestions on how to make a fight faster, more certain?

Clock: Just that a fish which has stars in its eyes should be gaffed as quickly as possible.

GWR: "Stars in its eyes"—what's that?

Clock: When a billfish comes up and shakes its head sluggishly back and forth just above the surface, we call that having stars in its eyes. It means the fish is gut-hooked and there'll be a period of five minutes or so when it's in shock and doesn't know what to do. We work that fish in as rapidly as possible and throw a gaff into him. Tournament anglers love such catches; to me, they're a wasted gamefish and a statistical evil.

GWR: After all our talk about buttons this afternoon, I meant to ask you, how many do you have?

Clock: I've got an albacore button from the Southern Cal Tuna Club and a marlin button from the Avalon Club. But I'm not a button fisherman. I don't fish for trophies. I've caught fish that could have earned additional buttons, but I didn't even bother to turn in the weight slips on them. I know some old-timers who may accuse me of breaking down the traditions by being so indifferent to awards. But that's not what saltwater angling is all about. At least, that's not the kind of tradition I'm interested in.

GWR: With the sardines gone and the live-bait situation generally deteriorated in Southern California, what will anglers do in coming years for their live-bait supplies?

Clock: The same thing they had to do before there was a live-bait industry: catch their own.

GWR: You mean small bottom fish? Are they that useful in marlin fishing?

Clock: They're all right when you can get them. But more popular and far more easily caught are California and Pacific jack mackerel. The former is quite similar in coloring and appearance to your tinker mackerel along the Atlantic coast. Both are good marlin baits, and the Pacific jack mackerel can frequently be caught in good numbers under floating kelp islands. Unfortunately, they're becoming increasingly attractive to the cat- and dog-food canners!

[172]

GWR: How do you catch them?

Clock: We use something called a Lucky Joe rig. It's a polished sinker with a small treblehook dangling below and four to six hooks tied above baited with nothing but a little bit of yarn. When you're lucky (hence the name), you drop the lure in the shade beneath the kelp and bring up five or six mackerel at a time.

GWR: How deep do you go?

Clock: Anywhere from the surface down to 100 feet. When you get one mackerel on, he starts dancing around, and that attracts the others. The only problem is that every so often, all the commotion attracts a cruising yellowtail that grabs one of your mackerel. Since your line is only 8- or 10-pound test, you generally lose the entire rig.

GWR: Marlin fishing is still a relatively expensive sport. And you indicated that bottom fishing is dying. What then is the future for saltwater angling in Southern California?

Clock: Fishing Baja. And I don't mean anything as exclusive as the fly-in, luxury hotels found around the Cape. Already we have half a dozen 85-foot fishing boats and a new 95- and a 105-foot boat that are making 3- to 14-day runs down along the Baja coast. Some of these boats cruise at 18½ knots fully loaded; and they carry 6,000 gallons of fuel, have two five-ton freezers for your fish, and have all interiors fully air-conditioned. The bigger boats even have some two dozen staterooms for couples. They cost roughly $50 a day, although excursions are pro-rated so that your expenses diminish the longer you're aboard.

This type of fishing is becoming very, very popular, and we're already gearing production of local tackle to suit the specialized uses of this market. Furthermore, I don't think the new Baja highway will be able to compete successfully with these boats. Development will still be slow down there because the Mexican Government doesn't want to see Baja ruined like California and Florida. So for many years to come, these new combination partyboat/fishing camps will be the best answer for any American angler who doesn't want to go through all the red tape and inconvenience of packing his own boat south.

GWR: Talking again of tackle production, tell me something about Sevenstrand's testing program. Do you use outdoor writers for this?

Clock: Tackle testing, as most people use the term, is a farce. The vast majority of outdoor writers who say they'd like to test your tackle are merely looking for handouts. It's laughable how few of them know anything at all about how to assess a new rod or reel once they have one. Probably the best 'tackle testing' we have going for Fenwick is done by some of our south Florida friends. And it consists of nothing more than putting our rods on their roofs. The sun and salt air in south Florida are worse than anywhere else in the country, and we've been able to make some tremendous improvements in our finishes just on the basis of these roof-top tests.

GWR: What about color evaluations for lures? Don't you depend on qualified field testers for these?

Clock: A conscientious report is always useful. But the most reliable test of the effectiveness of a color in a given area are sales figures. In the last analysis, the most dependable tackle tester you have working for you is the customer who actually shells out his money for a lure to catch fish. As a result, we know that on the Pacific coast, the colors green, yellow, and pastels are most successful in our knucklehead line— because they're the most popular—while hard colors, even purple and black, are more popular along the Atlantic coast. In the Gulf, they use a lot of red, black and white, and blue and white combinations. Of course, we do our own lure testing from time to time, and this is usually handled in a far more conscientious way than the average angler could manage or want to do. We'll run six lines with identical-model lures an equal distance from the boat—the only difference being their colors. Interestingly enough, we find some days, one color or color combination gets all the action, while the next day, in the same area, another color or combination is the right ticket for the same species of fish. There's just no way to predict results. Color differentiation and preference among different game-fishes are things we know next to nothing about.

It was getting late, but there was one last question I wanted to ask.

"Phil, you've sampled some of the best varieties of saltwater angling anywhere in the world. What's your favorite?"

"Well, I *don't* enjoy poor fishing. I'm far too restless for that. Each fishless day spent rolling around offshore verges on despair for me! And local fishing has become so poor in recent years that the only way for a California angler to maintain his optimism and interest in the sport is to save up his money for a week or 10-day trip to Mexico. Yet I suppose there is something of a paradox in my feelings, because one of my favorite pastimes involves the two-hour run to Catalina with my family and then the next day or two spent camping and fishing around the rocks for what the kids call 'funny fish.' I'd far rather be with my kids catching little kelp bass and hearing their squeals of excitement than be offshore hooked to a big marlin. I guess we go through something of a cycle in this regard: My father tells me he had the same feeling when we were kids."

As I drove back along the freeway to my hotel, I thought of the

[174]

generations of fishermen and how their interests peak and pulse, starting in one's own childhood and then linked to the childhood of one's children. And I recalled another interview made earlier that year with John P. Holman, one-time managing editor of *Forest and Stream*. John had many memories of our traditional frontier country, dating from early in this century. He remembered Anchorage, Alaska, when it was little more than a tent city, and he recalled British Columbia as the last great coastal wilderness of North America. But when it came to his memories of Southern California, it was then that I realized with a shock how little time it's taken to convert a continental wilderness to an endless plateau of shopping centers and freeways.

He referred to Los Angeles as a splendid town, quaint and rural, so perfectly adapted to its landscape: "The impression was one of great open spaces and wonderfully clean air—the kind of air that makes mountains 100 miles away seem like little hills close at hand. When you came across country, the sea eventually became your real destination no matter what other business had ostensibly brought you there. You arrived at the train station, and there were Indian porters to take your luggage and put it into the coach for the ride into town."

"Excuse me, John," I interrupted. "When was the last time you were in L A?"

"About 1910—I'm told it's changed a little since then. But I remember Los Angeles as a lovely town, with the most marvelous hunting and fishing right in your own backyard."

Now multiple lanes of traffic sped by me, racing over a landscape of garish light and unnatural shapes. Somewhere off to my left in the obliterated darkness lay the unseen Pacific, forgotten by all but a handful of men whose fathers came here because the sea was their real destination no matter what other business had brought them here.

Casting from the Rocks at Montauk

Section Three

INSHORE

ELEVEN

THE BEACHCOMBER

Oh, the weakfish am good
And the kingfish am great,
The striped bass am very, very fine;
But give me, oh, give me,
Oh, how I wish you would!
A channel bass a-hangin' on my line!
—Refrain from a song of the beaches sung by
fishermen at the turn of the century

Just as canine shows attract a host of fanciers who would be appalled to see a bulldog used in the context for which the breed was first developed, so surf casting attracts many admirers who would be amazed to see their heroes ever actually catch a fish.

The sport of competitive casting with surf rods and reels became popular in the years immediately preceding World War I. Suddenly a great number of people discovered that a revolving spool reel on a rod could be used to throw a sinker with more accuracy a longer distance than if it were twirled out with a handline or with the additional leverage provided by a cane pole with an eye at the top through which a fixed amount of line was cast.[1] Naturally, as soon as this lesson was

---

[1]The English writer "Wildfowler" described this method of casting from the beaches in 1879 in his collected *Shooting Adventures, Canine Lore, and Sea-Fishing Trips.*

learned, some anglers were compelled to see if they could outcast their neighbors. In 1914, J. E. Clayton set a mid-Atlantic record with a cast of 348 feet. By the early 1920's, some competition casters were regularly reaching out 450 feet.

Tackle manufacturers enjoyed this competition because, in the process, they learned much about the tolerances of their products, and they were thus able to make a great many improvements in rods and reels in a relatively brief span of angling history. Then, too, the publicity surrounding casting tournaments broadened popular interest in surf fishing and helped build a number of manufacturers from backyard tool shops to specialized plants and assembly lines devoted to the single task of turning out rods and reels.

Newspapers along the Jersey and Long Island shores featured articles on tournament casting to such a degree that reports on surf *fishing* were sometimes lost amid the banner headlines describing a new *casting* record. Naturally, there eventually appeared casters who had less interest in firing a lure *off* the beach than in sending a hookless version of it a specified number of feet *down* the beach. Vom Hofe, Meisselbach, and Ernest Holzman made reels especially for tournament casting; Leonard, Segar of Asbury Park and Corman of Ocean City, New Jersey, did the same for rods. And Ashaway introduced a special linen "Surfman Line" just before World War I that quickly became *de rigueur* for the tournament casting set.

The 1920's saw a flowering of tournament interest when the general public discovered the sport and came to view it with the same peculiar passion reserved for flag-pole sitting and dance marathons. In this decade, Vom Hofe, Bronson,[2] Pflueger, and Ocean City all appeared with special star-drag, surf-casting models. But the greatest success story of this period between the wars was the advent of Penn reels in Philadelphia, Pennsylvania. Combining ambition and the faith that he could build a better mouse trap, a young man by the name of Otto Henze left Ocean City after a brief apprenticeship to found Penn Tackle in 1932. His "Surf Master" series was an almost instant success, and the "Squidder" model, first introduced in 1936, is still the classic reel of the surf fisherman. His Senator series and, more recently, the International line, were all developed after Penn had made its reputation in surf casting.

---

[2]After the Bronson Reel Company absorbed J. A. Coxe, it for years produced a "Genuine Bronson-Coxe" reel for surf and bay fishermen. In June 1967, Bronson was in turn absorbed by the True Temper Corporation.

Another Philadelphia product to begin developing a reputation in this inter-war period and who ultimately became a significant influence on the development of saltwater angling was a gentleman by the name of Van Campen Heilner.

Some readers may think it frivolous to review the accomplishments of this giant of saltwater angling in a brief chapter devoted exclusively to shore fishing. But I believe Heilner would have approved the choice. Surf fishing was his first love, and he carried a torch for it long after he became famous as an all-oceans angler.

George C. Thomas III recalls that Heilner was with him in 1938 when he caught his first Atlantic bluefin tuna—a 715-pounder. Thomas tried to persuade Van to take his rod and catch one of the big bluefin himself. But Heilner refused.

"Perhaps it was simply courtesy," Thomas writes, "but I had the feeling that he did not want big tuna. He preferred smaller fishes: sailfish, bonefish—and particularly surf casting."[3]

Of all the species of littoral fishes, Heilner's special favorite was the channel bass. In 1934, when Eugene V. Connett asked Heilner to contribute a chapter on the bonefish for the Derrydale Press edition of *American Big Game Fishing*, Heilner agreed—but only if he could also write a chapter on the "bulldog of the sea":

Perhaps because this fish was associated with my early youth, or perhaps because he was the first large fish I ever caught, a 41-pounder by the way, the place he occupies in my heart is a near and dear one.

Memories of autumn days with the snipe trading down the beaches and the first flock of wild geese etched high against the sunset above the golden marshes, sea grass on the dunes bending against the kiss of the first northwester, spring days with the miles of rolling breakers creaming in across the bar and the nesting terns and laughing gulls setting up their ceaseless clamor in behind the thoroughfare—these all mean but one thing to me, that lovable old coppery warrior of the tides, *Sciaenops ocellatus*,[4] the channel bass.

Nowhere in angling literature is there a finer expression of the pleasures of surf fishing than in the writings of Van Campen Heilner. He fished the Atlantic, Gulf, and Pacific coasts of North America, and he fished throughout the Caribbean and South America. He was the

---

[3]From correspondence dated September 1, 1972.
[4]Some authorities use *ocellata* instead of *ocellatus*.

[180]

first American angler to own a home on Bimini, and he was a member and regular visitor to the Catalina Tuna Club. He caught and wrote about every gamefish from the summer flounder to the broadbill swordfish. Yet the greatest sport he experienced in the sea was surf fishing, and these are his reasons why:

Surf fishing is to saltwater angling what trout fishing is to fresh water. It is a one-man game from start to finish. You are the one and only factor. Here you are and there he is. If he runs out all the line, you can't pick up the oars or start the engine and follow him. No cushion or comfortable seat or chair supports your fundament, no thwarts against which to brace your feet, no companion to assist you or guide you. You must find your quarry yourself; you must rig and bait your hook yourself; you must become proficient in the art of casting so you may reach him; and you must bring him through a line of foaming breakers and singing tides until at last, whipped to a standstill, he lies gasping on the wet sands at your very feet. Then you must let him go because he deserves it.

Van Campen Heilner was born on July 1, 1899—heir to a Pennsylvania mining fortune. His youth was affected by the knowledge that he would never have to grub out a livelihood like most other mortals, and he drifted from school to school, trying to assign a goal to a life that was both prepaid and guaranteed.

Like many wealthy children of the Philadelphia Main Line, he spent his summers at the Jersey shore. In Heilner's youth, Atlantic City had already become a kind of oceanside suburb for well-heeled Philadelphians. But it was not the boardwalk, swimming, horse racing, or gambling opportunities that drew Heilner back to the coast season after season. Rather, it was the memory of the abundance and variety of sea fishes that fell so readily to his surf rod which remained with him during the winter months while he was away at school. In the last analysis, it was not the instructors at Phillips Academy or Lake Placid-Florida school who provided Heilner with his direction in life; it was the surf gang down at Corson's Inlet, New Jersey,[5]: Gus Wittkamp,

---

[5]In a 64-page booklet entitled *Fishing Around New York*, published in New York in 1909, the authors, J. W. Muller and Arthur Knowlson, recommend two places to go "trolling for very large [striped] bass: the mouth of the Susquehanna River, Maryland, and Corson's Inlet, New Jersey." However, "Corson's Inlet is much more reliable than the Susquehanna."

[181]

Link Roden, Jack Whatton, George Geiss,[6] Hartie I. Phillips,[7] Phil Mayer, Church Hungerford, Gus Meisselbach, George Mallory, and many, many more.

Heilner was something of a prodigy in outdoor writing. He began contributing surf fishing stories and articles to *American Angler, Field & Stream, Motor Boat, National Sportsman,* and *Sports Afield* before he was out of his teens, and by age 21, he had created a first book, *The Call of the Surf*—incidentally, the first book ever published devoted exclusively to surf fishing—with the help of his artist-friend and fellow angler, Frank Stick.

Stick came to New York from the Midwest shortly after the turn of the century to make his reputation as an artist. He had always loved the outdoors and had worked briefly as a guide before coming East. Since the community of outdoor writers and artists was a small one 70 years ago, Stick and Heilner quickly became acquainted, and Heilner showed the boy from Wisconsin what surf casting was all about. Stick became a frequent guest aboard young Heilner's cabin cruiser, the *Nepenthe*,[8] as it cruised up and down the Atlantic coast.[9] The artist quickly became as adept with a surf rod as he was with his brush, and it was a most natural outcome of these wanderings that the two young fishermen, Heilner and Stick, collaborated on *The Call of the Surf*, a 12-chapter volume of which Heilner wrote six chapters and Stick the other six, as well as contributing six paintings to illustrate it.

Two years later Heilner did another book called *Adventures in Angling*, using three of Frank Stick's paintings. But otherwise this book is all Heilner's, derived in large part from a variety of his articles contributed to *Field & Stream, Motor Boat, National Geographic, Recreation,* and *Wide World.*

This second book of saltwater angling takes the reader from the coast of Monterey for Pacific salmon, to Catalina for striped marlin,

---

[6]Van Campen Heilner once called this man "the greatest channel bass guide that ever lived.... If you cast where he told you to, you never missed." Heilner ascribed Geiss's greatness in part to the fact that he could *smell* the channel bass beneath the waves.

[7]Heilner and Frank Stick dedicated *The Call of the Surf* to this "pioneer in the sport of surf angling."

[8]Nepenthe was a drug used by the ancient Egyptians to help them forget their cares and misfortunes. Heilner thought it an appropriate name for a boat devoted to exploratory saltwater angling.

[9]It was partially through Heilner's good graces that Frank Stick made his first visit to the Long Key Fishing Camp in 1922—a visit immortalized in Zane Grey's "The Bonefish Brigade" (see *Zane Grey: Outdoorsman,* Englewood Cliffs, N.J., 1972).

to the Florida Everglades for tarpon, then finally to Bimini for sail-fishing. But the most stirring of all chapters is "The Sea Horse," describing a trip to a beautiful and uninhabited barrier island just south of Barnegat Bay. On this expedition, while surf fishing for that "coppery warrior"—the channel bass—Heilner finds and captures a feral horse, not unlike one of the so-called wild ponies of Assateague Island further south in Virginia. Heilner's horse becomes a symbol for a forgotten corner of America and an emblem for the wild spirit of the sea. Heilner and his friends realize there's no way for man to take such an animal back to the confines of civilization, and, at the end of the story, they release it:

We unhitched Pegasus and turned him loose. He turned and without so much as a glance in our direction, strode off. The last we saw of him was as he topped the crest of a great shaggy dune, stood for a moment silhouetted against the distant skyline, and was gone.

Where but an instant before his distant form had been the only living thing, now nothing broke the vast solitude of the sandy waste but the far-off moan of the sea and the whisper of the wind through the dry sedge.[10]

Heilner pleaded with his generation to release all such wild horses—the symbolic ones as well as the real equines—and leave the wonders of the barrier islands to the nesting seabirds and those few people willing to come by boat to fish, swim, and hunt. But his generation decided to cross the marshes with causeways, settle the barrier islands with towns, and still try to keep the wilderness. They failed, and today there are no wild horses left in New Jersey. As substitutes, the Chambers of Commerce of the manifold tourist towns strung out along the coast offer wooden facsimiles in amusement park merry-go-rounds open for the summer season.

Following publication of *Adventures in Angling*, Heilner's angling reputation began to soar. He became an associate editor of *Field & Stream* and a field representative in ichthyology for the American Museum of Natural History. On behalf of the museum, he participated in ichthyological expeditions to Peru and Ecuador in 1924–1925, to Alaska in 1927, and to Cuba in 1934–1935. After his first trip to Bimini in 1921, during which he took special pains to collect previously unknown fishes from tidal pools in the reefs, his close friend and

---

[10]*Adventures in Angling*, Van Campen Heilner, Cincinnati, 1922, page 37.

mentor, Dr. J. T. Nichols of the American Museum of Natural History, named two of the new species for Heilner and his boat: *Labrisomus heilneri* and *Eupomacentus nepenthe*.

Like another friend, Zane Grey, Heilner saw the advantage of motion picture film in discovering the world of travel and outdoors for millions of Americans who would never actually have the opportunity to visit foreign lands. But while ZG used the cinema to enlarge his own reputation, Heilner used it as a tool of science. As a result, while today we have a record of Zane Grey capturing sharks off New Zealand and Zane Grey catching marlin off Mexico, we have relatively little footage of Van Campen Heilner in similar moments of triumph. Instead, he left us such rare film as the first movies ever made of the nest building and feeding of the roseate spoonbill.

Following his return from Cuba in 1935, Heilner contributed two chapters on the channel bass and bonefish to *American Big Game Fishing*. Two years later he adapted these chapters and added 24 others ranging in subject from "Bottom Fish" to "Angling Around the World" for his definitive *Salt Water Fishing*, first issued by the Penn Publishing Company in Philadelphia. Feeling that fine art illustrations of angling scenes do as much to evoke feeling for the sport as does good writing, Heilner persuaded his publisher to let him use one of the outstanding outdoor artists of the day to provide *12* paintings for the book.

William Goadby Lawrence[11] had never met Heilner before being approached by him to illustrate *Salt Water Fishing*. Lawrence, of course, knew who Heilner was, but presumed that his artist-friend and angling companion, Lynn Bogue Hunt,[12] would be given this marvelous opportunity. But, at the time, Hunt had more than enough work to keep him busy, and Lawrence got the job.

Lawrence spent a year traveling up and down the coast gathering background materials and impressions for his paintings, and he even spent time aboard Heilner's boat at Barnegat, New Jersey. The results

[11]In the fall of 1972, angling writer Peter (*Big Fish and Blue Water*) Goadby went to Nova Scotia to captain the Australian Tuna Team in the Wedgeport competition. On his way home, he stopped off to visit his "distant cousin," William Goadby Lawrence, who now lives in Edgecomb, Maine. The two hope to collaborate on a book at some future date.

[12]Lynn Bogue Hunt was a writer as well as a painter who contributed the chapter on sailfish to *American Big Game Fishing*. (He also contributed all the art for the book.)

[184]

speak well of the effort, and sales figures for the book over the years have spoken well for the entire project. In fact, this publication was probably the first best seller in angling history since Izaak Walton's *The Compleat Angler*. It went through three printings before the end of 1937, six printings by 1940, and by the time Alfred A. Knopf picked it up in 1953, the book had sold tens of thousands of copies.

The Knopf edition included amendments in its version that illustrate change and development in saltwater angling during the 15 years between *Salt Water Fishing*'s first edition and Knopf's decision to reprint it. There is a new cover illustration and frontispiece by W. Goadby Lawrence, many new photographs of such angling personalities as the Lerners, the Farringtons, and Alfred Glassell with record catches, as well as Heilner's special assortment of gee-whiz and funny photos, and a new appendix about the International Game Fish Association, of which Van Campen Heilner was vice-president from its beginning. But probably the most significant difference between the 1937 edition and the 1953 version is the preface: the first by Zane Grey, the second by Ernest Hemingway.[13]

Of course, Zane Grey was no longer alive in 1953, and certainly the updated edition required an updated introduction. But Heilner was just as happy to bury the patronization of Zane Grey's preface that spoke more suggestively of Grey's own leading role in developing the sport than it gave any real credit to Heilner's accomplishments or the book's quality.[14] Grey's introduction implied that ocean fishing was a fraternity of anglers whose membership must be personally approved by ZG. Hemingway's preface, on the other hand, cites Heilner as a pioneer who "fished for sport rather than publicity." It goes on to attack the snobbery of ocean angling that excludes all but the very

---

[13]Although Ernest Hemingway and Van Campen Heilner's paths overlapped at many points in time (Bimini and Cuba) and on projects (both contributing articles to *American Big Game Fishing*), they apparently did not become familiar with one another until after they began to serve on the board of the newly-formed International Game Fish Association.

[14]ZG's patronage was a double-edged sword for more than one talented angler. After Mr. and Mrs. Eastham Guild, alias "Ham Fish" and "Carrie Finn," of Tahiti received some suggestions and gifts of equipment from Zane Grey, nothing they ever did thereafter as angler and anglerette, or outdoor writers, was treated by Zane Grey as anything more than the lesser work of "disciples." While they liked and respected Zane Grey as a pioneer angler, the Guilds quite naturally came to resent his treating their every new record or accomplishment as something inspired and personally orchestrated by ZG himself.

[185]

rich from the pleasures of tuna and swordfishing.[15] Finally, Hemingway commends Heilner for always fishing "as inexpensively as possible" and for sticking up for the inshore angler and his favorite quarry, the bonefish, the tarpon, and the surf fishes.

Following the first publication of *Salt Water Fishing*, there were more honors and expeditions. In 1937, he was decorated with the Order of Carlos Manuel de Cespeder by Cuba, and after World War II, he joined the Peabody Museum of Yale expedition to Tierra del Fuego and the Strait of Magellan. His publications were known abroad and earned him an honorary membership in the British Sea Anglers Society, fellowship in the Royal Geographic Society, and association with the Royal Anthropological Institute and the Bombay Natural History Society. At home, he was an honorary life member of the American Museum of Natural History, a life member of the Explorers Club, and an associate of the American Society of Ichthyologists and Herpetologists.

Salt Water Fishing was the last book on angling Heilner ever produced. He saw the uninhabited coasts he had explored in the 1910's and 1920's settled with countless summer residences, and he lost some of his enthusiasm for angling in general and surf fishing in particular. Then, too, Heilner was simply growing older. Unlike Zane Grey, who was more protective of his angling reputation the older he became, Heilner was content to rest on previously won laurels.

Yet Heilner never lost his interest in the outdoor world. He enjoyed corresponding with anglers of all ages and sharing their discoveries (which sometimes weren't really discoveries after all, but Van never let on), and trying to answer their many questions (some of which he himself had asked half a century earlier). Heilner maintained homes on Long Island and in the Bahamas, and he traveled widely. But his mailing address until the day he died remained simply care of *Field & Stream*, New York City.

One of the last, and certainly one of the most remarkable, articles he

---

[15]Hemingway was aware of the contrast he was making between Zane Grey's and his own introduction. We know from Hemingway's biographer, Carlos Baker, that EH was an avid reader of ZG's big-game fishing books as early as 1928— even buying them as gifts for his friends. But we also know through his correspondence with *Esquire*'s publisher-editor, Arnold Gingrich, that Hemingway considered himself a far superior sports writer to Zane Grey. All Grey sought, Hemingway pointed out, was that the world should marvel at his strength and skill, while he, Hemingway, stressed what the average man could do to participate in the sport and then what he could do to improve his chances once he was in.

ever published on saltwater angling was for the April 7, 1961, issue of *Life* magazine. The editors asked him for a comprehensive history of the sport—in 1,500 words or less! By touching base with half a dozen highlights during five centuries of effort, Heilner managed to come up with an amazing summary of what had been accomplished in salt water since Dame Juliana Berners wrote her *Treatyse of Fysshynge wyth an Angle* in 1496. (He always insisted that this first book of angling was actually a treatise on "flattie fishing" in disguise. For in a listing of common European fishes ideally suited for sport on hook and line, Dame Juliana includes the flounder, probably *Flesus flesus*.) Best of all, Heilner was able to work in his preference for inshore angling: After cataloging some of the achievements of high-seas sport fishermen, Heilner concluded his essay by reminding his readers that the largest fish ever taken on rod and reel anywhere in the world was caught by a surf caster! On April 21, 1959, Alfred Dean—without benefit of a fighting chair, or even a boat—landed a 2,664-pound white shark while fishing from the beach at Ceduna, South Australia.

Now *that* is fishing!

TWELVE

NEW ENGLAND—BETWEEN THE WARS

All good fishermen stay young until they die, for fishing is the only dream of youth that doth not grow stale with age.—J. W. Muller, writing in 1909

In Washington, D. C.'s, National Gallery, there is a painting by the nineteenth-century artist John Frederick Kensett showing Beacon Rock at Newport Harbor, Rhode Island. Dated 1857, the painting illustrates one type of American landscape art prior to the Civil War. But it does more. It shows a man fishing from the rocks with a cane pole for tautog.

No one knows how old this sport is, but Ollie Rodman remembers when it was still New England's most popular form of saltwater angling: "We used to hitch up our horse, Hazel, to the wagon—what we called a democrat wagon—two seats: one facing forward and one facing back with three or four people on each—and we'd set off for Point Judith about 12 to 15 miles from where we lived.

"Once we got there, we'd take out the bamboo poles strung with tarred marlin line, an egg-shaped sinker so we wouldn't lose the lead in the rocks, and two hooks. We used to tie up the hooks ourselves. They had no eyes. Just flattened heads on a shank. We'd tie them up with several half hitches and have them hang such a space apart they wouldn't catch or tangle one another. Still, while both hooks were rigged above the sinker, the lower one dangled below and was our true bottom hook.

"We used crabs for bait. And catching them was almost as much fun as fishing! At least we kids thought so. At that time, there was a brackish-water marsh near Wickford just loaded with fiddlers. On a low tide you would see hundreds upon thousands of them. So my brother, Robert, and I built a beam board in a V-shape about eight inches high, and we'd wait until the fiddlers were feeding some distance from their holes out on the mud flats. Then we'd toss the board between them and their holes and herd them toward our waiting buckets.

"Another good bait for tautog is the green crab. To get those, we'd go out early—usually fish the incoming tide—and then take all the fish heads and entrails from whatever we'd caught and tuck them under rocks in shallow water along the shore. We'd go up the beach a little way and sit down and wait. I smoked a cigarette—even at that age— and the ritual of lighting up and smoking it down to nothing took a good 10 or 15 minutes. Then we'd go back to where we'd left the fish heads and in no time at all collect a 10-quart bucketful of green crabs.

"When we went to the shore, it was always a picnic outing. My mother and sister made up a great hamper of sandwiches, and when we weren't fishing, we'd be eating!

"Everyone was given his own burlap sack to put fish in. We'd fish along the Point Judith breakwater, about fifteen to twenty yards apart. If you found a hole with quite a lot of fish in it, you'd sing out, and everyone would come over to fish with you in a great semi-circle, side by side. The fish ran anywhere from little guys the size of your hand on up to 7- and 8-pound lunkers.

"We'd always come home with at least one gunnysack full of fish. The next job, of course, was to clean them. We cut them across the throat, then down the stomach all the way to the tail. Also down the back on each side of the dorsal fin. Then when you pushed up on the pectoral bone on each side of the chin and ripped back, you could break loose the head and entrails all with one twist and pull. It was something of a trick, and you had to practice to develop the knack. Of course, some trips were so productive, you got all the practice you'd want.

"After the fish were filleted, we'd store them in covered earthenware crocks in the cellar. Put a layer of salt on the bottom of the crock, then a layer of fish, another layer of salt, and so on until you filled it up. That way we had enough fish to eat all winter long. You'd take the fish you'd need out the day before, put them in fresh water overnight, dry them on a towel, and they'd be just delicious at dinner the next day. I honestly believe that salting preserves a fish's flavor better than the deep freezing we do nowadays. Anyway, I've done a lot of fishing since my childhood on Narragansett Bay, and I don't think I have any finer memories."

Oliver Hazard Perry Rodman was born on April 1, 1905, in Lafayette, Rhode Island. His family had been in the woolen cloth manufacturing business in the same town for over 100 years, and Ollie's very first memories go back to the freshwater pond behind the family mill.

"One particular thing I remember," says Ollie, "was the time I'd just had the measles or some other darn thing. My father and brother went off trout fishing but wouldn't take me with them because I was just recuperating, and they didn't think I was strong enough to go. Anyway, they fished hard all day long and came back with half a dozen trout. Meanwhile, I'd gotten my mother's permission to walk the 200 yards down to the mill pond, where I caught a dozen or more nice trout practically in the middle of our village. That about floored my father and brother when they got back!"

Ollie's school years were uneventful—but regularly leavened by trips upcountry for trout and grouse with his father and brother or by trips to the coast with the entire family for tautog. Based on one of these coastal outings, Ollie sold his first outdoor story, on tautog fishing, to the Sunday supplement of the *Providence Journal*.

But there was also shore fishing for snapper blues and flounders. Or from Wickford harbor up Narragansett Bay as far as Providence, excellent weakfishing could be had from a boat anchored bow and stern across the tide. A chum line of grass shrimp was dribbled out, into which went your baited hook. The fish averaged a pound and a half, and occasionally a four-pounder was caught to make the day memorable.

Ollie went to Moses Brown prep school, Brown University, and when he finished, he thought he would like to try writing for a career. But his mother wanted him to study law. Ollie's father stepped in and worked out a compromise: The boy should give law school one full year. If he still was not satisfied after that time, he should go on with his writing.

"When I first came to Boston, I didn't know a soul. I registered at Boston University Law School—at that time a small building just behind the State House—and then had to find a place to stay. I asked a couple of boys standing outside the school where I could find a room for the night. One of them spoke up and said his roommate was away for two or three days, that he lived up on Newbury Street, and why didn't I come up and join him until I found a place of my own?

"Well, after he helped me settle in, I went out to buy a magazine and got a copy of *National Sportsman*. When I brought it back to the room to read, I noticed for the first time that out the window, directly across the street, were the offices of *National Sportsman*. So that first year I divided my time between law school and trying to write stories for *National Sportsman*. Somehow I managed to get credit for that first year of law, but the following fall I went to work in the advertising department of the magazine."

Today, nearly half a century later, Ollie Rodman is still active in advertising sales, now as the Boston representative of *The Sporting Goods Dealer*, a national trade publication. However, in the intervening years, he has contributed several classic titles to the literature of saltwater angling, been the publisher of both *Outdoors* and *Salt Water Sportsman* magazines, been an Executive Committee member of the American Wildlife Foundation as well as a director of both the Outdoor Writers Association of America and the Sportsmen's Club of America. He helped pioneer the first Atlantic Coast conservation laws to protect striped bass and other saltwater gamefish and has served as president (for too many years, he says) and chairman of the Salt Water Fishing Committee for the Massachusetts Fish and Game Association, America's oldest incorporated fish and game club.

Ollie recalls: "Our first attempt to put through a striped bass law here in the State of Massachusetts was when Dever was governor. We failed during his administration, but finally succeeded when Leverett Saltonstall was governor. I remember very well the meeting we had in the governor's office with some of the Boston Rod and Gun editors and photographers. We had arranged for the Cape Cod Chamber of Commerce to send us, in ice, the first striped bass taken from the Cape Cod Canal that season. After meeting with the governor, we presented him with this fish. He then thanked us and the next thing he did was to reach for the phone, call his wife, and tell her he was bringing home a huge striped bass that he wanted to have cooked for dinner that night!"

Perhaps, most marvelous of all, Ollie Rodman has accumulated memories of surf fishing during those decades when the exclusive memberships of the old New England striper clubs were dwindling and a new breed of shore angler emerged, carrying production rods and spinning reels stuck up on the front bumper of a beach buggie. Through just his fishing, Ollie has watched the world move from the nineteenth century into the present. And in his combined role as participant and reporter, he has become one of our most valuable chroniclers of the development of inshore saltwater angling.

"Rod and reel fishing just wasn't very common in the first two decades of this century. For that matter, saltwater fishing as sport just wasn't a very widespread notion. My family had fun when we went down to Point Judith for tautog. But we always had the ulterior motive of filling those earthenware crocks in the cellar with food. The same went for countless other people fishing for scup [porgy], flounder, weakfish, and blues. It was cane pole or handline fishing, and what you brought home for dinner was your prime indication of success—no matter how much fun you otherwise may have had. And I dare say for a legion of charter-boat and skiff-rental fishermen today, that's still true.

"Something else that retarded the development of sport fishing in the sea—at least along the New England coast—was the virtual disappearance of striped bass at the turn of the century. The majority of those gentlemen who fished from their private steel piers at Newport and Cuttyhunk used rods and reels, and the use of this specialized gear might have become better known to the masses sooner had those gentlemen's clubs, where such tackle was in use, remained with us a little longer. For a lack of fish and interest, Cuttyhunk finally closed its doors about 1907."

GWR: When was the first time you remember using a rod and reel?
Rodman: I was a boy. I don't recall my age. But I do remember that I first used such an outfit tautog fishing and naturally created quite a stir with it. Of course, rods and reels had been used in fresh water for many, many years. And the reason they were first introduced along the jetties and beaches was entirely functional and had nothing whatever to do with sport. Very simply, you could cover so much more ground with a rod and reel. With a cane pole, you couldn't fish more than ten or twelve feet from the rock you were standing on. But with

[192]

a rod and reel, you could cast 40 or more yards—a good distance in those days.

Naturally, such an obvious advantage caught on like wildfire. Everybody seemed to get into the tackle business about the same time. When people standing down the jetty saw you could reach areas they couldn't and saw you land big fish on what they at first thought was flimsy line, it didn't take *years* to get the ball rolling with rods and reels. In our area, a single season did the trick!

GWR: This was all tautog fishing?

Rodman: Yes.

GWR: What are your first memories of striped bass fishing?

Rodman: They go back to just about the time I went to work for *National Sportsman*. This publication started up in 1879, and when I joined the staff, the management had just started *Hunting and Fishing*. Both magazines sold for a nickel apiece, and we built up circulation with a form letter including a small card with an insert space for a quarter. Return the card with your quarter, and you had a year's subscription. We built up the circulation of *Hunting and Fishing* to around 400,000 when *Field & Stream* and *Outdoor Life* were still hovering around 200,000.[1]

Anyway, this was in the late twenties, and naturally I had to move up to Boston full-time to be on the magazine's staff. I married a local gal whose family had a place at Wellfleet on Cape Cod. We used to go down there for weekends and vacations, and since I'd read a lot about striped bass fishing at Cuttyhunk, I thought I'd give our beach at Wellfleet the benefit of the doubt and try a blend of my Rhode Island shore-fishing inexperience with what I learned about stripers in old books and magazines.

In those days there was no one—not a soul—fishing the beach on Cape Cod between Wellfleet and Provincetown. I know that may be hard to believe when today you practically have to elbow your way in to find a place to fish, but it's true. I was still a young fellow who didn't know that Cape residents might consider any fellow peculiar who spent a morning tossing a lead and baited hook into the surf. I just went out, got some squid, and that first day, caught a bass weighing about 25 pounds.

Of course, I had to take the fish into town and show everybody—convince them that surf casting was not only a reasonable but a profitable pursuit. Cape Codders are nothing if not reasonable folks, so the next day there were about a dozen people down on the beach—handlines and anything else that would approximate surf gear.

---

[1]Today, *Field & Stream* and *Outdoor Life* each have over 1,800,000 subscribers, while both *Hunting and Fishing* and *National Sportsman* are defunct.

There was one fellow in particular I remember well. We called him Billy Boots. He was a very likeable tramp who lived in a hole-in-the-wall in town with a little coal stove as his only furniture. Anyway, Billy Boots would walk the mile and a half or two miles from town across Gull Pond Road to the beach in a great pair of oversized boots, carrying an endless handline and a sinker that must have weighed about half as much as he did. I remember one day he came down near to where I was fishing, began to heave and twirl that sinker round and round over his head for the cast offshore. With all that line spread over the sand, and in all his jumping around, Billy stepped on the line, so the hook and sinker didn't even clear the first wave. It was right in the suds, maybe six or seven feet out.

Well, Billy started hopping up and down and cussing and was about to pull the line back in when it started out with a rush. Billy was a tiny fellow, and when he first took hold of the line, I thought he was going to be pulled right in after the fish! The bass was almost as strong as Billy, and just about the time he would start up the beach, the fish would trip him up and drag him back down to the water. You never saw such commotion! Finally, Billy put the line over his shoulder and started into the dunes and simply marched that fish up out of the sea! He didn't even unhook the bass; Billy just slung it over his shoulder, and dragging his line behind, he started back into town. The whole episode took less than 10 minutes.[2]

It amazed me how quickly the local Cape residents caught onto the spirit of surf casting. A retired shoemaker from Brockton, Eddie Beshong, who had a little cottage near town, used to come over from time to time to pass the time of day while I was fishing. It was all bottom bait fishing—sea worms or squid—in those days, so there was plenty of time for fishermen to reciprocate conversation. Anyway, this fellow just didn't understand how I could hold and catch fish on such fragile line. But he saw me do it often enough that one day he finally asked me if I'd pick him up a rod and reel next time I went to Boston. So we got him started, and in no time at all, he was casting well and catching as many fish as even the most experienced among us.

Another fellow, Kenny Baker, knew nothing but rabbit hunting

---

[2]Billy Boots was part of a tradition going back more than half a century when Ollie Rodman first saw this type of angling in action. Writing in 1878, George Brown Goode notes that "another mode [of fishing] which is growing in favor is that of heaving and hauling in the surf.... No rod is used, but the angler, standing on the beach or in the breakers, whirls his heavy jig about his head and casts it far into the sea, and having hooked his fish puts his shoulder to the line, and walks up the beach dragging his prize after him to the shore. This is practiced everywhere on exposed sand beaches, such as are found at Montauk, Monomoy, Newport, and Barnegat." *Game Fishes of the United States*, page 19.

until one day he came over on the beach and watched us catching fish. He was soon hooked on the sport and eventually became one of the most zealous surf fishermen I've ever known. He and I shared a beach buggie—the first one between Wellfleet and Provincetown—and you can imagine how delightful it was to cruise the deserted beaches of the 1930's looking for fish. It was an old Model A Ford, with over-sized tires which we still had to deflate when we went down on the sand. Then every time we returned to a hard-surfaced road, we'd have to get out and pump up the tires by hand. We used two pumps and worked out quite a system so it wouldn't take long. But you can imagine we puzzled more than a few passing motorists when they saw this car festooned with tackle and sometimes fish—looking like it had just rolled up out of the sea—and a couple of apparent lunatics in waders working like crazy over a pair of bicycle pumps!

I became so devoted to surf fishing that my wife and I moved to Duxbury where we wouldn't have such a long drive to the Cape on weekends. Then in Duxbury Bay itself, the fishing was good. When the stripers were not hitting, one of our favorite sports was to work up a school of mackerel with a jig. Then once they were around the boat, we'd cast to them with fly rods. They'd run from little tinkers on up to occasional three-pounders.

GWR: How about bluefish?

Rodman: I suppose I enjoyed some of the first surf casting for blue-fish on the Cape. In the course of my magazine work I met Dr. Mal-colm Johnston, who was just crazy about brook and brown trout fishing. I thought this was all he cared about. But one day when I went to his house for treatment, I saw a big surf rod on the wall, and we somehow got sidetracked and I almost forgot what I came to be treated for. Turned out he had been a surf-fishing buff for years. Then he took me into his confidence—said there had been a fantastic run of bluefish at Monomoy Point, Cape Cod, over the past several years, and that he'd take me along if I'd like to go. But that I musn't tell anybody else about it. "When do we go?!" was all I asked.

It was even better than Dr. Johnston described! He, a doctor friend of his, and I had Monomoy Point all to ourselves for several years— in the 1930's—and we never failed to do well with the then big blues of eight pounds or more. While you'll hear people claim larger blues for their favorite casting areas today, to be able to consistently catch bluefish that size was heaven by any standard.

GWR: Were you using lures by this time?

Rodman: Oh, yes. We used primarily metal squids—particularly for the blues. Doctor Johnston made a jig shaped something like the keel of a small boat with a free-swinging single hook behind that was

[195]

particularly successful. Then, of course, popping and swimming plugs came in later to revolutionize the sport.

GWR: Would you save your casting until you actually spotted fish feeding, or did you do a lot of blind casting?

Rodman: Blind casting was probably what it looked like. But we were always watching for feeding terns or gulls—a swirl—a slick. Of course, after you fish a beach awhile, you get to know where the holes and bars are—as well as the best time of the tide for each area.

GWR: Do you have any other special memories of those early beach-buggie days?

Rodman: Many of them! But one of my favorites was the time R. V. "Gadabout" Gaddis and I found a bunch of big stripers schooling bait about 80 yards offshore. Gadabout, by the way, lived in Florida, but he covered the New England area for Shakespeare Tackle and developed into a topflight surf caster. Anyway, it was shortly before dark with a beautiful sunset and a flat-calm ending to the day. The sea colored pink and gold and out where the fish were feeding, their movement and splashes gave the sea a molten quality. We patiently plugged those fish until we'd each taken three or four when along came another fellow, running like he was late for an appointment! His tackle wasn't very good and he just couldn't reach out to the fish. Every time his lure fell short, he'd crank in like mad, get so agitated, that his next cast fell even shorter than the one before! Finally, he couldn't stand it any longer. He ran up the beach, took off all his clothes, ran back to the surf and waded in to where he could still sling a lure. From our standpoint, all we could see was a head and shoulders! But he got a fish. Stark naked he played it! And stark naked he landed it!

GWR: Where else have you fished?

Rodman: Well, in the early 1930's I made a trip down to the Florida Keys—Pirate's Cove Fishing Camp. It was everything the advertising brochures promised it to be. We had tarpon fishing inside, and great variety over the reefs offshore.

Then, on another occasion, the National Wildlife Federation indirectly provided me with an interesting trip. Someone from Prince Edward Island in the Maritime Provinces asked someone else from the Federation how they could promote their fishing to anglers in the United States. The Wildlife Federation man suggested they get hold of an outdoor writer to visit the area and send back exciting reports. So I was picked to go up and see what I could do to develop Prince Edward Island's saltwater fishing reputation—this being in the days before they realized they had such fabulous bluefin tuna fishing offshore. I was sent to the northeast corner of the island, as that area allegedly had the best striped bass fishing. Actually the Provincial gov-

[196]

ernment had just established a park there, and they were hoping to publicize it.

So I fished the entire coast for 40 or 50 miles for over a week and never caught a striper! Happily the trip was saved by some outstanding freshwater trout fishing. But after I got back, I discovered that the best striped bass fishing on Prince Edward Island is actually on the inside of the island facing the mainland. The morale of the story is do your own pioneering!

My interview with Ollie Rodman took place in the study of his home in Brookline, Massachusetts. On the wall was Jack Murray's painting of a striper being landed on a Cuttyhunk bass boat off the rocky Massachusetts island that gave these boats their name. It was the same painting that Ollie had used as the frontispiece for his *Saltwater Fisherman's Favorite Four*, published in 1948—the definitive guide at that time to striped bass, weakfish, bluefish, and channel bass fishing along the Atlantic and Gulf coasts. There were other saltwater angling memorabilia in the room, and Ollie noticed me looking around.

"You know, you're sitting in the room where *Salt Water Sportsman* got its start," he said.

Seeing my look of amazement, Ollie continued: "Back in 1939, three of us working for the Tilton brothers—H. L. and L. O. (Harry L. as publisher of *National Sportsman* and *Hunting and Fishing* was the real power in the business)—decided to put out a little outdoor sheet of our own. Horace Tapply, better known as 'Tap' Tapply, was at that time editor of *National Sportsman*, and Hugh Grey was *National Sportsman*'s boating editor. These two shared with me an obsession for surf fishing, and we met here in the den to discuss the possibility of turning out a seasonal newsletter geared to other saltwater addicts like ourselves. Well, we started it up, and the journal became fairly successful. But old Harry Tilton got wind of it and thought we were spending more time on *Salt Water Sportsman* than we were on his publications, and demanded that we sell the operation. And we did.

"Tilton was generally fair-minded, but extremely tight-fisted and tough. He never paid you much, but you'd always get a nice Christmas bonus if you'd given him a good year's work. But on one occasion, I finally felt he went too far. When World War II broke out, he announced that we were all getting a severe salary cut. There was no reason for this—the war was merely an excuse. So I dug my heels in. I was young and brash and persuaded everyone else on the staff, but

[197]

one, that we stand up to Tilton and demand he maintain our salaries as they'd been. Well, we all got fired! That was on my birthday, by the way, and I really felt like something of an April Fool!

"Hugh Grey escaped the ax because he'd already gone to New York as editor of *Field & Stream*. An interesting footnote to his appointment is that one summer I had been invited to go goose hunting in Hudson Bay. I couldn't make the trip, so I asked Hugh to fill in for me, and he, of course, was delighted. On the trip he met Eltinge Warner, *Field & Stream*'s publisher, and the two got on so well together that when Hugh got back from Canada, he told us he was going to quit *National Sportsman* and go down to New York with *Field & Stream*. We wished him well—and well he did!

"Anyway, the day after our canning, Tap Tapply and I went fishing to talk things over. We decided that the quickest way to right ourselves after this little capsizing was to buy back *Salt Water Sportsman*—which we did."

GWR: How did Hal Lyman, the present publisher, ultimately come by the magazine?
Rodman: During the war, Hal Lyman's sister lived just two houses over from us. She'd married a doctor, and their children were about the same age as our three boys, so naturally we got to know one another pretty well. One day during a visit, she mentioned that her brother was coming home on leave from the Navy, and since he was an outdoorsman like myself, did I have any suggestions for entertaining him? It was March and offseason for practically everything, but I asked if she thought her brother would like to go crow shooting. "Oh, absolutely!" she said. So Hal and I first got to know one another on a chilly, damp day squatting in the bushes, tooting on a pair of crow calls.

He told me he'd be looking for work when he got out of the service, and did I think there was room for him on *Salt Water Sportsman?* "Sure," I said, "come on aboard." And that was it. He edited the newsletter for a few years, and then one day asked if he could buy it. So he bought it and has done a terrific job every since—building it into the finest saltwater magazine available. Hugh, Tap, and I all feel pretty pleased about it because when we first started out, we heard an awful lot of skeptical talk about there not being that many saltwater anglers to justify a publication aimed specifically at them. And besides, saltwater fishermen couldn't read anyway! Today, Hal has one of the classiest magazines on the newstands, with 75,000 regular readers. I think he has proven our point.

[198]

Ollie had stayed home this morning expressly for the interview. But I realized that he doubtless had a lot of work to take care of before getting to his downtown office (coincidentally just five floors above *Salt Water Sportsman*'s editorial offices at 10 High Street) in the afternoon. I had one last question:

GWR: Do you still fish much?
Rodman: Very little today. While the boys were growing up—as a family—we fished a lot together. My sons' childhoods by the sea were not unlike my own. But now they have their own children, responsibilities, and hobbies. Therefore, my wife and I don't fish as much as we used to. Time and age take their toll, you know. And as we grow older, we evolve into different people with different patterns than those of our youth or middle age. Besides, for over fifty years I've had my full share of fishing—and more!
GWR: But do you miss the sea?
Rodman: Of course! You never lose that.

THIRTEEN

NEW ENGLAND—SINCE WORLD WAR II

Sea-fishing is a sport where no man can stock
against his coming. He must take his chance
against everybody else.—Wildfowler in 1879

A suite on the third floor at 10 High Street in downtown Boston looks
more like an editorial office than do many of its more glamorous
counterparts in New York City. At least the traditional oak and
marble decor lends dignity to the office, and you feel that more substantial work is being done here than in the plastic spaces of Time,
Incorporated, or Hearst.

But editorial work is creative work, and Hal Lyman and his staff
believe that a fisherman does his best thinking on the water. Thus, it's
a rare event to find the publication team of Lyman, Woolner, An-
dresen, and Bramhall all in the office at the same time, and I therefore
felt a little privileged the day of my visit.

I spent some time talking with Hal Lyman about his advisory role
with both governmental and private agencies on behalf of the preservation of America's marine resources. Hal's particularly keen to see com-

mercial and sports fishermen stop their squabbling and join ranks to halt our common ills of pollution and coastal development. With all that he's accomplished on behalf of our sport, with all that he's seen and done as an angler, he's worthy of a profile in his own right.

But this chapter is devoted to the history and development of surf fishing, and for that, we turned to the grand master himself: Frank Middleton Woolner.

Frank was born on October 8, 1916, in the town of Worcester, Massachusetts. With older brother Ted, and two younger brothers Jack and Dick, Frank grew up fishing and hunting in what was then a part of small-town America. Today, reminiscences of those younger years, expanded by all they have learned since as professional reporters and outdoorsmen, make the weekly television show Frank does with Jack and Dick—the Woolner Brothers Outdoors—one of the most popular and knowledgeable sport shows in the New England area.

Frank became editor of *Salt Water Sportsman* in 1950 when Hal Lyman put back on his uniform to command a destroyer in the Korean War. Frank has been editor-in-chief ever since, and has collaborated with Lyman on three major saltwater books: *The Complete Book of Striped Bass Fishing*, *The Complete Book of Weakfishing*, and *Tackle Talk*. On his own, Frank has produced a number of books on a variety of subjects, but most important to the sea angler is the excellent *Modern Saltwater Sport Fishing*.

While one of the best informed writers in the outdoor business, Frank's largest contribution to saltwater angling may be in the dozens of young writers to whom he's given a helping hand. Name one reporter of consequence anywhere in North America who has ever tried his hand at saltwater angling and, odds are, he'll have a kind word and fond anecdote about Frank Woolner. Frank's only requisite for assistance is that the aspirant writer show some talent.

As the Woolner brothers grew up, they developed into top-notch amateur figure skaters and bicycle racers as well as outdoorsmen. Frank took Lucky 13 as his bicycle racing number and went on to become one of the best racers in New England—winning the state championship five years pedaling!

Frank's father was a carriage and then automobile painter, and Frank took up the trade as well. ("And I'll go back to it if they ever kick me out of the magazine business," he says.) But he was restless and

[201]

wanted something more. When World War II broke out, Frank responded to the draft call with enthusiasm. "In those days, we were all stupid: We wanted to go."

GWR: You were in armor. Did you volunteer for that branch?
Woolner: Sure. I thought tanks would be a blast. Well, they sure were, but not always in the most agreeable sense of that word! I joined the Third Armored Division when it was first formed, and we went to Camp Polk in Louisiana, on to Texas, the Mohave Desert, then Virginia, and finally Pennsylvania. At last, they sent us to England, and we went into Normandy on D-day plus 20. Everything went well that first day, thank God, but by the time we got into the Siegfried Line on September 12, a runner reached me and asked if I'd consider being transferred to headquarters, Third Armored Division, as a public relations man. Would I "consider"! After I said yes, it occurred to me that I actually might live through the war after all.
GWR: How did the PR job come about? Did the army know you were a writer?
Woolner: Right. When I first went into uniform, I was a $21-a-month private, and that wouldn't even pay for a night with—well, with the dice, or anything else. So I wrangled a typewriter and was shortly punching out $300 to $400 a month writing stories. All this stuff had to go through a censor, of course, and the division's censor was also it's public relations' officer—an awfully nice guy by the name of Haynes Dugan, who had been a newspaper man in Louisiana before the war.

As the war went into the homestretch, the Army became very public relations conscious, and headquarters decided they needed another writer on the staff. Since Haynes had been reading all my stuff as part of his job, I got the nod. Luckiest day in my life!
GWR: Did you really like the work?
Woolner: Absolutely. It's the only way to go to war. Every day I'd make a trip up front, get a story, and bring it back for the benefit of the civilian newsmen in the correspondents pool. Sometimes these guys would rewrite the material; sometimes they'd use it exactly like it was with their names on it. I didn't mind that so much; the important thing was that, at long last, I was out of the thick of it.

In addition, I'd go to all the high-level briefings, and I remember the day in late '44 when Courtney Hodges[1] told us he doubted we'd advance any further until next spring. I almost fell out of my chair! I

---

[1]Courtney Hicks Hodges (1887–1966), American general in command of the 1st Army, 1944–1945. "He was a little scrunched-up, wrinkled old soldier," says Woolner. "I always thought of him as the American Rundstedt."

couldn't believe it. After all, we'd come across France like a herd of turtles, and a lot of us assumed we'd have the war wrapped up by the end of the year. Later on, I came to appreciate the logistical problems involved in continuing the advance, but at the time, I tell you, I was shocked.

GWR: Did you come straight home after the war?

Woolner: I would have liked to, but a Colonel Andrew Barr, G-2, asked me to stay on six months to do a history of the division's part in the war. So I did—mostly hunting and fishing by day, and writing long hours into the night. The colonel saw to it that I stood no formations, ate when I wanted to, and had ample transportation, including a small plane and an antique Opal to run copy back and forth to Heidelberg. I wrote the narrative, and Major Murray H. Fowler, G-3, wrote the day-by-day combat reports. When the book was finished, it was called *Spearhead in the West*. But I didn't stay around to see it published. I was back home, a civilian, and at work as a daily rod and gun editor for the *Worcester Gazette* even before the Army had the book out of galley.

GWR: Had you done any surf fishing before the war?

Woolner: No, I hadn't. But during the war, I'd gotten a lot of correspondence from home telling me that something was developing there. In early 1946—it was too late in the season 1945 when I finally got out of uniform—I first tried my hand at surf fishing.

GWR: How'd you do?

Woolner: I caught stripers almost immediately—which was probably a misfortune. Because then it took me some time to accept the proposition that the striped bass is a damned unpredictable fish. You can't take dead aim at them. Nobody can. And this, of course, is part of what makes them interesting.

GWR: How have things changed in surf fishing since you began? What differences are you most aware of?

Woolner: [*Frank laughs.*] Cripes, you're talking close to three decades of change! As far as tackle development is concerned, 1945 is like a century ago. But for starters, we all used Calcutta or Burma cane poles. And since you could count on one breaking sometime or other during the season, most of us carried two or three rods. Our reels were all conventional, many of them poor—but there were good reels, too. The Penn Squidder, for example. Our line was all linen—Cuttyhunk linen —and when it wasn't burning hell out of your thumb on a cast or a fish, it was spraying water all over you. The stuff soaked up gallons of Neptune's finest, and every time you cast, you'd get showered. On top of that, you had to treat your lines like they were the Crown Jewels—rinsing and drying them after every trip, and then still expecting to bust off a fish every once in a while where the stuff had rotted. Nylon came in after the war, and there were some pretty funny episodes with the highly elastic lines they first produced. And early nylon cut your thumb as much as linen. But there wasn't one of us who had spent a little time with linen who didn't know that nylon and other synthetics, for all their drawbacks, would be the trend of the future.

GWR: Worcester is some distance from the coast. What kind of commuter problems did you have?

Woolner: Worcester is less than two hours from the Cape Cod Canal in a fast car, and 150 miles from Provincetown at the tip of the Cape. After I became editor for *Salt Water Sportsman* in 1950, I would sometimes drive down directly from Boston after work and this would save me even more time.

But Worcester is my home town, and we formed our first surf fishing club there. Being inland didn't hamper our effectiveness as anglers one whit. In fact, we're the only angling club to ever retire the Schaefer Trophy[2] after winning it five years in a row. That was for total poundage of striped bass, bluefish, and cod—but mostly stripers.

GWR: Did you found the club?

Woolner: No. But I was *one* of the founders, and I did help make the town striper-conscious through my daily newspaper columns. In time, we developed some of the best striped bass fishermen that world has ever seen.

There was Arnold Laine, for instance, of Templeton, Massachusetts —a lovely guy. He decided right after the war that he didn't want to work. He didn't want to do anything. But the work he ended up doing was harder than anything he might have found in a factory. He became a commercial rod-and-line fisherman and caught striped bass for the market. For several seasons running, he caught literally tons of striped bass for the Boston jobbers.[3]

Arnold was one of the most resourceful fishermen I've ever known. One day I saw him break a Burma cane pole while we were fishing the Cape Cod Canal. He didn't have a spare, but without blinking an eye, he rushed into the woods and cut down a birch sapling. He brought that back on a run, stripped it down and put a tip top on it and one line guide, and started catching stripers all over again! We've got some old movies of him doing it.

---

[2]The R. J. Schaefer Brewing Company established angling competitions and casting tournaments in a number of Atlantic coastal areas.

[3]Few fish marketed in New England actually stay there. Fish sales are handled by commercial jobbers and co-ops which send the fish to the Fulton Fish Market in New York City. Then, ironically, some of these same fish make their way back to stalls in Boston.

But Arnold never contributed to the Worcester Striper Club victories in the Schaefer Pageant because during his first year of competition he was challenged by someone at the Cape who said we couldn't use a professional—that is, a commercial fisherman. Well, this was just so much hogwash because very few of us in those days did not sell our surplus catch. Hell, it gave us money toward the next day's outing!

But Arnold was a sensitive guy, and he simply decided that if someone didn't want him fishing in the tournament, then he wouldn't. But Laine was one of the great ones who went down to the Cape at that time.

GWR: When did beach buggies first come into general use?

Woolner: There were a few buggies on the Cape before the war, and right afterward, a lot more began to appear. Mostly Model A Fords. But a few jeeps cropped up—souvenirs, so to speak, of the days in uniform. But no one drove anything new down on the beach. For one thing, none of us had the money to buy anything new. For another, we all knew that the salt air, water, and sand would make something old of something new in a hurry.

Several of us bought an old Model A Ford for $25 and did all the fixing up ourselves. We had welders and painters in our group, and a mechanic. And for a long while, that was it. One car for the bunch of us—sharing by turns or availability.

In the beginning, we used war-surplus airplane tires, which were no good because they wore out too fast on the open road going between beaches. Then we tried some surplus 900 × 13 sand tires, which were no good, because they wouldn't deflate properly for the light vehicles they supported. So we finally found our ideal buggy tire in the 820 × 15. It was perfect for the Model A, and with them the Model A became almost as effective as a jeep.

Today there're not many old Fords left on the beach. They're collector's items, and when you do see one out there, it's usually a complete wreck no collector would touch. But gradually other kinds of vehicles made their way out on the strand.

A few people tried panel trucks, and in the beginning, the rest of us said, "They'll never make it; those trucks are too heavy." But they used them, and they worked. Along about 1950, the first walk-in truck appeared on the beach. A fellow by the name of Bill Haynes, of Millbury, Massachusetts, bought an old Dodge bread truck down, and everyone told him he was out of his mind. He'd get stuck for sure on the first dune he tried to cross. But that Dodge went down on the beach beautifully. He had big tires for it—900 × 15, I guess—and all that storage and sleeping space made the rest of us jealous!

After that, big, elaborate, walk-in beach buggies began to crop up

[205]

regularly. With proper balance—which means getting most of your weight aft—and big enough tires, these things worked out pretty well. You don't travel fast, but then you don't want to travel fast because you'll end up breaking something of all the kitchen paraphernalia you're toting around to make life more comfortable.

At first we used gasoline camp stoves; now everyone uses propane. And by the early 1960's, new, specially designed trucks began to show up on the beach. Charley Whitney of Provincetown ordered a custom-made International Harvester, four-wheel drive, walk-in model—made of fiber glass, aluminum, and magnesium. It must have cost $8,000. We knew that surf fishing had arrived when something like this rolled down the beach!

I later bought that truck, kept it a few years, and sold it again. It really was a dosser! But by then I was already slipping behind the times. The latest rage were "chase cars." The idea was that you used a big beach buggy for a base camp and then roamed the beaches with a smaller car or jeep. And these so-called chase cars are precisely that. They can really make time along the beach, and many of them are equipped with CB[4] radio to keep others in your party informed about where the action is.

GWR: When did lightweight surf boats become popular?

Woolner: Oh, I suppose packing a boat atop your beach rig first became popular in the late 1950's. They were all aluminum, of course, and big at 14 feet. Anything bigger than that, and they were awkward to manhandle and darn near impossible to get on your truck.

Today, however, you'll see surf boats up to 19 feet with big motors. To launch these, you need a four-wheel-drive prime mover, often a chase car, and you push them into the surf with a padded surface attached to the left front bumper of the vehicle. Recovery is made at full throttle so that the boat slides well up on a sand beach. Power winches and tow ropes are employed to pull the heavy craft up above the high-tide mark and to rack it on a trailer. There is less and less manhandling these days.

GWR: The boom in surf fishing in the 1950's sounds like the boom in snowmobiling today. How did you regulate all this sudden growth?

Woolner: The Massachusetts Beach Buggy Association was the forerunner of a number of private clubs that pretty well handled the regulation amongst ourselves. It was pure self-defense. We knew that if we fishermen didn't do something about placing limitations and guidelines on our surf fishing activities, state and local government—with a whole lot of people who don't know one end of a fishing rod from

---

[4]Citizen's Band.

the other—would eventually step in to do the regulating for us. So the Massachusetts Beach Buggy Association got started in 1949 with 62 men like Francis W. "Sarge" Sargeant, who later became governor of the state, Howard Rogers, and myself, participating. And we wrote up a code of ethics and set standards of behavior for everything from keeping the beach clean to maintaining friendly relations with town authorities along the Cape. Rogers, who came from Orleans, became the first president of our association, and I took upon myself the job of secretary-treasurer, the nastiest job in any operation. I know, because I recall how much more pleasant life became when I was elected president the next year!

To identify our vehicles, we put 62 numbers in a hat, and passed the hat around.

GWR: Your buggy has always been 13. How did you arrange that?

Woolner: To be perfectly honest, we only put 60 names in the hat. We gave Sarge Sargeant, who, at the time, was Chief of Marine Fisheries for the State of Massachusetts, number 1. We liked him. Besides, it was good politics. Then I kept number 13 for myself. When I was a kid, my bicycle racing league number had been 13, and I raced all over the country with it and eventually became New England champion. So I figured 13 wouldn't be such a bad number in the beach buggy business either.

Anyway, we established very good relations with all the coastal communities, and even after both Cape Cod and the association grew in population, we had practically no friction anywhere.

GWR: "Practically" means you had some. Where?

Woolner: At Nauset Beach, Orleans, in the 1960's, local government passed ordinances which seemed to us first steps toward managing the public beach as a local concession, with fees we thought exorbitant and regulations considered (by us) inequitable. Naturally, this displeased a good many of our members. We were not unsympathetic to the arguments of town officials—there had been outlaw beach buggymen tearing up the dunes and leaving litter—but we felt the town officials should discriminate between the good guys and the bad. We never argued about intelligent controls, but we wanted regulations that applied to all hands, whether residents or visitors. There was a court case, which was settled out of court when MBBA and the Town of Orleans came to a meeting of minds. But then the town initiated new restrictions which transient beach buggy people thought unfair—and the dirt hit the fan again.

The whole thing came to a head when a group of summer residents, all women, dug a great pit such as Africans might dig to trap a rhino or elephant. They then camouflaged it over and hid up in the dunes.

[207]

Well, one of our members, a Portuguese immigrant who didn't understand English too well, drove down the beach that day and suddenly found the ground dropping from under his buggy. He slammed to an abrupt halt and has only the most dazed and terrifying memory of a swarm of Harpies rushing down out of the dunes to yell curses and insults at him! Needless to say, these games did nothing to endear local residents to any members of the MBBA.

GWR: Is this fighting still going on?

Woolner: Yes, but not at fever pitch. There are controls which some beach buggy people feel they can live with. A legislative bill to make Nauset Beach a state park led to a study commission which is examining the problem statewide. The federal government is in the act too, because vehicular traffic on National Seashores is being assessed. Some mechanized anglers think that local interests want to drive all transient beach buggies back into the hinterlands to assure motel trade and restaurant trade. There are excesses on both side.

While this is going on, beach buggy fishing is going through still another development, one that in a way is carrying it back to where it began. I think we'll see a slow phase-out of the huge live-in buggies and more chase cars working out of back-of-the-dunes motels and campsites.

GWR: Is this because there're so many restrictions against people staying on the beach these days?

Woolner: Yes. Many areas have such prohibitions. But the larger reason is that such big live-in rigs with a tin boat on top can get a little rich for the blood. Increasingly, surf fishermen are making the choice between a smaller rig and a boat. Fewer people are trying to combine both.

GWR: There's been a wonderful development in lures for saltwater fishing since the war, and a lot of it happened in surf casting. Would you describe some of this?

Woolner: Before World War II, the surf man's major artificial lure was the block tin squid. It was a great lure, but that one would be too expensive to produce today because of the price of tin. You'd polish it in the sand until it glowed like the dickens, and I'm not sure that these tin lures didn't have a richer, deeper shine to them than the chrome jobs we use today. Anyway, once upon a time, the block tin squid was your only alternative to casting out real squid or clams on a hook.

Plugs came in during the war. Oh, there were probably a few surf fishermen who used a big freshwater musky plug before the war. But the freshwater lures were too impractical for much saltwater use. The metal work would rust and corrode to hell and the hooks were too flimsy to hold the likes of a 30-pound striped bass.

During the war, most of the fishing centered around the Cape Cod Canal. It was off limits, because the Army was afraid of enemy sabotage. But that didn't seem to bother the fellows here at home. They knew there were fish in the canal, and they wanted them. Many of the fishermen wanted the fish to sell—an extra source of income—since the price was so high. Apparently, a kind of truce was finally worked out between the fishermen and the guards who used to bawl the fishermen out: "For God's sake, will you sit down in the rocks when I come by; I don't want to see you!"

About that time, someone made a clever discovery about the Creek Chub Pikie Minnow plug in muskellunge size. This medium-size wooden lure had been created as a diving lure, and a swimmer. A large metal lip angled out from the head and carried it under the surface when it was retrieved. But this first clever someone found that if you bent the metal lip of the plug straight down, it would operate on the surface with an awful lot of splash and commotion. They called it "The Blue Plug," and did that catch stripers!

About this same time Bob Pond in Attleboro came up with his first Striper Atom. The Atom was and is a big plug. At the time, everyone thought that the plug was too big. It was made of wood, but it was lightweight and relatively hard to cast. Nobody thought it would catch any fish at all, but immediately the regulars began to murder bass on it, and it became *the* striper plug.

We used to make modifications in all our lures and the Atom was no exception. We added weight to it and we——
GWR: This is after the war?
Woolner: Right. We were home by then. Anyway, when squid were in the canal, and we needed a red lure yet hated to paint our Atoms red, we'd cut a strip of red rubber, wrap it around the plug and cement it in place. Then when the squid were gone, we'd simply rip the rubber off again. The rubber also gave it additional weight so you could cast the plug a greater distance. Still nobody had the brains to turn the plug around backwards and make it look like a real squid.

That finally happened in 1951 on the beach at North Truro. Leo Perry from Worcester was out fishing with Arnold Laine and Bill Walton, who is still with us in the MBBA. Perry was tinkering, and he decided he was going to make a plug that looked just like a squid. So he took a wooden plug, turned it around and rigged it so the lure would come in tail first with most of the weight in the head. He put a bunch of rubber tentacles on the thing in place of bucktail and, without any hooks on it, he showed it around to the other fellows. Well, naturally they laughed at the God-darn thing. To test it, he put it on the end of his line and cast it out to the bar. First cast,

[209]

stripers came up from everywhere, trying to swallow the lure! Perry reeled it in like mad and spent a few feverish, fumbling minutes trying to get hooks into the plug. When he finished, the bass were still waiting, and he caught a nice bunch of fish.

Everybody then began experimenting with turned-around plugs. Since wood was so manageable, everybody worked with wooden lures. But Bill Walton decided to reverse one of the new amber plastic Atoms that Pond was manufacturing.

Bill took the lip off the lure, turned it around backwards, screwed a hole through the tail, and strung it. It cast and worked beautifully. Arnold Laine then looked at it and decided that it would do even better if it had more weight up forward. So they drilled two holes there. Since the lure is merely three hollow compartments fused together, the nose area filled with water and provided extra weight. Where the plug had worked beautifully before, now it was absolutely gorgeous! You merely cast it out and reeled it in as quick as you could turn the handle, and the stripers went beserk, breaking all over it!

Not long after this Reverse Atom design became popular and Bob Pond actually began to manufacture them that way, Bob came into my office and laid a few out across my desk. He told me that with the advent of the Reverse Atom, his business was at last out of the red— first time since he started making tackle.

There were many other good New England tackle manufacturers. Charlie Murat from Rhode Island, for example, put out some fine saltwater plugs starting in the mid-40's. And Stan Gibbs down on Buzzards Bay began to produce his own line about the same time. Stan is still making plugs, and some of his early plugs are still awfully good lures. His first was called the Castalure. And the Castalure is nothing more than a broomstick.

GWR: Literally, a broomstick?

Woolner: That's what we called them. Essentially they're a surface popper. The lure has a diagonal cut in the head, a weighted tail, and it swims. It cast a mile, and it caught fish. You actually could—and we did—make these out of broomsticks. Stan Gibbs simply made a more sophisticated version. He's always made great lures, but the problem is you have to be a real fisherman to successfully use some of his models. Take his Pencil Popper series, for instance—one of the greatest lures in the world for striped bass. Yet if you don't know how to use them, you'll never catch a fish. They have to be worked so they fishtail through the water. If you merely retrieve them as you would a swimming plug, the Pencil Popper comes in like a stick of wood. It takes a little experience to get the retrieve down just right.

[210]

Same with rigged eels. Here's a bait—yet not a bait—whose success depends entirely on how it's retrieved. All of us in the 40's and 50's kept a jug of eels somewhere in our buggy, and they always stunk like hell! But it was a good smell to us, because under the right conditions at night and with an educated retrieve, a rigged eel was unmitigated murder on bass.

When you cast out an eel after fishing other lures, it always felt like there was absolutely nothing on the end of your line. It slithered through the water as easily as when it was alive. But what you'd do is pump on your retrieve so the eel would swim forward, then settle back with a sinuous movement, then swim forward again, and so on. The bass would always clobber you on the drop-back.

GWR: Did you ever fish live eels?

Woolner: Yes. But not so much from the beach. We rig dead eels on two or three hooks depending on whether we're after a world's record or out for meat. Three hooks for one bait are prohibited by International Game Fish Association rules, but they do improve your odds for landing a fish once you're tied into him. Live eels are usually fished with a single hook placed through the nose, or in the eye socket and out the gills.

Another popular eel rig developed in New England after the war was the whistle-and-eel. The whistle was nothing but a piece of ⅝-inch copper tubing, flattened on one end, looking a little like a policeman's whistle, and attached to the head of a strung eel. The whistle gave the eel a diving plane and a little weight. When Al Reinfelder brought out his Alou eel, I took one look and told Al that he had created a "whistle" using an artificial eel. Being from New York, he didn't know what I was talking about. He'd never seen a whistle in his life. His lure had been patterned after the old squid-eel used on Long Island decades ago.

Today, Alou, Burke, and other plastic substitutes have just about put real eels out of business as striper baits. But there're still a few old-timers who insist that the bass can smell a true eel and therefore real eels are just so much more effective than imitations that they'll stick to their smelly jars of the real McCoy!

GWR: You test a lot of lures from many different manufacturers. During the past two decades, have you seen an overall improvement in quality? Or can most of what comes across your desk be categorized as junk?

Woolner: There's still a lot of junk. But gradually, knowledge and sophistication about saltwater requirements has percolated through the ranks of all the major tackle manufacturers. Creek Chub was one

[211]

of the first big firms with good lures. Now a number of other companies—East and West coasts—produce quality artificial lures for ocean angling.

Of course, you still get products designed by someone with a slide rule and no angling experience. Every year, I'm still sent lures that can't even swim, much less cast well. But overall, I think the proportion of these computer-designed lures is falling off.

GWR: Is there much interest in fly fishing in the surf, or is this too impractical?

Woolner: If you've got fish right in the surf—right in the suds—a saltwater fly or popping bug can be deadly. And I've caught as many striped bass on fly tackle in the surf as I've caught in rivers and along sod banks. But it's probably better sense to concentrate your fly fishing on tidal canals because there your tackle is more appropriate to the setting. Better yet, saltwater fly fishing is tops from a boat casting to the shore. It's just because I won't go anywhere in my beach buggy without a fly rod that I've gotten so many stripers in the surf over the past dozen summers. And if the fish are close where you can see them schooling and chasing bait, that's your time for fly tackle.

A fly rod can be a very powerful weapon on small bass. And when I say a small bass, I mean anything under 10 pounds. I've caught a good many six-pound stripers on fly rods, and, with a beefed-up tippet of 12-pound test, I've landed fish up to as many pounds. But I've never in my life even hooked a striper over 20 pounds on a fly rod.

I had a very big striper once swirl after a large divided-wing fly, but he didn't come back. And this is your basic problem with getting big East Coast bass on a fly. Mostly the fly is a school-fish lure. The small stripers are in all likelihood chasing a two-inch spearing when your two-inch fly drops in front of them. It's perfect! But except for a rare fish, you just can't interest a 30-pound striped bass in a two-inch lure when he's prowling around for one-pound mackerel or squid. And once you start making flies six and eight inches long, you've got an unwieldly lure that can't be cast worth a damn. But there're exceptions: West Coast fly fishermen are less worried about fly size than we are because their big bass often feed on very small bait.

Another problem with fly fishing in saltwater is that often you can't cast far enough to get your fly over the fish before they see you and go down. A great fly caster can grind out a hundred feet of line. But in all too many cases, that's still not enough.

A final drawback to fly tackle in saltwater is speed—or, rather, the lack of it—when retrieving the fly. No matter how fast you strip in line, many, many times it will be far too slow for, say, a bluefish on the attack. They'll charge in after the lure, then sheer away with something like disappointment when they realize how slow it's moving. You can't pull a fly away from any saltwater gamefish, no matter how fast you strip, so, of course, you lose their interest. This can be frustrating sport when your less-pure brethren are standing alongside you and clobbering the fish on spinning or revolving spool gear.

GWR: In essence, then, you don't think fly fishing will revolutionize the sport the way spinning has done?

Woolner: Right. But I do see a trend in the way the revolving spool is making a comeback among our more experienced surf fisherman. Spinning is delightful, and it recruited a legion of surf anglers who might not have had the patience to master the revolving spool. But your regular surf fisherman knows that spinning has its limitations. Then a few other anglers are turning to revolving spools because they want to recapture the flavor of the old-time sport.

The truth is that when fishing the high surf[5] with heavy lures, there's nothing that can touch the traditional squidding—or revolving spool—reel and rod. They're still areas where spinning rods and reels have never taken the place of conventional outfits for heavy work. Along the Outer Banks of North Carolina, for instance, surf fishermen need a long cast, and over the years, they've learned the efficiency of revolving spools on big sticks. Then, too, reel manufacturers have yet to develop a spinning reel drag as sure and efficient as the revolving spool's star drag. Once you learn how to handle a revolving spool, you have greater control under more different circumstances than you do with a spinning reel. It's good to see this traditional—or what we call up here, conventional—tackle making a comeback.

GWR: One last question, Frank: Do you have any special memories of surf fishing—any days or nights when fishing seemed to be about as good as anyone could ask?

Woolner: All my best memories merge into one retrospect of surf fishing as the highest kind of excitement the ocean can give. I've always felt that the difference between freshwater fishing and saltwater fishing is the difference between tranquility and fury. Saltwater angling is a furious game. Sure you find days on the ocean when it's like silk, and there's no wind. (But then the flies will bite hell out of you!) But mostly you have a breaking surf, and the wind whistling round your ears, and birds screaming overhead. It's furious sport!

If you're surf fishing, true surf fishing, you're wading the suds. And every now and then, you're going to get knocked down. You're always trying to wade out a little further for a longer cast, and suddenly a wave comes at you from the wrong direction and knocks you under.

---

[5]A term coined by Woolner many years ago to designate big open ocean surf as differing from the mild wash of sheltered bays.

[213]

So you wade in until you're over your waders and completely soaked. Then you come ashore, dump the water out of your waders, and wade back in again.

I remember a night on Nauset Beach with my kid brother, Dick, when we walked all alone down to a rock pile fairly close to Nauset Inlet. It was a black night with heavy surf rolling in, glowing like a wall of white in the darkness. Dick and I separated, and I went down to the water, made one cast and was suddenly picked up by a huge wave that came from nowhere and deposited me in a lump well up on the beach. Well, I got up and wandered over to Dick to see if that wave had gotten him, too. And he was just picking himself up, spitting out water. Well, those things happen. And after a little joking about it—to build up our courage again, I suppose—we went back into the surf. And we caught fish that night. We caught a lot of fish. It was like combat all night long! But that's the way the surf fisherman likes it. That's the soul of the sport.

FOURTEEN

MR. TIPSTER

"I wonder why there're three classes of tickets on an excursion fishing boat?" queried the tenderfoot, who had a third-class ticket.

Just then the anchor went down and the Captain sang out: "First class fishes; second class baits hooks; third class cleans fish!"—Nineteenth-century story of Sheepshead Bay

In the realm of outdoor writing, there are a handful of reporters who specialize in tips, hints, and columns devoted to the nuts and bolts of saltwater angling. Some of these writers have acquired large fan clubs of ordinary fishermen who regularly buy a given outdoor magazine or newspaper just to keep in touch with what their favorite columnist has to say about the sport. George Heinold, Mark Sosin, and Charles Waterman are names of such columnists that readily spring to mind.

Yet if I had to pick one name that stands out above all the rest as the "Mr. Tipster" of saltwater angling—the one man who has devoted his outdoor career to turning a host of eager amateurs into experts like himself—that name would be Vlad Evanoff.

I visited Vlad in his winter home at Pompano Beach, Florida.[1]

---

[1]Vlad has since moved and now lives in Fort Lauderdale.

Turning west from the strip of motels, gas stations, and instant eateries that Route 1 has become between Miami and Palm Beach, I entered a residential development of ranch-style homes planted with coffee and banana trees and other exotic flora. When the cold winds of fall send their first snow flurries across the lawn of Vlad's summer place near Belfast, Maine, he packs up his typewriter and drawing board and heads south. As he puts it, "I go from codfish to kingfish in less than 24 hours."

It is not warmth alone that Vlad values in his Florida setting. He feels that the light is better—truer—for the oil painting of marine game fishes and seascapes he has taken such an interest in during recent years.[2] Indeed, one of the reasons for Vlad's success in outdoor writing has been his talent for art and design. Unlike most of his contemporaries who are limited to the camera, Vlad frequently uses drawings to illustrate his tips and notions. "And drawing can be twice as effective as photography if you're really out to teach someone something," he observes.

The son of Russian immigrants who settled in New York City, Vlad was born on December 12, 1916. His father was a talented craftsman, like Vlad himself, who owned a musical instrument store on the Lower East Side that specialized in the manufacture and repair of accordions. ("My father was one of the top accordion tuners in the country," Vlad proudly recalls.)

However, while Evanoff's sister learned to play the instrument, Vlad never did. ("I was always more interested in the visual arts," he says. "And fishing.")

The Evanoff children got their first taste of the sport when their father took them fishing off Steeplechase Pier in Brooklyn. While an auspicious start for Vlad's saltwater career to follow, ironically, after this initial taste of brine, most of Vlad's adolescent experiences in angling were in fresh water.

"I used to work for the Schaefer Brewing Company in their booths at the outdoor shows in Madison Square Garden, and frequently when people found out that I was born in Manhattan and brought up in Brooklyn, they turned sarcastic and asked how could I know so much about fish, fishing, and natural history if I was brought up in the city. They figured the only real fisherman had to be a country boy.

"Well, I was a *part-time* country boy. My father arranged his business to have two months off every summer in order to take us all out

---

[2]Evanoff's major works regularly sell for $1,000 or more.

to the country to live on farms. And I learned a lot about fishing on those summer holidays."

GWR: Where were these farms?
Evanoff: New Jersey, Connecticut, and Pennsylvania. They were mostly owned by Russian or Polish immigrants like my parents. Today, a lot of that country I knew as a kid has been lost to roads and subdivisions.
GWR: What kind of fish would you catch?
Evanoff: That depended on where I spent the summer. Everything from trout to sunfish on cane poles to capturing suckers with our bare hands. So you see, I really had a most conventional upbringing in terms of outdoor exposure.

Evanoff went to Textile High, a secondary trade school in Manhattan, where he studied advertising art and design. And he attended Cooper Union night school for three years to acquire a background in drawing and painting.

Following school, and for six years before the outbreak of World War II, he worked as an artist in a variety of display houses and advertising agencies. ("I might still be in advertising, but going into uniform changed things for me—and for a lot of others, too.")

Vlad was drafted into the engineers in 1941, and for the next four years, the only "fishing" available to him was dynamiting North African canals for fresh fish for the mess, netting mullet in Sicily, and finally some honest trout fishing in the mountain streams of Italy.

When he got out of the Army, he found that the display house he had been working for before the war had closed down. So he made ends meet with free-lance art for comic books and occasional layout and lettering jobs in advertising. Then he decided to supplement this meager income by writing:

"I'd never done any writing, and I didn't know where to start. I only knew that to be good, you had to write about something you knew about. So my first book was about surf fishing. Since I had no previous writing credits and no particular connections in the publishing world, I did it the hard way—wrote the entire book on speculation. But I figured that if I did all my own illustrations, that would help sell the book. Anyway, I knew only one publisher who was also a bonafide fisherman, so I sent my manuscript to William Schaldach at A. S. Barnes in New York City. And he accepted it right off."

That first success was in 1948. Since then, Vlad has published more

[217]

than a dozen outdoor titles, most recently his extremely successful *1001 Fishing Tips and Tricks* and *Another 1001 Fishing Tips and Tricks*.

But let's back up a bit and hear how Vlad first got into saltwater fishing on his own:

"I was still in school at the time, and during the Depression, my family didn't have a car. So I'd go with a schoolmate or two by subway out to Coney Island to fish for whiting in winter or blackfish in the spring.

"Some of those winter expeditions got pretty chilly, and one night in December a bunch of us got trapped by the tide out on the end of a jetty. We found the highest rock we could stand on, yet the water still came up to our waists. We were really in a bad fix. Of course, we lost most of our fishing tackle, but we stuck it out, and after about four hours of standing in that freezing, surging water, the tide went down enough for us to get off. We didn't wear waders in those days, and with just street shoes and wool socks, my legs became so numb from the cold that I had a little trouble walking at first. But we all went back to the city that night by subway and the next day we all showed up at school. There wasn't even a runny nose in the bunch!

"I also started doing a little party-boat fishing out of Sheepshead Bay about the time I finished school. This was mostly bottom bouncing for sea bass, fluke, and porgy on the Tin Can Grounds and Cholera Banks. Bluefish were just beginning to taper off from one of their cyclic peaks, and there just wasn't as much party-boat interest in these fish 40 years ago as there is today.

"I was pretty obsessed with fishing, and I was most excited about surf casting, which was just beginning to grow. There were tackle stores all over the city where fishermen-craftsmen experimented with rod-and-reel designs or gathered in the evenings to talk about where they'd been fishing and what they'd caught. The tackle stores became the headquarters for a number of surf fishing clubs, and my favorite shop was Lou Epstein's down on Orchard Street on the Lower East Side.

"A whole gang of us would hang out there in the evenings and swap fishing tales and information. If you were a newcomer and had a little interest, first thing you knew, you'd be invited to go along on one of the trips to Long Beach or the Rockaways.

"I was still a kid at the time and stood in awe of some of the old-timers. But I had read practically everything I could get my hands on about fishing and thought I knew just about as much as some of them, even if I hadn't lived it. Anyway, one night a bunch asked me to tag along with them, and that's how I got my first real taste of surf casting.

"Every area, every year, has two or three fishermen who stand out—men who come back night after night with big striped bass. These guys are often the ones who do the least talking. And they are usually the ones the others pester for information or secretly follow out at night to see where they're fishing or what kind of lures they're using. William Mertz was one of these New York experts in the late 1930's. I never followed him around—I suppose I was afraid he'd catch me—but I did decide that if someday I could be half the fisherman Mertz was, I'd be something of a hotshot in my own right.

"Surf fishermen are loners. They fish in tight little cliques, and though they depend on one another for transportation and occasional companionship, they really prefer to fish alone once they reach the beach. Party-boat crowds just aren't their cup of tea.

"When I first began going out to the Island in the late Thirties, we'd get a group together in one car to save on expenses. Once we got there, you'd fish with a buddy or by yourself, but in either case, the entire night sometimes would pass without your speaking to another soul.

"We used miner's lamps, worn around our necks to signal to friends on other jetties. If you were close enough, you'd whistle when you got a fish or needed assistance. But generally we used a whole series of flashing signals to ask the other fellow how he was doing, to tell him you had a fish, or to call for help.

"It wasn't easy surf fishing in the Thirties because striped bass were very scarce, and we had only weakfish to rely on. We sometimes got tiderunners up to 10 pounds off the breakwater at Atlantic Beach or off the jetties at Rockaway.

"We fished bait more than we do today, and our only artificial lures were block tin squids we'd polish up with steel wool and wooden muskie or tarpon plugs made by Heddon. I preferred casting lures to bait fishing just because I'm such a restless cuss. Besides, it gave me a feeling that I was actually covering the area. I've seen a lure caster take fish from a point surrounded by bait fishermen too many times to feel that soaking a bait is the best way to get results. Frequently, a buddy and I would work out a pattern of attack: We'd take alternating jetties, and bypass one another as we fished along the shore. Once you've made a dozen casts into all the likely fishing zones, you're better off moving to another jetty. Though we doubtless missed a few fish doing it this way, we still skimmed the cream night after night and generally came home with more fish than the more methodical fishermen."

GWR: Do you remember your first striped bass?
Evanoff: Yes, I do. I caught it off Sea Gate in lower New York Bay. I caught it on a lure I had made from a plug body I had bought in the tackle store on Orchard Street. I painted the lure myself, put hooks on it, and then went out to Sea Gate, made a few casts, and—splash!— I got a striper weighing about 3½ pounds. Boy, was I on Cloud Nine! That was the first fish I ever actually took on an artificial from a beach. But the first fish I ever caught on an artificial lure was a bluefish. That happened about the same time as the striper incident. I used to fish off the Rockaway Point breakwater with clam baits for blackfish and porgy. One evening just before dark, I thought I'd make a few casts before going home, using a small metal sand-eel squid I had stored in the bottom of my tackle box. Same thing, I'd made just a few casts when—smash!—I hooked a three-pound bluefish. After these two experiences, I knew I was hooked on artificial lures and shore casting.
GWR: Did you ever fish anywhere else along the coast before going into uniform?
Evanoff: Yes. Just before I was drafted in 1941. I made a memorable trip down to the Outer Banks of North Carolina for channel bass. By that time I had a car, and I was a member of a surf fishing club with 13 members. This was the tail end of the Depression, and it seemed half our club members were out of work. Only a couple of cab drivers and myself had cars. But if the rest of the gang didn't have the money, they all had ample time for fishing. And, of course, their rationale for such recreation was that they were catching their supper. At any rate, I never lacked for companionship on the weekend forays I'd begun to make to places like Asbury Park or Long Branch in New Jersey or Shinnecock Inlet or Montauk on Long Island.

So, in the spring of 1941, we decided to make a trip to North Carolina. We heard that the channel bass, sea trout, and shark fishing was all pretty good in the surf, so I took a week off from work, and a group of us set off.

In those days there were no motels at Hatteras. In fact, there was no hard-surfaced road from Oregon Inlet to Hatteras proper—just sand. So we rented a Model A Ford beach buggy with balloon tires, and off we went. The entire week's rental cost just $24. Today they want $25 a day!

By the time we started out the sun was pretty low, and I was all for setting up camp a little way down the beach and getting a start for the run to Hatteras the next morning. But we had one of those I've-made-the-trip-before-and-I-can-lead-you-there-blindfolded guys aboard who insisted we could make the 40 or 50 mile run to Buxton without any complications—road or no road.

Well, that had to be the worst trip I've ever made in a car! We had all been up the previous night without sleep, and now we started off on this rutted, madcap marathon! First off, we came to a spot where a wooden bridge had been washed out by a new inlet. We tested up and down the shore until we found a place where the water wasn't too deep and we crossed. All in the dark, of course! Next we came to a spot where the road went off in two different directions. We flipped a coin and took off in the "heads" direction. Fortunately, we found out that all these various branches came together again further down the island. It's just that when beach buggies wore deep ruts in one road, drivers would create another. Of course, at night it was difficult to judge which was the better road, and it seemed that whichever one we took was always a disaster. Our Model A was so light that every time we got stuck, three of us would pile out and lift the car up and out to get it started again. Then, because we were afraid to stop once we had it moving again, the three who'd done the lifting would have to run alongside the car and leap in while it was under way. Again, all in the dark! I believe we got stuck 14 times before we made it to Buxton. The only reason we made it at all was because the four of us were youngsters and all in pretty good shape. If I tried the same thing today, I'm sure the trip would kill me!

Naturally, when we got there after midnight the little rooming house in Buxton was closed, and we had to spend the night in an abandoned Coast Guard station. Many of the surf fishermen, even in those days, camped out rather royally on the beach with large tents and other fine equipment. But our motley band from New York had brought barely enough blankets to go around. Yet, complaints aside, the trip turned out to be all we'd hoped for. And I caught my first channel bass.

Twenty years later, Vlad Evanoff made another trip to Hatteras, this time under the auspices of Time, Inc., with the specific mission of catching a large, photogenic channel bass for an article *Life* magazine was doing on "four masters of ocean fishing."[3]

---

[3]William R. duPont Carpenter and Michael Lerner were picked to represent the big-game angling world; Gus Zarkades represented the salmon fishermen of the Pacific Northwest, and Vlad Evanoff, the Atlantic coast surf fishermen. The article appeared in the April 7, 1961, issue of *Life*.

"I was living in Brooklyn at the time and received a letter from Bob Brigham, a *Life* reporter, saying that his magazine had selected me to make a trip to Hatteras for an article on saltwater angling. The letter said that I had been "highly recommended," and *Life* wanted me to come into the city for a preliminary interview. Naturally I was curious, and went to the old RCA building where *Time-Life* used to have their offices.[4] Brigham talked with me, and while I spent most of the interview trying to dissuade him from the project, he spent most of the interview building my ego.

"First, I suggested other worthy personalities like my friend Jerry Sylvester in Rhode Island, or Captain Bernie Ballance[5] down at Hatteras. No, Brigham said; Sylvester is a striper man, and Ballance may be death on channel bass, but your background encompasses both of these fish and more.

"Then I argued that it was fast approaching April and that there was barely time to catch the season at Hatteras. Besides, I was working on a book deadline and wouldn't have time to go.

"Again Brigham was persuasive—pointing out that if I wanted to sell many copies of my book, a story about the author in *Life* magazine would help sales. And as for the shortness of time, *Life* was willing to send me out immediately, first class, all expenses paid, to fish Cape Hatteras until I had my channel bass. They insisted that the fish must be a good one and caught by myself. They wouldn't pose me with any commercially caught fish or try to fake the fishing. And I suppose this is what persuaded me. I dislike faked shots and feel they're a crime against the profession of outdoor writing. The fact that *Life* would spare no expense to get the photographs of me actually playing and landing my own fish impressed me no end. In fact, Brigham said that he was determined that I catch a fish, because there'd be no story without one!

"Well, Brigham and Jerry Cooke, the photographer, flew down with me, and we checked into a motel and rented a jeep for a whole week—just to be safe. Yet the trip went off as if channel bass were paid members of the Magazine Guild! I caught a 52-pounder the first day, and a 32-pounder—for backup—the second day. We wrapped up the story in 48 hours and the two *Life* men took off. Jerry had been a little bored with the outing and was obviously delighted to get back to the

---

[4]Time, Inc., is now located in their own building on Sixth Avenue.

[5]Bernice R. Ballance once held the all-tackle channel bass record at 75½ pounds.

[222]

city. I tried to persuade Bob to stay around for another day or two of bluefishing, but he had to fly back to interview Elizabeth Taylor."

GWR: You mean he abandoned you and the bluefishing merely to interview some actress?

Evanoff: I know it's hard to believe, but that's what happened. But then neither of those guys was a real fisherman. The weather was chilly, and it gets pretty raw down there in April, and I think they preferred their apartments back in the city.

GWR: Vlad, you make that 52-pounder sound effortless. It couldn't have been as easy as merely making the trip down there and catching the fish to order. What's the full story?

Evanoff: Well, when we first arrived at Hatteras, I made a beeline to the beach and looked for Bernie Ballance. I found him fishing with two other anglers, and not one of them had a channel bass. They told me the classic: "You should have been here a couple of days ago, cause nothing's been doing since."

Next morning we got down to the beach at 9 A.M. Channel bass feed best on the top half of a rising tide, and just at the start of the out-going. There was not much point in getting out any earlier. It had been blowing for the past couple of days, and this was most likely what had dampened the fishing. That first morning out, the wind had moderated and the sky was clear, but the surf was still rough and dirty. As far as I'm concerned, that type of surf is always less than ideal for fishing. But then we had the story to do for *Life*.

At first I fished with a medium-weight nine-foot conventional surf rod with a standard two-foot wire leader and an 8/0 hook baited with half a mullet fillet. But by the peak of the tide, all I'd caught were two dogfish, a skate, and a small bluefish.

I'd been studying the water and noticed that it was brown until about 250 feet offshore. Even further out, I could see some birds working over baitfish probably chased to the surface by big bluefish. I went back to the jeep and brought out the heavy artillery—a surf rod a little over 11 feet long, capable of handling the heaviest baits or lures. I used a Penn Squidder reel with 200 yards of 36-pound test braided nylon, and I increased the weight of my sinker from four to six ounces.

My first cast landed just beyond the dirty-water line, and when the sinker hit bottom, I reeled up the slack and waited. A few minutes later something picked up the bait and began to move off at a slow but steady speed. When I struck, I felt a solid something living and knew that I was into a big fish.

The minute I hooked it, Jerry Cooke ran down alongside me and

[223]

began shooting pictures. Over and over again, he asked, "What is it? Is this a channel bass?" I was feeling enough pressure already without that! There're a lot of sharks in the surf at Cape Hatteras, and you can never be certain whether what you have on is a big channel bass or a shark until you work the fish in close.

This one acted strong enough to be a good-size shark. He worked me up the beach until I was in the rough, shallow water on the Point itself. And there he pulled me a few feet further into deeper water than I wanted to go—even for the cameraman! Finally, after quite a tug-of-war, I saw a crescent, pinkish tail break water above the suds about 50 feet out and knew that I had a channel bass.

GWR: Did you gaff him?

Evanoff: No. I don't like that. One of the local fishing guides ran down with one, but I waved him away. First of all, there're too many things that can go wrong with a strange gaffer wading around between you and your fish. Secondly, if something does go wrong, I want no one else to blame but myself.

I simply worked the fish in on the roll of the surf and waited for one last big wave to drop him on the sand. A wave will usually sweep the fish right up the beach to you and recede, leaving him high and dry. All I did then was to walk over and pick the bass up—though I'll admit my knees were shaking a little when I finally carried him up to the jeep for the ride back into town.

GWR: You used mullet for bait. Yet you said earlier that fishing with artificial lures was your favorite way to fish the surf. Since you wrote once that the striped bass was your favorite saltwater gamefish, is this preference for stripers over channel bass based on the greater likelihood of taking the striper on an artificial lure?

Evanoff: I think so. There's just so much more satisfaction in having a fish strike a lure than in hooking him after he nudges and fools around with your bait awhile. But let me quickly add that a channel bass can be a good artificial lure fish, too. But he has to be in a school, and then your best fishing for him is from a boat. Put a big Hopkins lure into the middle of a school of channel bass, and you'll have action every bit as solid as the best New England striper fishing. In fact, the afternoon of the day I got my 52-pounder, a big school of channel bass moved in along the beach, and a surf caster caught a 42-pounder on a Hopkins. I used bait because I wanted to be sure of getting a story for *Life.* Once they had their story, I was back down on the beach slinging lures with the best of them!

GWR: You mentioned Jerry Sylvester before, and I remember he wrote a book called *Salt-Water Fishing Is Easy.* Were you a good friend of his?

[224]

Evanoff: Yes, Jerry was a very good friend. And he was also one of the best striped bass fishermen this coast has ever seen. He was born in Maryland toward the end of the last century,[6] and when he was in his early twenties, he got a job in New York City as the chauffeur for the Thomas Ewing family. The Ewings had a summer place at Narragansett, Rhode Island, and Jerry went up there with them and had ample spare time to try the fishing. He became so addicted to striper fishing that he quit working for the Ewings and opened his own tackle shop in Narragansett. Actually Jerry's wife did most of the shop tending while Jerry continued to fish. His wife also kept a record of how many striped bass he caught surf casting, and when he produced that book, the tally was something like 22,000. By the time he died, the figure was close to 30,000.

GWR: What would he do with all the fish he caught?

Evanoff: Sell them. In those days, a lot of us sold our catch to make ends meet. Of course, I don't now, but, on the other hand, I don't have any feelings against those who do. Not long ago in *Salt Water Sportsman* there was an article about people who sold their catches, and the magazine staff received all kinds of angry mail about it. Most of the letters argued that it was good sportsmanship and sound conservation to let any fish go you couldn't actually use yourself. I agree with this. But ultimately, selling or not selling your catch is a matter of conscience. It's a personal thing.

I made such a personal choice many years ago. And though I felt pretty self-righteous for a while, it did me no good to try to convert others who still sold their catches. You can argue with the guy fishing down the beach from you who runs his load of fish into market as soon as the action slows down. But all the talking at him in the world won't change his mind unless you have the law to back you up. And here's the point. Instead of all those angry sportsmen wasting paper and ink writing magazines, why don't they write their state officials and congressmen instead? Here in Florida, the snook is a gamefish. The state figured this fish was more valuable as a tourist attraction and angling resource than it would ever be lying around on crushed ice. Well, that law has just about eliminated the commercial attitude toward the fish, and in another generation folks will be horrified at the thought that anyone ever actually netted snook for the marketplace. The same thing

---

[6]Sylvester was born in Port Deposit, Maryland, in 1896. When he was three months old, his parents took him back to Italy where he was raised on a farm. When he was 16, his family returned to America and settled in Waterbury, Connecticut. Besides *Salt Water Fishing Is Easy*, published in 1956, Sylvester is remembered for a variety of hardware contributions to the sport, most famous of which is his "flap-tail" plug.

could be done with striped bass, except probably too many states, and too many special interests, are involved. No state wants to make a game-fish of one species that another state still catches commercially: that only leads to illicit interstate traffic and sales like rumrunning in the days of Prohibition. —But now, where were we?

GWR: What kind of fishing do you do here and in Maine in the summer time?

Evanoff: In Maine, when I've done a day's work at the typewriter, I enjoy walking down to the shore not far from my house with my spinning rod to catch mackerel. It's amazing how many mackerel there are up there—good-size ones, too—and I don't think I was skunked but two or three times all last season.

In Florida, I like snook fishing best. The snook is a bridge and jetty fish—and a cruiser of shorelines you can catch at night—just like striped bass further north. They'll take lures and they fight well. They're a great gamefish.

GWR: What's your favorite fishing area or state?

Evanoff: Rhode Island. I got to know that coast pretty well by fishing with Sylvester. And the great thing about that state is that once you locate the holes and hiding places along a rocky coast, you can come back week after week, year after year, and take stripers there. With a sandy coast, there's just no way to do this. The underwater landscape is in such constant flux that the sandbar where you took a 20-pounder last week may not even be there next week.

Another reason I love Rhode Island is that I caught my two largest striped bass there—both contest winners.

GWR: You can't leave it hanging there. What's the rest of the story?

Evanoff: I had been going up to Rhode Island for years while I was still living in New York. Sometimes I'd take off a month at a time in September or October just to concentrate on striped bass fishing. Well, one year I went up and found they'd established a state-wide fishing contest with a $2 entry fee and a $500 Savings Bond for the biggest fish. Though I was technically a tourist, I felt I knew every rock and jetty in the Narragansett area and didn't really feel any disadvantage over being from out of state. When I arrived, there were only about four days left in the contest, with a 38-pound striper leading the pack. "Heck, I can do better than that," I decided, and added my two bucks to the till.

While I normally recommend that any man going surf fishing at night take a buddy, there're some nights when you just can't find anyone to go with you. Jerry was busy with the store that week, and the attitude among the rest of the fishermen was the big fish are all gone; this 38-pounder had the contest sewn up! So there was nobody to go with, and I ended up night fishing by myself. First night out I hooked a heavy fellow that cut me off in the rocks. That, by the way, is the disadvantage of fishing a rocky coast: you hook more, but then you lose more, too.

I didn't mention this big fish to anyone, but at least I knew they hadn't all moved out as I had been told. The following night after a squall, I went back there with a rigged eel bait—a whole eel rigged with two hooks—and cast it into that same spot. The result was a 42½-pound striper that won the contest.

Three years later I was up there fishing with a friend, Dick Lema. I had a beach buggy on that trip, and we used to patrol the beaches at night doing well on medium-size stripers and blues. That year the fish leading the contest weighed 47 or 48 pounds, and though I put my entry fee down, I didn't really believe I could do any better. But one night on Charlestown Beach, I again struck a big fish with a rigged eel bait, and when I finally brought it in through the surf, Dick ran down and grabbed the fish by the eyes, spanning the top of the head. He used to be able to gauge a fish's weight accurately that way, and he said, "Vlad, you've got a 50-pounder here!" Well, we could hardly wait until morning! As soon as the weighing station opened, Dick and I were on hand with that fish. Not quite fifty pounds—49½. But it earned me another $500 Savings Bond.

GWR: You seem to have a knack for taking big fish to order. What's the secret?

Evanoff: No one secret. Just a series of guidelines picked up over four decades of angling.

First of all, fall is your best time for big stripers. At least that's when they're least cautious in their feeding. Something in the cooler water temperature triggers an urge to put as much weight on as possible before winter, and even the wisest striped bass becomes vulnerable at that time of year.

Next, don't try to do it all in a weekend. Plan your trip as best you can according to weather and moon cycles, but allot at least a week to get the best advantage from the area you're fishing. Two weeks to a month are just that much better. A weekend may offer some recreation, but it's just too short a time for serious angling.

Obviously, too, get to know your water, your shoreline. A lot of blind casting over an underwater desert is just so much wasted effort.

Next, don't wear yourself down trying to fish impossible circumstances. Fall weather is tricky and can be harsh. When you get a storm surf where the water turns brown with a lot of suspended sand and grit, you might as well go back to the motel and break out the cards. Even though I know it's done, your chances of catching fish in dirty

[227]

water are so slim as to be untenable. That's another reason I recommend a week or more of fishing time; it takes into account the possibility of three or four days of bad weather.

GWR: Why don't the fish feed in a stormy surf? Is it because suspended sand gets in their gills?

Evanoff: No, I think it's because the fish just don't see the lure. Suspended sand alone won't keep stripers out of the surf. But murky water will.

Also, a storm surf usually means a lot of weed and other debris all over your lures and line. Not only is the fishing more hazardous and less productive in a storm, it's a downright nuisance to have to clean off your lure after every cast. I'm not saying you can't catch stripers in the middle of a hurricane; I've done it. It's just not an optimum time for trying.

My last recommendation for surf fishermen is that more of them do more night fishing. Despite all that's been written about how much better surf fishing is at night than by day—despite the average caster's recognition that big stripers which can't be reached by day often move inshore to water just a few feet deep at night—fewer and fewer fishermen, it seems, do their fishing at night. I don't know whether they feel television programs are all that good, or whether they prefer a little less risk to their sport, but I just don't find fishermen on the beach at night like I used to—which is all right by me.

GWR: Have you had any more narrow escapes since that night you and your schoolmates got stranded on a jetty?

Evanoff: Many. Night fishing—particularly night fishing from a jetty —is a dangerous game. As recently as two summers ago, I walked too far out on an exposed sandbar in Maine. Since it was night, I couldn't see clearly what was happening in back of me or exactly how far offshore I was getting. I caught a striper, put him on my stringer, turned around, and found myself surrounded by water. There was just enough moon that night so I could make out the shoreline and know that I was not wading further offshore. For that, I was lucky. My plan was to feel my way back as far as I could, then when I had to swim, cut loose the fish and go as long as I had some air in my waders. It's a funny thing, but until you get in a situation like that, you don't realize how helpless you are with waders on. In high school, I won a medal for swimming and was on the swimming team, but all that means little when weighted down by wet clothes and waders.

But in the end I was lucky. The water was deep for much of the way, but I finally had to swim only a matter of maybe 20 feet. I held on to my rod, and even saved the fish. But I was soaked and cold. Yet that's the risk of fishing at night—alone.

[228]

GWR: How did you get into the business of helpful hints for anglers?

Evanoff: Well, my books of tips are a combination of two columns I did for *Salt Water Sportsman* and the *Jersey Angler News* some years ago. When my book publisher found that many fishermen had cut out these columns and pasted them all together in scrapbooks, it gave them the idea for the hard-cover editions.

GWR: Did you use art in the original columns?

Evanoff: The *Salt Water Sportsman* stuff, yes. Not for the other. However, once we decided to do the book, I supplemented it with a great deal of art.

GWR: How did you come by all these tips and hints? Did you just keep your eyes and ears open while fishing around other people?

Evanoff: It's a little bit of everything. A little research—I've got a considerable file and library of nothing but tips and techniques from all over the world—and a lot of talking to other fishermen. Once people find I'm collecting such information, I even have tips sent to me in the mail.

GWR: Do you plan any more "tipster" books?

Evanoff: Yes. I find short paragraphs and simple illustrations the best way to communicate essential information about the sport. My books can also become a kind of reference how-to library for the average angler.

GWR: Vlad, one last but very difficult question: What attracts you most about saltwater angling?

Evanoff: That's not a difficult question to respond to, but the response is a little difficult to put into words. It's really a matter of feeling. It's how the sea and the sky all combine to enlarge something within you. When you're alone on a beach, you feel both very humble and like a giant. You can do nothing; you can do anything. Seeing the sun set, seeing the fish out there jumping, feeling a fish fighting on the end of your line—these sensations set off an ebb and flow of emotion just like the surge of surf around you.

One of my favorite books is Anne Morrow Lindbergh's *Gift from the Sea*. I think her writing is inspiring because the sea itself is. You can't commercialize the sea. And you can't reduce it to a 90-minute special. The sea is terrible or benign, but always infinite, and the surf fisherman feels this in the marrow of his bones.

FIFTEEN

GULF COAST—YESTERDAY AND TODAY

> The nice thing about coming to Texas is there're
> still more fish here than fishermen.—Overheard
> on the jetty at Port Aransas

National outdoor magazines are always adequately stocked with articles about Florida fishing. And readers see enough stories about angling along the New England and California coasts to make them feel it might be worthwhile to pack a rod next time they visit one of these areas. But until very recently, relatively little appeared in print outside regional publications on the excellent saltwater fishing along the Gulf Coast from the Florida panhandle to the Mexican border.

This lack of material from the Gulf is only partly attributable to those few editors who may never have heard of Aransas Pass or who feel that since they have relatively few readers in Alabama, there is no compelling reason to report on saltwater fishing in that state. Most editors I know are eager, if not downright desperate, for quality writing from and about the Gulf coast to lend support to their claims that their publications are national in scope. When Nim Marsh[1] of *Salt*

---

[1]Nim is now an editor of *National Fisherman*, published in Camden, Maine.

[230]

Water Sportsman heard I was planning a week-long trip along the Texas coast from Galveston to the Mexican border, he specifically asked that I keep an ear to the ground for competent reporters in the realm of saltwater angling.

One of the reasons for my trip was to visit an exception to the rule of limited reporting from the Gulf. Indeed, I decided to profile Curt Carpenter after reading a story of his in *Salt Water Sportsman* that described a fishing trip to Port Isabel with his sons and the changes he observed since fishing that area with his father and grandfather 30 years before.[2]

Curt was born in Port Isabel—the last coastal community in the United States before you reach the Rio Grande and the Mexican border—on June 2, 1929. He, three brothers, and three sisters were reared in a family where their father was both a charter skipper and a commercial fisherman—depending on the state of the economy during any given season. As a youngster, in hours sandwiched between time at school, Curt helped his father haul nets at night for speckled trout[3] or handlines by day for red snapper.

Curt's father, Guy L. Carpenter, first came to South Texas in the early 1920's as a construction worker, laying out and grading the roads for the new town of Point Isabel, later to be changed to Port Isabel. He liked the area, and when his job was done, he decided to stay around. But in those days, if you expected to make a living anywhere along the coast, there was only one type of work available: commercial fishing.

"My dad started out on a small scale—mostly trout and redfish in the bays—and he kept at it until Port Isabel became developed enough and sufficiently well known to support a charter boat business. A wealthy businessman named Bill Pattee moved into town, and my dad went to work for him as one of his guides—running a fast new clinker hull and fishing mainly for sailfish and tarpon."

"Were sailfish really such popular gamefish in Texas before World War II?" I asked.

"Yes. But the men who fished for them were mostly tourists from other parts of the country. The same was true of tarpon. Oh, a few

---

[2]"Return to Mother Bay," in the September 1970 issue of *Salt Water Sportsman*.

[3]Spotted sea trout are known along the Gulf coast as speckled trout; channel bass are called redfish or spot tails; cobia are ling; and snook sometimes become pike. Since the reader will have to accept these colloquialisms if and when he visits the area, I'll use them now so he can get used to them.

Texas men—doctors, lawyers, and the like—fished for tarpon and what we called deep-sea fishes. But the bulk of the anglers who came down to the coast were local ranchers and farmers intent on loading the boat with speckled trout, redfish, and red snapper. About the only difference between what they did for sport and what we did for a living was that they used classy rods and reels."

Curt was just 21 when the Korean War broke out, and after spending six months in California in basic training, he went off to serve in Korea and Japan. It was the first time he had been outside Texas, and the experience opened up a spectrum of new possibilities for him. After the war, instead of returning to commercial fishing, Curt went to work for the telephone company. He still fished, but now his interest was recreation. On his days off, he persuaded his father to take a busman's holiday and go along with him. And it was with special pride that Curt first introduced his dad to the satisfaction of taking bay fish on artificial lures.

The angling was fine, but at work Curt found himself too independent for the structured life of time clocks and office hours. Being brought up as a fisherman is not the best way to learn conformity. Curt quit his job with the telephone company and opened up a service station and garage. Being his own boss agreed with him, but here again, too much time was consumed in detail work that bored the restless young veteran. It was then he decided to try his hand at writing.

"It was an outrageously bold step," Curt recalls. "Here I was the product of a fishing village where we spoke better Spanish than English. But I had contributed some letters to the local paper while I was overseas, and this encouraged me to think I might have some talent. When I first went to the University of Houston on the G.I. Bill, I had been out of high school nine years and didn't even know what to major in. I told them I wanted to write, and they said you probably want to major in journalism, so that was it."

While in school, Curt asked if he could write an outdoor column for the university newspaper, *The Cougar*.

"Texans are nothing if not nuts about hunting and fishing, and I felt a little aggravated that the only sports coverage I saw was of football, baseball, and the other interscholastic specialties. So many newspaper editors appear to be parochial about this kind of thing. Probably more fishermen read any given newspaper than baseball or basketball fans, yet the editorial reasoning says that if it's not a spectator sport—that is, if there's no cost of admission—it's not worth reporting."

[232]

One of the grand old men of outdoor writing, L. A. Wilke,[4] saw Carpenter's work in *The Cougar* and interviewed him on behalf of the Texas Game and Fish Commission. As editor of *Texas Game and Fish*, Wilke, then in his early sixties, was looking for an ultimate successor. Carpenter agreed to come to work for the magazine as a special reporter, and within a matter of years had worked up to assistant editor, associate editor, and, when Wilke retired at age 65, Curt stepped into the editorship—a job he held for four years.

"I finally left when politics took over the old Game and Fish Commission. Industry decided to grab the last shell beds in Galveston Bay —they wanted the shell for construction and road-building projects— and our department opposed the action because the beds were vital to the welfare of the bay's fishery. One man in particular, Howard C. Dodgen, stood in industry's way, and they engineered his firing. One day he had a job; the next day he didn't. Dodgen was the best around. He couldn't be replaced then, and he still hasn't. I began job hunting —rather than be part of the political football game that was being played. It was a disgrace."

Next Curt became editor of *Oklahoma Wildlife*. He went up there to streamline and modernize the format, and he incidentally changed the name to *Outdoors Oklahoma*.

"But politics struck there, too, as it increasingly appears to be doing in all fish and game agencies across the country. These poor wildlife departments are suffering terribly from political pollution. Rather than continue fighting a losing battle, I decided to get out of state work entirely and find a job in private industry where I thought I would be free to write and work for better and more honest conservation."

From Oklahoma, Carpenter drifted to Outdoors Incorporated in Missouri, and he worked part-time for the Braniff Airline Council, which sponsors travel and recreation in South America, and served as an associate editor of the Mercury Motors outdoor magazine. Then he returned to Texas to edit the once-combined *Southern Outdoors and The Gulf Coast Fisherman*.

"When I worked for *Southern Outdoors*, I lived in Seabrook, Texas —right on the shores of East Galveston Bay. It was always so sad to think how great that bay had once been for speckled trout and redfish, and now how badly it's polluted. About the only thing you find

---

[4]Wilke is now in his seventies and still contributes to outdoor magazines. He started his reporting and photography back in the days of powder flash and glass negatives.

in Galveston Bay today are fat and happy mullet—and I mean lots of them! They grow big on all the algae in the bay which, of course, makes it uninhabitable for most other fishes. Oh, you still catch a few trout there. But you're reluctant to eat what you catch."

Today Curt is editor and publisher of *The Lake Livingston Sportsman*, a small newspaper in Livingston, Texas, located some 85 miles north of Houston. And it's here I found him living in a large, rambling, Victorian house with his wife and three boys. While the kids moved in and out of the house on mysterious errands known only to youngsters of any age, Curt and I sat near the tape recorder and talked:

GWR: When you were describing your father before, fishing offshore for sailfish, how far out did he have to go? And did he ever see or bring in any marlin?

Carpenter: Before the Rio Grande was dammed, we used to have the best combination of inshore and offshore sport fishing in the entire country. Marlin? We had an international game fishing tournament at Port Isabel back in the Thirties where you'd see big blue marlin brought in by the ton! There's still good marlin and sailfishing offshore. But it's not like the old days. It never is, I guess. But certainly the Japanese long-liners and Falcon Dam on the Rio Grande have done their share to eliminate the best of our fishing.

GWR: How did the damming hurt the fishing?

Carpenter: In two ways. First, by cutting off the flow of freshwater and nutrients down the Rio Grande into the sea, you eliminated the estaurine values that once gave the area such an abundance of life. Secondly, in the old days, the Rio Grande flowed with considerable force well out into the Gulf of Mexico. Consequently, the blue waters of the Gulf were drawn, as if in a vast eddy, close inshore. With the blue water would come the blue-water gamefish to feed on the shrimp and baitfish swept out by the river. Some days you'd see blue water right off the jetties, and you'd find dolphin and sailfish within a few miles of the beach. Today you have to run out a good 15 or 18 miles before you can find blue water, and the best deep-sea fishing is proportionately further offshore.

GWR: How was tarpon fishing affected by the dam?

Carpenter: In much the same way, except that the results were more quickly noticeable. We used to have tarpon fishing at Port Isabel every bit as good as Aransas had. There's even an area off Port Isabel called the Tarpon Hole. And we still get tarpon there. But it's nothing like

[234]

it was. The killing of the river, pollution, more boats, and more fishing pressure—all this was just too much change and pressure.

Funny thing about tarpon. They seem to be able to take a lot. When about the only other fish you have left in a bay are mullet and catfish, you sometimes see tarpon feeding among them. But then one day the tarpon are gone. Not just for the season but for good.

GWR: What was Port Isabel like as a town before the war?

Carpenter: It was something out of a novel by Mark Twain or John Steinbeck. It was a Texas version of Hannibal, Missouri, or Monterey, California. But it was more like the latter since its pace was linked to the rhythms and seasons of the sea.

Our community was filled with character and characters. Some were Mexicans, some Americans, and some bore names like Chewing Tobacco Bill, Pompano Red, and Pontoon Mack. Take Pontoon Mack, for example. He came to Port Isabel loaded with money. We figured he'd won it in a card game or, perhaps, had stolen it and wanted to live with us to hide out. Anyway, he moved into an old pontoon boat that had been pulled up on shore. The darn thing had its bottom rotted away. But that never bothered Mack. He wasn't planning to go anywhere anyway.

My grandfather was another one of the town's characters. Frank H. Carpenter lived in a kind of retirement. I mean, he didn't have to fish for a living like the rest of us. He'd do a lot of fishing, and he'd always sell the catch, but he did so because he didn't know what else to do with it.

He chewed tobacco and he drank Cokes. He couldn't make it through the day without some of both. He had been a professional cabinet-maker, and he'd still put together a fine cabinet for you if you kept him supplied with conversation, Cokes, and chewing tobacco.

Only trouble with conversation was that he was hard of hearing. In those days we didn't have hearing aids, so we spent a great deal of time shouting at one another. One day I was going to help him catch bait in the Brownsville ship channel. For some reason, shrimp used to congregate there in tremendous numbers, and with very little effort, you could catch all the bait you needed for a week or more. Anyway, my grandad had a penchant for dramatic starts with the cars and boats he owned. He used to rev up the car engine at a stoplight, and then when it changed, pop out the clutch and start off with a bang and jerk. Well, he did the same thing with boats. And that day while I was standing on the stern untying the lines, he yelled back to know if I was all untied. I had just finished—yelled back, "Yes"—and he immediately released the clutch and the boat shot out of the slip. Only

[235]

trouble was, he left me behind in mid-air! After I splashed in and came up, he was already halfway down the channel. And by the time I swam ashore and looked, he was just passing under the old railroad bridge.

That evening when I ran into him, I asked him whether he remembered I was supposed to go with him that day. He said that yes, just about the time he got into the port area, he realized I was no longer aboard. But since he had been traveling up until that time through a relatively narrow channel, and since he knew I swam like a fish, I was either safe ashore or drowned. In either case, there wasn't much he could do. So he figured the best thing to do was just to go on up and get his bait!

GWR: You used to help your father on his boat. What kind of work was that?

Carpenter: I helped haul the deep-water handlines for red snapper and the nets at night for speckled trout. I dreaded the former and loved the latter.

In the old days, all our red snapper fishing was by handline. It was only later that we developed bicycle gear hoists to help us move the line faster and easier. And today, of course, commercial boats use electric winches to get their deep lines in. But when I was a kid we fished half a dozen hooks per line with heavy sinkers, and about the time you'd reach bottom some 200 feet down, it was time to start up again—with the additional weight of several 5- to 10-pound fish. You'd finally get them up, swing 'em inboard, bait up, and go back down again. Some days, by late afternoon, you'd need help to bring your catch up. And when you got back to the dock, you were so bushed, you sometimes didn't even have the strength to protest when the wholesaler offered you less than the fair market value of your catch.

But the fishing I liked best was putting out our 3,600-foot net at night for speckled trout. We'd anchor one end and mark it with a lantern and then we'd run in a great circle and close the net into a corral. We had a great battery light suspended over the water at the stern, and then with the boat hung in the wind or downcurrent, we'd pull in the net, keeping the boat moving along the net with one hand, while plucking trout from the mesh with the other. You developed a knack over many nights to do this work smoothly, and it was my very favorite kind of fishing.

Most of the trout would be caught in the mesh. You'd just grab them by the gills and pull them through and throw them into the fish box behind you. But regularly you'd get a great, yellow-mouthed sow trout—10 pounds or more—too big to get caught by the net. She'd swim ahead of the boat as you retrieved the net, staying just out of arm's reach at the edge of the light, tempting you so that sometimes you lost the rhythm of the retrieve just watching her. When we had almost all the net in, there'd be a flurry of water as we went for her, and as she, of course, made her bid for freedom. About 50 percent of the time she got away.

Then usually on the way in, I'd go to sleep on the coiled nets, soothed by the steady sound and movement of the boat. I'd wake only when the engine was shut down and the boat bumped into the pilings at the dock.

GWR: How did you first get interested in sport fishing?

Carpenter: When I was a youngster, we used to fish entirely with cane poles, enormous cane poles some 25 feet in length. For terminal gear we had a popping cork and a whole shrimp bait. Back then, you'd plan on catching your bait on the way to the fishing grounds—there was just that much of it. Today you talk of pints and quarts of live shrimp; back then we didn't measure anything less than a gallon. We did a lot of chumming with the surplus—taking the shrimp from the bait well and squeezing them a little to stun them so they wouldn't swim off in a hurry. We'd anchor or put out a small anchor so it would drag, slow us down, and stir up the bottom like a school of feeding fish. Then we'd throw out the spare shrimp as far as possible behind the boat. Eventually trout would pick up the scent trail and work their way to within reach of our poles.

But that was the trouble with cane poles. You'd have to wait for the fish to work close enough before you could reach them. When rods and reels were first introduced down here, they were too clumsy and heavy to cast. But after their weight was reduced and when they were built with better proportion and balance, we found we could cast pretty well with them. Then we started using rods and reels to reach the trout on the perimeter of our chum zones, even before they worked up to the back of the boat.

Now if by switching to rods and reels just to get a little more distance we became sport fishermen, while angling with cane poles was not to be classified as sport, so be it. But I assure you, sporting interest —whatever that may mean—was not part of our thinking when we made the switch. It was very simply that there was so much waiting between fish while using cane poles—sometimes we had only 25 or 30 pounds of speckled trout in the boat after an hour's fishing—but after we started using rods and reels, we'd often have four times that amount in the same amount of time.

GWR: How about artificial lures? When and how did you start using those?

Carpenter: Well, again you have a practical, not a "sporting," reason for using artificial lures over natural bait. When your fish are schooling, you catch so many more with artificials simply because you don't have to rebait after every fish. There's no real consideration of the sport involved.

But there *is* a special satisfaction in fishing, especially casting, with lures. It's as though you were really catching the fish, and not the other way around. Big redfish—what we call "bull reds," sometimes weighing 35 pounds—are great excitement on spoons and plug-casting tackle. One of my best memories was getting my dad out with a spin-cast outfit one afternoon and seeing him tie into a huge red. Boy, he loved every minute of it!

GWR: What are your favorite spoons? Colors?

Carpenter: My favorites are the Rex, the Tony Accetta, and the Johnson. By the way, when people talk of the Johnson down here, they mean the Sprite. And since the Sprite is not weedless, I prefer the Rex, which has a single hook and two weed guards. It's a light, wide spoon with a lifelike action on a slow or fast retrieve. But I usually throw my reel into gear even before the spoon hits the water in order to start the lure back as soon as possible.

GWR: You skitter the spoon on the surface?

Carpenter: No. Just under it. But the water is shallow—sometimes little more than a foot. When the spoon crosses a hole—which you can determine by a difference in shading in the water—you let the lure sink and flutter to bottom. Maybe you bounce it around a little to persuade whatever's down there to grab hold. But if you don't have any luck, you whirl it out of there and continue to retrieve at a fast clip to keep the spoon above the thick grass growing on the flats.

In recent years, we've also started using some of the new plastic baits. Red, white, and red-and-white combinations are my favorites. And the darn things not only look like little fish, they have all the action of a live bait fish. Best of all, they outlast our old wooden lures. That is, if you don't lose one to a big red in the meantime.

GWR: Do you ever fish these artificials any other way than casting to schooling fish or into particular holes?

Carpenter: Sure. We also fish sandbars, shell beds, and sunken structures. You anchor downtide and cast your lure up on the bar and work it off as though it was a baitfish being swept out to the larger fish waiting in the deep water down current.

But probably the best way to fish the bays here is to drift. And mostly that's bait fishing. You cover more territory that way, and you can be a little lazier, too. If you get bored, you can also cast about with an artificial. That sometimes picks up the fish just coming into range of your shrimp and piggy fish.

[238]

GWR: Your what?

Carpenter: Piggy fish: a small, saltwater perch that looks something like a freshwater sunfish.

GWR: How about jigs? I would think they'd be quite effective bounced along the bottom.

Carpenter: They are. And in the past several years, they've become very, very popular. Especially with a plastic worm tail. I think we use these lures in a way most fishermen up north have never tried. We fish the worm jigs—as we call these combination jigs and plastic worms —below a conventional popping cork and live shrimp rig.

GWR: How does that work?

Carpenter: The live shrimp is hooked through the horn that projects from the carapace between its eyes. This doesn't injure the shrimp at all, and it keeps the creature in a forward-swimming, head-down position. Then the shrimp is suspended 8 to 12 inches below the cork with a longer leader running to the jig so that it drags on bottom as you drift. Or it hops along whenever you pop the cork. You tie the jig on the bottom leader instead of the other way around, because if you had this system reversed, your shrimp would be gobbled up in no time by the little bottom fish and crabs.

Well, every so often you'll have a fish grab the worm jig first. But mostly trout or redfish take the shrimp bait first. And then while your hooked fish dashes madly about on the end of the line, other fish in the school see the jig dashing madly about behind the hooked fish, and one of them will latch onto the lure. Fish are a little like ladies at a bargain sale: They can't always figure out what's going on, but if they see another one of their kind excited about something that seems to be good, they want to be in on it, too.

GWR: Do you have any other rigs or lures peculiar to the Gulf?

Carpenter: Probably quite a few. We have local manufacturers who make variations of baits you'll find in other parts of the country. But the differences are critical. For some reason, our Gulf fish will take a Gulf variation every time over a national model of the same lure. An example might be the Hump. It's made by Earl Humphreys, which is one reason for its name. The other is that these little one- to five-inch shrimp imitations have a little hump in them just behind the head. These lures look like half a hundred other shrimp lures, but that little hump in the shoulders makes all the difference in the action.

GWR: What would you use the little inch-long Humps for? Small speckled trout?

Carpenter: Not just the small trout. You see, speckled trout shed their teeth from time to time—mostly in the summer. They have fang-like teeth they use for gripping rather than cutting, and they periodic-

[239]

ally drop these to grow new ones—a little like a bird molting. Anyway, they feed less aggressively during these periods of the year when they're growing new teeth, and that's when the little baits worked slowly along the bottom like an injured grass shrimp really tear 'em up.

Then we have a unique mackerel-killing lure known as the Hootie. It's nothing more than strands of nylon or manila line wrapped round with wire—and sometimes with a tiny lead core head—with a 2/0 or 3/0 hook sticking out the middle. The lure is rigged directly to a lightweight wire leader about 12 inches long. Then sometimes a longer or shorter Hootie rig is fixed to the same swivel so you have two lures on the same line. The unequal length of the leaders keeps the hooks separated.

GWR: How is this used?

Carpenter: Merely dragged through the water 50 feet or so astern at six to eight knots. The Hootie is devastating on Spanish mackerel. The Spanish will move right in around the jetties in the fall, and at times you can catch all you'll want in an hour by trolling one Hootie, or a linked pair.

We used to fish two lines apiece with a single Hootie on each. As soon as your first line straightened out, you had a fish on. Well, you dropped back your second line before you retrieved your first line, because by the time your first is ready to go out again, you'd have a fish on your second line. We brought the mackerel up, swung him over a barrel or fish box, and jerked hard. The hook tore through the jaws of the fish, and he dropped into the barrel—we called it "hare-lipping" the mackerel—and the system was the quickest way to get your Hootie back in action again. With two or three people fishing four to six lines, you can imagine that it didn't take long to fill a pair of barrels.

And here again I'm reminded of how things have changed. I know some old-time conservationists don't like to admit there's so much difference between then and now because such an admission implies they haven't done all they could to prevent the worse abuses of Progress. Or maybe they don't want the present generation to get discouraged and give up on the future. But I have a very clear memory of fishing for Spanish mackerel, and very, very often filling our two barrels with fish before noon so that if we wanted to run in, sell the catch, and come out again—if the market would bear the strain—we could do so.

The same holds true for my memories of speckled trout fishing. Some days I'd row back to the docks with the boat so loaded that I prayed the wind didn't come up before I got in, or that a motorboat wouldn't pass to swamp me. Today, you just don't have fishing like that anymore. Oh, there're occasionally outstanding days for a handful of anglers, I suppose. But it's no longer true that a fleet of commercial fishermen can go back to one area, season after season, and fill their boats with fish. I'm sure overfishing—and I mean commercial fishing —may have played a hand in the demise of so much good that's gone from coastal angling. But I know that dams, channel dredging, and pollution played a still larger role.

GWR: When you say "channel dredging," are you talking about the removal of the shell beds?

Carpenter: That's bad. But, no, I was thinking how the digging of the intra-coastal waterway has altered the great bays like Laguna Madre. New tidal patterns and many dead zones in the bays were created by such dredging. I know that creating the channel was good for shipping and commerce, but I can't help believe that in many areas, the channel could have been designed both to accomplish the shipping goals and to minimize environmental damage. For instance, there's an area called the Graveyard next to the channel that runs through the bay just south of Corpus Christi. There's not much tidal exchange there, and the channel about eliminated what little was left. Consequently, during the summer at some low tides, the water used to get so shallow and warm in there that fish were trapped and died by the thousands. The sun beat down, and the water temperature rose with a loss of oxygen. Soon the fish were gasping and floundering at the surface. Most grotesque of all, a law in that particular county prohibited you from going in and netting these fish. So they died. I suppose the gulls benefited. But that was all. It seems to me the channel plan should have been studied in detail—even to making a mock-up model of the bay in that area—before the Corps of Engineers took out the first shovelful of spoil. But, perhaps, the formation of the federal Environmental Protection Agency may do some good. At least *another* canal was recently dredged into the Graveyard to alleviate some of the damage done by the *first* canal.

You know, a good many Texas sportsmen look forward to the occasional hurricanes that sweep our coast. These hurricanes sometimes show more sense than the Corps of Engineers, because they open up inlets where there should be inlets and close them where there shouldn't be. Best of all, these big winds flush much of the pollution from the bays. For a year or two following any one of our big storms, the fishing really improves.

GWR: What are some of the positive things being done for anglers along the Gulf coast that can be applied along the Atlantic or Pacific?

Carpenter: One of the most encouraging trends in recent years has been in the highway department's bridge construction program. While

I'm not always convinced we need new bridges every few years, I am pleased to see in many places where old bridges cross bays and estuaries, the highway people merely take out the center span to permit boat traffic to pass and convert the two remaining ends to fishing piers. Then they put the new bridge on a slight detour road alongside the old.

Another good development is found in the program to pave jetties for fishermen. I think we really have some of the best jetty fishing in the country here, and the tourists—especially the snowbirds who flock down here every winter from the Midwest—really enjoy the pier and jetty facilities. Near Galveston, the Texas City Dike stretches some five miles out into the bay. Someday if they get the bay waters cleaned up, they'll really have some top-notch fishing there!

The jetties are productive because when the fish move along the coast, they come to these obstructions and congregate there to feed, or, perhaps, they're temporarily stymied in their migration. At any rate, the feeding is always better around piled rock than over open sand, and some truly excellent strings of trout and sheepshead are caught off these structures.

GWR: With sheepshead, redfish, speckled trout, and tarpon—you have so many species in common with the Florida Gulf coast, I imagine you must have some pretty good snook fishing, too.

Carpenter: *Had* is the word. When the Brownsville ship channel first opened, we used to get quite a few pike there. But there're not many being caught today. For the very best pike, that is snook, fishing, you want to go to Mexico.

GWR: How are relations with Mexico in regards to fishing? When you were a youngster, do you recall any squabbling between Americans and Mexicans over fishing rights?

Carpenter: No. As I may have indicated, Port Isabel itself was half Mexican. All the commercial men just fished where the best fishing was—regardless which side of the border it was on. There was always plenty for all. Now there're just so many more people, and so many fewer fish, that's where the squabbles come in.

GWR: What other bay fishing do you have down here? How about fluke or flounder?

Carpenter: We have excellent flounder fishing—especially in the fall when the water temperature is dropping and the fish are really trying to pack it away before winter. But flounder are not really great gamefish. We do a lot more gigging for them at night than actual sport fishing.

However, I have had some excellent fun with flounder at Port O'Conner and Port Mansfield on spinning tackle and artificial lures. Especially at the new Padre Island pass at Port Mansfield. You can

[242]

walk along the shoreline and see where the flounder are lying in the shallows. Everything's covered but their eyes and the faintest outline of the fish in the sand. It's quite a trick to spot them. But when you do, you hop a jig across the bottom in front of them and watch them explode from the sand to grab the lure!

It's curious how such ordinary bay fishing builds better memories than any of my best days offshore. But I suppose I associate those deep-sea days with working as a mate or skipper on a charter boat and having to listen to the drunkenness, arguments, and profanity of countless customers. Perhaps, if I'd been wealthier and the patron, rather than the patronized, I would feel differently about it. After all, offshore angling is where an awful lot is happening in fishing today. More and more sportsmen are equipping themselves with fast hulls and electronic gear, and they're going out to the drilling rigs, the artificial reefs, and the ridges and bringing in nice catches of everything from cobia to broadbill swordfish.

GWR: Describe the ridges. Are these something new?

Carpenter: No. Most of them have been known for years. In the days of wooden ships and dead reckoning—when we'd merely set a compass course and run a certain number of hours until we estimated we were over a ridge or reef—we found these hot-spots almost as fast as do the fishermen today with their sophisticated depth recorders, loran, and radios. For example, the East Breaks off Port Aransas has been around a long time. Some of the older snapper fishermen probably went there half a century ago. However, recently a research boat from Texas A & M went out there and found tremendous schools of tuna and billfish, and the publicity put out by the university quickly attracted all kinds of sport fishermen. It was as though the college research ship had in fact discovered the banks. There're similar grounds elsewhere along the Gulf coast: the Choctaw Ridge off the miracle strip of the Florida panhandle, and the South Pass off Louisiana. Both these are now one-day runs in the new high-speed hulls they've developed, while in the old days, fishing these ridges would have been an entire weekend's effort.

GWR: Is most of the offshore fishing outrigger trolling?

Carpenter: Yes. However, kite fishing is becoming popular. Kite baits undeniably get more strikes than outrigger baits. But I don't know why. . . . Incidentally, a very popular bait along this coast, but which doesn't seem to be too well known elsewhere, is the cutlass or ribbonfish. This is a pretty frightening critter with long, fanglike teeth and a tail that is no tail at all. Its chief attraction as a bait is its polished chromelike color. Strips of it make excellent mackerel, dolphin, and marlin lures.

[243]

GWR: Curt, you've been both a commercial fisherman and a sports angler. Do you see any conflict of interest between the two—for yourself or for others?

Carpenter: No, I don't, as long as a man doesn't try to be both at the same time. The basic reason there's conflict is because there're more people and fewer fish—the same reason territorial arguments with our Mexican neighbors crop up. Rather than fighting, however, we should pull together to defeat common ills like mindless development and pollution.

But a man must make a choice between commercial and sport fishing. I heartily disapprove of any sportsman selling his catch in competition with commercial fishermen. The sportsman may use the rationale that he's merely making pin money so he can go on fishing, or that he's doing it so the fish won't be wasted. But it all comes down to the same thing: He's in direct competition with the commercial fisherman.

Now, your commercial man has a license and his life is directed toward bringing in enough fish, day after day, at a fair market price to keep his family going. The sportsman isn't in this situation. I think any sports angler who sells his catch should consider the paradox that a part of his day off from business is spent back in the marketplace which he's allegedly trying to get away from through fishing. In addition, when you add up all the sportsmen who "occasionally" sell their catch, it frequently amounts to tons daily. If I sell 25 pounds of speckled trout, and the next "sportsman" does the same thing, pretty soon, by the time the commercial fisherman comes in with his catch, the price of trout has dropped to nothing, and the fish are wasted anyway. Ultimately, you're driving that commercial man a little nearer to welfare.

I was pretty close to my father as a youngster, and I learned first-hand how rough the routine of a fisherman can be. All his life, my dad pulled anchors and heavy fish off bottom, he rowed and push-poled boats, and because of this his forearms looked like Alley Oop's. In addition to the usual number of cuts, breaks, and fractures, he endured tetanus, double pneumonia, and a black widow's bite. He was a talented guy who could have been a competent plumber, mechanic, or builder. He was great with tools and built all his own boats. He was also a wonderful storyteller. He could have gone into a dozen different professions and done well. But he chose the sea. It was not an easy living. But it was an independent one, and I believe his sons were made better for growing up in it.

GWR: How about your own boys? Do they feel the same way about fishing and the sea as you do?

[244]

Carpenter: They like it, but it's hard for me to determine their feelings. For one thing, my perception is layered over with feelings of disappointment between "what was" and "what is now," and I'm always afraid of destroying a family trip to the coast with a lot of frustrating reminiscences. My boys don't recall that things were better, and they have a perfectly fine time with what's theirs now. But I'm nonetheless haunted by memories of a finer environment and finer fishing. I suppose I'll have to learn to say more pleasant things about the few improvements we've made along the way.

But the most important thing is just to fish with your sons. It's a shared experience that you'll have years and years after they've grown up and moved away. It binds you together. And it teaches a man other values than just materialistic ones. I know this was true of my fishing with Dad. I hope it's the same now with my sons.

There's a little more to add to our Texas chapter. After visiting with Curt, I spent a week on the coast and took a boat through Laguna Madre from Port Aransas to Port Isabel—fishing some of the same areas he had once fished with his dad and granddad, and now fishes with his sons. The country is as wild and beautiful—and in some sections, as spoiled—as Curt described. However, my pilgrimage to the Texas coast was less to visit Curt's old haunts than to track down the history of a marvelous old settlement on the upper end of Mustang Island.

There was a time in America where certain classes of men knew the meaning of the word *leisure*. Prior to World War I, any angler who spent less than two weeks on a fishing trip was considered "uncivilized." Many professional men took off the entire summer to vacation with friends or family at some choice holiday spa where angling was the principal order of business. One of the most popular resorts in the Southwest was a spacious inn located in the quiet Gulfside town of Port Aransas.[5]

The first Tarpon Inn was built in 1886. It burned in 1900, was re-built, and then the second building was demolished by a hurricane in 1919. In 1925, the third Tarpon Inn was built on the site of the previous two, and so it still stands today, little changed by the growth of Port Aransas around about.

In fact, an interesting commentary on the substance of contemporary

---

[5]In one of those strange anomalies of place-naming, the inlet-sited settlement of Aransas became "Port Aransas," while the harbor town on the bay became "Aransas Pass."

American architecture can be made by noting that hurricane Celia in 1970 devastated Mustang Island and swept away many of the recently constructed summer homes and motels. However, the old Coast Guard Station and the Tarpon Inn, relics of the 1920's, stood unscathed.

While I was in town, I met William R. "Bill" Ellis, last member of the family who owned the Tarpon Inn since 1925. He has since sold the hotel to John Miller and now peddles real estate in a lawyer's office just down the street from the inn. However, I persuaded him to guide me through the newly remodeled hotel, and we started with the dining hall where there are mounted specimens of many of the salt-water gamefish of Texas. Then, as we walked along a shaded verandah, Bill told me that in the old days each guide flew his own identifying pennant and that landlubber guests could follow the progress of the day's sport with telescopes from the cupola[6] on the hotel roof. Even if the boat was too far off for the watchers to make out the occupants' faces, the craft's flag, coupled with the splashes of leaping tarpon, told the story.

Clearly, the area of the hotel Bill was most proud of was the reception room, where the walls are covered with countless tarpon scales, dated and signed by the guests who caught the fish. Some of the citations go back to the 1920's. The most interesting ones belong to Franklin Delano Roosevelt, Jr., and other members of his Presidential party when they stayed at the inn in 1937.

I later talked with Don Farley, the skipper who had taken FDR and his group out fishing. Don had been guiding for the Tarpon Inn since 1925, and it was entirely appropriate that this experienced skipper be selected to take out the President's party. Yet when I asked Don whether the assignment had been fun, he was evasive in his reply, saying that it had been a great honor to take the President of the United States fishing.

"But was the President a good fisherman?" I persisted. "Did he enjoy himself?"

"I suppose he enjoyed himself," Don said. "But there wasn't much for me to do."

"Why not?"

"Well," he began, as though uncertain he should tell the whole story, "when I got Roosevelt hooked up with his first tarpon, the fish started cavorting all over the ocean with Roosevelt not knowing step one what to do. He just kept swinging the rod around and yanking it

---

[6]Since removed.

every time the fish came out of the water. I went back to give him some advice on how to pump and reel, but he didn't hear me. He just kept yanking on the rod and shouting to his friends. I thought maybe he was hard of hearing and was about to repeat what I'd said, when one of the Navy captains[7] pulled me to one side and said: 'You can't teach that man anything; he's the President.'

"Well, when I saw that was the situation, I lost interest in the trip. I would have preferred taking out someone willing to learn something about fishing."

"But he and all his party got fish?"

"Oh, sure. In those days, you couldn't miss."

In the old days, a train brought guests from Corpus Christi to Aransas Pass. There the anglers would meet guides from the Tarpon Inn with their boats—usually the very ones with whom they'd be fishing for the duration of their stay—and then be ferried across to the hotel. Tarpon started moving in along the Texas coast in late spring, but the fishing didn't become dependable until early summer. May and June were the prime angling months—not because the fish weren't there in equal numbers in July and August but because the fishermen were not. Despite all the amenities of the Tarpon Inn, many anglers—particularly those from other parts of the country—didn't stay around to celebrate July 4th on the often sultry summer coast.

Tarpon apparently breed near Port Aransas. At least, they once did. Bill Ellis showed me a pair of tiny tarpon—1.9 and 3.9 inches long—that had been caught in a minnow seine in a shore pond in the Aransas National Wildlife Refuge in November 1950. The University of Texas Institute of Marine Science confirmed that these small herringlike creatures were baby tarpon, but there's been no similar capture of young tarpon since.

"Many of the old skippers," Bill told me, "were convinced that the fish used to come up here from Mexico just to breed. But if they did, that's all finished now."

The story I then heard from Bill Ellis was similar to the one Curt Carpenter had told: dammed rivers and dying estuaries, dredged shell bars and polluted grass beds.

"Tarpon are sensitive to noise," Bill added. "And where we once fished for them out of sailboats, rowboats, and then small inboard launches, suddenly there're great numbers of high-powered motorboats and outboards following the tarpon along the beaches, rushing into

---

[7]One of three Naval attachés in the President's retinue.

[247]

the schools and scattering them. Furthermore, I believe these fish are put off by the increased car and truck traffic on the beaches[8] and certainly by the hundreds of bathers. Even before our sand crabs disappeared from the surf, I think the tarpon had been made too skittish by all the splashing bodies to feed close inshore the way they did in the old days."

"Is tarpon angling finished now?"

"Yes," Bill replied. "Come to Port Aransas for our king mackerel runs, for the sailfish and marlin offshore, or for the red snapper and grouper fishing over the reefs. But if you want tarpon, you're better off going to Florida or Central America. We still get a few fish, mind you. But I think these survivors come here out of an ancestral compulsion of some sort. If we gave them half a chance, they'd probably reestablish themselves. But it seems we have fewer every year. If an angler wants assured action nowadays, he's better off going to Honduras or Costa Rica."

Thus the tarpon, the fish that led to the development of angling interest along the Gulf coast, has stepped down from the throne of prominence he occupied for more than 75 years. Despite ongoing tarpon tournaments and rodeos, this species is less important today to the annual angling activities of the Gulf than spotted sea trout in the bays or dolphin offshore. If this giving up of tarpon for dolphin was merely a matter of angling preference—if saltwater fishermen had just decided that leaping *dorado* were more fun to catch than jumping *savanilla*—then there would be no sorrow or shame. But the Silver King's uncrowning was not an abdication; it was assassination.

Tarpon have been eliminated by the abuses of human settlement and industry. And thus, this brief view of Texas fishing becomes more than one or two men's accounts of how it once was and how it is now. It becomes a plea on behalf of more thoughtful change everywhere, and in every context, so that the remaining coastal fisheries will belong to the future as well as today.

---

[8]Mustang Island's beach is firm, hard-packed sand—similar to the one at Daytona Beach, Florida, and just as attractive to drivers.

First Jump

THE GOLDEN YEARS
OF BIG-GAME ANGLING

SIXTEEN

THE LITERARY NATURALIST

A huge marlin had just been hoisted onto the dock at Bimini, and a small crowd of admirers gathered to watch the fish weighed in. A tipsy sailor from a visiting yacht pushed through the crowd, stared incredulously at the fish suspended from the scales, and declared, "The fella who caught that one is a liar!"

Every blue-water angler feels he knows Ernest Hemingway. A celebrity of the sporting world, literature, and three wars, Hemingway's swashbuckling independence appeals to men in a way that the computerized achievements of contemporary heroes like the astronauts never will. He did many different things well. He was self-made, not manufactured. And his chief value to saltwater fishing is that he articulated for every man—angler and nonangler alike—the grandeur of the oceans and the thrill of deep-sea fishing.

While Zane Grey, Kip Farrington, and others wrote about the pursuit of giant fishes, they wrote for the fraternity—for us anglers who know what they mean even when they forget to say it. Hemingway, on the other hand, didn't leave it to our experience or imaginations to fill in the gaps. He wrote for the uninitiated as well as aficionados. As a result, he speaks to all who want to comprehend blue-water angling —those of us who have done it, those who have thought about doing it,

[250]

or those who are merely curious to know why men risk their necks chasing after fish on the high seas:

In the first place, the Gulf Stream and the other great ocean currents are the last wild country there is left. Once you are out of sight of land and of the other boats you are more alone than you can ever be hunting, and the sea is the same as it has been since before men ever went on it in boats.

In a season fishing you will see it oily flat as the becalmed galleons saw it while they drifted to the westward; white-capped with a fresh breeze as they saw it running with the trades; and in high, rolling blue hills, the tops blowing off them like snow as they were punished by it, so that sometimes you will see three great hills of water with your fish jumping from the top of the farthest one and if you tried to make a turn to go with him without picking your chance, one of those breaking crests would roar down in on you with a thousand tons of water....

There is no danger from the fish, but anyone who goes on the sea the year around in a small powerboat does not seek danger. You may be absolutely sure that in a year you will have it without seeking, so you try always to avoid it all you can....

But there is great pleasure in being on the sea, in the unknown wild suddenness of a great fish; in his life and death which he lives for you in an hour while your strength is harnessed to his; and there is satisfaction in conquering this thing which rules the sea it lives in.[1]

Ernest Miller Hemingway was born on July 21, 1899, in Oak Park, Illinois. At age four, he joined the local branch of the Louis Agassiz Club, a nature-study group organized by his father, Dr. Clarence Edmonds ("Ed") Hemingway, and young Ernest proudly maintained this association for many years. At least, he was still an active member in September 1910 when he made his first visit to the sea, a trip to Nantucket Island where, according to his biographer, Carlos Baker, he fished for mackerel and sea bass and from which he shipped home a swordfish bill as a marine specimen for the Agassiz Club collection.

It is interesting to consider small parallels between young Hemingway and Charles Frederick Holder. Both men's fathers were physicians and both boys were shaped by association with Louis Agassiz, although in Hemingway's case, it was in name only. Both Hemingway and Holder had New England antecedents (Hemingway's mother's parents

---

[1]From "On the Blue Water: A Gulf Stream Letter," copyright 1936, Ernest Hemingway. Reprinted with permission of Charles Scribner's Sons.

had lived on Nantucket in the 1880's), and both their fathers were keen outdoorsmen who greatly influenced their sons' outdoor development. Finally, both Hemingway and Holder spent years fishing the Florida Keys with special attention on Key West and the Dry Tortugas.

However, Hemingway's first real angling experiences were in fresh water. His parents owned a summer cottage not far from the town of Petoskey, Michigan, and Hemingway grew up catching trout in the nearby streams and lakes. Years later, not long after *The Old Man and the Sea* was published, Hemingway revisited the area and had dinner with his childhood friend, Edwin "Dutch" Pailthorp. Dutch asked Hemingway whether he would ever come back to live in northern Michigan, and Hemingway—probably thinking how the wild trout of his youth have given way to the spawn of hatcheries, and how the frontier world he grew up in has been tamed by resorts—said, no, that northern Michigan was "too civilized" now.

This anecdote is revealing of much in Hemingway's life, including —indirectly—his love of the sea. While marine aquaculturists have managed to domesticate shrimp and shellfish, they haven't made much progress toward the artificial rearing of the great pelagic fishes. Such creatures require entire oceans for their development, and they are not so easily "managed" as brook or rainbow trout. The contrast between the two environments of fresh water and salt is basic to every angler's preference. Thus, while Hemingway felt *comfortable* fishing fresh water, he felt a *challenge* in fishing the sea.

In 1921, following a stint as an ambulance driver in World War I, his being wounded and convalescing in Italy and back home in Illinois and Michigan, Hemingway married Hadley Richardson and took her off on a honeymoon voyage to Europe. Their ship stopped for four hours at Vigo, Spain. And there in the harbor Hemingway saw six-foot tuna that "leaped clear of the water and fell again with a noise like horses jumping off a dock."

He and his wife then walked the cobblestoned streets of the town to the fish market where they found some of these great fish lying gutted on marble slabs. Anyone good enough to boat a giant tuna, Hemingway decided, should "enter unabashed into the presence of the very elder gods." This brief visit was written up as a column for a Canadian newspaper. And the experience of seeing such huge fish close at hand formed Hemingway's determination to land one for himself on rod and reel.

[252]

The opportunity to do so did not come for many years. The decade of the 1920's was the period in which Hemingway established his reputation as one of America's foremost novelists. The details of this period—his divorce and remarriage, his friendship with F. Scott Fitzgerald and other "lost generation" personalities, and his discovery of bullfighting—are all too well documented to belabor here. Our focus is on the sea and its influence on his life, and this really began in 1928 when he first visited Key West at the insistence of writer-friend John Dos Passos.

Almost at once Hemingway liked the town. He found it an absorbing hideaway where he could make friends with the "Conchs" (local watermen) without the interference of a press agent. He also made the first of many angling expeditions to the Marquesas and the Dry Tortugas. The antique marvel of Fort Jefferson had changed little since the days when Charles Frederick Holder had lived there. Only the quality of boats to get you there and the tackle to use once you arrived had improved, and Hemingway put both to good use catching sailfish in the cobalt depths of the dropoff and wrestling grouper from the reefs. Satisfied with nearly every aspect of the Keys, Hemingway bought his first permanent home there in the spring of 1931.

Set in a deep corner lot planted with sago, date palms, and banyan trees, the house was an 80-year-old Spanish Colonial-styled mansion when Hemingway first saw it, and he had to bring in a team of artisans merely to modernize the place with such amenities as running water and electricity. Today the house is a museum, but with something of a carnival flair. Mrs. Bernice Dickson, a local jeweler, bought the house four months after Hemingway's death in 1961 and now charges $1 admission (plus tax) for any tourist who wants to see it. In addition, she sells a variety of alleged Hemingway memorabilia including paving bricks "he may have once walked on." For $5, she will even sell you the Ernest Hemingway Home sign out front. ("You'd be surprised how many of those signs I sell," she confided to *Los Angeles Times* reporter Charles Hillinger.)

But while much of the house's decor may have been introduced since Hemingway's death—including the saltwater fly reel and mounted baby tarpon in his workroom—there is one detail too bizarre in terms of the famous author's popular reputation *not* to be genuine. Over the window seat in the workroom and permanently set in the wall is a cast of fish fossils—in part a reminder of his youthful days in the Agassiz

[253]

Club and in part an echo of the man who, although one of the world's great storytellers, was also a serious marine naturalist.

In 1932, Hemingway made his first visit to Cuba with Joe Russell, owner of Key West's Sloppy Joe's Bar, in Russell's 32-foot cabin cruiser, the *Anita*. Hemingway not only discovered Cuba, he discovered marlin. In 1935, Eugene V. Connett asked Hemingway to make a contribution to *American Big Game Fishing*—a sumptuous book published in Great Britain for the Derrydale Press and limited to 950 copies in its first, elegantly printed edition. All the artwork was provided by Lynn Bogue Hunt, and its various chapters were written by such angling experts as Van Campen Heilner, Charles Lehmann, Dave Newell, Otto Scheer, Kip Farrington, and George C. Thomas III. Payment was modest— some $75 for each author—but Hemingway viewed his chapter entitled "Marlin off Cuba" less in terms of his usual writer rates than as a contribution to science.

It is amazing how much Hemingway learned about marlin in the three brief seasons since he had caught his first one. He devoted himself to absorbing all he could about the fish with the same fervor that he had earlier approached the study of bullfighting or the craft of writing itself. He was aided in his marlin studies by a commercial fisherman named Carlos Gutiérrez and H. L. Woodward, Cuba's pioneer sports angler.

Woodward began his saltwater career in 1915, and by 1921, he had taken his first marlin from the Gulf Stream. He thereafter averaged some six or seven marlin a year, and by 1934, when Hemingway first fished with him, Woodward had caught between 75 and 100 of these great gamefish, including a 459-pounder.

However, in just three years, Hemingway had outdistanced the older man. In 1932, during his first visit to Cuba, Hemingway boated 19 fish; in 1933, during his second visit, he caught 34; and in 1934, he not only caught more marlin than during the previous season, he invited Charles M. B. Cadwalader, director of the Academy of Natural Sciences in Philadelphia, and Henry W. Fowler, the academy's chief ichthyologist, to spend the month of August fishing with him.

The scientists took pictures of every aspect of marlin fishing, from preparing the bait to gaffing and weighing the fish. (Hemingway used some of these pictures to illustrate his chapter for *American Big Game Fishing*.) They also dissected; took weights and measurements; made notes on wind, ocean temperature, and tide; and packed many specimens back to Philadelphia for mounting or further study. Hemingway looked over their shoulders every step of the way and supplemented their observations with those of his own.

Thus Hemingway's 26-page thesis on marlin fishing is less a manual on how to catch the fish than a complete natural history of their breeding and feeding habits, migration patterns, and incidental peculiarities—complete with two maps illustrating the marlin's distribution off Cuba and its distribution worldwide. Except for the fact that his classification of the different species does not jibe with modern classifications (but then ichthyologists still have problems classifying the various billfishes), the text of "Marlin Off Cuba" is instructive reading for today's students of marine science. The thoroughness of Hemingway's research, and the variety and interest of details couched in his lucid prose, make this chapter one of the most satisfying monographs ever written on a fish. Ultimately, "Marlin Off Cuba" is Hemingway's most notable offering to the memory of Louis Agassiz and his own naturalist father.[2]

In 1935, Hemingway made his first trip to Bimini. How he first heard about this island in the Stream is an interesting story in itself. Captain R. William ("Bill") Fagen, who is one of the grand old guides of Atlantic charter fishing, has this memory of his first encounter with the famous author:

I met Ernest Hemingway in February of 1929 at Key West after returning from a fishing trip to the Dry Tortugas. . . . I was at the dock cleaning tackle—had two 12/0, two 9/0, down to 1/0 reels, all Vom Hofe. (There were no Fin-Nor in those days.)

I heard a deep voice from the dock say something like, "What the hell do you do with reels that large?"

On looking up, I saw a young guy in torn shorts, no shirt, a beard,[3] and eyes that looked like they were on fire. He asked to come aboard, and I said sure. So he jumped at least 15 feet [down], landed like a cat and said, "Hemingway's the name."[4] He shook my hand and almost broke it. He had a beer and talked nothing but fishing for over two hours. I told him all about the Bimini and Cat Cay areas—that was

---

[2]Dr. Ed Hemingway committed suicide on December 6, 1928.

[3]Although Hemingway experimented with beards in 1930 and again in 1932, in 1929 Bill Fagen only saw a mustache and, possibly, a five-o'clock shadow.

[4]During a personal visit to Fagen's home in Miami's Coconut Grove, Bill told me that after Ernest introduced himself, Fagen thought he looked a little disappointed when the name obviously meant nothing special to him at the time.

where we needed the 12/0s[5]—and how long I had been fishing there.[6]

Hemingway kept in touch with fishing developments off Bimini through regular visits to the Key West docks or to Sloppy Joe's, where the chartermen sometimes came to drink. But he was still too preoccupied with Cuban marlin to pursue rumors of horse mackerel in the Bahamas.

Then marlin were caught off Bimini. The first was brought in on February 28, 1933, by Kip Farrington. It was a small blue—just 155 pounds—but it was, to use Kip's words, "an eye-opener." The marlin *were* there.

The next year, during Hemingway's summer research into the Cuban fishery, still more marlin were taken in the Bahamas. And there continued to be stories about giant tuna that passed the islands in the spring and destroyed everything in the way of tackle put out for them. Some folks even insisted these unknown denizens of the deep were enormous wahoo, or a species of super mackerel entirely new to science. A mystery like this was certainly worthy of Hemingway's time and attention!

His first attempt to get to Bimini was on April 7, 1935. Ernest, artist-friend Mike Strater, John Dos Passos and his wife, Katy, and two crewmen, Albert "Bread" Pinder and "Sacker" Adams, set forth in Hemingway's 38-foot Wheeler, the *Pilar*. They were not far offshore when three fish—a dolphin and two sharks—struck their trolled baits. When Hemingway brought his shark alongside, he gaffed it, held the shark in position with the gaff, and then began pumping bullets into it from a pistol he carried aboard. Suddenly the gaff handle broke. Hemingway lost his balance and shot himself through both legs.

Bread ran the boat back to Key West, and Dos Passos and Strater cleaned the wounds with boiled water and iodine while Hemingway threw up in a bucket. It was not only a painful and humiliating experi-

---

[5]This size was by no means as big as Vom Hofe was going to make reels for the Bimini trade. By 1935, 14/0 and 16/0 reels carrying 72-thread lines were aboard many boats bound for the Caribbean.

[6]From personal correspondence dated February 11, 1971. This probably *was* the first time Hemingway had heard about Bimini. Although Van Campen Heilner first went there in 1921, he was more interested in bonefishing than offshore angling, and it was not until some of the exploratory charters of the mid-1920's—frequently linked to the rum-running trade of the islands—that fishermen began to appreciate what a cornucopia of big game resided in Bimini's offshore waters.

ence but, for a superstitious Hemingway, a bad omen regarding his destination.

A week later they tried again with Charles Thompson (see footnote page 11) standing in for Mike Strater. When they reached Bimini, Hemingway's superstitious fear faded away, for the island was everything he had hoped it to be: primitive, desolate, and breathtakingly beautiful. Yet the tuna *were* hard to get. Not hard to hook, but hard to hold and hard to land before any of the abundant sharks reduced your catch to head, tail, and bones. Hemingway's first big tuna was so mutilated, and then Mike Strater,[7] despite (or because of) Ernest's assistance with a Thompson submachine gun, had a 12-foot marlin cut to pieces by sharks. The remains of this fish weighed 500 pounds, and the incident deeply impressed Hemingway. Not only was the fish a splendid record-breaker-that-might-have-been, but even in its mangled form, it outweighed Hemingway's Cuban record of 468 pounds. He still loved Cuba (and would one day live there), but the fact that huge marlin, as well as big tuna, could be found off the Bahamas' banks made him an angling devotee of the black and British world of Bimini.

Gradually, Hemingway evolved a theory for the successful capture of an unmutilated tuna. From the instant the fish took the bait, he argued, you simply had to fight the animal like there was no tomorrow. He believed that once any fish "understood" that it was dealing with superior force, then the job of landing it became half as hard. This all-or-nothing technique coupled with perseverance finally paid off. Despite several heartbreaking (as well as rod and line breaking) encounters, Hemingway landed the first two tuna—310 and 381 pounds—ever taken off Bimini without losing half the fish to "those murdering bastards," the sharks. Kip Farrington was the second man to break the jinx. Heeding Hemingway's go-for-broke advice, he brought three undamaged fish in weighing 330, 400, and 542 pounds. Most exciting of all, the fish could now be positively identified: They were *not* giant wahoo!

Years later, when Kip's wife, Chisie, became the first woman to catch a broadbill swordfish off the South American coast, Hemingway cabled his congratulations: "Perfection! The real record is to take the first one, because if you catch the biggest fish, someone eventually is going to catch a bigger one."

---

[7]He flew over to join the group in May.

While part of the point of this message may have been to remind Kip of Hemingway's own "first" off Bimini, he did truly view the real records in angling—as in hunting, hiking, or anything else—as belonging to those people who have done something before anyone else did it. When Hemingway fans tried to credit him with the largest sailfish ever caught in the Atlantic, he was quick to point out that the 119½-pounder had only been played and landed by him—Thomas J. S. McGrath had actually hooked it. Therefore, under IGFA rules, the fish was an illegal entry.[8] Today that would-have-been record has been broken several times, most recently by a 141-pounder caught off the east coast of Africa by Tony Burnand. This record in turn will probably be toppled one day. But Hemingway's bringing the first whole tuna into Bimini—while somewhat esoteric in category—is nonetheless unbeatable.

The spring of 1936 was even more exciting and glamorous in Bimini than the previous year. Tommy Shevlin, whom Ernest looked upon as a protégé since he had "advised" him about how to catch his 636-pound Atlantic blue marlin record of the previous year, was back with his wife, Lorraine. The Michael Lerners were there, along with the Kip Farringtons and the Nonie Briggses, another keen angling pair. There were even interesting spectators like novelist Marjorie Kinnan Rawlings (*The Yearling*) who was a guest aboard Mrs. Oliver C. Grinnell's yacht. Mrs. Grinnell, whose husband caught the first broadbill swordfish on rod and reel in the Atlantic, was an outstanding anglerette. Five years previous, she had followed in her husband's footsteps and become the first *woman* to take a broadbill in the Atlantic. She also contributed the introduction (and possibly some of the financing) to Connett's *American Big Game Fishing*.

If there was ever a Golden Era in big-game angling, the years of the mid-1930's were it. The tackle and boats in use from Nova Scotia to the Bahamas were not as sophisticated as those developed after World War II to hunt the giant marlin off Peru, but then the spirit of angling was less single-minded and mechanistic, and consequently more adventurous. Every day some new, often amazing, thing was learned about the world of deep-water fishes, and the angling areas involved were not yet so remote or so well publicized as to be either impossibly

---

[8]Although this fish was caught on May 23, 1934—five years before the formation of the International Game Fish Association—Hemingway later used the unusual circumstances of its capture to publicize IGFA rules, which rightly insist that all entries for record must be hooked, as well as played, by the angler concerned.

exclusive or downright tacky. Young guides of imagination like Bill Fagen, Sterling "Red" Stuart, the Cass brothers, and Tommy Gifford joined forces on days when they could not get a charter to explore new waters, or to experiment with new knots and new lures, or just to gather on the docks to trade ideas. Men fished from dawn to dusk with the enthusiasm of converts to a new religion. Then they stayed up all night talking about it, knowing that the next day would be even more exciting.

And you did not really have to be rich to participate. Certainly the guides were not. And Hemingway himself had to borrow $3,300 from Arnold Gingrich, publisher of *Esquire*, as an advance against future story sales to that magazine[9] in order to make the down payment on the boat he had fallen in love with in the Wheeler Shipyard catalog. Of course, this was the Depression, and $3,300 was a lot of money. But to borrow such a large amount with no collateral other than the adventure tales that might result from the boat's use was part of the exuberance of this era. While millions of Americans went to MGM musicals to forget hard times, Hemingway and a handful of others simply *ignored* the Depression and went fishing. And certainly Bimini was the kind of place where the only thing you had to fear was not fear itself, but whether you would be able to get a supply of fresh bonefish for the next day's trolling.

Yet even in the Golden Age, extreme competitiveness played its corrosive role as it had earlier at Catalina. Hemingway, for all his generosity, was frequently one of the worse offenders. At heart he knew that luck plays a large role in angling; it's the least satisfactory sport by which you may measure a man's strength or reflexes. But he was a competitive man by nature, and even when there was no one to stand against him, he sometimes turned on himself as his own best adversary.

Marjorie Rawlings recalls the day that Hemingway caught a 514-pound tuna that carried him from Gun Cay to the Issacs and took seven hours to land. Hemingway got "gloriously drunk" on the way in with the fish, and when the *Pilar* docked, he roared around for the visiting nonangler who had said not long previous that tuna fishing was easy. The entire island's population turned out to watch the big fish hoisted up for weighing, and the last anyone saw of Hemingway that night, he was using the tuna for a punching bag.

---

[9]This was no mean feat considering that *Esquire* itself was barely launched, having had its first issue the previous fall of 1933.

Incidentally, the waste of these great fish was something that began to rankle the consciences of a number of sportsmen as early as the 1936 season. The local Bahamians at most took a slab of tuna for dinner or a few sections as bait for their own fishing or as fertilizer for their gardens. Otherwise, the tuna, after being measured and weighed, was towed back out to sea. Occasional sport was had by shooting the sharks that sometimes swarmed after such towed taste treats. But even this "use" only aggravated the anxious feelings some anglers had about the waste of such fine gamefish. By the time the Cat Cay Tournament began in 1939, there were objections by a few pressmen and other observers about the "conspicuous consumption" of such a great resource. Some 42 anglers brought in 93,000 pounds of tuna, all of which were used for shark bait or otherwise wasted. To alleviate this criticism, a freezer ship was brought over from Miami to stand by during a later tournament in order to take aboard butchered fish after they had been weighed and entered in the contest. The frozen tuna were then taken back to Miami and distributed to orphanages, hospitals, and the like. For some reason or other, this plan did not work out. The situation was still so bad after the war, I can recall during my first flight to Bimini in 1948 that the small seaplane we took over had to pull up from its initial approach because of several floating tuna carcasses in the landing zone. Today the emphasis is on tagging and release programs without actually boating the fish brought alongside. While this is a most promising development, it is still not as widespread as needs be to give respite to the dwindling numbers of big bluefin that continue to barrel down "Tuna Alley" each spring.[10]

As early as 1928, a story began to percolate in Hemingway's mind. That year he met Carlos Gutiérrez on a fishing trip to the Dry Tortugas. Gutiérrez was in command of a fishing smack that had put into Tortugas to catch bait. Like many another Cuban fisherman, he drifted for marlin and broadbill swordfish off Coijimar[11] from mid-April until the first storms of October, and then during the winter months, he turned his attention to red snapper and bait fishing. Carlos had been following this pattern since 1884 when he first went to sea with his

---

[10]As recently as May 1972, a billfishing tournament was held at Hilton Head, South Carolina, during which 13 blue marlin were brought in, weighed, and then promptly cut up for use as compost at the Sea Pines Plantation's Heritage Farm. Tournament officials claimed that blue marlin are inedible and that this was the "only practical use" for them.

[11]A coastal village about 10 miles east of Havana.

[260]

father at the age of six. Certainly one of the reasons Hemingway eventually went to Cuba was to see for himself the fleets of small skiffs that Carlos had described as accounting for vast numbers of big marlin every year.

On his second trip to Havana, Hemingway sought out Carlos and made him his fishing adviser and guide. Then Hemingway systematically began to research the details of this marvelous Cuban fishery. He was amazed to find that the local fishermen did not consider 750 pounds of dressed-out marlin—that is, a fish with its head, guts, flanks, and tail removed—a remarkable catch. In fact, Hemingway shortly discovered a 1,175-pound dressed-out marlin that would have weighed close to a ton when alive. Such findings led to his conclusion in "Marlin Off Cuba" that "considering the size the fish attain, the present Atlantic records on marlin taken with rod and reel are ridiculous." Since the present world-record Atlantic blue marlin is only 845 pounds, Hemingway's assessment of the situation is still accurate.

Meanwhile, other saltwater researchers were beginning to show an interest in this Cuban fishery. Harlan Major was equally impressed by the size and number of marlin taken off the Cuban coast by the relatively simple technique of drift fishing, and his interest led to an essay in the February 1937 issue of *Motor Boating* entitled "Have You Tried Drifting?"

Some fishermen have attempted to reach large fish by drifting for them, but results were far from gratifying. The baits veered off at an angle instead of going straight down, and if there were other lines from the same boat they soon tangled. Then the fisherman would give up and go back to trolling with a kite or outrigger, or maybe go aloft to the crow's nest trying to get a glimpse of a fin or see the splash of a breaching fish in the distance.[12]

The unfortunate part of these attempts at drifting is that the fisherman has not realized it takes as much skill to drift a bait properly as it does to use kites or outriggers, as well as many of the tricks that experienced fishermen have mastered.

Probably the most difficult form of drifting is carried on by commercial fishermen who use this method in taking marlin off the north coast of Cuba between the ports of Cabanas and Santa Cruz del Norte. They call their nearly flat-bottomed skiffs *cachuchas*. A small sail carries these

---

[12]One angler who did not give up was Michael Lerner. In 1936, he spent 29 days drifting in an open skiff off Bimini trying to catch a big marlin. On the 29th day, he caught a 467-pounder and considered all the waiting worth the effort!

fifteen or eighteen-foot craft out to the fishing grounds but, once there, the mast is unstepped; the sail furled, and—it is up to the oarsman.

Three lines are used, the first known as *avio de mano* or hand tackle, and this is lowered to a depth of 90 fathoms. The second line is called *avio hondo* or depth tackle; and is lowered to 105 fathoms. The third, the *vuelo* or fly tackle, goes down 75 fathoms and is made fast to a stout cane pole which is projected from the bow of the skiff. Any activity on the forward line can be seen by watching the pole. The fisherman at the oar loops the medium line around his big toe and the long line is held by the second fisherman who is in the stern.

The most important work is done by the oarsman. He must maneuver the skiff so that all three lines lead straight down without tangling. The current may drift the lines more than it does the skiff, or the wind may be pushing the line in the opposite direction. This is where the skill comes in and the man at the oars must keep the skiff moving in the same direction and at the same speed as the current, so that his lines will remain in a vertical position.[13]

The Cuban pioneer H. L. Woodward was also a devotee of drift fishing, but Hemingway was not. In fact, one of their basic points of contention was Woodward's insistence that the very big marlin could only be caught on a deep-set line, while Hemingway argued that sooner or later all marlin, whatever size, spend time at the surface. And if they were found cruising at the surface, then they could be caught there, too, where sporting—*i.e.*, trolling—methods could be used to take them. Besides, who wanted to spend hours, if not days, rolling at sea waiting to bellyhook a marlin that might otherwise be hooked in the mouth after a thrilling surface rush and strike?

It was an interesting debate, and in the short run, Hemingway won. But when we consider the success of Japanese long-liners today using essentially a trot-line variation of the Cuban drift-fishing principle, when we recall that the biggest marlin caught by a sports fisherman in the Atlantic is still less than 1,000 pounds and that observers have seen *many* marlin exceeding this 1,000-pound mark in Caribbean freezer plants awaiting shipment to the Orient—then, perhaps, more creative angling can and should be done with deep-set baits.

But fishing techniques alone did not interest Hemingway. He was a storyteller who wanted to know all about the fish and especially about the men who pursued them. Less than a year after the publication of

---

[13]Reprinted with the permission of *Motor Boating & Sailing* magazine, copyright 1937 Hearst Corporation.

"Marlin Off Cuba," Hemingway wrote an article for the April 1936 issue of *Esquire* magazine. Titled "On the Blue Water: A Gulf Stream Letter," the piece is devoted to explaining the sport of big-game angling to someone who has never tried it. By way of illustrating the wonders of the sea, Hemingway includes a pair of anecdotes heard from or about Cuban fishermen:

Carlos Gutiérrez told Hemingway that one day he hooked an 80-pound white marlin that leaped twice and sounded. Suddenly a tremendous force took hold of the marlin and began to move off with it. Carlos described this whatever-it-was as though he was hooked to the bottom, but the bottom could move! Just as suddenly this force let go, and Carlos pulled up the white marlin, stone dead and with marks around its midriff indicating that another giant marlin had grabbed the seven-foot fish and crushed its insides. It was not a giant squid, Carlos insisted. There were no sucker marks and, besides, he knew the kind of bite a marlin made—but what a marlin this must have been!

The other story Hemingway told was of an old man fishing alone who had hooked a big fish, which dragged him far out to sea. Two days later the old man was picked up with the head and tail of the enormous fish lashed to his skiff. He had fought the marlin for two days and two nights with a handline, finally bringing it close enough to harpoon. Then, finding it too large to pull into his small boat, the old man had lashed it alongside. Sharks had arrived and despite stubborn fighting with clubs and gaffs, the old man had lost half his catch. When he was picked up, sharks still circled the boat, and the old man was sobbing in exhaustion and defeat. What remained of the fish weighed 800 pounds.

So here it was. The seed story of *The Old Man and the Sea*, some 16 years before it finally appeared in book form. In February 1939, Hemingway wrote his editor, Maxwell Perkins, that he was at last working on "the old man story." Properly presented, he predicted, it would be "great." And he planned to get out in a skiff with Carlos Gutiérrez to make sure all the details were correct.

That Christmas, Hemingway moved his residence to Finca Vigia, San Francisco de Paula, Cuba. But we do not know whether he ever actually made his planned authentication trip in the skiff with Carlos. The Cuban fisherman was then getting on in years, and even three years previous, Hemingway had complained that Carlos was "three-quarters blind and quite deaf."

Hemingway pecked at the notion of the old man and the big marlin for years. He kept taking it up, only to put it down after a few hours work. He fussed with the title some days instead of actually writing. Should he call it *The Dignity of Man* or *The Sea in Being?* Both sounded pompous, but he did keep the latter as a working title. Not until 1952 was the manuscript finally ready, and then he wrote Wallace Meyer[14] that, once launched, the book had taken him just eight weeks to complete with practically no rewriting.

The rest is literary history. *Life* magazine serialized the story and sold more than five million copies within 48 hours; Book-of-the-Month Club picked it up and provided Hemingway with millions more readers; finally, the Nobel Prize Committee in Sweden selected *The Old Man* and its author for its prize in literature. After getting word of each one of these new triumphs, Hemingway expressed his joy and satisfaction by going fishing. When the book really began to take hold in 1952, Hemingway made it a point to stay offshore as much as possible so as to avoid contact with the countless correspondents who began to hound him and the bags of mail that began to pile up. By the end of September, he had caught 29 marlin, and he wrote the art critic Bernard Berenson that "the leaving of the water and the entering into it of the huge fish moves me as much as the first time I ever saw it."

Less than 10 years later Hemingway was dead. He committed suicide with a favorite shotgun he usually reserved for pigeon shooting. All his life he had thought about death, and on many occasions he had given it the chance to take him with a flourish. But since Death seemed reluctant to accept his offer of compliance, Hemingway finally decided to make the final gesture himself.

On August 23, 1950, Ernest Hemingway made a very long, deep dive off the *Pilar* far out in the Gulf Stream. He decided this great river would be a most pleasant place to die. "It was awfully nice down there," he later told reporter Lillian Ross and he "was tempted to stay." But then, "the need to set a good example" for his children came to mind, and he surfaced. Eleven years later, his children were grown up, and Ernest Hemingway no longer felt the need.

---

[14]His new editor at Scribner's. Maxwell Perkins had died on June 17, 1947. The *Old Man and the Sea* was dedicated "To Charlie Scribner and to Max Perkins."

SEVENTEEN

THE AMATEUR EXPERT

> An expert angler isn't necessarily a guy who always does the right thing at the right second. But one thing he necessarily is, and that's a fishing man!—Crunch Adams in "The Expert"
>
> I'm only a moderately expert angler.
> —Philip Wylie in a letter dated February 1, 1971

The most persistent myth of deep-sea angling is that only the rich can afford it. The legend grew up in those early days when offshore trolling *was* a rich man's sport. But just about the time fishing cruisers reached a peak in luxury and cost—when a man could spend $120,000 on an angling platform and still not have paid for the bait—along came the mini-cruiser. Today, owners of 20- to 26-foot, trailerable, center-consoled utility hulls launch their $5,000 (fully equipped) rigs at public ramps and run sometimes 50 miles offshore in search of blue-water game. These anglers are as likely to be bakers as bankers, teachers as tycoons. And their presence offshore officially marks the end of an era that equated big money with big marlin.

New technologies are at the heart of this democratization of big-game angling. The advent of fiberglass mass production and the development of high-horsepower outboard motors and inexpensive, but reliable, communications and navigation systems have all played a part in

[265]

making billfish and bluefin tuna more accessible to the average salt-water angler.

But there has been a change of attitude, too. Had all the popular press and media maintained the myth that ocean angling was for the very rich alone, much of the impulse for developing vest-pocket fishing cruisers might never have materialized. Marlin might have remained the exclusive quarry of America's aristocracy (that is, our entertainers, sports stars, and the industrially wealthy) in the same way that Scottish grouse "belong" to Britain's nobility, or that all sturgeon in English waters are "owned" by the Crown.[1] Unless the public had come to share in some of the excitement and personal drama of deep-sea angling, there might have always remained a gulf of experience between people who fish for bullheads and those who pursue broadbill sword-fish. The writer who did most to dispel this myth of exclusivity, who helped persuade a majority of Americans—the readers of *The Saturday Evening Post* and the viewers of television—that deep-sea angling was something they could participate in, was a man by the name of Philip Gordon Wylie.

Wylie was born in Beverly, Massachusetts, on May 12, 1902. His father was a Presbyterian minister whose moves from parish to parish took his family from Massachusetts to Ohio and then back east to Delaware and Montclair, New Jersey, where young Philip finally graduated from high school. He had fished local runs and stone quarries from age eight on, but a small New Jersey lake gave him his first great angling experience.

The summer after Wylie's twelfth birthday, he and his parents stayed at a summer camp where the chief attraction was a lake in which big four- and five-pound large-mouth bass were regularly seen patrolling the shallows for food. For days on end, Wylie and the other youngsters in camp tried their best to catch one of these monsters. They used everything from live grasshoppers, worms, and frogs to artificial flies, plugs, and spoons. But nothing worked. Some of the bass—like the wiser mangrove snappers around a Florida dock—would eagerly rush at anything thrown their way without a hook in it. But attach even the most

---

[1]Or used to be. In February 1971, the British House of Lords acted to eliminate some of the ancient prerogatives of royalty—many dating back to the thirteenth century and the reign of Edward I. The sovereign's entitlement to all sturgeon in English waters was canceled, along with the Crown's claims to all whale tails washed up on the shores of England and any whale washed up in Scotland that proved too large to be dragged off on a "wain with six oxen" (*Time* magazine, February 8, 1971, page 37).

transparent gut leader, and the fish just could not be persuaded to bite.

One morning young Wylie was fishing all alone in a rowboat over a deep hole in the lake with a bluegill minnow let down to bottom on a splitshot—"just to see what would happen. I even forgot I was fishing."[2]

Well, you guessed it: Wylie hooked one of the huge bigmouths and after a titanic struggle, wrestled it aboard.

He then recalls how unbearable he was—parading through camp with the fish on a stringer, even straining a bit when lifting it to exaggerate the size. Naturally everyone wanted to know how he'd caught the fish, and Phil hesitated awhile before telling.

"Apple jelly," he finally confessed.

While most of the adults viewed this story as the ruse it was, Wylie's younger companions swallowed the tale hook, line, and sinker. Thus, for the rest of the summer, jars of apple jelly were seen in the hands of every urchin with a fishing pole—Wylie included. For to give his story verisimilitude, he carried around a jelly jar and regularly scooped out (and ate!) a portion of its contents. But when he rowed offshore to fish, he also carried a pail of baby bluegills sneaked aboard the previous night.

Despite such gross treachery—or, as Wylie the minister's son imagined, *because of it*—he did not catch another bass all summer.

When he was 18, a friend—Arthur Budlong Vreeland[3]—Wylie, and an Indian guide explored the then-virgin outback of Canada between Lake Kipawa and James Bay. They lived entirely on the fish and game they caught or shot, and the future writer of outdoor adventure stories considered this summer the most rigorous, and the most worthwhile, adventure of his life. When Wylie and Vreeland finally emerged from the woods, they visited Ottawa with the first maps government officials had ever seen of the area. Years later, during World War II, Wylie told a friend that one of the sad features of this shrinking world was that for future generations of young men, there never would be the opportunity to explore and leave their mark in the world in the way that he and young Vreeland had done in 1920.

That fall Wylie matriculated at Princeton University, a school strong

---

[2]This, and all following quoted material, is from personal correspondence with Wylie during January and February 1971.

[3]Son of Wylie's scoutmaster, Dr. Frederick King Vreeland, who was an "electrical engineer, naturalist, and explorer of Northwest and Northeast Canada and Alaska." Wylie was always most proud of his association with the Boy Scouts (ages 12 through 18), and he further describes Dr. Vreeland as having taught him "woodcraft, woodsmanship, the whole bit."

in Presbyterian traditions. He stayed until 1923, then quit. He wanted to write, and he decided in his junior year that he had had enough of formal schooling. Besides, there was the rebellious satisfaction of turning his back on a degree that was only nine months away, and on a potential career in one of the traditional professions of medicine, law, or the ministry.

Years later, after he had received an honorary Doctor of Literature from the University of Miami in Florida, he commented that such a degree awarded in recognition of accomplishment is more significant than any degree granted automatically at the conclusion of a four-year course of studies. However, he was always proud of his association with Princeton, and when he died on October 25, 1971, he left his papers to the university's Firestone Memorial Library.

The years between 1923 and 1930 were devoted to building an editorial and writing reputation in New York City. He joined the staff of *The New Yorker* in 1925, then became the advertising manager for the Cosmopolitan Book Corporation in 1927. He also produced a number of novels—among them *Heavy Laden, Babes and Sucklings*, and *Gladiator*—which eventually led to regular story assignments for Paramount Pictures and Metro-Goldwyn-Mayer.

But it was a winter visit to Coral Gables, Florida, in 1930 that really changed his life. Not only did the climate and pace of life agree with him, but he got his first taste of saltwater fishing. It was not much of a trip offshore. But he did catch several king mackerel[4] and was thereafter hooked on Florida fishing.

From 1931 to 1937, Wylie organized his life in such a way that he spent part of the year in Hollywood writing film scripts; part living in New York City and in East River, Connecticut, where he had bought a country home complete with a stocked brook and where he did most of his novel writing; and his winters in Florida, where he continued writing between fishing trips. His growing interest in reef and bluewater angling brought him into contact with many old-time Florida residents and anglers, and in 1936 he was asked to join the prestigious Rod and Reel Club in Miami Beach.

But 1937 was his most momentous year—at least regarding his growing devotion to saltwater fishing. He caught his first giant tuna; he

---

[4]I asked Philip Wylie exactly how many mackerel he caught that trip, but he could not remember. "Why? What difference does it make? I only needed one to convince me there was nothing in fresh water that could equal it!"

caught it with the girl who became his second wife and regular angling companion;[5] and he moved to Miami Beach full-time.[6]

First, the saga of the giant tuna:

Philip Wylie often went to Brielle, New Jersey, during the summer of 1937 to fish with George Fizell, whom Wylie described as "a stickler for form and rules, and a great skipper." One day when the weather was expected to be clear and calm, Miss Ballard was asked along. Captain Fizell left Manasquan Inlet and ran clear to Ambrose Light-ship, where he anchored and began to chum. Hours passed uneventfully while the sun rose and the day became hot and deathly still. About noon the wind came up in little cat's paws that wrinkled the surface. Then whitecaps began to freckle the ocean's face. When the anchored cruiser began to pitch, the group of three decided it might be wise to head home.

As Fizell moved forward to haul the anchor, Wylie saw the first of the telltale boils sent to the surface by feeding tuna. Some of the giants were working through the last of the chum as it drifted aft. Before anyone quite realized what was happening, a fish had taken the remaining bait left trailing in the tide, and Wylie was in the fighting chair rearing back to set the hook.

"It is quite a shock," he recalled, "even after sailfish and amberjack and sharks, to tangle with a big tuna."

The reel screamed, and the speed of the revolving spool was such that the reel oil heated up and oozed from the lubrication points. In one stunning run, line melted away so fast it seemed like something liquid rather than a true but fragile connection with a giant fish. The reel oil began to smoke, and water from a pail was doused over it and the angler.

Then the fish stopped, and Wylie began the job of working it back. The primitive slugfest between angler and giant fish had begun.

Wylie says of this first big fish that it was a nightmare—that he fantasied he was in the ring with Jack Dempsey in an everlasting grudge fight. But by the time the first hour had passed—and the second—and then the third, he felt as though he was a miner who had been working

---

[5]Wylie's first marriage to Johanna Ondeck ended in 1937. He then married Frederica ("Ricky") Ballard on April 27, 1938. She was the daughter of a country doctor in Rushford, New York, and a Cornell graduate. Wylie described their days of courtship as "she learned deep-sea fishing from me and with me and plug-casting as I learned [it]."

[6]Wylie built a new house on Di-Lido Island, part of the Venetian Causeway.

1,000 feet below the ground all his life and who no longer cared whether anyone remembered to blow the whistle to signal the end of his eternal shift. There was nothing else to do but to hold on when the fish ran, pump when it stopped, and hope that one day the whole thing might end.

By the time the fourth hour began, the wind was blowing strongly out of the southwest and the boat was having difficulty dealing with both the elements and the fish. On top of that, daylight was turning to twilight.

When the fish finally came within view at the outset of the fifth hour, Wylie still had enough energy left to feel a kind of panic at the thought of losing this hard-earned prize. The fight had taken them from within a few hundred yards of Ambrose Lightship to lower New York harbor, with the Manhattan skyscrapers in view. If worse came to worse, the captain announced, they could run for shelter up the Hudson or East River after they boated the tuna.

The line was reeled down to the swivel. Fizell grabbed the leader and brought the 500-pound fish close to the boat. With a lunge and a haul, the flying gaff was secured, and Wylie nearly fell out of the fighting chair with relief.

But then the real adventure began.

Captain Fizell had rigged a derrick affair to help load any heavy fish he might catch, and this was to be its maiden trial. With lines running out to the end of a boom supported by two steel rods on a turntable and then down to the flying gaff in the fish, the idea was that as soon as the giant was hoisted gunwale-high, the boom would be swung inboard to deposit the fish neatly into the cockpit.

The only trouble with the plan was the weather. Once the fish was sufficiently elevated for the roll of the boat to take over, what resulted was a grotesque parody of the pit and the pendulum! The great tuna began to swing—still shivering alive—first far out over the water against the sunset—then hurling back at Fizell, Miss Ballard, and Wylie with tremendous force. Incredibly, on the first few passes, nothing disastrous happened. Voices screamed, adrenalin pumped, and there may have been a near heart failure or two—but somehow both people and boat escaped harm.

Then both bolts anchoring the derrick snapped loose.

The steel braces supporting the boom flew back into the cabin, tearing out chunks of wood and smashing all the windows. Glass, wood, and metal fragments flew everywhere! It was as though a bomb had gone off. Yet, amazingly, no one was hurt.

The tuna meanwhile had depth-charged back into the sea and the gaff had come out. Despite its exhaustion and its unusual experience with levitation, the big fish was still alive and promptly began to swim off. But the hook was still in its mouth. Wylie retrieved the rod, and amid the confusion of trying to clear away some of the debris, worked the fish back to the surface.

This time when the gaff was reset, a more conventional boating procedure was adopted. The tuna was landed and the bedraggled and slightly shell-shocked crew at long last started in. But it was after midnight when they crept through a turbulent Manasquan Inlet and ran the boat uptide to her berth in Brielle. The docks were deserted, and there was some difficulty in arranging transportation back to the hotel. But the young lady said she was fine and had even found the day most exciting. For two days afterward, bellhops had to help Philip Wylie get dressed, but he had caught a giant tuna—and he had found someone who not only understood but actually shared his passion for fishing.

That next year he married Ricky, and they celebrated with the catch of his first blue marlin ("I had hung and lost nine previous") fishing out of the Key Largo Angler's Club. He also wrote his first Florida fishing story based on an event that actually happened to Mrs. Wylie and himself while fishing with skipper Harold Schmidt and his mate, John Smedburg. He changed the names of the characters, as they used to say, to protect the innocent. And he called his fictitious Captain and mate, Crunch and Des. But when this fishing duo later became the most famous and popular chartermen in the world, Schmidt used to advertise himself as "the original Crunch" on his dock signs wherever he fished.[7]

As Zane Grey's novels forever fixed in legend the campfire tales of Utah and Arizona, so Philip Wylie's stories of Crunch and Des record some of the traditions of the charter docks from Montauk to Key West. The main characters, Crunch Adams and his mate, Desmond or "Des-

---

[7] "'Crunch' and 'Des' have some characteristics of Harold Schmidt and John, but many qualities of assorted guides, too, for we fished with many of the guides at the Miami Beach Docks and Pier Five, Miami." From personal correspondence dated February 1, 1971. Another one of Wylie's favorite skippers was Crawford Edmund ("Eddie") Wall. Wylie used a photograph of himself taken aboard Wall's *Playmate* for the dust jacket of *Denizens of the Deep*.

perate" Smith, are part of every adventure. Other regulars include Crunch's wife, Sari, and his young son, Bill. There's also a dog named Noisy Groceries. The boat is the *Poseidon*,[8] which was once named *Evangeline IV* before Crunch and Des rescued it from the salvagers. And their home port is the Gulf Stream Dock, Miami, which bears a striking resemblance to the old Pier Five.

More than 100 Crunch and Des stories were written over a 20-year period ("the Thirties to Fifties—my saltwater interval," Wylie recalled). And they became so popular that several collections of these stories were published as books.[9] By 1956, when the television series first went on the air,[10] Crunch and Des had become as synonymous with saltwater angling as Holmes and Watson were with crime detection.

The best of Crunch and Des are great yarns written against the background of Wylie's love of sea angling, Miami, and the people of the charter fishing business—skippers and clients alike. The author also worked in his familiarity with such characters as Presbyterian ministers and towns with names like Antasquan, New Jersey. The stories are tailored for a mass audience and include such sagas as "Light Tackle," the tale of a lovely but lonely girl who has come to Florida for her health and who wins the heart of a crochety millionaire obsessed with breaking light-tackle records. Despite differences in temperament and background, the millionaire and the lonely girl fall in love, primarily because they both love fishing and because Crunch plays Cupid.

Then there are tales like "Fifty-Four, Forty and Fight" and "Crunch Catches One" in which our ex-boxer hero—Crunch fought professionally for two years to support his mother—takes on the forces of evil, be they the thugs who have just robbed the Golden Sands Hotel or racketeers who try to rig the fishing pool aboard Cap'n Collins' *Minerva*. There is nothing subtle about Crunch's justice: Black eyes and broken jaws are his instant remedies for malfeasance. But he is careful to match the extent of injury to the seriousness of the crime.

One of the reasons for Crunch's quick fist is that the world of chartermen is highly competitive, and on occasions, dangerously so. Wylie suggests that any man who enters this business must be, to put it mildly, self-reliant to survive. In one of the very first Crunch and Des

[8]Schmidt's original was the *Neptune*.
[9]*Salt Water Daffy* (1941), *Fish and Tin Fish* (1944), *Crunch and Des: Stories of Florida Fishing* (1948), *The Best of Crunch and Des* (1954), *The Big Ones Get Away!* (1954), *Treasure Cruise, and Other Crunch and Des Stories* (1956).
[10]The first showing in New York City was in September on WPIX.

adventures, a jealous skipper drills holes in the *Poseidon*'s hull and sinks her in an attempt to drive Crunch out of business. But virtue and industry and a strong left hook win out, and Crunch eventually earns his place in the sun at the Gulf Stream Docks.

Part of Crunch's defensive posture may have been a reflection of Philip Wylie's own. Not that Wylie ever got involved in any of the fist-fights down on Pier Five. But he knew that there were men down there who would have liked to provoke an incident with the famous author of Crunch and Des:

For me, [he writes], deep-sea angling was, first, private fun. [Then] it became a sort of vocation, separate from my other and vital ones, as "Crunch" and "Des" lent me an unexpected lustre as a sportsman and sports writer. From there, to various other posts and spots in that special limelight, the steps were unexpected, uncharacteristic, demanding, but still pleasant as novelty. Yet, for me, that identification was accidental, minor, and though valid enough, nothing at all like any similar sports identity was, would be, is, or will be for others.

My case was, not surprisingly, sometimes the cause of envy. And my reputation was abused as a means of diminishing the misery of the envious. They felt that here was a guy who didn't depend on a sport—or sport as such—for a living, either as a writer or a guide or the like. Here was a guy nobody had ever known about as an outdoor type who, suddenly, burst into renown as *The Saturday Evening Post*'s famous fishing-yarn author. And then this guy got all sorts of top spots in governing bodies like the International Game Fish Association. And no end of publicity—which he didn't need the way others did and do.

And these same envious souls looked on me as a big shot, authority, celebrity in their profession. They thought: "My years of hard learning even before this bastard ever wet a line qualify me in areas where this jerk isn't out of diapers!" (And that was true in many areas like fly-tying and the whole trout bit.) I used to feel very badly when old-timers showed such feelings. And I tried to understand when some of them tried to take a fall from me—even fouled a bit.

But for me fishing was fun. And the writing and work that went with it was an antic and unplanned area of my life. I enjoyed it all and incidentally found it highly remunerative. In fact, I'm probably the only deep-sea angler who spent up to 100 days a year fishing—and made more money out of it than I spent!

When I suggested he was being too modest about his contributions to the sport—that, in fact, Philip Gordon Wylie had done a lot to publicize light-tackle angling for once unpopular species like barracuda and jack crevalle even before the rest of the fishing fraternity was willing to acknowledge their value—he replied:

Sure I helped spread the light-tackle gospel. [But] others taught me the delights.[11] "Crunch" and "Des" made maybe a million or two new ocean anglers. But that part of it was spin-off and luck, not my life's aim. Just a side thing. In sum, I never had an axe to grind. I didn't need anything from the sport or need to write about it. [My reputation] often embarrassed me. But I must add, I did my homework, and you will not fault anything I ever wrote about fishing. The *SatEvePost* used to have the best and most finicky editorial typographical people extant. They questioned hundreds of things in the many years—the many Crunch and Des tales, articles, etc.—I did. In that mass of words, they caught me wrong twice: once, matter of latitude (foolish error); second time, length of the dorsal fin of a permit. Real blunder by me. But that's one reason the yarns were popular: stories plausible, data exact.

Keeping the sport honest—hence, "sportsmen"—was my personal concern. This also was Mike Lerner's. Many other men—and women—had other and differing stakes. Guides had obvious stakes and related angles. So did some other writers who depended on fishing—writing as their main or major source of income or, at least, of public attention. Still others pathologically used (and misused) angling and related activities for ends I call sick.

And there was the glory of records that misled or even debauched a few men of note in business. There was inconceivable rivalry and jealousy. Thus the "history" of salt-water angling is like all history, and few reliable witnesses existed at the time, let alone survive and remember clearly.

Ultimately, Philip Wylie's proudest associations with fishing were legislative and scientific. He met Michael Lerner for the first time in the mid-1930's in Bimini where the Lerners owned a house.

And with my wife we four became and remain very fast and close pals. We fished together endless times out of Bimini. The International Game Fish Association was a going concern when Mike asked me to become one of its officials. Then for many years after I did much of the actual work, along with Erl Roman[12] and Mike, of writing and

[11]Wylie spoke especially well of guide Leo Johnson of Islamorada, Florida Keys, with whom he did much of his "plugging for everything that would hit."

[12]Author of *Fishing for Fun in Salty Waters* (1940), Erl Roman served for many years as the angling editor of *The Miami Herald*.

re-writing rules, reviewing world record claims, correspondence, et cetera.

Every man on the IGFA is so honest it's sometimes painful. So, too, with our worldwide representatives. We, and they, spend endless time and vast travel, checking claims we think might be mistaken, perhaps phoney, possibly unclear, perhaps with insufficient data. I never knew people so insistent on integrity in awarding records for proper claims.

For years as claims came in, two or three of us inspected them, and records were established only when at least two of us were absolutely satisfied. All lines submitted for record are tested commercially by two different firms. Any doubt or question, and our work began.

I also helped revise rules as our feelings and information suggested we do. The IGFA was set up to enable people, world-wide, to fish the oceans with adequate sporting tackle. And that meant we couldn't tighten rules to the fantastic and super-sporting degree some few rich deep-sea clubs go by. Those rules usually mean additional expense for the angler, and we wanted the average man of any nation to have a decent chance at a record.

That IGFA rules are strictly enforced can be seen in the following true anecdote:

Two apparently well-known—but when I asked Philip Wylie who they were, he diplomatically declined to give their names—light-tackle enthusiasts were fishing together for sailfish off Mexico. One was using three-thread or approximately nine-pound test line; the other, six-thread or eighteen-pound test. A huge sailfish rushed up behind their trolled baits and took both of them before the men could react.[13] Both lines came tight about the same time and reels screamed. The six-thread fisherman made an almost instant decision: the fish was a big one and likely to be a record on either line. However, it would be so much more of a record on three-thread. Hence, the six-thread sports-man tightens his drag and pops off the fish.

After an arduous, but cautious, battle, Mr. Three-Thread lands the fish. It is a record—that is, if the IGFA approves—which both anglers can only imagine will be a matter of form. So the extensive question-

---

[13]This happens from time to time with blue-water gamefish. Once trolling with my father off Hollywood, Florida, with four lines out, a school of dolphin suddenly appeared leaping in our wake. All four baits were struck nearly simultaneously. It took us several minutes to determine that the same bull dolphin of about 25 pounds was at the end of three of the lines, and a smaller fish of nearly 10 pounds was at the end of the fourth line. You can imagine the resulting tangle before we finally got those fish in.

naire and applications are filled out, and the weighmaster's affidavit properly notarized. A sample of the line is included with the various forms, and the two men sit back to await the new entry in the annual listings of the association.

But no! The application is refused! The rules state very clearly that the fish must be hooked and fought *unaided and without interference.* The fact that the sailfish was on Mr. Six-Thread's line, too, even though only a matter of seconds, disqualifies the catch. Although Mr. Six-Thread's gesture was magnanimous and, perhaps in a storybook version of the catch, would be immortalized along with Mr. Three-Thread's record, in real life the gesture is reduced only to the satisfaction it gave these two friends. Unfair? Not if you are to have standards and maintain them.

The Second World War changed Philip Wylie's life. For starters, in Wylie's words, it "threw a block at fishing."

However early on, with Mike Lerner, Erl Roman and many scientists, we did a very fancy job of designing "life-saving fishing gear" for the armed forces. The stuff the Navy had when the war came was strictly Captain Ahab vintage. Our kit updated and condensed what was available and probably saved hundreds of men after their ships had been sunk or their planes cracked up at sea. Since the sailors and soldiers started swiping these kits from the life rafts, we also later designed a "recreational fishing kit." Mike paid for the first 100,000 himself, after which the Red Cross started providing for them.

This contact with government service and Philip Wylie's own skeptical sensibilities joined forces after the war to move him increasingly away from sport fishing per se and into the realm of marine research.

[When] I resumed fishing . . . I soon caught a biggish blue marlin and the next day, looking at the carcass, I decided I didn't need to kill any more big fish for fun. After hunting to eat (summer of 1920) I never again found hunting a sport! My satisfaction became—and still is—to take other people fishing now and again.

In 1948, Charles M. Breder, Jr., head of the American Museum of Natural History Department of Fishes, Michael Lerner, and Philip Wylie established the museum's field station in Bimini. For all the rest

[276]

of his life Wylie was a member of the museum-appointed committee, directing the facility's research operations. Also from the start, Philip Wylie was a consultant to Taylor A. Pryor's Sea Life Park and the Ocean Institute in Hawaii. And it was only incidental that "Tap" Pryor happened to be Wylie's son-in-law, for Wylie always treated his appointments seriously and guided developments with devotion.

But Wylie's interest in marine science, on at least one occasion, caused a conflict with some fans. This is how he described the incident:

After reading some hydrodynamic math on fish power, I decided the bonefish was overrated and seemed swift only because his runs were visible, near at hand, and in clear, shoal water. Bob Monroe who at that time was the fishing columnist for the *Miami Daily News*, got so mad, he challenged me to prove my claim that a six-pound bonefish couldn't break a six-pound test line if you prohibited the fish from taking line, thereby building up speed and momentum. If any angler will clamp down his reel and hold it at full stop before the bonefish gets going, the fish will be compelled to run in a circle around the boat until pooped, when it can be easily reeled in and netted.

I accepted the challenge, and Bob got some AP photographers in a charter boat, and we got in a skiff. And sure enough, I hooked a six-pound bonefish. I refused to let it run and exactly as predicted, the fish circled the boat a few times at the distance at which it had been hooked. When it was done, I reeled it in near belly up. It was a real shock to Bob and to quite a few of his readers, for Bob ran a true account of what happened with pictures to back it up.

But the myth lives on!

When I asked Philip Wylie whether he preferred the bay, flats, and light-tackle fishing that he frequently championed over blue-water game, he replied:

I liked the big ones best. But I wrote a great deal in praise of lesser breeds than marlin, horse mackerel, *et al*, because
1) I liked that fishing too,
2) a guy writing a fishing series for the [*Saturday Evening*] *Post* for 20 years and articles for everybody else, cannot have his people catch monsters every time out, and
3) a very great many people, fresh-water anglers, cannot afford deep-water charterboat fishing, but *can* afford the light tackle, bait and fly casting varieties.

[277]

Writers, like doctors, are often paid with promises, and sometimes with goods. . . . But the following Wylie anecdote surely represents one of the most pleasant, but unusual, payments ever received by writer:

Right after the war, the *Ford Times* asked me to do a general Florida ocean fishing piece—how and where, how much, et cetera—for a dealer's convention to be [held in] Miami Beach. I wrote an extensive piece and the editor wired he was going to run it in two installments, [and] I was offered double my regular price.

I had no car—having sold my last Zephyr in wartime— [and] I asked my agent[14] if they'd send me a Ford instead of the money.

The editor [then] wired he'd send me a Mercury and asked only, "What color?" Color [was] no object in my dire straits—I was a year back on the waiting lists—I just needed a car, any car! I got it—black, I recall.

One unfortunate aspect of Philip Wylie's saltwater angling was his notoriously bad luck. Ultimately, however, through an ability to smile at himself, he turned the trait about to enhance his fame and popularity.

The poor luck really had nothing to do with his competence. He was frequently selected to serve on tournament teams and to defend the honor of his club in angling competitions—nothing a dunderhead would be chosen to do, celebrity or not. But one nonetheless suspects that his teammates did the chosing with the hope that *this time*, things would be different!

Probably my favorite story of Wylie misfortune concerns his two-week-long blue marlin expedition to Bimini with Harold Schmidt aboard the *Neptune*. The first week of his charter, Wylie put in long and utterly fruitless days trolling the Atlantic. The boat would run out at dawn, Wylie would sit and stare at the splashing baits for hours on end, and at sunset, the boat would head in. Some days the subtropic sun was so bright and hot that any metal surfaces on the boat or tackle burned like fire to the touch. And the sun's glare off the water filtered even through sunglasses so that you felt as though your brains were beginning to fry behind your eyes after just an hour's concentrated bait watching. A week of this—and he did not even have a false albacore to show for his time and money.

Finally, on the seventh day, there was a strike. One of the outrigger bonefish baits was cut in half by a barracuda. Wylie went to the fishing

---

[14]Harold Ober Associates, his agent since 1930.

chair, took the heavy rod from its holder, set it in the chair gimbal, and began to reel in the bisected bait so that a fresh one could be put on.

Just as he brought the mutilated bonefish to the stern, the barracuda made another pass at it. Wylie then decided to catch this consolation prize to at least have *something* to show for seven days at sea.

He threw his reel into free spool, and the bait drifted back and sank. Suddenly the line began to run out fast. Deciding that the 'cuda really had it now, Wylie threw on the drag to set the hook.

But he never had a chance, for he had misjudged the speed of the racing line. An ordinary fish would have given him a precious instant in which to readjust his grip for the strike. But as soon as the drag lever clicked into place, some $800 worth of rod and reel shot from the gimbal and Wylie's tenuous grip, banged once on the transom, and vanished into the sea.

Bewildered by the unbelievable power of a mere barracuda and dumbstruck by the terrible loss of his prized tackle, Wylie stared incredulously at the ocean. Suddenly a *tremendous* blue marlin lunged 15 feet into the air not 50 feet astern. While both Wylie and Schmidt stood helplessly by, the fish made half a dozen more magnificent leaps in an effort to shake loose the weight it was dragging. Then it vanished.

That night Wylie radio telephoned Miami for some more equipment, but the next week of his stay was as marlin-less as the first week had been.

This he called Wylie's Luck.

Sharing his tales of bad luck with others, and finding that all anglers have some sad stories of their own to tell, Philip Wylie decided to institutionalize this phenomenon of fishing (in which luck—bad or good —plays a more vital role than in any other sport) with the Philip Wylie Hard Luck Trophy. Since he was a member of the board that ran the Greater Miami Fishing Tournament,[15] he suggested they make the annual award to that tournament angler who put forth "grim effort in the face of hopeless predicament" or who had the "worse break." The first year of the award was 1941, and it went to Jim Scully, a fellow who wanted an IGFA record more than anything else in the world—and who caught a world-record amberjack one afternoon, only to lose it within the hour to a fishing companion, Bert Harborn, who took another amberjack just 5½ pounds heavier. To add insult to injury,

---

[15]Now the Metropolitan Miami Fishing Tournament, including not only Miami but the Florida Keys, Everglades area, and the Bahamas.

Harborn was not even interested in whether his fish was a record or not!

I teased Philip Wylie into telling me some of the *lucky* things that had happened to him while angling. He said he could recall two (but just two!) lucky days:

As you know, it's hard to hook a tarpon on a plug and 10- or 12-pound test line. . . . [Yet] one day in the Bay of Florida with Leo Johnson, I saw and/or he saw exactly six tarpon "rises." And I cast to all six—hooked, boated, and released all six—missed nothing, the full day's score. We weighed the biggest before releasing: 37 pounds. And afterward that place in the Bay along Nine-Mile Bank, Leo named "Wylie's Bight." For that six-in-a-row with no misses was . . . exceptional.

And that first blue marlin I got—the ninth or tenth I'd hooked—as soon as it finished its first wild run, [it] swam back, took aim, and rammed guide Art Wills' boat, the *Sea Queen*. Drove its bill through the two-inch mahogany stern and broke it off.

Wills later moved to Puerto Rico. But he had the marlin bill cut trim with the stern planking, sanded, varnished, and looking like a knothole to show customers where the author's first blue marlin had rammed his boat.

But these are good luck anecdotes. I could give you many more bad luck tales. All true. Many incredible—had I time.

Elsewhere in this same letter, he comments apropos of nothing in our correspondence, "My time's running out."

And so it was. Within nine months, Philip Wylie was dead.

He once wrote that fishermen are philosophical men, not because of their patience—the usual explanation—but because we all know that angling is a lifetime recreation (with the emphasis on *re*-creation)—not like white-water canoeing or mountaineering, things for our youth alone. While time may alter the degree or kind of angling we do, it never alters our opportunity. Or as he put it more personally in his last letter:

It could be that . . . I tend to take up things with an intense, all-out fascination: practice-learn-engage-in-them for a while, even many years, and then go on to something else. But I've had a long and varied and extremely great life, and the part that has been fishing was part of its greatness, and so remains—though at longer intervals and reduced catches. . . .

Regards and good luck,

Phil Wylie

[280]

EIGHTEEN

THE SCIENTIFIC ANGLER

I have laid aside business and gone a-fishing.
—Izaak Walton

Of all men associated with the golden age of deep-sea angling, the name of Michael Lerner looms largest. When I described the scope of my project to Hal Lyman in 1970, he said, "You've *got* to include a section on Michael Lerner." And when I began corresponding with Philip Wylie about his part in the story, he wrote back, "No history of deep-sea sport fishing would be worthy of the designation without a chapter gotten from Mike Lerner, that father and grandfather of the sport." Finally in conversation with guide Johnny Cass, who was among the first to fish with the Lerners in the Bahamas, he spoke of Mike in words more suitable to a legend than a living man.

If I wondered why these men were so emphatic about the big-game angling world's most illustrious member, I soon found out when I tried to set up an interview with him. These other fishermen had meant: "Get Lerner if you can; it won't be easy!"

Thus, the saga of my pursuit of Michael Lerner is only slightly less

[281]

awesome than the story of his own pursuit of giant billfish around the world! However, after considerable correspondence and with the aid of mutual friends, I finally stood before the door of the Lerner Marine Laboratory on a hot Miami morning.

The door was opened by a husky, blue-eyed man who looks far younger than his eighty-odd years. His face is ruddy from sun and salty wind, and his reddish hair has not entirely turned grey. My dread vanished when he smiled—a funny small smile that's both friendly and shy, and slightly amused by something, possibly himself. Then in a quiet voice he said,

"Come in. We're in the other room."

He and Francesca LaMonte had been to a board meeting of the International Game Fish Association and as Mike's wife, Helen, was still recuperating from a hospital stay, Fran had agreed to stand by during the interview as a possible memory prop.

The session started slowly for, although he quickly put me at ease, I still felt awkward about asking Michael Lerner apparently trivial questions about the fabulous angling expeditions he led so many years ago. In addition, it was quickly evident that though he is wonderfully cordial to strangers, he values privacy and has no desire to become a public figure. This fact was brought home to me rather dramatically after the interview when I drove Fran LaMonte to the airport. She commented almost casually,

"You know, I think you're the first journalist to see him in over a decade. A *Life* magazine photographer was permitted to take some pictures in 1960, but that's been all for about 25 years now."

The interview was made even more delicate when I discovered that Michael Lerner believes angling is a private affair—one that has little bearing on the public unless the angler seeks to establish a record for a particularly large fish. Then he must come within the purview of a specified code of conduct and equipment. Indeed, it was Mike's desire to see the formalization of such standards for the sport throughout the world that caused him to temporarily abandon his own privacy in 1939 in order to help found the International Game Fish Association.

But this was much later in his life's story. In the beginning, in those first days of sea angling at the turn of the century, there was only Mike and his father on afternoon outings to Sheepshead Bay where they caught flounder and porgy. The sounds of the tide passing beneath their anchored skiff, the quiet and the open spaces accented by gulls' wings over the marsh and bay, and the frantic tattoo on the floorboards

[282]

of freshly caught fish, are youthful impressions which were only enlarged in later years when Michael Lerner fished more distant waters.

Early in the 1920's, he experienced a kind of angling apotheosis when he caught his first bluefin tuna off the south coast of Long Island. Although only about 70 pounds, the fish's speed, strength, and stamina so enthralled Lerner that although he maintained an interest in all fish species henceforth, he became especially devoted to the pursuit of large blue-water gamefish.

He fished the Florida Keys later in the decade, and like many another angler in those days, he heard rumors of an even greater fishing ground across the Gulf Stream. Curious, the Lerners made their first trip to Bimini in the early thirties. That visit turned into a lifelong love affair with the island.

Most fishermen visiting an area leave few reminders of their stay once they're gone. They meet people; they catch fish; they spend money. But once they leave, their presence fades from memory so that local residents have only a blurred impression of many such comings and goings. But from the outset, Michael Lerner's relationship with Bimini was different.

This wasn't just because he returned to the island year after year. Nor that he and his wife[1] became Bimini's foremost angling couple. Rather it was because, right from the start, he adopted the island and felt a sincere interest in the welfare of its people. Following the devastation of the 1935 hurricane, for instance, Lerner was on hand with relief even before the British government rallied with aid. And after he built a home there, it became a kind of unofficial American Embassy in the Bahamas.

Lerner was a personable ambassador. One of his favorite stories concerns the visit of Prince Wilhelm of Sweden, the King's brother, who arrived in Bimini with two friends, all quite formally dressed. Mike sensed the Prince's discomfort, and one evening when Wilhelm was visiting the Lerner home, Mike said to him, "Your Highness, no one dresses formally here at the Anchorage. We just wear open-necked fishing shirts."

Next Mike suggested that if Prince Wilhelm wanted to do some

---

[1]A petite woman, Helen Lerner had nonetheless caught 17 blue marlin up to 460 pounds by the end of her fifth summer in the Islands. After World War II, she received the gold medal from France's *Académie des Sports* for catching the first giant tuna on rod and reel ever taken off the coast of Brittany. Among the handful of other American sportswomen ever to receive this award was Gertrude Ederle, the first woman to swim the English Channel.

fishing, he should meet Mike at his boat early the next morning. The Prince did so, and Lerner and he left Bimini harbor before the rest of the island was awake.

Wilhelm had a successful day offshore, and some years later, when the Lerners visited him at the royal residence in Stockholm, it was Mike's turn to be concerned about what to wear to lunch at the palace. He finally decided on a dark suit, a white shirt, and a conservative tie.

The Prince took one look and said:

"Mike! Take your tie off. You *must* take your tie off. Look! I have on my Bimini shirt."

Mike then took a second look at what His Royal Highness was wearing, and, sure enough, beneath the sport jacket was an open-necked fishing shirt!

The Lerners fished off other southern islands besides Bimini. Their friendship with Julio Sanchez and Ernest Hemingway[2] led to an invitation to fish Cuban waters, and in June 1936, Lerner did what Kip Farrington called (in slight hyperbole) "the most remarkable feat ever performed in the saltwater fishing history of the world." Lerner caught a 48-pound white marlin on 3-thread (9-pound test) line. While an outstanding catch of the day that did much to publicize the potential of light-tackle fishing, one can measure how far the sport has progressed by the fact that such remarkable catches are presently made annually in light-tackle tournaments from the Florida Keys to Australia.

In fishing around, Lerner heard much talk about a single gamefish that was revered above all others. Kip Farrington made a virtue of the fact that he had fished for six seasons before catching his first. Even Ernest Hemingway could be shaken in his devotion to giant blue marlin when conversation turned to the legendary broadbill swordfish.

It wasn't just the fish's size and power that intrigued Lerner. It was its elusiveness and mystery: Where did the broadbill spawn? How fast did it grow? How deep did it run? What were its migration routes, and where were its feeding grounds and concentration points? Why was it so much harder to bait and hook than any other pelagic gamester?

These questions interested all big-game anglers, but they ultimately shaped a career for Michael Lerner. During my interview I asked him

---

[2]In 1936, with more and more tourist anglers coming to the island, the regulars who had been fishing Bimini for several seasons put together an informal Bahamas Marlin and Tuna Club to institutionalize their pioneering achievements. The club officers were Ernest Hemingway, president; Michael Lerner, Thomas Shevlin, and Anthony Baldridge, vice-presidents; Julio Sanchez, treasurer; Kip Farrington, secretary; and Erl Roman, historian.

[284]

what his favorite gamefish is. Lerner's reply reflected a curiosity about all fishes and a sensitivity to the slighting of one of their reputations over another.

"They're all grand," he said. "From the little reef fish to the biggest billfish, they all provide pleasure or excitement—each in its own way."

"But don't you have a special fondness for the broadbill?" I prompted.

For a moment he was thoughtful. Then he smiled and nodded and made a gesture that was part affirmation and part apology to all other species. There was such contentment in his expression, I was reminded of Kip Farrington's anecdote that Lerner once passed up, by actual count, 51 tailing marlin in a single day off Tocopilla, Chile, in order to continue his search for finning broadbill.

Actually Lerner's passion for broadbill swordfishing is rooted in his devotion to all the billfishes. One noon in early 1935, a guard at the front entrance of the American Museum of Natural History in New York City telephoned the Department of Fishes on the fifth floor that "There's a man here who wants to give the museum a fish."

The Department's secretary said that the staff were all at lunch, but if the gentleman would wait, she would try to locate someone who could help. After a lengthy search, the secretary found Francesca La-Monte, Associate Curator of Fishes, in the staff dining room.

Fran met Lerner in the foyer where he explained in a tone bordering on apology that he had caught a large blue marlin off Bimini, that Al Pflueger in Miami had mounted it, and that he now wanted to donate the fish to the museum for exhibit in the Hall of Fishes of the World.[3] She immediately took him to see James Clark, then Chairman of the Department of Preparation and Exhibition, and this was the start of Lerner's long-time association with the museum.[4]

One day later that year while planning a fishing trip to Louisburg, Nova Scotia, he mentioned to Dr. William King Gregory, Chairman of the Fish Department, that if some of the museum staff members "would like to go along," he'd be delighted to have them as his guests. There was a large commercial broadbill swordfishery at Cape Breton, and the expedition members would be able to examine not only specimens

---

[3]First opened in 1928, the Hall was demolished in the 1960's.

[4]For a while the mounted marlin was exhibited on a pedestal. It stood nearly vertical, as if tailwalking. But Mike soon provided a setting with plaster waves and a specially lighted background as he did for all his other single mounts such as the bluefin tuna, mako shark, et cetera.

[285]

brought in by the harpooners, but do intensive work on those fish that Mike and Helen brought in.

Dr. Gregory was impressed by Lerner. He realized Mike was not a casual angler who took big fish without any interest in the larger implications of the sport. It was evident Lerner was gathering and retaining quite a bit of useful and exact information about the fishes he caught.

Dr. Gregory then asked the rest of the staff whether any of them would like to go. Would they! Eventually chosen were Francesca La-Monte and G. Miles Conrad, both then young Associate Curators—Fran in the Department of Fishes and Miles in the Department of Comparative Anatomy; John Treadwell Nichols, Curator of Recent Fishes, and Harry C. Raven, a Comparative Anatomist—both older scientists who had done considerable field work and were, therefore, of inestimable help to the less experienced members. Also included was a museum preparator to take charge of casts made, and a recent Princeton graduate, Anthony Q. Keasbey, who had been doing volunteer work in the museum's Department of Comparative Anatomy. This group headed north with the Lerners and their boatmen in August 1936.

Louisburg occupies a windswept place on the Atlantic side of Cape Breton. Because of the climate, none of the houses have blinds and few are painted—most having walls of grey shingle siding. The townspeople are all of Scot or Welsh descent, and news of Louisburg in the mid-Thirties was found in a column written in Gaelic in a Sydney paper. In the window of one store in town there was a sign: "The dentist will be here Friday." Since there was no inn in this town of 500 people, the Lerner group stayed in a local farmhouse. And since Cape Bretons are a sea-faring. God-fearing people, the sail-loft laboratory used by the museum personnel was always locked on Sunday, and the seventh day became an enforced period of rest.

The scientists depended primarily on swordfish caught by Mike and Helen Lerner. Those the commercial fishermen brought in usually arrived minus head, fins, tail, and gutted in order to conserve space in their small boats at sea. Mike kept a close and kindly eye on the museum staff and saw to it that whatever they needed was quickly provided. He had made sure in advance that the laboratory was set up with a skylight and electricity. It occupied the top floor of a sail loft with a door at one end that led into open space—like the loft door of a barn. The dock was immediately below, and when the boats came in, the staff could stand

[286]

and watch the hosing down of the fish and their transport to the weighing-in station where agents for Canadian and U.S. dealers stood by to bid on the fish. Then when Mike brought in a whole specimen to work on, the mewing of the gulls was a kind of background music to the work at a long central table in the loft.

After five weeks in Louisburg, several of the expedition members went down to Wedgeport where Mike had pioneered the bluefin tuna fishing. Before the establishment of the International Tuna Cup Matches, Wedgeport was a quaint French-Canadian town with many ancient customs intact from the days when the boats of Brittany and Normandy would winter over after a season on the Grand Banks. Though primarily herring fishermen in this century, the men would frequently bring in giant tuna that had become tangled in their nets or which they had harpooned at the surface. The fish were brought in whole, and this is what the members of the Lerner expedition went down to see. They were given specimens to work on, and laboratory space was provided in a shed on the dock.

Overall, the summer was very productive and the local fishing communities were tremendously helpful. The day before the Lerner group left Louisburg, the townspeople gave them a farewell party filled with the warmth and sentiment associated with the completion of any shared adventure. At the end, everyone stood arm and arm and sang "Auld Lang Syne." In the introduction to her first fish book, *North American Game Fishes* (published in 1945, with foreword by Philip Wylie), Fran LaMonte returned the compliment by thanking the entire town of Louisburg for the part it had played in the summer's success.

That first year's work led to three of the museum's staff (two scientists, and a preparator) spending much of the following summer with the Lerners in Bimini working on marlins in a sun-baked tent located at the edge of the Queen's Highway—little more than a sandy path back then. In the few intervals from work, the three young people enjoyed going down to the Lerner dock where they fished for snappers, grunts, and angelfish with handlines.

In 1938, the Lerners returned to Louisburg for more swordfishing—and three of the 1936 scientific team went with them—primarily seeking answers to questions raised by their findings during the first summer's work. Then in 1939, Michael Lerner underwrote the American Museum of Natural History's expedition to New Zealand, Australia, and Bali. While in Australia Mike Lerner, with blue-water guide Bill Hatch at the helm, dazzled his hosts by single-handedly fighting and landing two black marlin at the same time. Each weighed over 300 pounds. This event was not planned as a stunt: Lerner merely happened to be fishing alone when the two fish struck simultaneously. Rather than cut off one or the other, and curious to see both, Mike successfully fought both to the finish.

During this trip, the International Game Fish Association was formed. Actually the idea of an international governing body for salt-water angling had been discussed in America, and particularly in Great Britain and her colonies, for some time. However, Mike Lerner carried this idea from the discussion stage to concrete plans in private talks with Dr. Gregory and Clive Firth, one of Australia's foremost sportsmen. Firth was most enthusiastic, but suggested the organization be American-based because of threatening war in Europe and the Far East. Lerner agreed, underwrote the expenses for the establishment of this international body, and its first organizational meeting was held in an office of the American Museum of Natural History on June 7, 1939. Those present were Dr. Gregory (who served as the organization's first president), Michael Lerner, Ernest Hemingway, Van Campen Heilner, and Francesca LaMonte. Shortly afterward, Philip Wylie was asked to be its first field representative. The following year, Mike Lerner succeeded Dr. Gregory as president.

Over the next few years, Dr. T. Harold Pettit of New Zealand did much to expand the IGFA's effectiveness in the South Pacific, while Michael Lerner and his colleagues concentrated on enlarging its bases in Europe, Africa, and North and South America. By 1943—and despite the war—the IGFA had 24 representatives, 8 member scientific institutions, and 27 member clubs. By 1970, the organization had grown with 81 representatives in 43 nations or island groups, 24 member scientific institutions, and 802 member clubs.

From the beginning, the IGFA has had a very real interest in serving marine science. This had included assistance to scientific institutions, educators, fisheries personnel, and conservation workers.

In the late 1950's, the organization grew too large for the Museum's space, and it was moved to the Alfred I. duPont Building in Miami. Michael Lerner was its president at that time, and he assumed all support for the IGFA, including publication of the IGFA yearbooks, record charts, and a journal called *Ichthyological Contributions of the IGFA*. (This latter was discontinued when its material was found to be acceptable to the regular scientific publications of the museum.)

In 1961 when William K. Carpenter—an active angler and an out-

[288]

standing tuna sportfisherman—succeeded Mike as president, he took over the organization's financial burden while Lerner continues to serve as chairman of the board. The organization's headquarters were later moved from Mike's stomping grounds in Miami to 3000 East Las Olas Boulevard in Fort Lauderdale, Florida, 33316.

One of the charter regulations of the International Game Fish Association prohibits any officer of the organization from holding a world record. Some men have turned down a chance to become officers because of this ruling. But such a prohibition helps ensure fair-mindedness in record keeping. It also takes the pressure off board members who merely want to fish and not compete every time they put a line over the side. Certainly Mike Lerner enjoyed this aspect of the by-laws as he set about organizing the American Museum's first angling expedition to Chile and Peru in the spring of 1940.

An Englishman living in the port of Tocopilla was the first angler to give the world notice that there was spectacular billfishing available not far from his front door. Mr. W. E. S. Tuker (who later became the IGFA representative for Chile) invited Kip Farrington and his wife to try the sport, and in 1939, the Farringtons—fishing separately—sighted no less than 73 broadbill swordfish, presented baits to 37 of them, had strikes from 26, hooked 19 and caught four. The Farringtons were overjoyed; in nearly a decade of fishing, Kip had caught only one "albacora" previous to his Chilean trip. Their host, however, was most apologetic; never had he known anyone to have poorer luck while fishing off Chile.

Meanwhile, in 1939, Mr. George P. ("Ted") Seeley, a New York businessman whose work took him to Peru, tried fishing off a little-known cape 26 miles north of Talara. His tackle was primitive and the boats he used were more so. But he landed two black marlin in three weeks of fishing at Cabo Blanco—both over 700 pounds.

These successes on the west coast of South America confirmed marine scientists in their faith that the upwelling Humboldt Current would produce major concentrations of bait and gamefish found in few other places on earth. With all available charts and reports in hand and with the blessings of the American Museum of Natural History, the Lerners set off for South America in the spring of 1940.

The preparations for such an odyssey were immense. Two fishing boats were sent down in advance. Then all tackle—including enormous quantities of line, leaders, hooks, lures, teasers, spare rods and reels, fighting chairs, etc., etc.—went with expedition personnel aboard the

Grace Line steamer. Cases, 40-quart milk cans, collecting jars, chemicals and associated materials went along for specimens, and specially-made wooden tanks lined with metal were included so that large items could be kept and shipped home in preservative.

In addition to clothes, notebooks, paper, instruments, *et al.*, the expedition carried a great deal of camera equipment and film—all of which had to be declared at the Varick Street customs facility in Manhattan the day before sailing. In all, there were 162 pieces of luggage that accompanied the Lerner expedition to South America, and the camera equipment alone occupied a stateroom unto itself. Twice during the trip, that part of the expeditionary force which accompanied the luggage went over their lists to make sure nothing had been forgotten.

In Guayaquil, Francesca LaMonte, photographers C. Irving Hartley and Vibo Valenzio, and guides Bill Hatch and Douglas Osborn, who were all traveling aboard the steamer, were met by the Lerners and photographer David Douglas Duncan who came aboard to see that all was going well. Later when the ship stopped at Talara, Peru, the shipbound crew found that Mike had arranged for them to have the freedom of the port without going through the usual customs and immigrations formalities. A day's sailing from this port, Fran met once again with the guides and photographers in a corner of the ship's lounge to make sure that all the required equipment was still aboard. She had a large notebook containing the master list, and each man responsible for a particular item would check it off and account for its location. The newly appointed U.S. Ambassador to Peru, R. Henry Norweb, was in the lounge and witnessed the ceremony, and later at dinner, he asked Fran whether she had been conducting a prayer meeting!

Everywhere the expeditions went, the Lerners made detailed advance preparations. There was always a place to work in, boats to fish and collect from, and comfortable living quarters. What local help was needed or required by law was already assigned when the expedition arrived.

Lerner gives his orders quietly—more as if they were requests. But if they are not carried out expeditiously, a considerably forceful personality replaces the smile and gentle voice. When I used the word "adventure" to describe one of the events in a Lerner expedition, Mike hastened to correct me by quoting Roy Chapman Andrews[5] to the effect

[5]American naturalist, explorer, and author, Andrews headed expeditions of the American Museum of Natural History from 1916 to 1930 to Tibet, China, Burma,

that an expedition which has "adventures" is an expedition that has not been well planned.

On returning from a trip, expedition members accompanying equipment were customarily met by the museum's bonding agent and one of the museum staff who had been on the trip. The long plaster molds for fish mounts were checked and, if satisfactory, immediately shipped to Al Pflueger's in Miami. Microscopes and photographic equipment were carefully offloaded by hand, and all tanks, cases, cartons, and jars were duly registered and sent to the Museum's bonding room where their contents would be examined by a customs agent.

This became a notorious ritual. A lab assistant and someone from the department's scientific staff attended the ceremony. First the lab man opened a tank, and then he and the staff member put their arms in up to their shoulders to fish out a specimen. However, usually even before the specimen was all the way out, the customs official had retreated into the corridor, shedding tears and gagging from the smell of formalin. He would return at intervals to do his duty, sometimes with a handkerchief across his nose and mouth. But he also urged that the work be done as quickly as possible and that no more specimens be removed from the tanks.

This first South American expedition resulted in a number of outstanding catches. Helen Lerner became the first woman angler to take a broadbill in both the Atlantic and the Pacific, and she also caught a world record 403-pound striped marlin. Mike performed the rare feat of landing two broadbill in the same day, and the number of swordfish taken, along with various other fishes—from huge roosterfish to a new species of grouper—kept the museum staff working longer hours than they had on any previous trip.

Yet the most awesome—certainly the most exotic—angling Lerner did while in South America was for giant squid off Peru. The advent of this angling was entirely accidental. The first night out, Mike had merely been pursuing a local rumor about an area of the sea off Talara where great concentrations of squid could be found. Lerner had no idea of the size of these squid, but he reasoned that since these 10-armed cephalopods were one of the broadbill's favorite foods, such a concentration zone would undoubtedly attract many big billfish. However, some natives indicated the squid were monstrous, and local fisher-

Mongolia, and Central Asia, where his most famous find was dinosaur eggs in the Gobi Desert. Born in 1884, associated with the Museum from 1906 and its director from 1935 to 1941, Roy Chapman Andrews died in 1960.

men refused to go near the area in their small boats. But Lerner and his American crew put this down to superstition and set off one evening to see if they could hook a swordfish or two.

Every ocean angler should experience night fishing. Running out from a port at night is an adventure in itself. The darkness accentuates any noise and all silence. It exaggerates your sense of proportion so that near lights seem far away and an ordinary mile becomes a league. You must rely on instruments, not instincts.

Night fishing makes any fish you hook a little larger, a little more difficult to land. The contemplative light of the stars is matched by the phosphorescence of the sea, and you frequently find yourself with a wholly new perspective of time and tides.

The first squid Lerner hooked was a mystery. Something attacked his bait, ran with it, and then his line went slack. Suddenly the line rushed off again, only to go slack again. It was a most unfishlike performance, and after this was repeated still another time, Lerner finally managed to get the *whatever* close to the boat's lights. There, as a 20-foot squid thrashed on the surface fighting the wire leader, the amazed angler and his crew learned what the rush-and-stop fight was all about. As soon as one squid hooked itself and started away, others attacked it, tore it apart, and in the process another was hooked—only to be attacked and devoured in turn! The guide got his gaff into one of the survivors, only to be liberally sprayed with ink and clutched by sucker-disks that tore the skin from his arms and hands. The squid finally broke loose and escaped.

Lerner and his crew were horrified. In the darkness around them, they could hear water breaking as vast numbers of these eerie creatures fed on fish—and each other. They had all seen the notorious feeding frenzy of sharks, but never before had they felt so certain that a slip in the dark with one of them overboard would mean an immediate and gruesome death. Yet fascinated, they went on fishing.

Eager to see how large these creatures were, and to collect specimens for the museum, Lerner returned the next night armed with pillow-cases with eyeholes to keep himself and his crew from being drowned in the ink that was sprayed every time one of the squid was brought alongside. After a repetition of the previous evening's experience of hooking huge squid that were immediately attacked by a horde of lesser brethren, Lerner finally landed a giant. But he knew that he'd had on even larger ones. Years later he compared the sucker disks of a 30-foot squid on exhibit in the American Museum of Natural History with sucker imprints on the side of another museum specimen, a sperm whale. The imprints, or scars, indicated disks about three times larger than those of the 30-foot squid! Thus, those engravings of long ago depicting attacks on small ships by giant squid fully as large as the ships themselves might be grounded, after all, in something other than fantasy.

While the Lerners were in Talara, the Nazis invaded Norway. Though concerned and made cautious by this turn of events, the expedition members did not want to waste the opportunity of being so well equipped for marine research in such productive waters. So they pushed on to Chile. While there, an amusing incident occurred as a small relief to their growing anxiety. It concerns the only other interview Michael Lerner has ever given.

A voice, speaking quite fluent English, telephoned from Antofagasta that their leading newspaper wanted very, very much to send a reporter to interview Mr. Lerner. Mike, amused by the notion and mellowed by the hospitality of his host nation, gave way to the charm and persistence of the caller and agreed to see the reporter.

It was late in the morning when the fellow arrived and Mike discovered with something of a shock that the gentleman spoke no English. Most everybody else was already aboard the boats, including David Duncan, the expedition's Spanish linguist. Fran LaMonte rallied with a Spanish dictionary and a limited vocabulary of words and phrases utterly detached from any kind of grammar. However, she had studied Italian in Rome, and by combining elements of English, Spanish, and Italian, the interview seemed to proceed fairly well.

When it was over, Fran and Mike escorted the reporter to the huge front doors of the Grace House where the reporter shook hands and said thanks and good-bye all around. Then just as he stepped through the open door, he turned, cocked a thumb at Michael Lerner and yielded his only English:

"Some baby!"

The days of work in Chile followed a pattern: Everyone was up well before dawn. Breakfast was at 4:30 A.M. with all hands present so that the plan of the day could be discussed and details settled. Then as soon as there was sufficient light, the boats went out with at least one expedition member left ashore to take ship-to-shore messages, run errands in town or finish up photographic work. Some days, however, everyone went out on the boats.

It was on one of these days Fran witnessed a moment that, perhaps

[293]

better than any other, defines the spirit of Helen Lerner, a marvelous anglerette. Every guide who fished with her speaks of Mrs. Lerner with admiration, and on this occasion, she hooked a large marlin in mid-morning and fought it skillfully for over seven hours. It grew dark, but still she kept on. Suddenly the fish rushed to the surface and in a final leap, threw the hook—as simple as that. Helen was perfectly calm. She just turned in her fighting chair and smiled at the others aboard.

Late in the afternoon, around 6 P.M. the fish were brought in for weighing and photographing and then transferred from the dock to the Grace House coal shed by horse-drawn cart. By then it was time to clean up for the long Chilean dinner, after which, while the captains worked on equipment or dried line in the entrance hall and the photographers reported on what they'd taken—and what they'd missed,[6] Fran returned to the coal shed—accompanied by a watchman and an over-enthusiastic yellow cat—and worked on the fish until midnight. While the specimen was still fresh, color notes had to be made along with measurements, fin counts, and a thorough outer examination. Then a long, low lateral cut was made in the thick body wall. The wall below the cut was pulled down and secured, and the upper part pulled up and similarly fixed. Then the soft organs were examined. Sex was determined, and stomach contents and parasites examined for possible clues as to the depth and possible migration routes the fish was following when caught.

If there were a number of specimens to go through, everyone helped out. And Lerner himself, by this date both a field associate and a trustee of the American Museum of Natural History, was a competent assistant in making the scientifically prescribed set of measurements. When such preliminary work was done, the specimens were covered against insects and the cat for further work the following day. Then to bed and up again before dawn.

The expedition wasn't all work and no play. One evening after a particularly successful day offshore and after Helen Lerner had already landed, the group was startled to hear Mike serenading her through a megaphone from a small boat beyond the surf. Others joined in and soon the words of "All the things you are" and one that ran "When you hear my name, will you feel the same? Will your heart beat for me?" chorused out over the bay. The songfest idea caught on, and Mike had

---

[6]All was noted in a daily log and, because of the damp climate (it was winter south of the Equator), the exposed film was immediately prepared for shipment to Eastman headquarters in the United States.

[294]

selections printed on pink sheets so that everyone could participate. "Roll Out the Barrel" became especially popular while transferring fish from the boats to the dock for weighing-in.

On another occasion Mike gave a delightful surprise when he announced a two-week vacation for everyone. Some members of the expedition went to Lima and to the San Lorenzo Islands, while the Lerners, Fran, and one photographer went off to Lake Titicaca, to Cuzco, and then on to the Incan ruins of Machu Picchu. Although every one of this latter group was a seasoned traveler, none had seen anything like Machu Picchu. Standing in the ruins of this fabulous and all-but-forgotten civilization, the war in Europe seemed even more pathetic and surreal than usual.

By the time the Lerner expedition arrived in Tocopilla, the radio yielded only broadcasts from California and Russia. The Lerners and Fran, who had had some experience with a previous war, decided they better enlarge their supply of American currency and speed up the photographic work. Antofagasta, the nearest city, was something of a provincial German outpost. Indeed, the local bank was a branch of the Deutsche Bank where only German and Spanish were spoken. It was decided that since Fran had been to school in Munich as a child, she better go for the money. The road to Antofagasta was under repair after being washed out by heavy rains, so she ended up going over the mountain in a Grace Line truck. The next day she came back by road, bringing another photographer and the American currency. There was no way Lerner could have anticipated such problems raised by war. Thus, despite the advice of Roy Andrews, the expedition did have its "adventures."

When I was a youngster and my parents still lived in Forest Hills, Long Island, it was a weekend ritual for the family to visit the American Museum of Natural History. We'd drive into the city through deserted Sunday streets, and my father always found ample parking space alongside the Museum. Sometimes we'd see a special movie or a new exhibit. But mostly we just wandered the spacious corridors to gaze into the miniature worlds of far-away found in gallery after gallery.

My very favorite place was the Hall of Fishes. While dioramas of life beneath the sea are more difficult to compose and probably less popular than scenes of African animals or South American birds, I still found the size, design, and metallic hues of the great ocean gamefishes set against paintings of the undersea world my very favorite displays. The ocean as a vast frontier for study and sport appealed to my young mind as mightily as space travel appeals to some youngsters today.

At the time, I was too young to care about the names of the various donors of the Museum galleries. Now that the Hall of Fishes of the World has been replaced by impersonal filmstrip devices which incessantly talk at the visitor, I more readily appreciate the imagination implicit in the older format and the personality provided in each display by its donor, plus the talent of painters, taxidermists, and preparators shown in the backgrounds and mounts.

Among the Lerners' gifts to the American Museum of Natural History were two particularly impressive cases. One contained beautifully mounted specimens of marlin caught on the Australian-New Zealand expedition, and the other (labeled as a gift of the IGFA) contained the mount of a huge broadbill swordfish, the skeleton of another, and a growth series from the egg into adult sizes of still other broadbill. Many of the individuals in this series had been gifts of the *Istituto Talassografico* when the Lerners visited Messina, Italy—the Straits of which have a complete life cycle of *Xiphias gladius*.

These gifts were not only of interest to casual visitors such as myself, but back before World War II when the museum staff was small, such exhibits became essential aids for the instruction of future generations of marine scientists. For example, Dr. William King Gregory was both Chairman of the Museum's Department of Ichthyology as well as Chairman of the Department of Comparative Anatomy (also, Professor of Palaeontology at Columbia University). He gave his graduate student lectures in a large classroom adjoining his office in the museum. A similar situation involved Harry Raven who served on the staff of Johns Hopkins University in Baltimore as well as with the American Museum of Natural History.

As the museum staff grew following World War II, the Department of Fishes grew proportionately short of areas for research and teaching. But Mike Lerner was once again prepared to help out. During the Thirties—and whenever he could get over during the war years—Lerner had been developing in Bimini something approaching a marine biologist's Shangri-la. The work started in the mid-Thirties with a few pens off the docks of his home to keep live fishes for study. Mike had experimented with everything from live tuna and marlin to little reef fish. (Needless to say, the reef fishes fared better than the marlins!) And although the primary function of the Lerner pens was research, they fulfilled some of the same entertainment and basic education tasks of

[296]

a Marineland or Seaquarium when a visit to Bimini became incomplete without a visit to the Lerners' dock. As a youngster, I spent many hours enthralled there, looking down on the circling fish and intrigued by the fact that the sharks didn't immediately eat all the other fish in the pens with them.

Concerned about complaints of overcrowding in the museum's labs in New York City, Mike Lerner announced one day in the 1940's that he was turning over docks and a marine laboratory he was building to the American Museum of Natural History to serve as its Caribbean field station. This announcement was the fulfillment of a dream reaching back even before the Museum's first field trip to Bimini in 1937. Mike had long felt the need for closer communications between people working with the why and how of fishes, and he had always hoped to provide a vital link in that chain of communication. Possibly as early as his initial purchase of property in Bimini had such a contribution been in Mike's mind.

The original laboratory property ran from the King's Highway, which fronts the harbor, across the narrow island to the Queen's Highway, which fronts the open Atlantic. It included a good-sized house, an attached shed, an old stone building, and a separate storage shed. The house became the Lerner Marine Laboratory "Residence," while the stone building was used as an office and library to which were added a series of laboratory rooms. Later on, separate cottages for the superintendent and resident director were built on the grounds. Finally, and in addition to the docks, Lerner provided a large boat and several skiffs.

In the 1960's, when Mike perceived that scientists working at the laboratory were too numerous to house or provide with adequate research facilities, a larger Lerner Marine Laboratory was constructed with modern equipment and very fine living quarters overlooking the Atlantic. Such has been the progress since the early days when Mike kept a few live fish dockside for the amusement of visitors.

After the founding of the IGFA and the establishment of the Lerner Marine Laboratory, Mike's proudest achievement as an ocean angler was the part he played in the development of survival fishing kits for lifeboats and life rafts during World War II. Survival equipment was extremely limited at the outbreak of the war. Emphasis was on having enough life preservers or space aboard life rafts and lifeboats—not on survival thereafter. The assumption was that if men could survive being shot down or torpedoed, their rescue would be effected within a matter of hours. However, circumstances didn't bear out this assumption, and

[297]

a grim feature of rescue operations in 1942 was the discovery of rafts days after a disaster with men aboard who had starved or died of thirst.

Lerner became very much concerned after hearing some of these stories from Gifford Pinchot.[7] It was reasoned that, in many cases, had there been proper fishing tackle aboard, the men might have survived —catching fish from which they could have extracted body fluids for moisture and meat for food. Working closely with fellow anglers Kip Farrington and Philip Wylie, and charter skippers Bill Hatch and Eddie Wall, Lerner applied his own many years of angling experience to the problem of condensing into a single, lightweight but durable kit everything that a sailor or airman would need for survival, no matter over what ocean he flew or sailed. Since petroleum was rationed, Lerner did much of his tackle testing off Miami's Government Cut in a dory. And on at least one occasion, with wind and tide against him, his simulated course in survival nearly became a reality!

The kits were designed and assembled at the Ashaway Line and Twine Company in Ashaway, Rhode Island. Two sizes were created: the large kit was supplied by the U.S. government to all ships' lifeboats and rafts, while the smaller kit was made part of the inflatable life rafts aboard all planes. When Mike discovered that one of the most popular pastimes among servicemen was fishing, he designed a recreational fishing kit. He then headed an IGFA committee to raise funds through a nationwide campaign to manufacture the kit, which was then distributed by the Red Cross. The government, seeing the popularity of these recreational kits, later assumed distribution to overseas areas of occupation.

After the war, General H. H. ("Hap") Arnold[8] sent Lerner a copy of his book *Global Mission* with this inscription:

To Michael Lerner—in appreciation of the work that you did with life rafts during World War II. Your efforts contributed greatly to saving many lives of our combat crew and passengers.

Also during the war, the USO sponsored tours for popular baseball

---

[7]Pinchot (1865–1946) was America's first professional forester, chief of the U.S. Forest Service (1898–1910), professor of forestry at Yale (1903–1936), and Governor of Pennsylvania (1923–27, 1931–35.) He was also the author of such angling and adventure books as *To the South Seas* (1930) and *Just Fishing Talk* (1936).

[8]Henry Harley Arnold (1886–1950) was made chief of the U.S. air forces in June 1941; general of the army in December 1944; and general of the air force in May 1949.

stars to various overseas areas. The G.I.'s proved even more receptive to sporting personalities than anticipated, and the USO asked Michael and Helen Lerner to go to North Africa and Italy to talk about fishing. The Lerners took with them Captain Eddie Wall, and while he showed the troops various types of tackle and illustrated their uses, Mike and Helen talked, showed motion pictures made during their trips, and answered questions. These "angling clinics" were always crowded and frequently lasted well into the next morning.

In all, Michael Lerner sponsored seven expeditions for the American Museum of Natural History. Among the many honors commemorating his angling triumphs and scientific contributions, Mike is particularly fond of a rosewood plaque from the government of Nova Scotia where he is an honorary citizen, as he is of the province of Brittany, France. He was made a Comendador of the order "Al Merito" by the Chilean government, was presented with the President's Certificate of Merit by Harry S Truman, and has received an honorary Doctor of Science degree from the University of Miami in Florida.[9] Mike also received the Gold Medal Angler's Award given for the first time by the International Oceanographic Foundation for being "the sportfisherman who has accomplished most for marine science."

In looking back on a life of angling, any fisherman remembers details that can only be meaningful to himself. And so it is with Michael Lerner. It wasn't catching one of the largest mako sharks ever brought into Bimini that Mike recalls; it's the fact that inside that shark, neatly cut into small pieces as though a butcher had done the job, was a small broadbill swordfish—the first indication the world had that there was a spawning area for this species somewhere in the western Atlantic.

And it wasn't always the big fish lifted by the crane onto the dock at Cabo Blanco or Tocopilla that Mike remembers; it's the still larger ones that cruised imperiously past his bonito baits. It's also the booming sound of the surf along deserted coasts, the chatter of native crewmen as they prepare the boat for a day's outing, and the catching of bait that could be as much fun as the catching of the swordfish themselves. There was, also, the sight of the graceful frigate birds linked in memory to the gulls of Sheepshead Bay from so many, many years ago.

---

[9]His good friend Philip Wylie received his honorary Doctor of Letters degree from the University of Miami that same day: June 9, 1952.

NINETEEN

THE STORMY PETREL

If my father had held onto 30 acres of Signal
Hill, I might have been a millionaire. But then
I might have ended up like half the mugwumps
who've crossed my stern, and what good would
that have done me?—Tommy Gifford

Big-game angling has a brief history, but
Tommy Gifford's name is sharply etched on
every page.—Raymond Camp

I was still working in New York City then, enclosed in a tiny editorial
office made of moveable panels and frosted glass. That morning my
stall was invaded by the art director, who needed a title *immediately*,
and the production chief, who wanted copy *now*. The phone kept
ringing. Finally they left, and I lifted the receiver.

"Mr. George Reiger?" the operator asked.

"Yes"—probably a woman in New Jersey calling to tell me her husband caught a big sea bass over the weekend; or possibly a man in
Florida trying to find out how to replace a busted shear pin.

"George, this is Lyman Spire. Tommy's dying."

My breath stopped.

"He's back in Georgetown Hospital, and Dr. Ashburn gives him less
than a week."

Stunned, my mind wandered.

[300]

The bell buoy off Key Largo's Ocean Reef Club was always good for barracuda. Not only were the fish plentiful there, stacked up like cordwood in the shade of the buoy, but the fish were sometimes huge. Tommy Gifford once cajoled a monster into taking a live pinfish bait. My younger brother John hooked the fish, but on its first leap, the barracuda showed itself to be so large as to have difficulty heaving its bulk from the water. John, amazed and confused, clutched his reel into free spool and popped the fish off in the resultant tangle.

"The last picture I saw of Tommy, he looked terrible," Dr. Spire continued. "He's gone through so much hell with these operations that it's a wonder he's survived to date."

I'll have to let John know. He had been only 9 when he first met Tommy, age 55, but they cottoned to one another as though they were old schoolmates. John was the kind of kid who would get up at six each morning to walk the seawalls with a spear looking for mullet or stingrays—or mostly just looking down into the once-transparent waters of Biscayne Bay, thrilled by every new thing he saw. Tommy knew John was that kind of kid, and he liked that. Tommy had been that kind of kid himself.

"Can I call Tommy and talk to him?" I asked.
"No, he wouldn't even recognize you now. He's under sedation, and . . ."

Tommy once ran my two brothers and me far out off Miami's Government Cut. He stopped the engine, rigged up a balao bait and leader to three sash weights, and dropped the whole combination over on his monster or "wampus-cat" rod and reel. He told us we were tilefishing. Al Pflueger needed a tilefish specimen to mount, and we were going to catch one for him. Although youngsters, we were pretty well versed in marine science, and we knew that tilefish were rare and exotic.[1]

---

[1] A deep-water species sometimes found at depths exceeding 1,000 feet, the tilefish (*Lopholatilus chamaeleonticeps*) was first caught commercially in 1879 off the Nantucket Shoals Lightship. In 1882, when commercial interest in the fish was just becoming significant, a sudden temperature change over a vast area destroyed many thousands and resulted in some 4,250 square miles of the Atlantic being covered with dead tilefish. Since the species then disappeared for many years, it was popularly assumed to have become extinct. However, a modest commercial fishery for tilefish revived following World War II, and in the last few years, regular sport-fishing excursions for the species have started, mostly from ports along the North Jersey shore.

[301]

However, Tommy said we were going to catch one on the wampus-cat rig, and we knew it would be so.

"Here he is now"—just like that—and Tommy buckled John into the fighting chair and told him to crank until he got tired. I was next, and then Tony. Then John again. There was an occasional jerk of life at the other end of the line, but the combined load of fish, sash weights, and several hundred feet of line out made slow work for the triumvirate of youngsters laboring aboard the *Stormy Petrel*.

"Wait until the boat rolls," he coached. "Then crank on the down roll. Always use the sea to help you catch your fish."

Finally, the fish was alongside—distended, green, and weird. Perhaps a more exotic kind of cod. Tommy swung the tilefish inboard and immediately started the engine for the run home. We had not been out half a day. It was like a dream—except John went around for weeks afterward claiming he had caught the fish since he had spent more time on the reel than either Tony or myself!

"Don't forget to do all you can to publicize the hospital trust fund. Tommy'll need every bit of money he can get, and Esther can certainly use what's left over," Dr. Spire advised.

Tommy's wife, Esther, often caught the pinfish he used during his kite-angling forays. But whenever we stayed down at Key Largo, my brothers and I took over the bait-catching chores from her. To us, it was half the fun of fishing

Tommy seemed to know all there was to know about catching and rigging different kinds of baits. His very favorite was live balao, and we spent many a morning circling schools of "half-beaks" over the reefs with a surface seine and then loading the live well and spare buckets with wriggling bait, which we later converted to sport with every conceivable species of gamefish in Florida waters. We even once had a white marlin jump the gun and charge in behind the boat while we were still loading balao and—thunk! into the stern with his bill in determined pursuit of a stray baitfish that sought sanctuary under our keel.

Luther D. Miller, Jr., Rector of Saint David's Episcopal Church in Washington, D. C., told me the saddest story of Tommy's fight with cancer. In one convalescing period between operations, Tommy was taken for a boat ride on Chesapeake Bay. At first, he showed great improvement and was his old talkative self. But soon he tired and became

[302]

silent. Finally, on the way in, he turned to the nurse who was with him and said, "I know I'll never be able to run a boat offshore again. But do you think I can get well enough to catch bait for the others?"

"Sorry to bother you at work," said Dr. Spire. "But I thought you'd want to know." He sounded reluctant to hang up, as though he, too, had memories he wanted to share. But then, "So long now."

I hung up and stared at the frosted glass panel before me. So many memories. So little time. I was sitting, staring at the wall, when the art director returned for his title. Dragged from the edge of reminiscence, I thus returned to the *now* that practical men call reality.

Before he died on November 15, 1970, Tommy Gifford had spent half a century serving as guide and consultant to some of the most glamorous names in saltwater angling. One afternoon in Tommy's last home at Red Hook, on St. Thomas in the Virgin Islands, I was reading through his copy of *American Big Game Angling* when I came across the following inscription:

To Tommy Gifford who was catching them off Cuba when we first began. Who kept on catching them, bigger and bigger. From his friend and admirer, Ernest Hemingway.

Havana, Wedgeport, Bimini, Montauk, and a dozen other place names are resonant with the angling fame Tommy helped create for them—and for himself. Essential saltwater equipment such as the outrigger, fighting chair, flying gaff, and even the star-drag reel all owe debts to Tommy's rambunctious thinking. He ranks with George Farnsworth and Bill Hatch as being among the most creative and popular big-game guides of all time.

But Tommy's reputation was leavened by controversy. Unlike Farnsworth and Hatch, he lacked two ingredients of the "perfect" guide: restraint and discretion. When a charter captain spends all day, every day, for extensive periods of time, with the man who hires him, his first obligation—after a decent day's work—is silence regarding the personal vices of his patron or any differences of opinion between them. Tommy, unfortunately, was all too willing to share with the world the details of his latest disagreement with Michael Lerner, or his outright hostility toward Kip Farrington. And ultimately Gifford's fame was built more by the sporting press—and by those women and children

[303]

he championed as anglers—than by the famous fishermen he guided, many of whom he competed with for the limelight.

Part of Tommy's fondness for publicity was based in the fact that by the time he got into the guiding business after World War I, competition among the various chartermen was considerably keener than it had been 20 years earlier. Every angler wanted to fish with a well-known guide. And who had ever heard of a 23-year-old kid named Gifford working out of Miami in 1920? Tommy's answer to that question was to be a little more daring, a little more imaginative than the next man. And if he did not initially have the support of that well-heeled fraternity of sportsmen who frequent salt water, well, he would certainly recruit a little attention through his friends in the press.

But the habit stuck, and years later when Tommy had all the charters he could ask for—when men were flying him cross-country for just a few days of fishing—he still could not keep his mouth shut. Energy, enthusiasm, and imagination were all qualities of this stormy petrel. Discretion was not.

The Reiger boys first met Tommy in 1951 at the peak of his angling reputation. However, two dozen world records caught aboard Gifford's boats meant little to three cocky kids who had done a little ocean angling of their own. At ages 15, 12, and 9, Tony, myself, and John were pretty sure we knew all there was to know about the sport.

I caught my first sailfish when I was eight, and the story was featured in newspapers up and down the Florida coast (for several weeks following, I was unbearable to live with!). A year later, I refined that initial feat by taking a sail on regulation bait-casting tackle. Christmases at the Pelican Hotel in Stuart, Florida, were annual events for the Reiger family, and when we boys first met Tommy, we still had vivid memories of one afternoon when we had caught and released 17 sailfish.

I had seen giant tuna hauled from Wedgeport's Soldiers Rip (and when the tide slackened, my father had let me fish bottom for cod). And I had watched the clipper fleets of sportfishing boats surge from Bimini harbor to the drop-off where sleek migrant bluefin were found. (And in the evenings, after the weighings in, the rejoicing and the arguments—after the crowds dispersed to the bar or to their boats, some of the mates showed me how to catch mangrove snappers in the shadow of the dock lights.)

Off Bimini I watched "Red" Stuart use a technique Tommy had helped develop (although I did not know this at the time) of herding a hooked tuna into the shallows and keeping it there without sufficient room to move or dive so as to literally suffocate this fish that requires a steady flow of oxygenated water over its gills. Thus Stuart, always a superb boat handler, helped my father land a 570-pound fish in 15 minutes.

In 1951, our family moved from New York City to North Miami Beach, and to make the transition more agreeable to his three sons, my father decided to spoil us with a boat. Since he still maintained an active medical practice in New York, my father was limited to weekend visits to Florida, so he asked Tommy Gifford to help us hunt up something respectable in the way of a 16-foot inboard.

After fishing itself, Tommy was most fond of women and kids who liked to fish. Since we fell into the latter category, Tom spent an inordinate amount of time helping us three youngsters settle on a second-hand plywood "character-style" boat with a dependable but low-power inboard engine barely strong enough to get us in and out of Baker's Haulover Inlet—which we had been expressly forbidden to go near, but where we inevitably strayed.

We were discovered one afternoon in this breach of contract by our mother when she happened to drive over the old Haulover bridge at the precise moment we were battling a 60-pound tarpon—and some pretty fierce waves!

But the water's wrath was nothing compared to our mother's! Our story that the fish had towed us out the inlet only doubled our dose of punishment. And only Tommy's laughter when he heard of the incident and our father's curiosity about the king mackerel fishing we had discovered offshore the Kenilworth Hotel saved us from losing the boat entirely. Some weeks later we took our father out—"just to see how we handled the boat in the inlet"—and the trip was blessed by a sizeable catch of kings. Thereafter, we were cleared for ocean angling.

A ritual of those early years in Miami were spring and fall pilgrimages to Key Largo's Ocean Reef Club, where Tommy showed us the best reef and Gulf Stream fishing we will ever know. And he was always an excellent teacher.

He taught us the importance of live baits and how best to catch them—from cast-netting mullet to diving for spiny lobster (in those days we frequently used the tails to catch yellowtail and crushed up the heads for chum).

In our diving adventures, Tommy spurned flippers and face mask and the new spring-powered spear guns that were just then coming on the market. The only clothes he wore were a pair of Japanese goggles, and he carried a sling spear which fired a sharpened 7-foot metal rod through a hollow length of bamboo by means of flexed surgical rubber tubing. I remember his excitement one day when he brought back an unusual spiny lobster colored coal black with red spots, and I recall how we laughed at his comic appearance, standing there in the nude with water still streaming down his body while he solemnly declared he would name the new species of crawfish after his pet dog!

On another occasion we smiled at his insistence that the olfactory senses of the average fish made the best bird dog's nose seem weak in comparison. We ridiculed the notion that smell could play much of a role in the response of an oceangoing gamefish to a lure racing by his line of sight.

Then some days later we encountered a widely scattered school of cero mackerel feeding along the edge of a reef. Merely by baiting one feather jig with a plug of shrimp and leaving an identical lure unbaited, and then by fishing both lures an equal distance from the boat, Tommy proved how essential the sense of smell is—even to a fast-moving gamefish like the mackerel. The baited lure caught more than *four times* as many fish as the unbaited lure!

Tommy also taught us how to debone mullet and how to prepare bonito, mackerel, or dolphin belly strip-baits. We were taught that a kite can catch fish on days when no other technique will take them. And we learned tricks that made little sense unless you were there to see them work.

Like the slow day Tommy ran us to an amberjack hole where a couple of "friends" lived. Live pinfish baits lured them to the surface—huge fish weighing better than 70 pounds apiece—but neither the pinfish nor an assortment of lures or special retrieves could make them hit.

"I've caught these rascals before," Tommy explained.

He ordered in all the lines but the two with pinfish on them—"to keep 'em interested," he said. Taking a Spanish mackerel from the fish box, he hooked it through the nose and lower jaw and cast it out on one of the 6/0 outfits we normally held in reserve for grouper. The mackerel landed beyond the patrolling amberjacks, and Tommy skipped the dead fish back over their heads as fast as he could reel. He sailed the rig into the boat alongside some pretty startled anglers!

"Get ready!" he ordered. "And when I bring the mackerel in this time, get the pinfish out of the water."

Again he cast. The pinfish came in, and the amberjack turned toward the commotion of skittering mackerel. Not just the stripes through their eyes, but their brows and backs, too, flushed black as the amber-

[306]

jacks raced the mackerel to the boat. Just as one was about to nip the bait, Gifford whipped the rig from the water.

"You ready?" Tommy asked. Were we! Tony and I trembled with excitement while watching the show and trying to keep our pinfish separated in the bait well.

Again the mackerel went out, and this time Tommy was reeling even before the fish hit the water. Again the amberjacks raced for the mackerel, swirled after it, and nearly caught the decoy in their rush to the boat. Zing—slap! We all ducked the incoming mackerel.

"Now!" Tommy yelled.

Our pinfish went out. Smash, boom! Barrels of water went all over everyone, and two reels shrieked as they never had before.

Forty-five minutes and one broken line later, a huge fish lay exhausted alongside the boat. Tommy gently unhooked the amberjack, patted its head affectionately, and said, "See you again, big boy."

The fish wagged its tail away out of sight.

Tommy never lost his zest for the sea and the creatures in it. Even when he did not have a charter, he and his wife would often go offshore on a busman's holiday of exploration and experimentation. And he so much more preferred a youthful squeal of appreciation for a leaping sailfish than the ho-hum—I've-done-this-kind-of-thing-before reaction, that he once turned down a lucrative charter simply because his prospective client had become jaded with big-game angling and only fished for business reasons. Tommy delighted in wrangling records for women and children just to irritate male chauvinist anglers who felt that big tuna and marlin were only for the likes of them.

In 1936, Kip Farrington went out on a limb by predicting that any woman who tried to bring in a giant tuna would be taken back to Miami in a box that was in the front hall of the Compleat Angler Hotel in Bimini. In a stunning season, combining rare angling ability and superb boatmanship, Helen Lerner, with Tommy Gifford at the helm, boated 11 such bluefin in 1938. Then, in 1941, Tommy went out with Mrs. Marian Hasler and came back with a 374-pound tuna on 15-thread, the first such size fish ever taken on such relatively light line —by a man or woman. The next month he was with Mrs. Hasler off Cape Breton and helped her land a world-record 530-pound broadbill swordfish on 24-thread; then a month later a 246-pound swordfish record on 9-thread (27-pound test!)

"That was a *great* summer," Tommy said about the last fine fishing he was to know before being caught up in World War II.

During World War I, Tommy had served with the Coast Guard in the Mediterranean. In 1943, he was recalled as a warrant officer but was soon made a lieutenant junior grade and sent to the Cay Sol Bank to break up the commerce there between Cuban "fishermen" and German U-boats. This he succeeded in doing so well that he was promoted to senior lieutenant and packed off to the Pacific for duty with light tankers carrying aviation fuels.

Tommy was reticent about those days in the Western Pacific. But James A. Mulcahey, a former vice-president of Harrington and Richardson who served with Tommy, has these memories: "You can sum up Tommy's life in the Pacific with one word: boredom. Probably his greatest achievement was in constructing a Rube Goldberg-type washing machine so his men could have clean clothes. But he himself never wore much more than a pair of khaki shorts. And it wasn't easy tracking him down during duty hours. He spent most of his time diving over the reefs of the different islands we visited, collecting shells and coral for stateside museums. The decks were always littered with a great variety of marine flora and fauna drying in the sun."

Despite this laissez-faire approach to service, Gifford was asked to stay on after the war, and was even tempted with a lieutenant commandership. But he argued that sport fishing was a higher calling, and by the winter of 1945, Tommy was back trolling Atlantic waters.

Ten months before his death, I visited Tommy in the Virgin Islands. He was recently back from Miami, where a malignant growth in his neck had been removed—the first of many operations that attempted to stem the tide of cancer. Leery about calling on a convalescent man his age, his wife reassured me, saying, "Oh, he's always well enough to talk your head off! Besides, the visit will do him good. The doctor has postponed his fishing plans indefinitely, and he's starting to leave claw marks on the wall!"

The operation had sapped much of Tommy's energy. Normally restless and rambunctious in his conversation, for once the indomitable Gifford was in a reflective mood. However, he could still be cantankerous about people or circumstances that he felt had treated him unfairly. When I asked a question about his book, *Anglers and Muscleheads*,[2] Tommy launched into a tirade about how the book was now a collector's item worth several times its original value and how he had never made a penny on the project.

I changed the subject: "Bill Hatch is credited with originating the drop-back technique for catching sailfish as early as 1915, but you're

---

[2]Published in 1960.

the man generally honored with fixing the principle into the outrigger. How did the idea come about?"

"Well," replied Tommy. "I was going to the Bahamas and was going to use some big heavy reels. And I couldn't see why the party should sit there on their pants all day long holding one of those big reels.

"So I got the idea from a grove of Florida bamboo. I cut down three or four of them, but by the time I cut them down to where they were fairly straight, they were too darn short! 'Well, that's that,' I thought. But I hung them up to dry and went on down to Miami. There in a hardware store I discovered some of those old 25- and 30-foot Japanese cane poles. So I took a brass sleeve and drove my Japanese ends into my Florida butts and came up with a pole 50 feet long!

"Well, I lashed the things to the side of my boat—the crudest damn things you ever laid your eyes on—and out offshore I went. I hadn't been out there 10 minutes before I had the goldarndest crew of boats following along at a respectful distance!

"I was using ballyhoo.[3] And those bamboo poles were so much like 50-foot fly rods and the boat was flat-bottomed so that when she'd fall off a sea, the outrigger on one side would skip the bait out of the water and send it sailing across to land 20 feet in front of the boat on the other side!

"Well, I knew then I'd have to put steadying things on her. So I put sets of spreaders made from bamboo, took a little piece about an inch and a quarter, forced it over and glued it and wrapped it with about a million miles of string! And that was the outrigger that caught the first giant blue marlin ever taken in the Atlantic."

I told Tommy I'd seen an ancient Fin-Nor reel with his name on the side plate along with a calendar of other outstanding names from the 1930's. And that Fin-Nor's representative had told me it was the second Fin-Nor ever made.

"Nope, that was the *first* one" he said. "The second one, I've got here [in St. Thomas]. I had both at one time and loaned that one you describe to Dave Meyers [vice-president of Fin-Nor] many, many years ago. The first fish that reel caught was the start of a great many years of untroubled fish catching! The old Vom Hofes and the old Coxes and the old Hardies—they used to be sent to somebody like Mike Lerner to be 'tested.' Well, he'd look at me, and I'd look at him [Tommy

---

[3]While ballyhoo (*Hemiramphus brasiliensis*) and balao (*Hemiramphus balao*) are different fish, these look-alikes are viewed by most anglers and guides as one and the same.

giggled in reminiscence], and he'd say, 'Tom, let's go out and tear the darn things up!' [laughter].

"Sure enough, we'd go out and tear the guts out of those reels on big fish and bring them in a bunch of rattling parts. The foreman mechanic at Vom Hofe's—well, I took him one of his 12/0's that had frozen, and he absolutely refused to admit it was frozen. Big German boy. 'Ach! De reel, it is not froze up!' Well, in those days, the way reels were built, there was no reason in the world why they wouldn't freeze up.

"Well, I tore the reel apart, right down to the darn place where we had to use a Stilson wrench on the bronze bushing that held the post— and, sure enough, it was frozen. Yet that lunkhead *still* said it was not frozen!

"Well, I got so Goddamn mad, I scooped the whole lot of parts into a bag and said, 'You know what I'm going to do with this reel'—to show you how rough I was in those days—Mike Lerner standing right there and the manager just came in, somebody by the name of Sutton or something, and I said to them all, 'You know what I'm going to do with this reel?'

" 'Are you going to leave it with us for overhaul?' the manager asked.

" 'Heck no, I'm not!' I said. 'I'm going to pay for it with my own money and I'm going to take it to Miami, going to borrow a friend's speedboat, and I'm going to take it four miles offshore and drop it overboard!'

"Then I waved the drawings of this reel that you're talking about— the one with the names on it. And it was so simple that even somebody like me who's not a draftsman could draw a half-baked likeness of it— and I waved the drawing under the foreman's nose and told him, 'I have something 10 years ahead of its time.' And the foreman let out a couple of grunts and said, 'I'm not interested in anything 10 years ahead of its time.' And I said, 'It's certainly a cinch to know I can't do anything more with you,' and walked out."

Tommy wiggled his finger at me, and the shadow of his hand wiggled back from the floor: "Remember, it don't matter how ornery you are if you're right. And if you're right, don't worry about people thinking you're ornery. Besides, sometimes it's the only way to get anything done."

Tommy settled back and went on with the story: "One day sometime later, one of my best competitors—one of the Cass boys—told me about a terrific mechanic who didn't merely repair automobiles, he *rebuilt* them! My friend said, 'I bet you he could build a reel.' So I went to

[310]

the mechanic and he said, 'Yes, sir, we can build that reel.' And, boy, it was the most wonderful feeling using that first reel! I don't recall whether it was a tuna or a marlin we caught first, but we sure started tearing 'em loose from then on in!"

Tommy did not invent kite fishing. But he did use the technique in 1927, shortly after Harlan Major brought it from the West Coast.

"One day on the docks at Montauk, Harlan Major walked out to go fishing with a kite in his hand, and one of the neighboring chartermen said, 'Oh, look at the pretty man coming with his pretty kite.' And the charterman hollered over to a buddy, 'Did you bring your jacks today?' You know, ignorant sarcasm. But Major was not a man to take sarcasm. He was an extremely serious-minded guy, and he had put an awful lot into building those kites. So he turned on his heel and headed off the dock.

"When he got opposite me, I said, 'Gosh, that's a lovely swordfish kite.'—'So you know what it is?' he asked, sarcastic as hell! Boy, was he mad! But just then my party showed up, and it ended with him going out with us. And we caught the first bluefin tuna and the first white marlin taken on kites off Montauk *that trip!* And I learned a lot about kite fishing from Major, and even if it's no magic formula for those occasional dull days we all get, still it was something that always interested my parties."

The generation that produced Tommy, his friends and clients, is almost gone. And some of the survivors, he wouldn't talk about.

Tommy's feelings for men—fondness or fury—stemmed from their attitudes and conduct in fishing. Tommy's opinion of one well-known angler is frankly, unprintable. Tommy alleged this famous fisherman once tried to hush up the fact he had been beaten by a big fish—the further implication being that the man had even tried to buy his crew's silence.

On the other hand, Ernest Hemingway, in Tommy's opinion, was one of the finest men ever to troll a line in blue water. He, too, was once beaten by a huge fish, and readily admitted the fact.

"Ernest was a real gentleman and a very great angler. He was one of the most wonderful people I've ever known. He was loveable, he was—well, most important, he was the kind of man who would never accept a lie for truth. It was one of the greatest shocks of my life when I heard he was dead."

Other favorites of Tommy's were Charlie Lehmann, George Thomas III, Tony Hulman, Joe Peeler, Maury Webster, and Van Campen

Heilner. One of the small disappointments of Tommy's life was that he came within an ace of guiding Heilner to a marlin catch when that writer lived in Bimini.

Perhaps the most consistent theme of Tommy's life was his insistence on using light tackle whenever and wherever possible. In recognition of Tommy's presence in the islands and his contributions to light-tackle angling, the Virgin Islands established a Tommy Gifford Award: the Masters for anyone catching the islands' big five—blue marlin, white marlin, sailfish, Allison (yellowfin) tuna, and wahoo—on 20-pound tackle, and the Grandmasters for anyone taking these same fish on 10-pound tackle. The first angler to qualify for the Grandmasters was Dr. Lyman J. Spire of Syracuse, New York.

This is how Tommy talked about his love of light tackle:

"I always enjoyed poking fun at fellows who caught small fish on big tackle. I wiped out the chartermen who had mugwumps[5] come down to fish who thought they knew how to fish light tackle. When they tried to fish light tackle, the mugwumps went home without any fish, and the chartermen came in without any tackle.

"But some fish aren't meant for the light stuff. When the Allison tuna and big wahoo are running good here [the Virgin Islands], a reel of 30-pound line lasts me about two weeks. A 50-pound line will last maybe two months.

"But if you've got the chance—say with sailfishing—not only do you have more fun with the fish on 20-pound test than with 50 or 80, but it's a heck of a lot easier to hook the fish in the first place because you use a hook so small and sharp, the hook easily penetrates and holds.

"That's why I was able to have such terrific luck with my sailfishing at the Ocean Reef Club. I used a 4/0 Wright & McGill hook that was so light that when it was in a live pilchard—well, I've seen a sailfish mumble a pilchard around in his mouth for three solid minutes. He pulled it off the kite and he was swimming into the current, and at the end of three or four minutes, all of a sudden the hook finally lodged in a tender spot. And when the fish finally came out of the water, he was hooked. None of my parties ever hooked their fish. The fish would come out of the water, and I'd say, 'Oh, look, you've got a sailfish on.'

"Then I used number 5 or 6 wire so that when I wanted to release a fish, all I had to do was reach out, get ahold of the leader, give it a sharp little pop, and it would either straighten the hook or break the

---

[5]Tommy's use of this word has nothing to do with the dictionary's definition. It denoted anything he wanted it to mean, depending on how he used it.

wire. That way you don't have to grab the wire and have the fish thrash himself against the side of the boat in the usual so-called 'release.' Ninety-nine percent of the sailfish I release, I guarantee you, live to bite another day. But not—well, the other day by the time my mate [Vincente] got through raising hell with a sailfish, I gave *him* hell! I said, when we're using number 7 wire or number 8 wire on account of the blue marlin in the area, don't you *ever* pull a sailfish up along-side the boat and grab him by the bill and try to wrestle the hook out! Just cut the hook right at the mouth."

When it came to landing big fish, Tommy preferred an A-frame rigged over the cockpit rather than try to use a gin pole. These were his reasons:

"First of all, any man who ropes a giant marlin or tuna by the tail is asking for trouble. For starters, if the fish has any life left in him, you can't kill him by hitting the tail!

"I have on board my boat a heavy-duty shark hook filed down sharp as a razor with a big bronze ring welded in it. And through that ring I've run a ¾-inch rope about 10 feet long. The minute we get the fish up alongside, we start the boat moving ahead at two or three miles an hour. If it's a big fish, first we get him with the flying gaff just back of the dorsal fin. Then we drive that shark hook in above the nose and give it one half-hitch, two half-hitches, three half-hitches. The instant those three half-hitches are on, there's one chance in fifty-five million— there's no chance—that we'll lose that fish. Now with the A-frame you can lay that fish anywhere and land him either side or even right over the stern. Remember, you can't always bring a fish up any side you want to. If the gin pole's on the far side of your fish, and there're sharks around, you've got troubles. I've never *ever* lost a blue marlin along-side the boat to sharks! I've seen 'em lost on a dozen boats where they had the fish round the tail and were trying to drag him all the way around to the gin pole on the other side. With the A-frame sitting up over your deck, with the block and fall tucked in here [demonstrating], and a cable support running forward to a big fitting in the bow—with a floodlight mounted atop the frame and with the frame supported by a pair of three-inch aluminum pipes sitting on foundations at the sides, you've got something that's practical, that's no more in the way than a gin pole is, and something that will *never* break.

"I've seen gin poles smashed all to hell by big fish. I saw one fish pulled up, and he was so big they couldn't get his head out of the water, and when they got him up as far as they could and before one of us could jump aboard and help 'em pull the head around and into the boat, that fish went into a frenzy and when he got through, he had done over $1,000 worth of damage to the boat. . . . You can have the gin pole!"

A rod-handling technique that Tommy has taught a good many of his anglers is what he calls the "short pump."

"All you do is rock back and forth and get the big fish started up, instead of waiting half an hour between pumps, thereby giving the fish a chance to get his head down again.

"Mrs. Phyllis Bass learned this one *beautiful* moonlit night when she had a 340-pound blue marlin on 50-pound line 1,700 feet straight down and hooked in the back. Three times she tried to raise him, and three times she missed him.

"Finally, I said, 'The only way we're going to do it is for you to raise him a little bit at a time. You can raise him, can't you?' 'Yes,' she answered. 'All right,' I said. 'This time when you raise him up, *snap* down and get a half turn, a *quarter turn*, I don't care if it's a fifth turn!' And she did. She said, 'It works!'—'Well,' I said, 'keep right on going.' All this while her husband was 200 yards away fighting a world-record 104-pound fish on 12-pound test. He landed his fish a little bit sooner than she did, but when she pumped hers up, it was a world record, too, and both boats ran back to port with our horns going to wake up the town!"

Toward the end of my visit, I asked Tommy about big-game fishing in the Virgin Islands—how it compared with what he had known off Bimini. His reply was laced with the kind of enthusiasm that would make even the local Chamber of Commerce blush.

"That country [the Bahamas] is good and has rapidly developed into one of the best marlin spots anywhere—especially being so close to Miami. I understand now there's about 70 to 80 boats running out of Bimini and South Bimini together.

"But this place here—well, last year [1969] fishing two months, I didn't raise 31 marlin, I *boated* 31 blue marlin in 60 days! That's a fish every other day. And one of those was 570 pounds!

"This is the only part of the world I've ever been where an enormous number of people fishing with Captain Johnny,[6] myself, and our other

---

[6]Johnny Harms, one-time protégé of Gifford, persuaded Tommy to join him in the Virgin Islands for a joint sport-fishing assault and pioneer effort to discover what the islands had to offer.

[314]

chartermen catch blue marlin *every doggoned month of the year*! [He rapped the table for emphasis.] You just don't do that anywhere else.

"And another thing, I've laid at the dock up north [in Florida and in the Bahamas] during the winter months and figured the wind was going to blow the boat right away from the dock. But in four years here, honestly now, I've had four days when I didn't want to go fishing. Never saw anything like it! Most steady, even climate.

GWR: Do you ever use live baits here?
Gifford: No, you don't need to. Small barracuda, bonito, mullet, mackerel, bonefish—they're all good trolled. Artificial lures work right well, too, *if* they're supple enough. Hell, we had one marlin follow our boat half a mile while trying to swallow one of those rubber toys! But our party kept jerking it away from him. Fish finally got discouraged and swam off.
GWR: Summer's your best marlin season. What's your slowest month?
Gifford: Well, month of January I only got three blue marlin, but that was in catching a lot of wahoo. Up north I caught wahoo for 18 years, and 50 to 60 pounds was the average. Here I've got 30 wahoo over 80 pounds and one 114. Every year we get a great winter run. Just last week one of my brother fishermen brought in one 100 pounds.
GWR: What kind of tackle do you use for wahoo?
Gifford: Wahoo are strictly 20-pound test fish. If you catch them on anything heavier than 20, you're not priding yourself on doing anything exceptional. But there's a big difference down to 12-pound test. You take Dr. Spire—he's one of our favorite anglers here. I think he went through 25 or 30 wahoo before he caught one on 12. Of course, like I say, these are big average fish.

Another thing, when a man goes out off Miami or off the Bahamas, once in a great while, if he should catch four or five wahoo, everybody gets excited about it. Johnny [Harms] twice—he has a very fast, big boat and he can *go.* There's a spot 45 miles from here, right out through here [pulling out a chart and tapping a section of ocean northeast of St. Thomas called the Sea Mound]—and twice he has brought in 21 wahoo up to just under 100 pounds. [I whistled in appreciation.] Yep, it's one of the great wahoo spots of the world.

Then, besides wahoo, we have our own run of dolphin in March, April, and May.
GWR: Big ones?
Gifford: Big ones. Oh, yeah. Up to 50 pounds. And every once in a while you see the one that gets away which is twice as big as that.

[315]

Last year I had out a man that I love very much, and he's a light-tackle boy. Well, you guessed it. We hooked a dolphin that looked to me like it was eight feet long. Jesus, what a monster! He finally broke off. It was just too much fish for 10-pound test.

GWR: How about the reefs? The reefs of the Florida Keys are so rich with snapper, grouper, mackerel, and so forth. Is this comparable here?

Gifford: No. Though, here again, I believe if I actually went to work and studied the spots, I could give you some very wonderful grouper and barracuda and kingfish. Like the other day we went out, I had people who I knew weren't going to be able to go way offshore, so we stayed close and caught 22 kingfish. We went out another day and got 18. We have a spot out here called the Kingfish Bank. Then we have another place called the Barracuda Bank. At certain times these give us very, very good fishing.

GWR: I know there're a lot of small barracuda inshore. But are there any really large fish off these banks?

Gifford: [Tommy smiled] Lots of folks think that the further away in the world they are, the bigger the fish are going to have to be. [Then seriously] But I did see something last summer that had my mate walking around in a daze for nearly a week. I saw a blue marlin that would have gone better than 2,500 pounds. [A long, long whistle from me. I didn't doubt the size for a minute. Tommy had an amazing ability to judge live 100-weight fish within half a pound.]

We have had so goddamned many fish on over 1,000 pounds! But those fish—well, the annoying thing about it is that people say there are no thousand-pound blue marlin, because if there were, why haven't you caught one? Well, what they do, they make the mistake of comparing blue marlin and black marlin. And there's no more damned comparison between those fish than there is between the sun and the moon!

Years and years and years ago, fishing out of Kona [Hawaii], I caught a 325-pound blue marlin in the morning and a 325-pound black marlin in the afternoon. Both fish were hooked in the corner of the jaw; both hooked on heavy tackle. Well, the blue marlin just fought the pants off the black marlin!

There've been a number of black marlin now landed over 1,000 pounds, and no angler—no *good* angler—has ever had any trouble with them. But right off the island of Bimini, there've been two or three dozen fights with blue marlin 800 to 1,200 pounds—hooked and lost. And just last summer, Johnny [Harms] hooked a big blue on 80-pound line and lost him eight hours later. Fish was about 1,000 pounds. From a standing start, the blue marlin will run circles around the black

[316]

marlin! And in running away from you, that's when he breaks loose.

GWR: Do you think anyone's ever going to get one of these monster blues?

Gifford: Of course they are! When I was out in Hawaii, one of my Japanese-American friends got a 2,550-pounder on a heavy handline. He was catching bonito while patrolling his long-line and this marlin came right up to the boat. He stuck one of the bonitos on a great big hook, and the marlin swallowed it up to his ass—[Suddenly embarrassed by the tape recorder, Tommy changed the subject.] All I want— I was hoping—I was up in Florida not so long ago, and I saw something that made me drool. I've always been a lover of small boats for the simple damn reason that you don't use a draft horse to play polo. And you don't use a great big clumsy boat for that extra special marlin.

Now I know how many Johnny Harms has lost. And I know how many I've lost. Well, I've got a 42-foot boat——

GWR: The *Caribe Maid?*

Gifford: Yep. She's beautiful, and she's big, and she's clumsy. Now, when I was up in Florida, I saw a boat sitting in Forrest Johnson's yard —you know he built the 26-footer I made my reputation on . . .

GWR: The *Stormy Petrel.*

Gifford: *Stormy Petrel,* the 26-foot Prowler. Well, Forrest was now working on a 31-foot, 6-inch glass hull that with a pair of V-8 Cummins diesels represents the ultra, ultra, ultra, ultra in big-game fishing boats. Now, right away some millionaire mugwumps will holler: "Too damned small!" And just you look at some of these new boats coming out 47, 48 feet long. Every once in a while a 50-footer. Hell, you've got to put 350- to 400-horsepower engines in them just to make them get out of their own damn way!

Now, I'm hoping before I'm through fishing that I can use that kind of boat here one summer from June to November. [Wistfully] Oh, gee, I've lost two or three beautiful fish—fish so much bigger than I've ever caught before. But we'll catch them, by golly. We'll catch them! You come back in July and August, and we'll rewrite the record books!

Obituaries for Tommy Gifford were carried in newspapers and magazines—including *Newsweek* and *The New York Times*—in every coastal state of the union. On November 30, 1970, a procession of 17 fishing boats led by Johnny Harms's *Savana Bay* (shortly after to be lost in a dockside fire) and Tommy's own *Caribe Maid* carried Captain Gifford's ashes to sea. The flotilla plowed through heavy swells north of St. Thomas on the familiar sport-fishing route between Thatch and Grass Carp. At last, the *Savana Bay* stopped engines, and while the other boats slowly circled, a brief ceremony was read by Father John M. Hennessy. The ashes were scattered and the memorial wreaths were cast on the waters, and the long procession of fishing boats turned back to Redhook.

I'll never now have the chance to rewrite the record books with Tommy as we had hoped. But another of Gifford's disciples is on hand in St. Thomas, and she seems to have that possibility well in hand. Maintaining Tommy's tradition of enthusiasm, cussedness, and determination, Eleanor Heckert regularly cruises the waters of the Virgin Islands in a 37-foot Striker with a keen-eyed mate named Lincoln. Ellie has a little ritual that mystifies, and even startles, some guests. When some time passes without any action, she borrows a coin, tosses it overboard, and yells to the heavens: "Tommy, you old bastard, send us some fish."

Strangely, it sometimes works.

Missed Strike on the Flats

Section Five

TODAY—EAST, WEST, AND ABROAD

TWENTY

LIGHT-TACKLE CONVERT

All men are equal before fish.—Herbert Hoover

Fly casting for ocean fishes is nearly as old as American angling itself. Yet some outdoor authorities believe saltwater fly fishing only began after World War II. But if my history-poor colleagues had said that the sport has only become *popular* in the last three decades, they would have been closer to the truth. For the cult of saltwater fly fishing is as much a result of the substitution of fiberglass for bamboo and nylon for silk, as it is a growing awareness that you do not need telephone poles and winches to make respectable catches in the sea.

Up until the 1920's, fly fishing in Florida was generally thought to be a wealthy eccentric's pastime. And while occasional river tarpon were taken on fly rods, blue-water fish were never approached with anything less than 3/6 tackle—and even this was considered foolish or daring, depending on your point of view.

[320]

However, outdoor writer Stewart Miller began to popularize salt-water fly fishing,[1] and in 1931, Miller wrote: "Fly fishing has taken hold in Florida like fire on a sun-baked prairie. Where, years ago, the fly rod was just something to gather dust in the tackle shops, it is today considered a reliable source of revenue." He then told of a doctor-friend from Baltimore who was converted from Atlantic salmon by his first dolphin on a fly rod. The fish weighed 17½ pounds and came to net only after "26 death-defying leaps." Thus, although much of this early oceanic "fly fishing" was merely another form of light tackle endeavor—with trolled strip baits substituted for cast flies—the adaptation of trout and salmon tackle for blue-water angling was well underway before World War II.

After the war, spinning competed with fly gear for the attention of light-tackle advocates. Bob McChristian, Jr., who later built the Seamaster reel, opened Captain Mac's Fishing Shack in November 1946, the first place you could buy spinning tackle in all of Florida.

"DuPont developed monofilament as early as 1932," says Bob, "but that first stuff was impossibly stiff. You had to use a tiny stiletto to tie and untie your knots.

"In reels we sold the Swiss *Fix*, English *Ambidex*, Swedish *Staro*, and the French *Centaur*, early *Mitchell*, and *Ru-Mer*. The *Centaur* was the first reel to use a finger pickup, and then all the French reels had it. The first full bail came out on the Italian *Pelican*, which was a forerunner of the *Orvis*. We also sold the American-made *Basch-Brown*, *Unicaster*, and *Bradco*—but these came later on."

On September 15, 1949, Bob and his wife provided a remarkable first for ultra-light spinning tackle by taking a pair of bonefish on 2.5-pound (tested) line. In 1950, he, his wife, and an apprentice in his shop won respectively the U.S. Men's, U.S. Women's, and U.S. Junior's Distance Casting Championships with spinning gear. Bob also caught the first permit ever taken on spinning tackle, and his 69-pound cobia

---

[1]In writing his chapter on "Fly Fishing" for the *Salt Water Tackle Digest* (edited by Lou S. Caine in 1947), Erl Roman credits Stewart Miller and Henry U. Birdseye of Miami with getting fly fishing going in South Florida. Together they designed a "special ocean fly rod" 10 feet in overall length with the reel seat above the hand. The rod weighed 10 ounces complete with double-handed butt, and became commercially available through James Heddon's Sons in Dowagiac, Michigan. Writing in 1935, angling-artist Lynn Bogue Hunt says, "All my sailfishing these days is done with the Stewart Miller-Heddon salt-water fly rod on which, because of its lightness and quality, I use a Pflueger Capitol reel of 300 yards, 9-thread capacity."

on 12-pound test, and his wife's 51-pound, 8-ounce wahoo on 10-pound test, further popularized spinning gear for big game.

Soon, many South Florida guides, appreciating the simplicity and convenience of this tackle, carried a spinning rod aboard for any of the light to welterweight fish they might encounter offshore. A blue runner caught on six-pound test spinning went a long way toward soothing the disappointment of an otherwise fishless day.

Today, fly and spinning are no longer viewed as competitive. Rather, they are complementary. As fewer of Florida's tourist-anglers feel the need to catch a sailfish, more are discovering the thrill of flats fishing. In some ways, a flats angler resembles a hunter, for he is judged more by his accuracy and the success of his stalk than by the weight of his kill. Of course, some of the flats fishermen are youngsters in furiously fast boats who may cover 100 miles a day in their search for the one big fish they hope will distinguish them from all other mortals. But there are old-timers, too, many with fabulous blue-water memories, who now prefer the quiet cuts and channels of scattered mangrove keys, and tropic sunsets on their shoulders as they turn home with nothing more than a small redfish or a pair of snappers for dinner.

One of the best of these mature anglers is a former deep-water charterman who has lost most of his older clients to death and taxes. Rather than try to compete with the spiraling costs of maintaining an offshore cruiser at a metropolitan dock—yet rather than give up the charter business entirely as some of his friends have done to work in boatyards, tend marinas, or manage motels—Johnny Cass traded in his blue-water boat some years ago for a houseboat named *Cassamar*.

This craft is a light-tackle base camp from which Johnny scouts the nearby Keys for gamefish. And by giving up his offshore career for the flats, he mirrors the prevailing trend in saltwater angling away from a select few seeking giant tuna to the increasing many after their first tarpon on a fly rod.

Aries must be a good astrological sign for successful chartermen, for Bill Fagen and Tommy Gifford were both born on April 11, and Johnny Cass was born the thirteenth of that month, 1908. The youngest of six boys, four of whom became charter boatmen, John Jenkins Cass matured into the most famous of the brood. Only his brother Archie—retired now and famous as the guide who founded the remarkable tarpon and permit sport fishery in Miami's harbor inlet, the Government Cut—rivals Johnny for family laurels.

[322]

Charles and Louise Jane Cass moved their family to Florida from Berwyn, Pennsylvania, in 1913. They first settled in the inland town of Palatka on the St. Johns River. While chicken farming helped make ends meet, Johnny's father, a skilled mason, began to find more and more of his work to the south in the towns that Henry Flagler was building. Charles Cass's first assignment came about when a wealthy Palatka neighbor asked him to build the fireplace in his new home in Miami. The elder Cass quickly became skilled in the special art of Cochina shell masonry, and by 1921 it was abundantly clear that the family's future lay south of Palatka. Converting their four-room bungalow into a pontoon type houseboat with all the pontoons covered with concrete (Charles Cass was a mason, after all), the family towed their residence with two small skiffs (one powered by a five-horse, the other by an eight-horsepower inboard engine) down the newly completed intracoastal waterway to Fort Lauderdale. The hurricane of 1926 later destroyed the houseboat, but the sons went into the mangroves to find the pieces and then rebuilt their home on land.

Johnny apparently enjoyed the houseboat living of his youth, for his present home is a 70-foot housebarge, which he calls a "yachtel."

"When I started building her in December 1958, my mother came down to the dock one day, looked about, and snorted something about, 'Oh, Lord, not *another* houseboat in the family!' But when I got the *Cassamar* done, she came aboard to try out the accommodations and got downright comfortable about houseboating again. Ed Moore[2] is retired on one, lives over in Coconut Grove."

I had called Johnny in early November for an interview. He was in the process of converting the *Cassamar*'s roof into a floor for two master bedrooms and a lounge, making his barge into a palatial doubledecker. And he was trying to have her ready by the first week in December when he would set off in her for the Keys. Work came first, and there was some question about when we could get together. Sunday morning seemed best.

"Come by at 6:30 if you don't mind getting up early. We'll talk while we have breakfast and before I have to go back to work."

As you drive north over the Miami River on the 27th Street bridge, the *Cassamar* (when not on its "working" location behind Riding Key) is sometimes berthed beneath an enormous banyan just to your right. I parked in front of the house that shields the boat from North River

[2]Another of the great early charter skippers.

[323]

Road, and while collecting pad and pencil, someone said, "Good morning."

Johnny Cass is a ruggedly handsome man whose most distinguished feature is a pair of bright blue eyes that radiate goodwill. He is a confident man, and his confidence puts you at ease.

"Come on along," he said. "I'd like to show you the boat."

The *Cassamar* is built along conventional, although spacious (27-foot wide), houseboat lines. There is nothing racy about her; she has no engines. Comfort is the keynote.

"Why the name *Cassamar?*" I asked.

"Well, it comes from *Cass*, my name; *A* for Ann, my former wife's name; and *mar*, meaning the sea. The whole word without the double *s* means 'house' or 'castle on the sea' in Spanish. I also have a twin-engine commuter skiff, for running between Cudjoe Key and my anchorage, called the *Little Cassamar*. It's a modified Chris Craft kit with a low profile and lots of beam—the perfect workboat. I also use it to tow the *Cassamar* south in December."

"How'd you get started in deep-sea fishing?"

"Well, all of us—Archie, Sam, Harvey, and myself—were interested in fishing early on. We fished together, and we mated for men who already had their own boats. For instance, I mated for Captain James Vrelan out of Fort Lauderdale, and I worked with Tommy Gifford for a while. But our big break came when Edward Schmidheiser from Atlantic City and Philadelphia decided to sponsor us. He gave Archie his first boat, the *Boy-Mac*; Sam, the *For-Tuna*; and me, the *Dolphin*. He was a remarkable man who, even when he didn't go fishing with us, would send his chauffeur down to the dock with seven crisp-new five-dollar bills. That was our going rate back then: $35 a day."

"Did you ever fish him in the Bahamas?"

"No. Only off Miami. Once I took him to Everglades City for tarpon. We got a 135-pounder on 50-pound test line, which was considered quite a feat in those days."

"Did you ever fish people besides Mr. Schmidheiser?"

"Oh, sure. He was our regular charter for about 12 years, but he didn't care what fishing we did when he wasn't there. He knew the more we fished, the more we learned, the better his fishing would be when he came down."

"Is that when you made your first trip to Bimini?"

"Right. We worked out of Pier 5 then, but we tried to persuade our charters to run over with us for a day or two and even up to a week at a time."

"What year was that?"

"Oh, 1929, 1930—right on to 1932."

[324]

"What was the advantage of taking charters so far from Miami? Wasn't the fishing good here?"

"Adequate's more like it. Nothing compared with Bimini in those days. We first went over to see if we could land any of the big horse mackerel that were tearing up everybody's tackle."

"Is that when the first Fin-Nor reel was developed?"

"Right."

"Did Tommy Gifford design that first reel?"

"You heard that from Tommy?" He smiled. Johnny knew Tommy liked to boast, but there was no sarcasm in Johnny's question. He was one of the guides who organized a collection of funds in the Miami area to help defray Tommy's expenses while he was in the hospital. "Actually, we all had a hand with that first reel. We all knew what was needed. But Edward Lloyd Knowles, who mated for Tommy and who was a first-class mechanic, actually built the first reel. Fin-Nor's Fred Greitin further developed it, and then promoted it. After we had the reel, Tommy's achievement was in taking the first giant bluefin in one piece on 80-pound test tackle, and then on 50-pound test."

"When you say 'in one piece,' you're talking about sharks?"

"Yes, indeed. When we first started, if the tuna didn't destroy your tackle, the sharks destroyed your tuna."

"Can you remember any unusual moments from those early charter days?"

"If you mean by 'unusual,' funny things, yes. Plenty. One day, two ladies came to the dock in Miami and asked to go sailfishing. I couldn't find a mate, but I decided I could take the two gals out by myself since they seemed to know something about fishing. So we went out and trolled—each lady holding a rod on a flatline—that's straight back in the wake, not up in an outrigger. I told them that if they felt a tap, they should free spool the line immediately. They nodded and seemed to understand. Well, on toward noon, I felt nature's call, and told the ladies to holler for assistance if they got a strike. I was below just a few minutes, then came back on deck, and one of the ladies said: 'Oh, Captain, while you were gone, there was some kind of fish with a stick in his mouth hitting my bait!'

"But the worst thing happened to skipper Harry Hill. He was running his boat from the flying bridge one day when one of his anglers got a sailfish strike.

" 'Let him have it!' Harry called down. 'Let him have it!'—meaning free spool, of course.

"Well, you guessed it. The confused angler stood up, hesitated just a moment, and then threw his rod and reel overboard!"[3]

[3]Philip Wylie used this anecdote in a Crunch and Des story called "The Reelistic Viewpoint."

[325]

"What do you think about flatlines versus outriggers? Which gets the most fish?"

"Unquestionably, the flatline. But you've got to have the right angler to fish it. Outriggers are great for the average man who prefers day-dreaming to fishing. A flatline angler must be alert 100 percent of the time."

"Do flatlines *really* get that many more strikes?"

"Absolutely. You'll catch more big fish within 30 feet of the boat than you ever will 120 feet out. And you have better control. One day, a 719-pound tuna[4] jumped at one of our flatline baits and missed. He made five more passes before he finally took hold. The point is this: My angler was able to keep his bait reacting like a live fish and was ready to strike when the fish finally grabbed it. You can't have that kind of control with an outrigger."

"New York and New Jersey anglers find that tuna are susceptible to lures close in the prop wash," I said. "But will marlin take a bait so close to the boat?"

"I've taken more big marlin within 40 feet of the boat than I ever did on an outrigger. No one should ever fish for any fish more than 90 feet out."

"What's the reason for this? Do you think the wake turbulence excites curiosity?"

"Probably. And the churned-up water also helps hide the leader."

"You and your brothers were fortunate in your patronage. Do you think high taxes have made such generosity impossible today?"

"It's a little more difficult for the young skipper today. But it's not impossible. Wealthy individuals supported our efforts 40 years ago; corporations can do the same today."

"Do you have any hints or advice for young chartermen just getting started?"

"Mostly a complaint. I think any charterman who takes a party out all day, hooks every fish for them, and then doesn't stop the boat to give the fish a chance or allow the angler some sport is doing a tre-mendous disservice to the entire future of deep-sea fishing. A man who hooks a fish and then gives the rod to another is like a fellow playing golf who knocks the ball down the fairway and then hands the beginner the club to carry. If a tourist doesn't know anything about fishing, he's got to make his own mistakes to learn. Few of the young charter guys seem interested in developing anglers, and I think the sport may suffer in the long run."

"What's the advantage of keeping a boat moving with a fish on?"

"It avoids a slack line and helps the fisherman land his fish. And a

---

[4]This is the 719-pound fish referred to in the next footnote.

[326]

moving boat makes a little kingfish or barracuda on oversize tackle seem a whole lot bigger. Heck, you get just as much sport out of dragging a broomstick or bucket! There's no reason in the world why a brand-new fisherman can't go out with a little instruction and handle his first sailfish on 20-pound tackle. But 50 and 80 seem standard on a lot of so-called 'sport-fishing' boats."

"Who was your most important patron?"

"George A. Lyon, Senior."

"How long were you with him?"

"Eighteen and a half years. Based at Paradise Point, Bimini."

"Did you ever catch any records together?"

Johnny smiles at the question. He clearly does not think records make the angler. "Yes. Two world and one Bahamian."

"Any of these still standing?"

"I'm sure the Bahamian record has been broken by now.[5] And so has the 85-pound white marlin Mr. Lyon caught on three-thread tackle in February 1949. But you saw that Atlantic blue marlin in the picture downstairs? I believe that one's still on the books for 30-pound test.[6] Mr. Lyon caught that fish July 23 off Bimini—the same year the white marlin was caught. It weighed 480 pounds."

"There's a picture of a mako shark that was caught on your boat in the receptionist's office at the Fin-Nor/Tycoon Tackle plant. Wasn't that a record?"

"Norton Conway of New York City caught that one in 1935 or 1936. It weighed 798 pounds, but we didn't enter it for a record because it had to be shot.[7] A few days later we had a mako 1,500 or 1,600 pounds jump at the bait and miss. I don't know what we would have done if we'd hooked that one and got it alongside the boat!"

"Do you think the IGFA is wrong in prohibiting the shooting of sharks?"

"No boatman likes to see his transom chewed up, but he's got to take those risks if he wants a record.[8] No, I don't think there should

---

[5]In 1948, George A. Lyon won the Cat Cay Tuna Tournament with a total of 5,575 pounds of fish. His biggest single tuna was a 719-pounder, which was the largest fish ever taken during a Cat Cay Tuna Tournament until June 1970, when Bud Hittig and George Matthews tied for largest fish honors with two 745-pounders. George A. Lyons, again guided by Johnny Cass, took second place in the 1949 Cat Cay Tuna Tournament with 1,381 pounds of fish.

[6]It is.

[7]The International Game Fish Association does not recognize any fish that has been shot, harpooned, or otherwise mutilated.

[8]While the IGFA does not recognize shot sharks for records, the Miami Metropolitan Fishing Tournament will permit a skipper to shoot or employ a "bang stick" on a shark *after* it has been gaffed to help subdue the fish and save wear and tear on his boat.

be any exceptions made on big sharks. In fact, it's sad freshwater rules still allow the use of guns, for I know muskie fishermen up north who won't boat a fish without shooting it. Now a big muskie's no different than a hefty barracuda, and there's just no reason in the world to pack a pistol for a fish like that."

"What's the bigger element in successfully playing a big fish on light tackle—skill or luck?"

Johnny laughs. "Oh, there's no denying you've got to get breaks on all the big fish. But skill, endurance—that's what make the difference. The fact Mr. Lyon's 480-pound marlin somehow threw a perfect clove hitch in the wire near the tip of its bill certainly helped land that fish —but it hurt the angler, too. Every time that fish swung its head, Mr. Lyon's rod tip was slammed down about six feet. You can imagine the leverage behind those swings when you consider the line was tied to one end of a 12-foot marlin. Mr. Lyon had to stand up and play the fish next to the gunwale whenever it sounded. If he hadn't, the jerk of the marlin's head would have smashed the rod against the side of the boat. You can appreciate the punishment my angler took, standing in a choppy sea, fighting a big marlin that slammed the rod tip into the water every time it shook its head."

"What's the largest marlin you ever boated?"

"A 606-pounder off Bimini. Mrs. Harley J. Earle caught it."

"Ever had on a 1,000-pounder?"

"Every charterman who fishes Bimini regularly gets a crack at one of those really big fish."

"What's the best way to handle one of the giants?"

"That all depends on how they're hooked. If it comes up spitting blood or shaking its head from side to side like it's sick, the fish is hooked deep and has to be played carefully. A jaw-hooked fish can be worked a little harder."

"Why wouldn't a deep-hooked, badly-injured fish be easier to catch than one that's only bothered by a hook in its jaw?"

"Because deep hooks pull out more easily. I watched Ernest Hemingway one evening lose a marlin between 1,200 and 1,400 pounds because he worked it too hard. You could tell by the way the fish tossed its head, he was sick. But Ernest always fought everything as though the sharks were after it, and he wouldn't ease up on that fish either. He was fishing 54- or 72-thread line, and he finally pulled his hook right out of the fish.

"Another time, I had a party on my boat with a 512-pounder I could see was deep hooked. I begged the angler to ease up on the fish, and I'd show him why when we got the fish in—if we got the fish in. Sometime after nightfall we slid that marlin into the cockpit and I held a flashlight for my angler so he could look down the fish's throat and see. Sure enough, the hook was barely held by a quarter-inch of throat skin. 'How'd you know?' he asked. I didn't for certain. But when you see your fish bleeding, or tossing his head, it's a pretty safe assumption.

"In contrast, Mr. Lyon's 30-pound test record was hooked right in the corner of its jaw and jumped 45 times—counted leaps, mind you—and was landed in just one hour and fifteen minutes. An active fish will often do a lot of his own catching, and you can work him harder."

"Did you ever charter for Ernest Hemingway?"

"No. But I did go fishing with him as his guest on the *Pilar*. He first came over in the early 1930's and wanted to learn some of the tricks we used. Of course, when you were Ernest's guest, it was understood he did all the fishing."

"Did he make any outstanding catches while you were aboard?"

"No world records. I was with him when he caught one of his first big tuna—a fish about 300 pounds. He spent five hours on it, and we came in after dark."

"Any other adventures?"

"Yes. We used to have fun with the sharks. In those days off Bimini some really huge sharks would get into the middle of schools of feeding bonito and actually stick their heads up out of the water waiting for something to jump by. We'd cruise up to those monsters and pour lead down their throats from machine guns. Sharks don't seem to wait around with their heads out of water over there anymore!

"But fish are always changing habits. Not only will grounds that were hot 10 years ago be dead today, but, for instance, big tuna in the Bahamas: They don't run as close inshore as they used to. We used to be able to catch some of them in pretty shoal water. And they never had anything in their stomachs in the old days. Nothing. Today, they're gorged with tiny porcupine fish."

"Porcupine fish?"

"Right. Stuffed with thousands and thousands of them. Red Stuart first told me about it. There're schools of a lot of things we don't know about in deep water."

"But where would the tuna get the porcupine fish if not in the shallows?"

Johnny shrugs. For me, it is a mystery that should be examined; for Johnny, it is just another marvel of the sea that one should accept.

"Red Stuart's great claim to fame are the giant black marlin he helped Alfred Glassell catch off Peru. Do you have any particular memories of either of them in Bimini?"

"Only that Red was always a strong contender in every tournament. He lived hard and didn't take care of himself the way he should have—especially as he got older."

"Did you ever fish Michael Lerner?"

"Yes. In 1933 and 1934 at Bimini."

"The Farringtons?"

"Mrs. Farrington's one of the finest anglerettes I've ever seen."

"What other female anglers have you particularly admired?"

"Mrs. Lerner was the best anglerette I ever knew, and one of the best fishing people—man or woman—in salt water. I used to put the spyglasses on her while she was working a fish. But my personal favorite was Connie Earl of West Palm Beach. She caught 13 blue marlin with me on 30-pound test tackle up to 412 pounds. She refused even to hold a 50-pound outfit in her hand."

"Who was your favorite male angler?"

"Mr. Lyon. He was the finest sportsman I ever knew. Even in competition angling when he'd lose a big fish—sometimes right alongside the boat—he'd stand up, take off his hat, and call after the lost fish, 'You're a better tuna than I am an angler!'

"He developed the offset butt when he was 74 years of age. Since he had a bad back but strong legs, and since a dead tuna's the devil's own work to raise, the offset provided a certain leverage. With a foot brace and harness, he could use his entire body to lift the fish. We made the first offset butt out of bronze; then we experimented with laminated wood. Now they're made out of cast aluminum. The IGFA once considered them to be unethical, but now they've been cleared for records."

"Did you leave Mr. Lyon to build the *Cassamar?*"

"Not right away. Mr. Lyon's doctor told me not to take him tuna fishing anymore, no matter what. But he just couldn't stay away from the fish. One day he turned to me and asked, 'Johnny, are you going to take me out for tuna or not?' I said, 'No, sir, I can't. Your doctor won't allow it.' And he told me if I wouldn't take him out, he'd have to find someone who would."

"How old was he when he died?"

"Oh, I think he was 79."

"Why did you turn to the flats? And to generally smaller fish?"

"Tournament fishing was exciting stuff, and we had some great men in the beginning. I always liked Steve Bancroft, for instance. He was a Pan American pilot and a great angler who fished with Tommy [Gifford] a lot and won at least one tournament.[9] And the society of anglers was smaller then. Everyone knew one another and all the boatmen, too. And the Bahamas themselves were better islands then. And maybe I was getting older. So were many of my clients. We began to enjoy fishing the mangroves more than bumping around offshore every day. Cecil Keith had done some pioneering of the flats fishing near Marathon. He, too, had started with big game. Also Lloyd Knowles.

[9]In 1941, Steve Bancroft took first place at Cat Cay with a total catch of 5,441 pounds.

Anyway, a number of people had proved there was charterable interest in flats fishing. When I first told people about the houseboat idea and started building the *Cassamar*, I got a lot of help. In fact, after just a few seasons, I found we were booked up five years in advance. Many of my old blue-water clients came down to fish with me—some from 35 years back. Robert Sealey, for example—he's over 80—has gotten his share of bonefish, tarpon, and permit with me, all on 8- and 10-pound tackle."

"Did you ever fish the Bimini flats for bonefish?"

"No. The Bahamians developed most of that themselves. Some of the local boys became really expert. People like Bonefish Sam."

"What else is different in your fishing today than 40 years ago?"

"Well, most of the folks I fish today aren't so competitive as they probably once were. A lot of times we watch big tarpon rolling, and no one will even throw a hook at 'em. We're just content to watch them roll. One fellow who fishes with me regularly pinches the barbs back on his hooks and casts to these big fish just to get one or two jumps out of them. 'Just to look them over,' he says, and that's it. Going after a 100-pound tarpon is work, and most of my clients just want to relax. They also want to release the fish they catch. We release 90 percent of everything we bring to the boat. That's one of the most pleasant things about the fishing I do nowadays, particularly when I go to Key West and see the awful waste of fine gamefish that goes on there. Beautiful cobia, barracuda—all brought in and then thrown away."

"Do you fly cast for bonefish?"

"Fly and spin." Johnny smiled and leaned forward. "Strictly between us, bonefish are a pushover on a fly. I caught three the first morning I tried."

"How about permit?"

"Oh, that's another story."

"Ever get one with a fly?"

"Not yet."

"Tarpon?"

"Sure. Quite a few on fly. I have a little trick that helps new people get hook-ups on tarpon nearly every time."

"I'm listening."

"It's very simple. Just remember to strike straight overhead and not off to one side or the other. The inside of a tarpon's mouth is like metal, but if you strike straight up, you'll get pretty nearly every fish that takes your fly, 'cause a tarpon's got a tender nose. Of course, you sacrifice something in the play of the fish. Nose-hooked tarpon don't jump as well as jaw-hooked fish."

"What other fish do you regularly catch?"

[331]

"Chiro—ladyfish—are a great gamefish that need to be written up more. There must be millions of them in the Keys, but they're overshadowed by everything else down there. Believe me, a three-pound ladyfish on six- or eight-pound tackle has terrific stamina and jumps like mad.

"Then we go jewfishing occasionally. Particularly if we want some good chowder. One time Otto Geralyn, a brass foundry executive, wanted to try jewfishing in the Ten Thousand Islands, so we ran to a spot I was pretty sure would give us a 40- or 50-pounder. Well, he hooked one, and the fish ran straight back into a hole in some brush, and rather than disturb the hole, we cut the line. Mr. Geralyn hooked another fish, and this one did the same thing. But we decided to see if we could get this one out. We drifted into the brush, and though we finally had to cut the line, we managed to get it untangled and land the fish. Then somebody noticed another line in the brush, so we untangled that one and found it belonged to our first fish. We brought him in, too. Then Mr. Geralyn began to reel in the slack line that had spilled over the side in the confusion, and darned if a third jewfish hadn't gotten himself tangled up in that—around the fins and in the gills—and we landed him, too! A lot of folks won't believe that story, but it's true."

"Have you ever fished outside Florida or the Bahamas?"

"Just up and down the Atlantic coast. I spent the summer of 1939 working for the state of Virginia trying to find a deep-sea fishery there. Captain Bill Hatch had been asked up by the Townsend brothers to explore offshore Maryland, and he had discovered the Jackspot[10] and helped publicize the white marlin fishing out of Ocean City. The state of Virginia was hoping I could do the same for them.

"I started at Cape Henry—Little Creek was the only harbor we had then—and worked offshore and north all summer running out of Wachapreague and Chincoteague on the Eastern Shore up to the Maryland line. I got our first marlin just north of the Chesapeake Lightship, and on July 4—Pony Penning Day—we brought 11 white marlin into Chincoteague. They sure stole the show from the ponies! The state had the fish photographed a dozen different ways and then shipped them to Richmond for display."[11]

"So there're white marlin grounds off Virginia?"

---

[10]Originally called the Jack's Pot after an old Maryland market fisherman, this shoal bank, some seven miles in length, was pioneered by Paul and Jack Townsend in 1935, with Captain Bill Hatch as their guide.

[11]The Virginians had cause to celebrate. This was the largest number of white marlin ever taken by one boat in a single day's fishing. The previous record was a tie of seven fish apiece between the Townsend brothers fishing off Maryland and Ernest Hemingway fishing off Havana.

"Not really. Food concentrates those fish. Dense schools of sand eels and squid. And as the bait shifts, so do the marlin. The day we caught the 11, I started just 20 miles offshore and six or seven miles south of Winter Quarter Lightship. I never saw so many marlin in all my life! We counted more than 2,000! But there's no guarantee those fish will hold in one area from day to day. I understand even the Jackspot isn't what it used to be. Chartermen in the area are supposed to be running to a zone 45 miles offshore Lewes, Delaware, now. And even if that's straight offshore, that's a little too far for the average angler.

"And there's another drawback to Delmarva white marlin fishing: The white's the best gamefish in the sea—*if* he's caught in the Tropics. Off Florida it's rare to find a white that won't jump at least 30 times if he's hooked on the right tackle. But those middle Atlantic marlin are just so full of food, they can't fight. Fifteen jumps is good action on the fish up there.[12] Same reason a lean, hardened, 600-pound Bimini tuna is one of the toughest gamefish in the sea, and a whole lot tougher than the 800- to 1,000-pound hogs they become by the time they get to Nova Scotia."

Boats were now moving up and down the Miami River, and I was losing Johnny's attention. I could see he was thinking about getting back to work on his own boat. We went below, and I asked him to pose on the stern of the boat, so I could get pictures of Johnny Cass in his "natural habitat." He grinned, did so, and between film advances pointed out baitfish in the shade of the boat ("see, the Miami River is not so bad off after all") and a pair of cruising needlefish ("they make excellent marlin bait, and there's something of an art to catching them").

Then I got in my car and drove south over the 27th Street bridge. When I looked back, I saw Johnny already at work, preparing the *Cassamar* for her next season in the Keys.

---

[12]There's at least one other theory to explain this popularly noted phenomenon of a marlin's superior defense in Southern waters compared to his resistance further north. Donald Leek, president of the Alglass Corporation which makes Pacemaker yachts and sportfishing boats, is a devoted marlin angler who has caught an estimated 200 whites and perhaps 50 blues. He has fished the entire Atlantic coast, but prefers the fishing off Ocean City, Maryland, and the Bahamas. He feels the reason a marlin fights better in the Bahamas is that "a marlin is basically a tropical fish and has a metabolism best suited for tropical waters. As the fish migrate north, the water temperature may fall only a few degrees, but it seems to make a difference in its actions." *How the Experts Catch Trophy Fish,* Heinz Ulrich, Cranbury, N. J., 1969, page 152.

[333]

TWENTY-ONE

THE IMPRESARIO

The pleasantest angling is to see the fish ...
greedily devour the treacherous bait.—William
Shakespeare

As the Cass brothers were fortunate in having wealthy patrons, Bernard
Victor Kreh, better known as Lefty, was fortunate in having a pair of
talented teachers. And to repay the assistance given him by Joe Brooks
and Tom McNally when Lefty was first getting started in outdoor writing, Lefty in turn has helped any and all newcomers to the field.
Among notable angling reporters who have come within the purview of
his help and influence are C. Boyd Pfeiffer, Mark Sosin, and Bob
Stearns.

Lefty was born on February 26, 1925, in Frederick, Maryland. His
father died when Lefty was six, in the midst of the Depression. There
were three sons, and as soon as Lefty was able, he was out supplement-
ing the family's income by bush bobbing for catfish in the summertime
and trapping mink and muskrat in the winter. Meanwhile, at school,
he was earning the nickname that forever replaced Bernard Victor.

"I'm ambidextrous and also have what they call crystal vision, so

[334]

that when I was a kid playing basketball I could throw a ball left-handed to one corner while watching an opponent in another who expected the ball to come off my right hand. Pretty soon some of the players on rival teams in town started calling me Lefty. It stuck."

There are other advantages to being ambidextrous:

"When you're in a boat with another fellow on the paddle or push pole, and you're casting to a mangrove edge on your left, you should always cast right-handed to keep the fly over the water. When you turn around and come back, then you switch to your left hand to keep from having to bring the fly between you and the guy handling the boat.

"I really prefer casting left-handed. But I learned to fly cast with my right hand to teach people at casting clinics. It confuses right-handed beginners to demonstrate with my left hand. But when they see how easy it is for me to cast equally well with either hand, it gives them the confidence they need to be effective casters with just one."

Lefty is a born teacher. He enjoys working with kids and has frequently served as a nature counselor, worked at local YMCAs, and been an instructor at the annual Summit membership meetings of the National Wildlife Federation. As one of America's foremost fly casters, he has for the last several years instructed at various national casting clinics. He has enormous confidence in his own abilities, and he loves to share the fruits of his skill and knowledge with anyone interested in learning. Since he makes so much of his own equipment or refines what is given him, he is stronger than most outdoor writers in the mechanics of angling. And since he came to salt water with few preconceptions, his inquiries into *how, what,* and *why* have taught him things and showed him places in the few years he has been in Florida that even old-time residents do not know.

Today, Lefty stands at the center of light-tackle—particularly fly fishing—interest in south Florida, where he serves as director of the Metropolitan Miami Fishing Tournament.[1] Honorary member of at least two angling fraternities, his job prohibits him from more binding allegiances, and he feels this is just as well.

"There's terrific competition down here among the different clubs, and out of that competition has come everything that's new and exciting in light-tackle fishing. Being a neutral observer, I avoid all the sound and fury of competition. But I'm right there just the same when something new is developed."

Lefty does a lot of innovative work of his own. Rather than merely

---

[1] Lefty recently became the outdoor editor for *The St. Petersburg Times.*

be a spectator to other people's achievements, Lefty often finds himself at the center of get-togethers when the unofficial members of the Who's Who of saltwater angling in Florida drop by his house to find what new things he is working on. His inventiveness, and his goodwill in sharing these inventions with other anglers, have made him one of the most popular sportsmen in the writing business.

But he does not share all his secrets. He has learned through unhappy experience that a man is a fool to show his best fishing spots to mere acquaintances.

"All fishermen have special, secret places, and I'd be unkind to my friends or myself if I took a casual visitor to any of these. In my work [with the Metropolitan Miami Fishing Tournament], I play host to as many as 40 or 50 outdoor writers a year. Some of them have been assigned the outdoor beat by their editors and don't know one end of a fish from the other. They're happy to catch pinfish just so long as they get to tell their readers they've been fishing in Florida. Well, we take 'em pinfishing!

"Others are good tackle men, but they've never fished salt water before. We'll show them good flats fishing—but not enough to keep them from going home. Saltwater fish are so much stronger and more spectacular than anything they have in fresh water that if we took out a man from Montana and had him bust up all his tackle the first day, he'd either never forgive us or he'd never want to leave Florida!

"Generally speaking, if you're an outdoor writer from the South, likely to get back to Miami more than once or twice a year, we'll show you *good* fishing. If you're an editor from New York or the West Coast and the trip down is a special occasion, we'll try to show you *better* fishing. But it takes a lot of getting to know you before we'll take you to those flats where we're likely to see 1,000 tailing permit at a time. And you can be sure that if we do, you'll be sworn to secrecy through a blood pact and threatened with death if you ever breathe a word about the area!"

How does a man become a major writer? This is Lefty's story, but it starts with Joseph W. Brooks, Jr.[2]

"Joe got started writing when he worked for a little daily in Towson, Maryland—a suburb of Baltimore. He got his big break right after the war when millions of soldiers were coming home who were starved for

---

[2]After a long illness, Joe Brooks, *Outdoor Life's* angling editor for many years, passed away on September 20, 1972.

angling information. He proposed a fishing trip through the provinces to the Canadian government, and they helped him with most of the arrangements. The Canadians were happy to have him publicize their angling, and the boys back home were eager to read about it. He got so busy free-lancing, he soon didn't have time for the Towson column. So Joe knew a younger fellow working in the local Montgomery Ward sporting goods department and asked him if he'd take the column. And that's how Tom McNally got his start.

"I was real friendly with both Tom and Joe, and we used to go fishing together a lot. In fact, I learned to fly cast with those guys. I guess it was back in 1947 or 1948. Joe had already moved away, but one weekend when he came back, the three of us were going to fish for bass in some ponds on the Eastern Shore.[3] I was staying at McNally's house, and we were driving over the next day in my old Model A Ford with the canoe on top. Anyway, at dinner the night before, I told them I'd seen Jack Sharkey at the Washington Boat Show knocking cigarettes out of a guy's mouth with the end of a fly line and how fantastic I thought that was. Well, they both laughed at me and said there was nothing to it. And to prove the point, the next morning they took me down to Tarkington Sporting Goods, helped me pick out a good fly outfit, including a Medallist reel—which I still have, and I must have caught 5,000 fish with it by now. And they took me to Herring Run Park, and within 30 minutes they had me knocking cigarettes out of Joe's mouth. Well, I just couldn't believe it!

"Meanwhile, Tom had been encouraging me to write. I'd been brought up on a farm and had gotten to be an Eagle Scout and knew the outdoors pretty well. Tom reasoned that it takes a lifetime to learn the outdoors, but you can learn to write in six months if you apply yourself. So when McNally left for the *Chicago Tribune*, I inherited his job on the *Towson News*. And if the Towson paper hadn't been sold about eight years later, I might have been Daddy to an outdoor writer of my own!

"In the meantime, I'd started an outdoor column for a Frederick paper, one for a Hagerstown paper, another one in Winchester, Virginia, and still another one in the *Montgomery County Sentinel*, which is just outside Washington. I also did some stuff for the *Washington Post*. Now, all this time I was working as a bacteriologist at the Bio-

---

[3]The Delmarva Peninsula, made up of portions of *Delaware, Maryland*, and *Virginia*.

logical Warfare Station at Fort Detrick, Maryland.[4] By my own request I'd work all night, which enabled me to be on the water six or seven days a week. I guess I fished and hunted more in five years up there than the average guy does in a lifetime."

GWR: When did you sleep?
Kreh: Sleep really didn't seem necessary then. But I don't know if I could do it again today. The job was great because sometimes they'd let me go double shifts so I could get off Friday, Saturday, Sunday, and until four in the afternoon on Monday. In essence, I was getting off four days a week, and I promise you, I knew every back road, every stream, and every pond in the state of Maryland. In fact, we were doing something back then that people are still missing out on—using two-pound test tackle on tiny streams and getting all kinds of wonderful fishing!

So, for a while there, I was doing 11 newspaper columns, free-lancing to magazines, working for the government five days a week, and making a TV film series called "Chesapeake Outdoors." It kept me busy.

GWR: How did you first come to salt water? Did you use fly tackle from the start?
Kreh: Right. On striped bass—both wading and from boats. I fished all over the Chesapeake Bay, but found two areas especially productive. One is the Susquehanna River just below Conowingo Dam. You fish the stripers the same way you'd fish for freshwater bass. When the dam gates are open, the water comes through fast—too fast. But when the gates are shut, the water goes down and collects in pools, confining the stripers so you're better able to locate them. Then the water gets very still, and any big plug that hits the surface scares the fish. It's perfect streamer-fly water. And incidentally, despite all I've read about the success of popping plugs on striped bass, I find streamer flies to be far more effective—especially in shallow water.

The other outstanding striper area is formed by two very deep basins separated by a kind of ridge lying between Pocomoke Sound and Tangier Sound. There're all kinds of marshy islands in there with strong tidal currents, and you can either drift from a boat or pull your boat up on the banks and walk the edges. But there aren't really big fish in those areas.

GWR: What size?
Kreh: If you saw a 15- or 20-pounder, you'd seen one heck of a fish.

---

[4]On April 1, 1971, the federal government transferred this facility from the Department of Defense to the Department of Agriculture, and research on plant diseases is now its primary mission.

I must have caught 5,000 striped bass on flies, and I've never caught one over 13 pounds. And I don't think I ever caught more than four or five over 10 pounds. Ten pounds was about the limit.

Now, those were the two best areas you could always count on. But in October the entire bay comes alive with striped bass and bluefish. I don't know if you've ever seen it.

GWR: Yes. We usually fish the mouth of the Choptank River.

Kreh: Right. The Choptank's a good spot. Well, most of those fish are two to four pounds, and years ago we learned to approach the breaking schools with fly tackle in a way that saved us time and gave us much more opportunity to take fish before a school moved on. Nowadays, I use the same trick down here on breaking bonito and school tuna. I strip the amount of fly line I think I'm going to cast. If I think I'll need 70 feet of line, I pull off that amount and stream it behind the boat while we're racing to the fish. If you hold your rod tip high enough, the speed of the boat keeps the line straight out behind.

You should always approach a school of fish with the wind behind you, and you should be positioned so the fly line streams outboard of other people in the boat. For instance, if a school of fish is feeding in a northerly direction, and the wind is blowing from the west, you should approach the school from the west, and you should be in the stern on the starboard side—if you're right-handed, that is. If you cast with your left hand, you should be on the port side. Anyway, your line is trailing along behind the boat, and when you race up to the fish, just double haul and shoot the works to them.

But a lot of anglers don't really know how to use the double haul.

GWR: How so?

Kreh: Remember I told you that Brooks and McNally gave me my first fly-casting lessons? Well, after I got the basics from these two giants, they went off and left me to learn the rest on my own. So I read everything I could on the subject and took pictures of myself practicing to see what I was doing wrong. And eventually I learned to double haul by putting *The Wise Fishermen's Encyclopedia* on the lawn in front of me and going through the motions diagramed in the book. And I suspect I began to develop my own style then because there was nobody there to give me bad advice. Today I can throw a 100 feet of fly line with either hand while keeping the other one in my pocket.[5]

What all this means is that I learned some things about fly fishing that

---

[5]After our session with the tape recorder, Lefty took me out in front of his house in South Miami and casually flicked the gutter of his roof with the tip end of his fly line while standing 100 feet away—and with one hand in his pocket. He then topped this by casting better than 80 feet with his *bare hand*. Lefty's youthful awe of Jack Sharkey's casting skill was nothing compared to my own of Lefty's!

most anglers never realize simply because they do as they've been taught to do or have seen others do. Now with a double haul, very few casters know that as their loop opens, their line falls. Very few people understand this. And you open your loop by the distance through which you exert power in the stroke. The shorter the stroke, the tighter the loop; the longer the stroke, the more the loop opens. If you make a cast and just swing the rod tip to the ground, your entire loop goes straight up in the air and collapses.

Okay, the average person learns to throw a line with the loop opening about 35 feet away so the end of his line falls about 37 or 38 feet away. Then he learns the double haul. Now, the double haul only increases line speed, nothing more. It has nothing to do with loops, leaders, or anything. So let's assume it takes you four seconds to cast 35 feet—that is, from the time you turn your wrist over to see your line go 35 feet and open up. Then you learn to double haul, and you double your speed. Now instead of casting 35 feet in four seconds, you're reaching 70 feet in four seconds—but your loop is still opening in four seconds. Follow me? The point is, regardless of how much *power* you put in a cast, your loop is going to open in the same amount of time it always has. You've doubled your line speed, not altered the loop factor. So you're really just throwing your original casting mistakes over a longer distance faster.

I maintain that you should learn to control your loop *before* you learn to double haul. If you learn to control your loop, you'll be able to throw 100 feet *without* double hauling. And then double hauling merely becomes the means to get your fly to a fish faster—not a way to give you extra distance. But most guys never realize that the rod hand is about 85 percent of the effort, and when they double haul, they pull from their eyebrows to their knees—they go way down like this [demonstrating], and on the way up they trip over their underwear and everything else! Actually, the only time the double haul is doing you any good is when you turn your wrist over to make the loop.

The most important lesson in fly casting is that the fly is never going to move until your line is straight. It's like a garden hose zigzagging across the lawn to a sprinkler. If you want to move that sprinkler by the near or spigot end of the hose, you have to pull all the bends and curves out of the hose before the sprinkler will move. The same thing is true of a fly line. In order to get an effective back cast—and forward cast—you have to make sure your line is completely straight so your fly will move. If there's the least wrinkle in your fly line, your rod will have to remove that wrinkle before anything can be done with the fly. So one of the secrets of successful fly casting is *not* to do what every book on fly casting tells you to do. They say to wait until you feel the tug before you start to reverse your cast. But when

[340]

you feel the tug, your cast is over! The line has already started to fall to the ground.

What you really want to do is start coming forward a fraction of a second before all your line gets straight behind you. You don't take a spinning rod and lay it softly over your shoulder and then come forward. No, you make the back cast, put a bow in the rod and then make your forward cast. The same with a plug rod. And the same with a fly rod—except that you start coming forward with your fly rod while your line is still going the other way. Then, by the time you're into a full forward cast, your line is straight behind you and your rod is bowed and cocked—ready to shoot the works over to a tailing permit.

GWR: When did you first come to Florida?

Kreh: I came down with Tom Cofield in 1954. I used to go to Canada twice or three times a year. After I made my first trip to the Florida Keys, I vowed I'd never again spend another nickel of my own money to go north of Maryland! And while I've been back to Canada since on government-sponsored trips, I still prefer light tackle in the Tropics to anything up north. There're just so many more fish down here, and anything in salt water can drag the best freshwater fish around by the tail.

GWR: When did you move down here full-time?

Kreh: Joe Brooks called me in Maryland late in the summer of 1964 and asked me if I'd like to be the director of the Metropolitan Miami Fishing Tournament. So I asked, "What's that?" And he explained it was like being the mayor of fishing in south Florida, and that I'd work eight months and be off four. Since I was already a consultant for Fenwick and Scientific Anglers, and since they seemed pleased with the prospect, and since it was the kind of job that would provide me with tremendous contacts, travel opportunities, and free time, I said, "Heck, yes!" Well, there were 32 applicants for the job, but I'm pretty sure that since Joe Brooks recommended me, they decided I was probably the best risk. It's worked out great!

You know, I've helped about a dozen outdoor writers improve their photography, and whenever they started to thank me, I said, "Don't thank me. Thank Joe Brooks." I couldn't do anything for that guy; but when I helped those other people, and they went to Joe and said thanks because Lefty helped us, it gave Joe a big kick. And it's the only way I knew of repaying him. He was one of the finest people in my life.

GWR: You've had a considerable influence on saltwater fly fishing in the seven years you've been down here. How do you explain that?

Kreh: Well, certainly my job helps. But I think it really all began when the Tropical Anglers Club invited me over one evening not long after I arrived for a demonstration. They're one of the three best angling clubs in south Florida—the Rod and Reel Club over on Miami

[341]

Beach and the Miami Sport Fishing Club being the other two. I figured they had a few outstanding casters in Tropical Anglers and that they were really inviting me over to see what this reputed hot-shot from Maryland was all about. So I figured I had to do something pretty unusual to impress them.

Sure enough, we got out by the pool, and here were all these serious, skeptical faces standing around with their arms folded as if to say, "Let's see what you know." So I began to strip out line, and pretty soon I was casting the entire fly line. That was just the start, but I could see some of those fellows had never seen anything like that before. I mean, their arms unfolded and so did a few mouths. Then I cast the whole fly line just using the tip section and then just using my bare hands. Finally, I was out there throwing 80 feet with just two fingers, and they all looked so goggle-eyed I figured I'd passed the test!

But what I found out was that most of those guys couldn't cast worth a darn. Except for Chico Fernandez, who is really a good caster, the average Tropical Angler couldn't get out 40 feet. Or, if he did, he considered that a long cast. They had never heard of anybody throwing a whole fly line before. They thought it was impossible. Well, a number of these fellows like John Emery, Tom Rich, and Bob Stearns really got hooked. They had formerly been slinging big bunches of feathers and corks down on the water and getting the fish to take them, and they thought that was saltwater fly fishing. They came to my house in the evenings during the next few months, and in no time at all, some of them were getting to be pretty darned good. All of a sudden, they wanted lighter tackle. They had been using number eleven rods—I mean, you could pole a boat with those things!—and numbers eleven, twelve, and thirteen lines. They'd been using weight to propel their flies instead of timing and line speed.

That was nine years ago, and up until then few of the really difficult fish to get on a fly, like the bonefish or permit, were showing up in the Met records. Any fish you could lure within 20 feet of the boat, like an amberjack, cobia, or shark—they were being caught. But as soon as these guys got interested in distance and accuracy, well, all kinds of hell broke loose. Today, there're at least two dozen top-notch fly casters in the Miami area, and they're new ones all the time.

Just last Saturday I ran into Chico Fernandez and Norman Duncan over at Flamingo. They were fishing a trail for redfish.[6] They had 10 fish up to 11 pounds all caught on six-pound test. No shock leader or anything. You see, they now appreciate the real finesse in light-tackle fishing. A Florida redfish has absolutely no chance to break a 12-pound

---

[6]Channel bass.

[342]

tippet. But half that pound test, and you've got a fair fight and some excitement.

GWR: Do you think part of the new interest in saltwater fly fishing is because anglers feel most of the records on traditional tackle have been set? For instance, there're certain species not even on the fly-rod record books yet.

Kreh: Here in South Florida, that might be true. We have a great variety of fish species and year-round fair weather that encourages anglers to experiment in new areas with new tackle. But that doesn't explain why fly fishing for striped bass has caught on so well in, say, New England where you have only half a dozen gamefish capable of taking a fly and just six months out of every year to catch them. I suspect the destruction of a good many freshwater rivers and streams near our big coastal cities is part of the reason you're getting an influx of fly fishermen. They no longer have any fresh water to cast over. The good small streams are now all private, and you need permission or have to pay a fee to fish the farm ponds. Most of the lakes have gone to developments, and the few rivers left are fished so hard, you don't catch much out of them anyhow. Ultimately, trout fishing, as it was once practiced, is a fading phenomenon.

GWR: Is all your saltwater fishing with fly tackle, or do you ever use plug and spin gear?

Kreh: Oh, yes, I do a lot of plug casting, and we always have spinning tackle aboard. Particularly when I take out other people. Everybody seems to be able to handle spinning tackle, but it takes a little savvy to use a fly or plug rod.

GWR: What pound test do you use in plug casting?

Kreh: Six-pound.

GWR: Isn't that a little light?

Kreh: Once in a while when we're going for tarpon—a lot of tarpon —we go to heavier line. But at Flamingo, on redfish, snook, and tarpon up to 30 and 40 pounds, you don't need more than six-pound test line if you know what you're doing. And if you've got a good drag.

GWR: We were talking this afternoon about bail-less spinning reels.[7] Do you ever use them?

Kreh: No, but primarily because I've got to think of the people I fish

---

[7] I had met Lefty in his office at the *Miami Herald*, and we had spent part of the afternoon at lunch and then shopping for old saltwater fishing books at a secondhand bookstore he knew of. This bookstore had inherited the library of Erl Roman, a former *Herald* outdoor editor and one of the first regular saltwater angling writers in south Florida. Lefty had showed Joe Brooks this gold mine of out-of-print bargains before me, and I confess that I stripped the shelves of everything Brooks had been unable to cart away!

with as much as my own inclinations. As I mentioned, I fish with a great many outdoor writers every year. And I also take out a lot of public relations people in conjunction with my job at the Met tourney. Now, the problem is they've all got to do everything *today*. And they usually need all the help they can get. Many of 'em have never seen a bonefish or permit before. Just the shock of this first encounter knocks off their timing. So, for all these reasons, we usually keep bailed reels on board.

Still, I prefer bail-less reel for my own fishing—not because they're more efficient or easier to cast but because they're equipped with the only rollers that roll.

GWR: Better explain that.

Kreh: When you hook a big fish and get him near the boat, there's usually a lot of seesawing about 25 feet out as the fish realizes its problems have something to do with the boat. You gain six feet; the fish takes out six feet. You gain it back; the fish takes it out again. And so forth. That's where you break off your good fish. My brother-in-law lost a 35-pound permit this way a couple of weeks ago. We brought that fish up to the boat six different times, but the tide was going out, and the fish had that big flat body of his against the tide, and every time the permit got within a few feet and saw the boat, it would work away again and have to be brought back. My brother-in-law was using his own fishing reel, and the roller wouldn't roll. I just knew what was going to happen, and, sure enough, his stretched line went back and forth across that static roller and scored itself. Ping! The fish was gone.

Garcia markets an absolutely beautiful manual roller. The whole thing is mounted in oil with ball bearings. It's also shaped in a deep *V* so the line is held on two sides instead of resting along an inverted point at the bottom. Now these rollers are noisy as heck when you get a fast fish on! With the ball bearings racing around, it sounds like the whole reel's coming apart. But we found that if you substitute STP for Garcia's lubricant, the roller rolls more smoothly and is a lot quieter.

You need manual rollers on big fish. We use spinning reels primarily for deep jigging when we're hooking big groupers and king mackerel on 6-, 8-, and 10-pound test monofilament. And those big fish are so strong, they'll actually heat up the rollers with the speed of their runs. Freshwater anglers just don't understand what saltwater fish can do to their tackle—and that goes double for most tackle manufacturers. A few years ago, a new reel was sent down for me to test, and I took just one look at its guts and realized the thing wouldn't hold up. So I called Mark Sosin, since he lived not too far from the manufacturer. And I explained that this reel had a spool with a smooth inside surface that was rubbing against some French-motorcycle brake lining sitting on the shaft. Instead of having the heat flash off on the shaft and the air around it, the brake lining was storing it up in the spool. Mark knew what I was talking about right away. And both of us knew what was going to happen if you got this reel tied into a strong fish. But the company insisted everything would work perfectly.

So, sure enough, I went out and blew up three reels on the first three amberjacks I hooked. The company still wouldn't listen. Besides, by this time they were already tooled up for production, and they couldn't afford to listen. You know how that goes.

But any decent drag system must use alternating soft and hard parts together. In salt water you just can't have two hard parts riding cheek by jowl. Friction and heat will build up and score your metal every time. But we still use that company's reels. We just cut out a piece of Teflon to replace the motorcycle brake lining. Works real well. But do you think we can get the company to do something like that? Not on your life! This business of being a field tester sometimes boils down to a company wanting you to publicize their product—and nothing more!

One interesting thing I've discovered in consultant work is that tackle which works well in Florida might not work well in Maine. For example, the color fly line you use in the Tropics should be totally different from the color line you use in New England. I found that when you drop a dark-colored fly line on the deck of a fiberglass boat and let it lie there in the hot sun, the dark line picks up so much heat and becomes so limber that it's nearly impossible to cast—like trying to cast wet noodles! By the same token, a white line up north might become so stiff as to be equally unmanageable. Ideally, a tackle manufacturer should have consultants both north and south.

GWR: Which do you think is the most difficult fish to stalk, the hardest to hook, and the toughest fish to play in salt water on fly tackle?

Kreh: Certainly permit are the most difficult to stalk and the most difficult to get to take a lure. I don't think anyone would question that. But, of course, there're exceptions. Jim Lopez once caught 15 permit on fly tackle in just two days of fishing over a wreck. Sometimes when you get huge schools of these fish on wrecks, they get careless. But on the flats, they've got to be the toughest fish going. Last weekend I cast to over 80 of them, and not one showed the slightest interest in a fly. And I changed flies three times. In fact, I've probably cast to 2,000 or 3,000 permit, and I've had just three hook-ups and caught one. Stu Apte[8] has probably cast to 5,000 fish and had only one take his fly. Catching a permit on fly tackle on the flats involves enormous time, skill, and patience—all seasoned with massive doses of luck!

A more common fish on fly tackle, and yet the one I consider to be

---

[8]A co-pilot on Pan American 747's, Apte works as a part-time light-tackle guide in the Florida Keys.

the most difficult fish overall to take, is the shark. He's not easy to hook because a shark's vision is so poor he can only see things alongside him. Most people fail with sharks because they drop their fly in front of his nose and continue stripping the fly right in front of him. The shark doesn't hit simply because he never knows the fly's there. You've got to present the fly alongside a shark's eye. If you drop it too far away, he doesn't see it; if you drop it on top of him, he's liable to spook.

Then when the shark strikes, about the only time you can depend on a hook-up is when he swings his head sideways to get the fly. If he happens to lunge forward, he often misses because he can't keep track of the fly—and it's not a particularly large thing to strike at. So you've always got to approach a shark from the front. From the rear, a retrieved fly will pass his eye too quickly for him to register interest. You approach from the front, cast beside him, and strip in so as to keep the fly riding alongside his eye until he strikes at it. But then you've got to avoid leading the shark right into the boat, because you'll spook him sure. Position the boat slightly to one side and then make your cast as perfect as you can—which means into an area no bigger than a 12-quart bucket. And for that kind of cast and follow-up control, 35 feet is an absolute limit for consistent accuracy.

Now, say you've hooked one. Flats' sharks range from 50 to 150 pounds, and they're all cartilage and muscle. On top of that, they have sandpapery hides, and teeth that can cut through nearly anything. So the first thing you've got to remember is on which side of the mouth he's hooked. In fighting him, you've got to try to stay on his hooked side, because if you get the line across his back or head, you'll lose that shark nearly as fast as if he cut the leader with his teeth.

GWR: Do you use a wire shock leader?

Kreh: Right, solid wire about number six or seven.

GWR: Why not braided wire? I would think that would give you greater flexibility.

Kreh: I prefer solid wire, because over the period of a long fight, a shark can chew through one strand at a time of braided wire and weaken it enough so that it breaks.

GWR: How long is your wire trace?

Kreh: Saltwater fly fishing rules stipulate a leader at least six feet long. Somewhere in that length you must have at least 12 inches of leader material which does not exceed the category in which you want to compete—6-, 10-, 12-, or 15-pound test. That is, if you want to enter your fish in a contest. Now you can have a shock leader in the forward part of the tippet, but it cannot exceed 12 inches, including knots. For sharks, you try to get it about 11¾ inches long, because every fraction of an inch may keep you from losing your fish when he starts rolling or thrashing about. And, all of this is, of course, complicated by the inevitable strands of grass you pick up on your line. All things considered, a 100-plus-pound shark is one of the toughest flats fish you can take on a fly rod.

GWR: How about handling fish at boatside? Angling from a small open boat must raise some interesting situations with big fish.

Kreh: It does. And it teaches you some interesting things about gaffing. I've talked with Stu Apte, George Hommell, and eight or nine other of the top guides in the Keys, and they all agree on certain rules —like never put a gaff in front of the line because the fish might surge forward and tangle it. And never stop coming with the gaff once the fish is struck.

But I learned something else, ever more important. I found that each man has his own gaffing style which reflects his temperament. For example, Dan Schooler's one of the best gaffers going. But he gaffs fish like he does everything else—*fast*. Dan says you don't fool around with 'em. You bring a snook alongside Dan's boat, and suddenly the snook's in the boat with you! Just like that.

Ralph Delph, on the other hand, is a more methodical guy. He says you've got to get everything lined up just so and don't make any sudden moves to alarm the fish. And he, too, is one of the best gaffers going. Dan and Ralph handle fish completely different. Yet they're both expert and would probably argue like heck about which is the correct way to do it. The point is, each does it according to his own style and temperament—and that's the way it should be done.

One thing the best gaffers agree on is that a big fish should always be gaffed in the center of its body. That way you've got equal amounts of weight levering on either side of your fulcrum: the gaff. If you gaff an 80-pound amberjack in the head, you've got 80 pounds of energy on the end of a pole. But if you stick him in the center, you've got 40 pounds on either side seesawing back and forth. It's still awkward, but it sure beats the head-on predicament.

Now, there are further variations to this. Stu Apte gaffs tarpon differently from anyone else, and he always does a very effective job. He gaffs underneath in the belly and turns the fish upside down. Stu maintains that a fish turned over on his back is disoriented and can't swim normally. Hence, the fish loses his full thrusting capability.

Other guides maintain the belly's too soft, that it's better to hit a tarpon in the muscle along the back. Boy, let me tell you from experience that after you've slammed into a big tarpon to get the gaff point into his back, that fish is in a perfect position to beat the tar out of you and the boat—particularly since for a moment or two you're still a little off-balance from having wound up for the strike in the first place!

[347]

Let me give you an example of the kind of power a big tarpon has. A few years ago, Jack Kertz won the Islamorada Fly Fishing Tournament with a 132½-pounder.

GWR: Is that better than the one you have over there on the wall?

Kreh: That's only 108.

GWR: That's a huge fish. Are 100 pounds the standard you shoot for?

Kreh: Right. If you take a tarpon over 100 pounds on a fly rod, you're in! Anyway, Jack's guide was Cecil Keith, who is a burly, powerful guy about five-feet-ten but built like an ape. He's been pushing a one-ton boat around the flats for years. So Jack got his fish near the boat, and a big shark came by, and naturally Jack was afraid the shark might get his tarpon. This was, also, during the Gold Cup Tournament, which has rules stating that the longer time you spend on a fish, the fewer points you earn.

Cecil thought the tarpon was pretty green, but he decided to take him. He got out his killer gaff with a five- or six-inch hook on an eight-foot pole about two inches thick, and he sunk it into the fish. Well, the tarpon started down along the boat, dragging Keith end-over-end right into the bay! There was considerable splashing and roiling of mud, and Jack worried that this would excite the shark. In a moment Cecil came up—water streaming everywhere, but minus the gaff. Remarkably, the line hadn't broken.

The fish was half a mile away by now, but Cecil had another gaff aboard, and about 20 minutes later, Jack had the fish alongside again. This time after Keith hit the fish and was dragged the length of the boat, he managed to jump in with the fish, rather than be hauled overboard! There was furious thrashing and much confusion, and Jack saw the gaff go flying off. But the man and the fish stayed together. Fortunately, the shark was no longer around, for it took a little while for things to quiet down. When it was all over, Cecil came up blowing like a whale, but he had one hand running up under a gill cover and out through the tarpon's mouth. "Gimme a rope," he said, "I got this son-of-a-bitch!"

Well, they landed the fish, but Cecil's arm was terribly scratched up from the gill rakers, and he had a sore back for days.

GWR: Does anyone ever use super-size gaffs on the flats—like those you'd use offshore with a 10- or 11-inch spread?

Kreh: No, there's rarely any need for such a heavy weapon. And flying gaffs are no longer legal for fly fishing. A crisis occurred a few years ago in saltwater fly fishing when one angler caught a truly enormous jewfish on a 12-pound tippet. Rumor said this marvelous catch was made while the jewfish was lying in a hole in the flats, that the fish inhaled the fly in the process of breathing rather than striking it, and that a flying gaff was used to reach down to capture the creature after

[348]

it refused to budge despite the angler's efforts to make the fish aware that it was hooked. In essence, a majority of the fishing fraternity figured that since the fish had not moved during the "contest"—indeed, probably hadn't even intended to inhale the fly—that using a flying gaff on it was equivalent to harpooning a free-swimming fish. The resulting furor over this incident led to a banning of the flying gaff in saltwater fly fishing. Six-inch spans fixed on a two-inch pole are about our maximum. After all, a gaff's not expected to kill a big fish—it's merely to hold and subdue it.

Norman Jansik designed a beauty which I use now and find ideal for shark fishing. As you know, sharks twist and roll when they're stuck, and it's awkward as the devil trying to manage a big pole when it wants to flail about. Well, Norman slid a piece of grey D/C plastic tubing about a foot long down over his gaff and centered it on the pole with two smaller pieces of tubing locked at either end of the larger piece like wedding bands. The big piece in the center then revolved completely around the gaff pole while the two smaller, fixed pieces kept it from sliding up or down. Thus, when you strike a fish that wants to spin, you slide your hand quickly down to this plastic sleeve and let the fish spin all it wants. The spinning doesn't affect you in the least. When the fish is done with his gyrations, you can grip the gaff normally and haul him in.

GWR: That's a great idea! What other tips have you got for a saltwater fly rodder?

Kreh: Well, one idea that has saved me a lot of fish on the strike while I've still got a lot of loose line lying all over the foredeck is to make an O-ring with the thumb and forefinger of my line hand to guide all that loose, rushing line up into the first guide of the fly rod and overboard. After a fish takes your fly and you've snubbed him, you shouldn't worry about keeping a tight line until you've got all your loose line overboard. And the finger-made O-ring helps.

Another thing, freshwater men often come to Florida and go right out and buy one of the better saltwater fly reels made down here—a Seamaster or FinNor—sometimes an expense they can barely afford on top of the cost of their dream trip to the Keys. Naturally, they have no time to fish with the new reel and become accustomed to the drag system before going out after bonefish and tarpon. Consequently, these fellows reared on hatchery trout and smallmouth bass break off nearly every fish they hook. They finally get discouraged and turn to spinning on the last day of their vacation in order to have at least one tarpon to talk about when they get home. Now, a few might return North determined to come back to do better next time. But many go back bitter and broadcast their disappointment against all saltwater fly fishing. If only more people would bring down the equipment they

[349]

already own and know—a few modifications and more backing would do the trick—or if they want a good saltwater reel, get one well in advance of their trip, and use it, and learn to understand drags, and maybe even find a way to practice on bluefish or mackerel, and eat with it and sleep with it, until they know the new reel *better* than "ole dependable" in the closet—then their once-in-a-lifetime trip to Florida would mean something to them, and we'd have even more converts to this business of fly fishing for saltwater gamefish.

GWR: Are there any specific lessons you've learned from saltwater fly fishing that a hypothetical freshwater angler can take back to Indiana after a week in the Keys?

Kreh: Oh, yes. First off, he'll learn how important his knots are. When you're straining tackle to the utmost on strong, *strong* fish, and your knots are not 100 percent strength, you soon learn to tie those few knots which are![9]

Next, in fresh water he probably gets away without sharpening his hooks because he's using relatively fine diameter wire to begin with—which is sharp even when you buy it in the store—and because the mouth of a bass or a pike or a trout is very vulnerable, with a lot of spongy areas in which a hook can get caught. But in salt water, where your 2/0 or 3/0 streamer hook has four times the diameter of the hook in a comparable fly in fresh water—coupled with the fact that saltwater gamefish have leathery or iron-hard mouths, or at least hard scraping teeth—then you must *constantly*, and I stress that word, keep after your points. And when I say points, I don't just mean bringing the tip of your hook to needle sharpness. I mean keeping a cutting edge on the point's face so you end up with a scalpel/needle combination and not just a puncturing tool.

A third thing, most freshwater men make the mistake of manipulating the lure with the rod. Of course, I'm not talking about dry-fly fishing, where you're not trying to move the fly at all. I'm describing popping-bug or streamer anglers who twitch the lure along with their rod tip. This is a mistake.

How many times have you heard some smallmouth fan complain about the number of bass that are spitting out his poppers?

GWR: Me, for one.

Kreh: Well, what's happening is you're flopping the rod up in the air to pop the bug and then coming down as the bass strikes. Those bass aren't spitting out your bugs; they're simply striking the bugs on a slack line. You can't control a fly rod retrieve with the rod tip.

In fresh water this is not crucial. Sloppy handling will catch you

---

[9]In 1972 Lefty published *Practical Fishing Knots* in collaboration with Mark Sosin.

enough fish to confirm you in your bad habits. But retrieve is crucial in saltwater angling, and once you learn to point your rod low and in the line's direction and use your fingers for the retrieve, you'll take that knowledge back to your inland lakes and do five times as well.
GWR: Why is the retrieve so crucial in salt water? Because of the greater speed of the fish?
Kreh: Yes. Often you'll have to strip line in hand-over-hand with the rod butt and reel stuck between your knees in order to keep a streamer moving fast enough to interest a fish like a bonito. But control is really the crux of the matter. What you have in the way of fingertip reflexes cannot possibly be duplicated by the wrist, rod tip, and all that loose line. There's not a fish in fresh water that can take and reject a streamer as fast as a wary permit. And after you've lived with the frustration of this awhile, a trout or smallmouth bass seems like a pushover.

A final lesson of salt water useful to take back to fresh concerns timing and accuracy. You always have to be alert on the flats. Even if you're fishing spinning tackle, and you're standing in the bow of a boat with a rod in your hands and you see a permit—if you have to open the bail before you make your cast, you probably won't get that permit. The time it takes to glance down at the reel, open the bail, and ready the cast is too long. You lose the opportunity.
GWR: Lefty, my last question: You have been a consultant to some of the best tackle manufacturers in the business, and you've been associated with a variety of national and international angling and conservation groups. What affiliation are you most proud of?
Kreh: I think being selected adviser to the Fly Fishing Federation. This is one of the greatest organizations and certainly the most progressive fly-fishing outfit in America today. It's an enormous honor to be associated with them.

Another group is the Salt Water Fly Rodders, and I take some pride in having been one of about seven people—including Joe Brooks, Frank Woolner, and Harold Gibbs—that Fred Shriver asked to Barnegat to fly fish and talk about the formation of the SWFR. But I fear this organization has too limited a view of the world of saltwater fly fishing. Everything it does is done from the perspective of a relatively small clique of men living near Tom's River, New Jersey.

Not long ago they wrote me to ask for something they could print *before the coming fishing season*. That really struck me with how out of touch they are. There's just no such thing as a "coming fishing season" in Florida! Nor in California, Mexico, or half a globe full of fishermen.

In contrast, the Fly Fishing Federation has participating voting chapters from Alaska to Alabama. Furthermore, though Salt Water Fly Rodders was formed the same year—practically the same month—as

[351]

the Federation, today the Federation has over 25,000 active members, while the Fly Rodders has only about 2,000 names on a membership list.

The point is this: A world of light-tackle angling has been opened up in the past decade, and countless thousands of fishermen are now flocking to the coasts to try new skills in a new environment. If we're to have standards in the sport against which all anglers may measure themselves, we must have a supervisory organization led by men with vision. Of all the angling agencies in this country and abroad, the Fly Fishing Federation comes closest to meeting this description.

TWENTY-TWO

PACIFIC NORTHWEST

> The two times fishing is best is just before
> you arrived and just after you left.—Anon.

Donald Raymond Holm introduces his *Pacific North! Adventures in Sportfishing* with an opinion of Secretary of State John Hay that "the Mediterranean is the ocean of the past; the Atlantic is the ocean of the present; and the Pacific is the ocean of the future."

However, like many men of the Pacific Northwest, Don's childhood memories are midcontinental, and it was only in his early adult life that he completed the migration his ancestors had started toward the western sea.

Born on January 3, 1918, in Velva, North Dakota—a town of about 800 people—Don grew up fishing and trapping the little streams of this still wild country. His father was the local blacksmith and a farmer. After finishing high school in North Dakota, Don set off for the University of Texas, where he studied part of one year before running out of money in a burgeoning Depression. He drifted off to California, north to Alaska, and finally back to Washington. Here he logged

[353]

timber, worked in mines, and helped construct some of the early dams across the Columbia River. "I worked on the Grand Coulee—that was the first of them. It blocked the entire Columbia upstream, but none of us thought about that then. We didn't think of the damage a dam could do to the salmon runs. In fact, some of us thought the dams were a boondoggle, that nobody could ever use all the electricity they'd produce. Of course, we hadn't figured on aluminum plants moving in, and the gradual urbanization and industrialization of this country ever since. Now we've got some 500 dams up here, and everything's changed. And, of course, the fishing and hunting aren't what they used to be. Back when Zane Grey fished the Rogue, it was not exceptional to catch a 50-pound salmon. Today a 20-pounder is a big fish."

Don served in the Navy during World War II, and while most of his comrades-in-arms spent their money on liberties, Don saved most of what he earned for schooling after the war and invested the rest in some property near Portland, Oregon. When the war ended, Don was discharged in Bremerton, Washington, and immediately returned to Oregon to be near his new home. He has been there ever since.

Today, as wildlife editor of the *Portland Oregonian*, Don has one of the most widely read outdoor columns in the Pacific Northwest, and he probably has more fan mail than any other writer for the newspaper—including "Dear Abby." He is especially fond of sea fishing and is the correspondent most responsible for making Oregonians aware of the excitement of launching dories through the surf for runs offshore to the albacore grounds, the fun of bottom fishing for lingcod and halibut, and the peace—and piscatorial productivity—of Oregon's 400 miles of public beaches. Perhaps it is significant that Don's guide, *101 Best Fishing Trips in Oregon*, starts with a story of surfperch fishing at New River and ends with a description of baits for "alongshore" species like kelp greenling and cabezon at Stonewall Bank.

Appreciating the growing interest of ocean angling in the Pacific Northwest, a publisher asked Don in 1969 to do a book on the subject. And, oh yes, could he have it ready for publication in a month's time? Working feverishly night and day, Don finished in three weeks the handsomest book to date on coastal fishing from California to Alaska.

Pacific North! opens with a review of the historical, geological, and biological attributes of the North Pacific basins. Then Don unites these different subjects with the real theme of his book:

[354]

Most fishermen—be they sports or be they motivated by profit (or both) —are singularly curious, inquiring, individualistic, and sensitive persons constantly seeking attunement to their environment; and therefore they are not content with mere manuals of technique, catalogues of equipment, and essays by Old Local Experts on the finer points of baiting a hook. They respond to total involvement of ecology and esthetics and abstractions of their world, if the writers of "fishing books" would only know.

I met Don at his desk on the third floor of the *Oregonian* building. As is all too common in editorial-management relationships, and despite the popularity of Don's column, he is allotted no more than a small corner of the entire sports room. With the clacking of type-writers and news-service machines overriding the sound of a TV set where one reporter was "covering" a football game, I could barely hear Don, who is a big man but soft-spoken. I suggested we find a quieter place to talk. Outside, a steady December drizzle had started, the kind that continues all day—sometimes mist, sometimes rain.

"Too bad the weather's so poor," he said as we walked along. "We hadn't had any rain for nearly a week, and with the streams starting to clear up, we were starting to catch some steelhead. This rain will likely kill that."

A newcomer to the Pacific Northwest is sometimes confused by the inversion of Atlantic perspectives on particular species. While the rainbow trout in the East is often a hatchery-reared midget, pale in color, rarely more than a pound in weight, and most unlikely to be found downstream of the dam above which it was planted, the rainbow of the Far West regularly strays to the sea and returns a brilliantly colored and aggressive giant known by the pugnacious name of "steelhead." And while the Atlantic salmon is angled for in Nova Scotian streams against a green pine and silver birch backdrop, the Pacific salmon is usually sought on white-capped waves with surf on a distant headland. Scolding kingfishers and jays accompany the Eastern salmon angler; the insults of gulls and terns are his chorus in the West.

"As soon as a Pacific salmon enters fresh water, he starts to deteriorate," says Don. "The fish turn dark and are called smokers. But they're not used for smoking; they're not fit to eat. Some folks in Idaho consider any salmon a prize, and I've seen them caught there, dark, hook-nosed, and with the flesh beginning to fall away from their sides. But the locals think this is okay. They take the salmon home, get some

[355]

pictures—even eat the fish. But as far as I'm concerned, a salmon is finished then. And though you'll find bright fish sometimes hundreds of miles inland, the prize Pacific salmon is an ocean fish.

"On the other hand, the littoral striped bass of the Atlantic coast, a species which is synonymous with beaches and bridges from Maryland to Maine and wet nights off Montauk and Cuttyhunk, is generally regarded as a river fish in the West—and sometimes unwanted at that.

"Striped bass were introduced into the Sacramento River system in the 1880's," Don says, "and within a very short while, Californians had a commercial fishery with them. The fish gradually spread northward into some of the Oregon rivers, and for a long time we had a tremendous striped bass fishery here—especially in places like the Coos River. But residents there considered them trash fish, and worse yet, rumors started going around that striped bass were destroying the salmon, which, of course, was not true. But it's the same kind of story you hear around San Francisco Bay: that stripers have killed all the crabs. Sometimes anglers cut open their fish and find them chock-full of crabs. And this then makes it doubly difficult to persuade West Coast anglers that over-fishing and destruction of their habitat has caused the reduction in crab and salmon catches and not the introduction of striped bass. A lot of people are partial to the victims of certain predators, and they give the predator a bad name. And it's a bitter irony that with the tremendous rise in water pollution, logging, trash thrown in rivers, silting, land filling, garbage dumped in streams, that stripers are still being blamed for poor runs of salmon or steelhead, and poor hauls of shad and crab. Striped bass in the Coos Bay area hang on by a fin through all the filth, but because they are better able to tolerate pollution than other fish and are about the only species left down there, they're still being blamed for depleting the other stocks. Commercial fishermen still have shad nets in the rivers, and the shad nets are taking occasional stripers by mistake—some really nice-size ones, up to 60 and 70 pounds. But these fish are treated with contempt and are thrown up on the banks to die and rot. When the shad and stripers are both gone, I wonder who or what next we'll find to blame —except ourselves, of course."

Compared with other parts of the country, the Pacific Northwest is most like New England. The vast middle Atlantic and Gulf Coast mergers of fertile marsh with the sea have few counterparts in the West. Rather, there is an abrupt, even determined shoreline, bulwarking the coast from compelling fogs and often fierce seas. Rivers run through

[356]

rocky gorges and well-banked plains, until suddenly they are joined with the ocean. The North Pacific coast is somehow familiar to New Englanders. Perhaps that is why so many Oregonians are descended from New England stock.

"Don, why has Oregon escaped overcrowding and the worst kinds of coastal development to date?"

"It's primarily a matter of being a little bit further up the coast—our weather's not as ideal as down south. Unless you have a feeling for this country, California's still the promised land for most Easterners moving west. But I'm afraid that as more people are coming out and seeing the mess made of things down there, they're starting to bend north to Oregon and Washington State. We'll see big changes here in the next decade or two.

"But we've escaped the worse kinds of development California has seen because of a wise old bird of a governor here about 50 years ago. Oswald West saw that our population was destined to grow, and he wanted everybody to have a share in the beauty of the Oregon beaches. At that time, just 29 miles of coastline were privately owned, so he managed to maneuver the other 400 miles into the state's Roads Department and to get them classified as a public highway.

"As a result, we still have the most extensive, the finest public beaches in the United States. Of course, as with any fine thing of value, you've got to be prepared to defend it from the ugly who think *value* means only money. As pressure from the south begins to build up here, we're finding that our wonderfully lonely beaches are being sought by real estate promoters. Lots of money is starting to flow into the state—in some cases, legislators have worked behind the scenes for their private profit; in other cases, legal help is being recruited to find loopholes in the law. Thus, in the past five years, public ownership of the beaches has been lost in several places, and private developments have crept out over the sand.

"However, this misfortune may hopefully do some good. Our public has been made aware of the threat, and we're getting protective laws strengthened, better defined. But it's still going to be a fight."

GWR: Does Washington State have a similar coastal ownership situation?
Holm: No. A good deal of their oceanfront is held in large private tracts. And other large sections are in Indian reservations. But the Indians arc toughening their position, and just last year, some of the

tribal councils voted to bar white men from coming to the beaches because of their litter.

GWR: Can an angler still approach the beaches from offshore in a boat?

Holm: Yes, you can. But our west coast is quite rugged and not a Sunday boater's dream.

GWR: When did saltwater angling begin out here?

Holm: [He laughs] That's easy to answer if you're talking about documentation. [Seeing my puzzlement, Don smiled and explained.] Lewis and Clark spent the winter of 1805/1806 at Astoria, and there're government acquisition records showing that before the expedition left Philadelphia, it purchased rods and reels from a dealer there. One of the party was a fellow by the name of Goodrich, who was an avid sportsman, and though the records don't exactly state that whenever Goodrich went fishing, he used such and such a thread line and type reel, you can be near certain he fished with the rods and reels the expedition had requisitioned. And we know they caught salmon at the mouth of the Columbia, and steelhead, searun cutthroat, and sturgeon, too. And they dipped great quantities of smelt.

Of course, other European anglers might have been here even before Lewis and Clark. You Easterners tend to forget that a regularly scheduled Spanish galleon service was in operation between Manila and Acapulco a century before the Pilgrims ever got around to finding Plymouth Rock. And we know Chinese mariners visited the Pacific coast centuries before Columbus got the backing he needed for his much shorter trip across the Atlantic. Who knows who the first salt-water angler was out here? For centuries, the coastal Indians used elk and deer sinew lines and bone lures to catch fish. And since they preferred halibut to salmon, and since you have to go some little distance offshore to get the really big fish, the Indians must have managed some pretty navigation in their big dugout canoes.

GWR: So right from the start settlers converted their covered wagons to boats and went fishing?

Holm: Not quite. American pioneers first settled the interior valleys and only later spilled out along the coasts. The coast has a harsher climate and is not so well suited for agriculture. But the men who settled the coasts were mostly transplanted New Englanders, and they brought with them their equipment and techniques. In fact, our popular Oregon dories evolved from New England models.

But circumstances were very different at the start of the last century. For one thing, the Indians had settlements at most of the river mouths and, in the beginning, when there were still many Indians and few white men, white men honored these settlements. There simply wasn't that much free access to the sea just anywhere along the coast.

[358]

For another thing, there was no real salmon fishery out here—either sport or commercial—until the coming of the canneries after the Civil War. Settlers didn't need to fish for salmon; the salmon practically fished for the settlers! You could dip or spear anywhere along the rivers and find fish. Old-timers used to tell me of taking their spring wagons down to the river and using pitchforks to load up with salmon, and then taking the entire load into the fields for fertilizer. Up-country, the salmon were regarded as a nuisance because after they spawned and died, their carcasses would so badly pollute the headwaters you couldn't draw water fit to drink, the entire valley would stink to high heaven, and you were liable to have your animals poisoned if any of them ate the rotting fish. Any dude coming west before 1870 who talked about sport fishing for salmon would have been laughed back to Pittsburgh!

Actually, the first sports fishery here would have been for steelhead. They were called "salmon trout" for a long time, beginning with Lewis and Clark, who thought they looked like trout but were big like salmon. And that's a fair description. After all, searun rainbow trout are closely related to the Atlantic salmon. The former is *Salmo gairdneri*; the latter is *salmo salar*. Anyway, we have records going back to 1837 showing there were people who enjoyed sport fishing for steelhead. That year Jason Lee and his bride spent their honeymoon with another couple on the coast near the Salmon River and caught all kinds of fish. Missionaries, honeymooning farmers and their brides, and occasional vacationers all through the 1840's and 1850's made sport-fishing trips to the coast from interior valleys. They crossed the mountains over Indian trails and sometimes they were guided by an old mountain man or trapper.

GWR: What about the commercial fishery for salmon? That's had such a tremendous influence on the history of the Pacific Northwest—when did that begin?

Holm: Commercial fishery operations were begun in 1834 by Nathaniel Wyeth from New York. He sent one party overland and came with another around the Horn and set up a salmon mill and curing operation on Sauvie Island at the mouth of the Columbia. At that time, Indians still lived there, and they called it Wapatato Island after a kind of tuber that grew in the swamps. Something like a potato.

Wyeth set up his salmon curing station and did very well. Of course, his raw product cost him nothing. Salmon were everywhere abundant. Pretty soon he had salted shipments going back to the East Coast, to Europe, and to Asia. This was the first commercial exploitation of salmon, and it was so successful, the Hudson's Bay Company moved in and ran Wyeth out of business.

Then in the 1860's, after the Civil War, some fellows from New

[359]

England came to California with the idea of canning salmon to sell to men working the gold fields. First efforts were quite crude, but it worked. They expanded the operation northward and discovered there were salmon in the Columbia in quantities never before dreamed of, and salmon canning really got underway as big business. After the operation moved north to include Alaska, salmon was king for better than half a century.

GWR: Was all this done by netting?

Holm: Yes, all gill netting until about 1900. Then the fishermen began to troll as well. You see, a hook-caught fish is a finer fish to eat than one bruised up in a net. So the men trolled for fish even before they had motors. In fact, Captain Joshua Slocum, first man to sail solo around the world, worked for a while on the Columbia River, and he's generally credited with designing and building the first big sailers they used for commercial trolling. In the 1920's, motors started coming into use, and trollers began working farther offshore for their salmon.

GWR: When did the offshore sport fishery develop?

Holm: The sportsman's story is tied to the commercial man's. Trolling is, or rather was, a commercial sports fishery. Without doubt, trolling got started because the guy loved to fish and didn't have enough money to buy a net. So he just went out and started taking king salmon with hook and line. Today, some of the trollers have fancy rigs costing up to $60,000, but in the beginning, anybody with a sail or even a pair of oars could go into business.

GWR: How heavy is the sport fishing tackle you use for salmon?

Holm: That depends on the salmon. One of the best ways we have for taking coho is to use a saltwater streamer fly—we call it the coho fly—and we troll it on very light tackle in the boat's wake, running about five or six miles an hour. The flies are right up on the surface on the edge of the wake. The coho go crazy trying to catch 'em!

GWR: Where did this technique come from?

Holm: The Canadians have been using saltwater streamers for 50 years or more to catch coho. But I probably brought the idea to Oregon. I fished streamers for coho in the Campbell River, British Columbia, just after the war, and we had such luck on ones made from polar bear hair that I brought three or four with me when I came down to Oregon. I took them to the mouth of the Siletz River the fall I returned, to use with light spinning gear—which was also new at the time. I went down to the river where it flows into the surf, and there was a crowd of local people who had fished for coho all their lives with big poles—logging gear, I call it—50-pound test line and eight-ounce sinkers. So I muscled my way between a couple of these guys who looked over my little coffee grinder with five-pound test line, and they started laughing. And they said, "What are you going to do with that?"

[360]

And I said, "I don't know. Fish for salmon, I guess." And everyone up and down the line started ha-haing. I made one cast just to get the feel of the outfit and to get the kinks out of the line and to see how the current was running. The streamer sailed out a country mile, clean across the channel. On my second cast, I hooked a salmon, and after a spectacular fight landed it down the beach. A 16-pounder. No one was laughing anymore, but a few of the guys started making cracks about "Jesus, some guys getting all the luck" and "He sure came out smelling like a rose," and so on. So I made my third cast and hooked another coho. A 15-pounder. That did it. I'm sure there were at least a dozen converts on the beach that day. I've researched the thing, and as best as I can find, that was the first time anybody ever used a coho streamer fly along the Oregon coast.

GWR: What other lures are used for salmon?

Holm: The McMahon and Reekers spoons are standard items which probably originated with the first commercial trollers, though their antecedents probably date back to things the Indians made out of bone.

GWR: Are there any special plug shapes unique to the West Coast?

Holm: Yes. The Lucky Louie was designed by Les Davis in Tacoma, Washington. It was the first successful wooden plug for salmon. Probably again the Indians used something similar first. The Lucky Louie looks like an early Pflueger casting plug but it is stockier and more torpedo-shaped. I think color is its most important feature. The Lucky Louie has a silvery cream color with a tinge of pink or blue along the side. The Pink Lady is a successful variation which looks like a fat herring with its head cut off at an angle. And, of course, herring is one of our best fresh baits. What we call a cut plug, or plug cut, bait is one in which the herring's head is cut off on a bias and a double hook harness inserted and fixed in such a way that the bait wobbles through the water like a crippled fish.

GWR: What about motion? What's the best action in a salmon lure?

Holm: There're two theories about that. Both produce fish. One says that the more natural the bait, the more the salmon like it. The other says a crippled or spinning bait is best. I'm partial to this theory. The spoons all wobble like a crippled fish—so do the plug-cut herrings. In fact, another wobbling lure experimented with some years ago was made from a woman's hair curler. Now it's got a trade name and patent, but its first inspiration was the curler.

GWR: A number of articles have been written about "mooching." Would you describe that?

Holm: Yes. As far as I can determine, mooching originated in Puget Sound and was brought here about 1950. Up until that time, salmon fishermen had only been trolling with plugs and spoons. Some of the Puget Sound boys came down here and really cleaned up. And you can bet when one or two fellows walk off with all the big prizes in the Salmon Derby, everyone else learns what they're doing in a hurry!

In mooching, you use a crescent sinker ranging in weight from one-half to two ounces. I'd say two ounces is about your limit, and you only use that in the really heavy tide rips off the Columbia. Then I prefer an eight-pound test leader about 18 to 30 inches long. Some fellows use heavier rigs and, of course, the guys with rented tackle have to take what's available, which is always too heavy in my book.

Now, there's a little technique to fishing this rig. You cast it out and let it sink to bottom. Then you lift the rod slowly and then let back to enable the tide to tumble the bait around. A salmon feeds by knocking the corners off a school of balled herring and stunning a lot with his tail. After he's eaten the ones he's run down, he'll turn and pick up the cripples he's knocked out. It's the same way a marlin uses his bill.

Anyway, you'll often feel a strange vibration on your line, or a kind of nibbling. This may be the salmon hitting your bait with his tail or mouthing your bait tentatively. In either case, let the first vibration or so pass until it becomes a steady thing—then set the hook.

We also have a technique called "motor mooching," which is a combination of mooching with very slow trolling. Actually, you're using your motor to keep your position in the current rather than actually making any ground speed.

GWR: You've done a lot of work publicizing the albacore sport fishery here. How did this fishing first come to light?

Holm: Oh, it's been known about in a small way for years. Recently, however, satellites and other sophisticated electronic gear have been used to track schools, and we've discovered that Pacific albacore swim a kind of counter-clockwise migration around the entire sea basin, feeding and breeding along the way.

Apparently they're born in the South Pacific, and by the time they're off California and Oregon, they weigh between 15 and 30 pounds. Then they circle round to Japan, and by the time they get there, the 15-pounder of California may be pushing 90 pounds. Then the circuit begins again.

The Japanese have done most of the research, but Scripps Institute, NASA, Oregon State, and the Bureau of Commercial Fisheries are all involved now. When they first discovered albacore off here in the early 1930's, the salmon fishermen thought they were trash and threw them away, until someone identified them as albacore. Sometime in the mid-1930's, a few fishermen began to bring in commercial landings of the fish, but World War II halted that. However, since the war, it's grown up enormously. Today we have thousands of bait boats operating off the West Coast, and the bulk of the catch is made off Oregon.

[362]

GWR: Are there other fish with the albacore?

Holm: Yes, big eye tuna, and even bluefin. But whether these fish travel with the albacore or have migration patterns of their own are things our scientists are still trying to find out. The albacore range from 10 miles offshore to nearly 400 miles out, and seem to prefer a temperature gradient between 58 and 65 degrees Fahrenheit.

GWR: When did the sportsman get in on this?

Holm: Right from the start there were adventurous souls who went after albacore for sport. Then, after World War II, one or two charter boats started going out. Usually what would happen, the charter boat would be fishing salmon on a slow day and hear on the R/T of an albacore school not far away. Then the skipper would ask his customers if they'd like to go off, and they might say "sure" and go. Few people deliberately fished for albacore then.

One problem is that few charter boats are licensed by the Coast Guard for operation more than 100 miles from shore. And, of course, the albacore are often found further out. So to date we still have fewer than a dozen boats which specialize in this fishing.

GWR: What about the Kiwanda dory fishing for albacore I've heard so much about? Would you describe that?

Holm: Well, that's a variation on the dash for blue water made by the larger albacore boats, except dory fishing is about 100 times more adventurous and exciting. You launch these big flat-bottomed dories right into the surf at Cape Kiwanda, and once you're over the first breaker, you drop your outboard into the motor well and pray she starts on the first crank! Then you're off, holding on for dear life, greyhounding and being pounded to death on every swell! You have to watch your weather in these little boats, and even on calm days, you're usually grateful to get home. As a precaution, we always go out in pairs with CB radio. But it's the most exhilarating fishing I know.

GWR: Have you ever tried live bait fishing for albacore?

Holm: No. Live bait's not so readily available up here as it is off California. So the most common practice is trolling a jig.

GWR: How about surf fishing? What's the most important fish along the coast?

Holm: The sea perch. There're about 50 or 60 varieties that look something like an Atlantic porgy. The most common variety is the red-tailed perch. It's an excellent eating fish, and very often you catch 'em right behind the first wave.

GWR: What's the bait?

Holm: Clams. And you use tiny bits of clam and shells to chum them up to a particular spot along the beach. And the beauty of this fishing is that you can go to almost any spot along our coast and be sure to get action. The beaches are deserted for 20 miles in either direction

[363]

and you've got it all by yourself, or with your friends or family. It's wonderful fishing.

GWR: And at the rocky points you get lingcod.

Holm: The rocky points do get the lings and rockfish. There're about 50 varieties of rockfish, and a good dozen varieties are quite common along the coast.

GWR: When you say varieties, are you speaking of color types or different species?

Holm: Different species. They belong to the same family, however.

GWR: But you don't bother to discriminate between them?

Holm: No, we don't. Even marine scientists can't often tell 'em apart. China rockfish, red rockfish, snappers—they all look alike.

GWR: What are the size of these surf fish? Seaperch, for instance?

Holm: They reach a maximum of about eight pounds.

GWR: Is that a rare catch?

Holm: Yes, that would be a rare fish. But I just did a story on a 93-year-old lady who caught one that big.

GWR: What's the average size?

Holm: Two, two and a half, three pounds. Anywhere from one pound to four pounds is pretty common.

GWR: How much larger are the lingcod?

Holm: They'll run to 20 pounds. They're strong fish, and they have teeth like needles. They're the most horrible looking things you've ever seen, and probably one of the best eating. We call them Toothy Critters. And you soon learn not to put your fingers in their mouths. If you do, it's like having a razor across your thumb. You put your fingers in their eye sockets to lift them. But with the snapper, it's just the other way around. You can put your thumb in the mouth, but not in the eye socket. It has sharp horns around the eyes that will cut you.

GWR: It sounds like you need someone familiar with these fish just to help you unhook them!

Holm: Oh, even I forget from time to time. I was brought up in fresh water where we held fish by the lower jaw or over the back by the gills. Unfortunately, these holds can lead to a lot of pain and bleeding along the coast.

GWR: Are sturgeon considered to be a coastal fish?

Holm: Now, yes. The white sturgeon is North America's largest freshwater fish, but because of the dams, today it's mostly found in tidal areas. The lower Columbia all the way to the sea is the last great stronghold of the white sturgeon. Then there's a green sturgeon that's even more of an estuary fish—really a saltwater fish.

GWR: I know California has certain size restrictions on sturgeon. Any restrictions up here?

Holm: None on the green sturgeon. But the whites can only be kept

[364]

between three to six feet. Anything under or over must be released.

GWR: In your *101 Best Fishing Trips in Oregon* there's a picture of more than 20 sturgeon caught in the lower Columbia by one party of fishermen. Are such catches unusual?

Holm: Yes. Recently white sturgeon have suffered from overfishing —sport and commercial. Few anglers try for green sturgeon as yet. It's sad to think that there were once some real monsters in the Columbia. I mean, 1,400-pound fish. The early people—the Hudson Bay trappers and traders—preferred the sturgeon to salmon. But today it's a senior citizen's fish. Hundreds of retirees sit in their boats year round fishing for sturgeon to help make ends meet. Then every so often they'll go smelt fishing just to catch bait for sturgeon fishing.

GWR: What kind of rig do they use?

Holm: Bottom fishing with an egg sinker and a free-running line, hook and leader. The fish sucks in the smelt, and you have to let him run with it.

GWR: What baits other than smelt and herring can you get locally?

Holm: Sometimes we have pretty good pilchard runs. Last year at Chetco harbor, for instance, the pilchards ran right up the river from the ocean with the salmon right behind. The bay was filled with pilchards and salmon, and the anglers had a ball.

When you get runs like this, you can scoop out a few for live bait. But normally keeping live bait is a problem. Our anchovies mostly come in frozen packages shipped from California. And if you try to keep ocean smelt or herring alive in a live bait well on your boat or at a bait station, the fish die pretty fast because the water's just too sweet for them once you get into the harbors. The Columbia's such a powerful river that it creates a relatively warm, freshwater area for miles offshore. This even affects the use of live bait offshore, so naturally our ability to bring bait into harbors and keep them alive from day to day is greatly impaired.

GWR: Do you have many halibut here?

Holm: Not as many as in the old days. We've been pretty well cleaned out by the trawlers. But we regularly catch 6-, 12-, or 20-pounders, and every so often, a fisherman comes in with a 40- or 50-pound fish. But it's nothing like up in Alaska. You regularly see them there a hundred pounds or more.

Hopefully, the restrictions we have now will improve the halibut fishing. If a commercial fisherman gets a halibut on today, his safest course is to cut the line straight off. If any commercial man brings a halibut in to market out of season, he's hauled into court and fined so fast his head swims!

GWR: Are there any sport-fishing restrictions on halibut?

Holm: No, none. In fact, there're no restrictions of any kind for

[365]

saltwater sportsmen in Washington and Oregon with the exception of stripers and salmon. With salmon, it's three a day and nothing under 20 inches. And a license and tag are required. Any salmon smaller than that is shaken off the hook. Hence, the nickname we use for these juveniles of "shaker." Stripers are open all year round with a 24-hour limit of five fish, 16 inches and over. But it's not easy to get a limit. During one extended period when I was after a striped-bass story, I made seven consecutive trips without even seeing a fish.

GWR: Don, would you say that saltwater angling was one of the fastest growing sports out here—not to ask a leading question, that is.

Holm: That's easy. We've been doing a little research at the newspaper and have determined that saltwater angling is growing about 20 percent every year out here, which means that every five years saltwater angling interest doubles. This growth is more than twice as fast as freshwater fishing—which, incidentally, is our most popular outdoor sport.

With a big influx of outsiders coming in as new residents, we have a new breed of sportsmen who haven't been conditioned from birth to think of salmon and steelhead as the only gamefish. In many cases, they've come from areas where the fishing hasn't been so good or varied —where any fish that struggles a bit and is good to eat becomes a prize. For instance, in California you'll find anglers who will drive 500 miles to get the kind of fishing local folks here turn their backs on. But as new families come in, they create new interest in all kinds of fishing.

GWR: Where would you recommend a sea-angling visitor start in Oregon?

Holm: There're just so many harbors and good places to fish along the Pacific Northwest it would take me the rest of the afternoon to tell you the ports in Oregon alone. Why not tell your readers to spend a few weeks out here exploring for themselves? They'll have a grand time, and you can't go wrong anywhere along the coast. You might end up staying on. We don't mind newcomers—as long as they're fishermen!

TWENTY-THREE

VAGABUNDO DEL MAR

> For every day a man spends fishing, Allah does
> not subtract that day from his allotted span.
> —An ancient Moslem saying

Aeronaves de Mexico has two mid-afternoon flights into La Paz, and not certain which flight I'd taken from the States, Ray Cannon arrived early at the airport. Ray enjoys the colorful flow of tourists through this Baja California port of entry, and he insisted there was no hardship in waiting the hour between the arrival of the flight I might have been on and the one that actually brought me nonstop from Los Angeles.

"It gave me a chance to watch book sales at the magazine stand. Why, we sold six copies of *The Sea of Cortez* in the hour! The darn thing's in its seventh printing and just keeps going.[1]"

As if to dramatize these words, actor William Holden came over while we were waiting for my luggage and asked Ray to autograph his copy of *The Sea of Cortez*. A former film star in his own right, Ray

---

[1]Ray's monumental travel, history, and outdoor guide to Baja California was first published in 1966 and was revised in 1972.

was nonetheless pleased to be sought out by a current Hollywood celebrity.

When we finally claimed my two bags and fishing rods and started across the lobby, I was amazed by the number of people who seemed to know Ray—tourists tugged one another's sleeves and pointed our way; clerks and porters smiled broadly with "Buenos días, Señor Cannon"; and other folks just grinned and waved.

"Looks like all your relatives are here, Ray," I teased as we started across a stretch of runway to where the private planes were parked.

He grinned, obviously pleased with the recognition his beard, blue blazer, and yachting cap receive everywhere in Lower California.

"Ah, but people don't know the real Ray Cannon," he replied. "They see the cap and these whiskers"—tugging at the silvery fur on his chin—"and that's what they call Ray Cannon. Many of these people first learned about Mexico from my writings, and now when they see me—recognize me—they think, 'Now we must really be in Mexico!' But they don't know me. And they don't know Mexico. We're both about the same age and equally inscrutable."

Ray stopped to laugh. He cocked his head and looked up at me to see if I appreciated his humor. Apparently satisfied, we continued walking.

"But the thing I find most wonderful is that after the tourists tell me they've read my book and that they love my column in *Western Outdoors*, then they ask me where and how to catch fish!"

Ray stopped and laughed again. His cap was squashed down over large ears, making them seem even larger than they are. Silvery thatch stuck out around the cap edges, and there was dust on his blue blazer —a wholly inappropriate costume for the chalk-dry climate of La Paz in February. Ray seemed like an unkept youngster—but one nearly 80 years of age.

The sun shimmered in heat waves off the pavement, causing the nearby landscape of cactus to tremble and swim in your vision. Ray stood a little longer, then went on with his thoughts: "It isn't just the ones who have read—but somehow not read—my book who intrigue me. I'm fascinated, too, by those who expect you to be up on fishing everywhere and at all times. They ask me how fishing is down at the Cape, and when I tell them I haven't been to the Cape in two weeks, they seem puzzled, as though my reply is no reply at all."

He chuckled again and we continued walking.

"The point is—"we stopped—"I want people to know I'm an au-

[368]

thority, not an expert." Ray cocked a drooping-lidded eye at me. "You understand the difference?"

I said I thought so, and we finally made it to the plane.

There we met Gil Kimball, manager of the sport-fishing fleet at the Camino Real Hotel near the tip of Cabo San Lucas. After hurried hellos, Gil nodded in the direction of the sun and indicated we would have to hurry in order to have sufficient light to land at the Cape. Without further ado, we climbed aboard his little Cessna—Ray in back, myself in the co-pilot's seat—and taxied to the runway.

"Which way do you want to go?" Gil asked above the engine's noise. "Over the mountains or down along the coast?"

"The coast, of course," I replied.

When we got airborne, the plane banked smoothly over the desert and headed west. Ray smiled happily in the back seat. He had not heard our conversation, but he knew that our direction meant we would soon be over the Pacific.

We swung south over the ocean's edge. The air was suddenly more chill, and on the horizon lay an ominous, endless fog bank. Below the plane, innumerable dark patches of water reminded me of kelp beds, and I pointed them out to Ray.

"There isn't any kelp this far south," he said, swiveling about to look down and see what I'd seen.

"Those are schools of small forage fish!" he exclaimed. "Mama mía, look at them—as far as the eye can see!"

Gil nosed the Cessna down and we roared several hundred feet lower. Sure enough, as far as we could see up and down the coast, my "kelp beds" turned out to have ruffled surfaces with occasional bursts of white water as some larger fish slashed into the baitfish.

"Look there! Yellowtail. Oh, I bet there're thousands of them down there!"

Birds drifted dispassionately over the schools or sat off to one side, digesting what they had already eaten. Only further along did we find a pair of pelicans seriously attacking a school—lumbering into the air, circling and then gliding in for the return crash near the spot they had just left. Their activity aroused the interest of other birds, and we saw several new birds flying toward this school as we went on.

We passed a gull sitting in the midst of a dark patch of sardines. Just as we flew by, yellowtail began to attack savagely from all sides. With something bordering on alarm, the gull took off and followed us down the coast.

[369]

Ray was beside himself: "Look at those fish! By the millions! All those yellowtail, and not a boat in sight. And there—look, tuna!"

A little further offshore, another kind of school was working. Leaping fish characterized this area—leaping fish of considerable size.

"Yellowfin tuna!" Ray exclaimed. "Aren't they beautiful?!" Then he tapped me on the arm and pointed down to the sea.

"This is the way the entire Pacific coast used to be 60 years ago. The fish used to come up off California—our U.S. California—like this. Look, whales! What a day! Watch the spouts. Sometimes you can tell by the spout whether it's a finback or a sperm."

"What's the difference?" I asked.

"The sperm spouts like an umbrella—up and then out—its blowhole is narrower or something. The finback spouts like a *V*—the air goes to all sides."

Ahead a pair of spouts appeared as mist, then blew away.

"I can't tell what kind they are," I said.

"They're sperms. I got a look at one before it blew."

Gil, with a grin of amazement on his face, flew the plane low over the submerged leviathans gliding pale blue beneath the surface. High, blunt foreheads identified them as sperm whales.

"Beautiful," Ray whispered. "I wish there was enough light for pictures."

"Light!" said Gil, coming out of a trance. "We'd better hurry if we're going to have any for landing."

He heeled the plane toward shore. Ahead was Cabo San Lucas, and around the Cape steamed a tuna clipper.

"Well, that's the end of my beautiful afternoon," said Ray. "Some fellow with a plane saw the fish and called the cannery in for the kill." Ray settled back with a frown and took no more interest in the passing scene.

Man-of-war birds roost like sea vultures around the cliffs of Cape St. Luke, and Gil had to dodge to avoid hitting one startled by our sudden appearance. We circled once to let another plane land ahead of us. Then with shadows filling the valley and lights already coming on in the few houses that make up the town, Gil brought us in for a perfect—albeit dusty—landing.

As we climbed from the plane, I thanked him for waiting at the airport and hoped that the extra hour hadn't been too much of a nuisance.

"Even if it was, I've been more than amply repaid," he said. "I

[370]

make that flight 10 times a week and twice that often in my sleep. Tonight, Ray Cannon showed me a sea full of fish I've never noticed before. I should be thanking both of you."

The waters of Baja are not always so rich in visible sea life. During my first visit to the country south of La Paz in 1964, a friend and I spent two weeks camping and fishing along the coast from Todos Santos on the Pacific side south to Cabo San Lucas and then north to Bahía de Palmas, where I caught my first black marlin. Besides billfish, we saw seals, turtles, small schools of tuna, and even a pair of killer whales that spent some little time playing tag with our boat. But in 10 days of fishing we never saw half as much sea life as Ray, Gil, and I scanned from the air in a single half hour's flight. It was a glorious experience and, like Gil, I felt lucky to have been along. But then you expect that kind of luck and adventure when traveling with Ray Cannon.

Ray was born in Union County, Tennessee, on September 1, 1892. Both parents were part Cherokee, and Ray, two brothers, and a sister grew up among people who viewed hunting and fishing as naturally as today's parents view television. They lived by a river in the Cumberland mountains, and Ray started catching dinners for the family at an early age. When later in his youth—as part of an initiation ceremony to manhood—Ray's father sent the boy alone into the woods for a period of three weeks to learn survival and self-reliance, Ray passed the test with flying colors and even wanted to extend his stay to avoid the routine of family chores.

His first sampling of life beyond the Tennessee hills came in 1900 when his parents moved to Oklahoma to accept two quarter sections[2] of land from the government as part of the Cherokee claims settlement. The family stayed there a year, until a great malaria epidemic drove them back to Tennessee.

The rest of Ray's childhood was a rambunctious affair, for even as a youth, Ray exhibited those nonconformist traits that have colored his entire life. His father, a Baptist preacher, hoped that Ray would take to the cloth. But the elder Cannon's ambition for his son was unrealistic. After two years in a Baptist school, Ray left—at the school's request.

He joined a summer stock company in Knoxville and learned the

---

[2] A section is one square mile or 640 acres. Each adult person of Cherokee ancestry was entitled to a quarter section. The offer expired in 1906.

[371]

fundamentals of acting. But he was restless to explore the world beyond Tennessee that he had briefly sampled in Oklahoma and that he regularly studied through the plays he read and acted in. So when Ray was 17, he set off for Oklahoma City, and from there decided to go to Dallas, Texas. But he was still inexperienced in hoboing, and somehow the train he hopped went to Fort Worth instead of Dallas. But no matter—he got a job as a reporter with the *Fort Worth Record* and then eventually shifted base to his original destination and worked for a Dallas paper. Through his own initiative and an unexpected break (the owner of the Dallas paper died and left it in Ray's hands), Ray was soon a prosperous 19-year-old businessman. He was so successful that he and a couple of cohorts decided they were well enough off to retire and go live in Tahiti. So selling their various investments, the three boys set off for Long Beach, California, where they hoped to find a boat heading for the South Seas. Instead, they found girls every bit as beautiful, accommodating, and plentiful as any they had imagined could be found in Papeete. So Ray decided to settle in Long Beach. He joined the stock company of the Bentley Grand Theater and spent all his leisure hours *chercher les femmes*.

"But darn, if it didn't get so bad, they started chasing me! At first I liked it. But then they started driving me crazy, and I just had to get out of there."

Once again he abandoned the theater and moved north to the deserted beaches of Santa Monica, where the only settlement was a small Japanese fishing village. He pitched his tent close to the village in order to be near the general store. But he quickly realized he had made a mistake when the fishermen started bringing in boatloads of Pacific mackerel. The fish were planked and hung in the sun to dry.

"To my Japanese friends," Ray recalls, "the smell of those fish was the sweetest thing on earth. But for me, it was nearer high heaven!"

Ray moved about a mile away. However, he maintained regular contact with the village and frequently went out on one or another of the small fishing boats. Most of the fishing was with multihooked handlines for bottom species, but occasionally the Japanese would find a school of bluefin tuna.

"We trolled a kind of bone jig for these fish. Sometimes the lure had feathers attached. The tuna were not big ones—maybe up to 60 pounds."

"Did you learn much about fishing on these commercial forays?"

"Yes, it was terrific experience. I even knew that at the time. I turned down a number of interesting adventures ashore to go fishing

[372]

with my Japanese friends. I probably wouldn't have attempted writing that first book[3] without the background of those days offshore. It was quite an education."

One day in 1913, a film director appeared not far from where Ray was camped to shoot a movie. The director needed a diver to play a drowning elderly man, and Ray, always available for any new kind of adventure, happily volunteered. Barely 21, Ray played the part so convincingly, he was signed up for other movies.

A few years and several films later, the great D. W. Griffith invited Ray down to Hollywood to start a long and serious career in the movie business. Over the next several years Ray appeared in literally dozens of films alongside such stars as Theda Bara and Charlie Chaplin. Under Griffith's direction, he played the male lead in *The Great Love* with Dorothy and Lillian Gish, and then during World War I, Ray became Griffith's assistant in making a series of American propaganda films.[4]

In his off-camera hours, Ray started to write. He published a prototype movie magazine called *Camera*. In addition to supplying all the copy, Ray had to be his own ad man and art director. But the publication was a wonderful success, and a major publisher later bought it as the foundation for a chain of Hollywood-oriented magazines.

With what little spare time he had, Ray started turning out scripts for a variety of stars such as Buster Keaton, Edward Everett Horton, Bebe Daniels and Clara Bow. He wrote the popular comedy *Never Say Die*, and by 1927 he was in such demand that he made the Ten Best Motion Picture Writers list.

But even writing, editing, and acting were not enough for Ray's abundant talents. He took up directing as well. Among the many movies that carry his credit line, film *aficionados* most readily recall *Life's Like That* with Grant Withers, *Red Wine* with Conrad Nagel, and *Cradle Snatchers*, a successful musical comedy.

Naturally this busy schedule left little time for fishing. However, Ray did make a point to work in an angling break at the conclusion of each directorial assignment. "I usually celebrated the finish of a film with an offshore outing for all the writers involved, and then a big fish fry at my place afterward. It got to be such a ritual that some writers would start asking where we'd be going weeks before the film was done.

"Sometimes I'd make a trip to Catalina to do some big-game fishing,

---

[3]*How to Fish the Pacific Coast*, first published in 1953.

[4]The Nationalist Chinese admired these films so much that in 1932 Ray was invited to China to make similar movies for Chiang Kai-shck.

[373]

and I went out a few times with R. C. Grey, Zane Grey's brother. But that was a rather exclusive world over there, and the fact that I worked in the motion picture industry was against me. You either had to represent big money or be a big-name star to be accepted at Catalina.

"That changed eventually. Other tuna clubs were created on the mainland, which took some of the exclusiveness and glory away from Catalina. And, of course, most fishermen went fishing without joining a club. By World War II, tens of thousands of California anglers enjoyed outings for yellowtail and barracuda who had never even heard of the Catalina Tuna group."

Following the war, these ranks of West Coast anglers swelled even larger. One of the most significant full-time additions was Ray himself. In 1947, after a serious stomach operation for ulcers, his doctor told him that if he did not get off the Hollywood treadmill, he would not live out the decade.

"That was 25 years ago. And all I've done in the meantime is fish. I'm having so much fun, I figure I'm good for another 25 years!"

Actually, not all of Ray's time has been spent fishing. A year in retirement was all his restless temperament could take. Thus, during one angling expedition off the rocks at Point Dume, Ray caught a fish that eventually gave him a new career.

"I got two of the things—about seven pounds apiece—and they had the most beautiful blue eyes. Carla Laemmle, my secretary,[5] got one as well. It put up such a terrific fight, she nearly lost her footing and went in the water! Well, I was naturally curious to know what these wonderful fish were. So I took them to a couple of local tackle stores and asked the men there. They didn't know. Next, I stopped by a sportsman's club, and they didn't know. I was disappointed to find so many fishermen who knew so very little about seafishes in general. One of them told me he called our fish 'Catalina blues,' while another fellow said they were 'Jack Benny fish.' Now, I just knew that couldn't be right!

"Next, Carla and I went to the local library to see what the fish authorities had to say. We consulted Jordan and Evermann and found a fish that seemed like the one we had caught, with a popular name of 'seaperch.' But I wasn't satisfied with that. And as events proved, my hunch was right.

"Finally, since it was getting late, we took some pictures of the fish,

---

[5]A former ballerina and actress, her drawings illustrate *How to Fish the Pacific Coast.*

cleaned our catch, and had one for dinner. At least then we knew one thing positively: They were great to eat! Later, I found time to take the pictures to the Marine Division of the California Fish and Game Department and showed them to Dr. Frances N. Clark. She said: 'Yes, we know this fish well, but we're not exactly sure how to classify it. We call it the opaleye because its eyes have such a lovely opalesque color.'

"So that was it. *Girella nigricans*, the opaleye. Most people call it a perch, but it's in no way related—though commercial fishermen take them by the ton in six- to eight-inch sizes and sell them in the markets as 'perch.' If the market men held off another year, these same fish would weigh up to seven pounds and be of great value to both commercial *and* sport fishermen. But farsightedness has never been one of man's strong points when dealing with sea resources.

"This episode taught me two things: One, that there were common ocean creatures we still didn't know much about. Two, that fishermen were among the most ill-informed people going about what they brought—or didn't bring—home to the dinner table. Instead of setting an example in knowledge and interest, a great many just didn't care. And worse, those who did had practically nothing in the way of a non-scientific but authoritative guide to fish and fishing along the Pacific coast. So that's when I started collecting material for a book."

In 1949, J. Charles Davis II,[6] wrote *California Salt Water Fishing*.[7] Despite an introductory chapter on "Pacific Coast Fishing" and the inclusion of some few fish caught outside Southern California, this book was written by a man based in Los Angeles for other Los Angeles sportsmen. The illustrations are generally weak, and while new developments in big-game fishing are reported, this section is written with less authority than the George Thomases' book, *Game Fish of the Pacific*, published 20 years earlier.

However, Davis's effort is significant for being one of the first West Coast publications to concern itself with the small boat and pier fisherman. Davis seemed to recognize that there were more people capable of catching kelp bass than bluefin tuna. In addition, while more than

<hr>

[6]Davis was the son of journalist Colonel J. Charles Davis and a frequent contributor to outdoor magazines. After a career in advertising, movie production, and promotion, Davis junior became the Pacific Coast editor for *Sports Afield* magazine.

[7]When the publisher reprinted this book in 1964, he changed the title and asked Davis to expand its concept to include all *Salt Water Fishing on the Pacific Coast*. However, with few revisions or additions, this is the same (1949) *California Salt Water Fishing*.

30 years after surf fishing had become popular in the East, Davis's book is one of the first to outline its activity in the West.

But, all in all, *California Salt Water Fishing* only pointed up the need for a truly comprehensive guide to fishing from British Columbia to Mexico—for everything from grunion to broadbill swordfish. Ray Cannon's *How to Fish the Pacific Coast* helped fill this void four years later. With specific sections on geography, bait, tackle, and boats, Ray leads the novitiate angler into the sport. Then, for the more experienced fisherman—the one who has already caught a fish and wants to know what it is—Ray created the first popular guide to Pacific species identification done up until that time. Working closely with 20 different marine scientists—including such respected names as Dr. Carl L. Hubbs of the Scripps Institution of Oceanography; W. I. Follett, Curator of Fishes at the California Academy of Sciences in San Francisco; and special friend Dr. Boyd W. Walker of the University of California in Los Angeles—Ray provided a key to classification and then a brief description of all the most common Pacific coast fishes with their popular names, coloration, size, range, bait and tackle, and special comments touching everything from gee-whiz facts about their sex life to pleas for conservation of certain jeopardized species. It was an enormous undertaking and an outstanding achievement for a man 60 years old with a couple of careers already behind him.

Meanwhile, Ray had discovered the Sea of Cortez. The Mexican government was studying the possibility of a new road from Mexicale to San Felipe, and Abelardo L. Rodriguez, former provisional president of Mexico,[8] asked Ray down to research the sport-fishing opportunities in the upper end of the Gulf of California. Rodriguez owned much of the land around San Felipe, and he hoped to see the area developed. He figured (correctly) that if the government in Mexico City thought American sportsmen could be persuaded to visit San Felipe, it would put up the money for the road.

Such research was no work at all for Ray; he performed his duty faithfully and fished every day, filing reports with the local constable and Dr. Boyd Walker in Los Angeles. One of the most amazing fishes he encountered was the well-nigh legendary totuava, largest member of the croaker clan.

"Some scientists will tell you this fish only gets up to about six feet and maybe 200 pounds. Well, we caught literally dozens of 200-

---

[8]From 1932 to 1934. By profession, Rodriguez was a general, active in a number of revolutions. Born in 1889, he died in 1967.

pounders, and the largest one I ever weighed—brought in by one of the commercial men—was 303 pounds."

GWR: What were these fish used for? Were there that many people in San Felipe to feed?

Cannon: In the beginning, believe it or not, the fish was caught almost exclusively for its air bladder. The bladder was dried, ground up, and then shipped to the Orient for use as a soup condiment. In fact, there was a Chinese merchant in San Felipe who handled the trade and made a fortune out of it.

Then some Americans found out about the meat of those huge fish just going to waste on the Mexican beaches, so they began to truck the carcasses to the Los Angeles market. It's only a 150-mile run, and even with the poor roads and inadequate refrigeration in those days, you could make the trip overnight and drop all this fine fish flesh in the LA market early the next morning. By nightfall, you'd be back in San Felipe for another load.

When the Mexicans found out how much money this fly-by-night operation was making, they passed restrictions that soon eliminated anybody who wasn't Mexican from the totuava trade. In fact, they eliminated everyone but the Chinese fellow who had started the whole thing off in the first place. He was already a Mexican citizen and, therefore, continued to export the air bladders.

GWR: Is this trade still going on?

Cannon: Almost finished. The fish are protected now in the upper Cortez, and there's a closed season from March to May. But still a couple of hundred small totuava are caught annually. Our Chinese friend got rich and returned to China. Today others are marketing shark livers, skins, and even jaws for the tourist trade. They put the jaws of the larger sharks in a chicken wire cage and set the cages out overnight in the water. Copepods come up and clean the jaws faster and more thoroughly than any man can do.

One of the great pleasures of angling with Ray is hearing anecdotes like these. Cruising slowly over the cobalt-colored Gulf while watching for tailing marlin or leaping sailfish, Ray fills the time wonderfully with reminiscences of his early days of fishing off Baja.

"One of my very favorite anglers was Eddie Urban, from whom I learned most of what I know about albacore fishing. Eddie was an opera singer and a Lebanese Christian who also knew the Koran. He often made trips with me to San Felipe in the early days, and we fished together with a small Mexican crew on a small shrimp boat that was loaned to me for my research. Eddie was like an unpaid assistant—he just came along for the ride and the fishing.

"He was a huge fellow with an immense voice and an exuberant nature. Every morning as we went fishing with the sun just emerging out of the sea, Eddie couldn't contain himself. He'd climb on top of the cabin roof and chant, in that magnificent operatic voice, the Moslem call to prayer in Arabic. It was an awesome thing, and Eddie did it out of the sheer joy of being alive. But our Mexican crew never had any idea what it was all about. They sensed it was something solemn and very holy, and they'd always get down on their knees, cross themselves, and pray, while I was the only one left to run the boat!"

One of the wonderful features of being an Atlantic coast angler in the Sea of Cortez is the variety of new fishes you encounter. Although cabrilla remind you of an Atlantic grouper, you know they are something different. Even more wonderful is to hook a fish with all the stubbornness of a jack crevalle, but with greater speed, and find that when you have brought your quarry boatside, lo and behold, you have caught your first roosterfish.

But there is satisfaction, too, in finding a number of fish familiar from the Atlantic—pelagic species like the dolphin and oceanic bonito. You even come across some inshore varieties recalled from home, and one of the highlights of my first camping trip to Baja was catching palometa or gafftopsail pompano[9] from the beaches. My companion was less of an angler than I, and he preferred wading beyond the mild surf in the early morning, bending down and peering around underwater with a face mask, and then spearing a pair of the curious fish for our breakfast when they came to investigate his legs. All pompano are delicious, but I suspect those breakfasts were especially so because the fish were fresh caught—and because they brought to mind other palometa, and other meals, when I was a youngster living in Florida.

Thus, when Ray said one day that he had developed a surefire way to catch pompano in the Sea of Cortez, he immediately had my undivided attention.

GWR: When you say "pompano," you mean the true pompano, not the butterfish?
Cannon: Right. The one I'm talking about is a member of the Carangidae or jack family—the very same fish you're charged $3 to $5 apiece for back in the New York markets. One evening, I was sitting

---

[9]*Trachinotus glaucus*, not *Palometa simillima*, the California butterfish sometimes called pompano.

in my camp above San Felipe watching the mullet jump when I noticed a large, flat fish jumping with them. I had never seen a pompano jump before, but I'd caught them in the Caribbean, and I had a hunch that might be what the jumpers were.

So I tried fishing for them. I suppose I tried everything in the way of conventional bottom baits from shrimp to crabs to pieces of fish. But all without success. Then one of the Mexican boys speared one for me and, after confirming that it was indeed a pompano, I opened its stomach to find it full of little fish about an inch and a half long. Well, I couldn't get any bait that small, so I decided to imitate the little fish. I cut tiny strip baits from a bonito belly and tried drifting them from a small boat just offshore. No luck. Then I tried casting them. Still no good. Then I decided to troll them. But they were so light, my bait started to skim along the surface. I thought that was bad, so I put on a small clamp-on sinker. Then I began to work the sinker-strip bait combination behind the trolling boat like it was a jig lure. Well, I guess I worked the combination too vigorously, because the sinker came off and the strip popped to the surface and began to ski along beautifully on top of the water again. Before I could do anything about it—wham!—I had a pompano. He came right off the bottom, hit the lure at the surface, and then went about two feet in the air. What a lovely strike!

So I had my fish, but I still wasn't sure I had a technique for getting more. I experimented with other ideas, but every time I came back to the tiny "ski bait," I got a pompano. In fact, I loaded the boat, while the Mexicans never caught one. They were astonished to see me bring in so many fine fish. But I gave them little hooks and taught them how to make and use a ski bait, and soon they, too, were catching fish as fast as me. And now they use this technique for catching a variety of other species as well.

On our last day of fishing, we trolled up the coast to San José del Cabo and passed what looked like a small freighter run aground on the rocky shore. I asked Ray what had happened.

"One thing I like about Baja," he began, "is that the local people don't like to wait for decisions to be made by the federal government. If they see a local injustice, they act to remedy it themselves. Baja California Sur is still a Territory, after all, not a State. And the folks down here are independent in ways peculiar to people living on the frontier.

"When the Japanese began to long-line this coast several years ago, they trespassed inside the 12-mile fisheries limit with impunity. To save the Mexican government's face, the Japanese carried out most of this work at night. But still the Baja California fishermen knew what was going on, knew it was illegal, and worse, knew that they were losing their livelihoods to foreign competition.

"The Japanese would sneak within a few miles of shore, set out their immense trot lines,[10] buoy the ends, and attach tiny radio transmitters and radar reflectors so they could locate the buoys in the dark the next night. Then they'd run offshore to do some 'honest' fishing by day before sneaking in the next night to load up with illegally caught fish.

"Of course, the local Mexicans started out by protesting to the national government. But you can imagine how effective that was. People with prime jobs in capital cities are usually so involved with the 'big picture,' they're rarely of much use to anyone—particularly those people whose interests they represent.

"Anyway, the Japanese depredations continued despite local retaliation by pulling some of the long-lines and recovering the catch for themselves. Then one brilliant, anonymous Mexican had an idea: He went out, cut loose one of the buoys with its radio transmitter intact and brought it ashore, taking it about half a mile inland. The next night, the Japanese long-liner followed the transmitter beeps right onto the beach where you see her now. Since it was a relatively calm night, the captain and his crew were arrested for drunken navigation as well as trespassing, and charged enormous fines eventually paid by the Japanese government. The Mexican authorities insisted that no navigator could have run his ship aground with such force at right angles to the beach on a quiet night and still have been sober!

"Since that incident, the Japanese long-liners have shown greater respect for the territorial waters of Mexico."

Before leaving Baja, we stayed one night at Rancho Buena Vista on the Bay of Palms. One of the finest resorts south of La Paz, it has grown considerably since I first saw it in 1964, but it retains a family boarding-house atmosphere at its communal dining tables and a simplicity in accommodations that does not overwhelm either the visitor or the surrounding landscape. It is a comfortable place to spend a week or 10 days, and the clientele is completely devoted to fishing.

The minute we arrived, Ray was once again the celebrity. People brought him copies of his book to sign, and little groups of ladies gathered to ask him about his early days in Hollywood, while the men mostly asked where they could catch big marlin. One family from

---

[10]Each boat normally handles six lines, each 11 miles in length.

Nebraska, on their first angling expedition outside the states, adopted him, and at one point I found Ray entertaining the youngsters with an elaborate tale of how long it takes billfish to grow a new spear once they have lost the original in the side of a boat or shark. He gave me a happy wink over the tops of their heads as I passed on my way to the dining room.

If fishing south of the border—from Baja to British Honduras, from the Virgin Islands to Venezuela—is a large part of the future of salt-water angling in the western world, then I can only hope that all the resorts-to-be have a resident "sea vagabond" with the warmth and humor of Ray Cannon.

TWENTY-FOUR

THE COMMANDO

An old fisherman has few regrets; a young fisherman has none.—Anon.
Reinfelder's definition of "true hungry": To want fish and fishing so bad you can't sleep at night for dreaming of it.

Demographers tell us that before the end of this century, over half the world's population will reside in major cities. In North America, the proportion will be closer to 80 percent. Since tradition has it that urban living and fishing tend to exclude one another, such demographic forecasts would seem to spell the end of saltwater angling for all but the wealthy who can continue to get away from it all.

But just as weeds sometimes find sufficient soil and, therefore, life in the cracks of a city sidewalk, so tomorrow's anglers may find inspiration in the remaining tidal streams and estuaries in the heart of megalopolis. The odds against survival are great. More than ever, these remnant natural areas are hard-pressed by pollution and urban growth. In addition, the sheer number of people seeking relief from the unnatural world of the city puts tremendous pressure on these few oases, stifling the solitude of any fishing to be found there. As a result, many potential young anglers turn back to the midnight streets where they can at least create the illusion of privacy and control.

[382]

Finally, there is the matter of law. Many of the best fishing spots are off limits because—unlike the beaches of Oregon and Hawaii—shorelines are considered personal property in the East. Even highway bridges, which sometimes provide outstanding angling, are often restricted by state or city officials who—without hearings—decide unilaterally that such public structures are actually meant to serve just one type of taxpayer: the motorist. The bureaucrats justify this action by saying it is for the "fisherman's own good" to protect him from passing cars. As a result, either an angler has a boat, or he goes not only fishless but without even the opportunity to fish. And, of course, anglers who can afford boats do not usually choose to fish in megalopolis anyway.

Thus, to become an angler today when you are born and brought up in the heart of a big city not only requires infinite faith and determination, but a willingness to break a few of society's rules. It is an upstream struggle, but a few men do make it. And to round out this collection of angling profiles, I have selected a story about a boy from Manhattan who successfully challenged inertia and ignorance to find fame and fortune as a fisherman.

Alfred Reinfelder was born on July 9, 1937, in Gotham Hospital not far from where his family lived on the East Side at 88th Street and Third Avenue. His father was a waiter in the Waldorf Astoria Hotel and a nonangler. Yet, somehow, Al was born with a craving to catch fish.

"When I was nine years old, I didn't even know what fishing was. But I told my mother, 'You have to get me a fishing outfit.' I didn't even know what a fishing outfit was! But she said, 'All right,' and bought me one of those diversionary toys that look like a rod and reel but which even Al McClane[1] couldn't catch an eel on! It was a wooden stick with a wooden spool nailed in one side. The spool turned on the nail with a little handle, and that was your reel. The stick was your rod. And then there was some linen line with a rubber grasshopper at one end with a hook in it.

"Of course, I thought this was pretty hot stuff, and I begged my parents to take me fishing. Finally, my mother agreed to take me to Staten Island where my aunt and uncle lived. We went by subway and had to transfer at Grand Central Station. A man there had dropped

---

[1]Executive editor of *Field & Stream* and creator of *McClane's Standard Fishing Encyclopedia.*

a parcel onto the tracks, and my mother said she'd get it with her son's fishing outfit. So she proceeded to fish for the package with my rubber grasshopper. She finally caught it, and was a heroine, of course. But my outfit was a mess! It was so tangled and bent out of shape I couldn't even use it.

"When we got to Staten Island, my aunt gave me some string and a bent pin—the classic and completely unrealistic tools of the beginner. I went out to a very shallow tidal creek near the house, where there were perhaps a few mummichogs,[2] but that was all. I caught nothing and was very discouraged. But when I went back to the house, my uncle had come in from work, and he said he'd take me down to the jetty for eels. We fished with handlines, and after I threw mine out and held it, I just *knew* what a fish was going to feel like! It was something electric, and I felt destined to be a fisherman! When I got my first eel, I pulled it up and ran all the way back along the rickety wooden jetty to show everyone back at the house. Later we caught eels on rods and reels. That was even better. I was now thoroughly obsessed with fishing."

During the next several years, Al's parents got summer work in Colorado, and Al learned to fish fresh water as well as salt. But his first love was the sea, and as he moved into his teens, he became fired with the ambition to catch a *real* saltwater gamefish: the fabled bluefish or the even more elusive striped bass.

"My first experiments in striped bass fishing were unqualified failures. I fished with friends and their fathers who were actually after blackfish or flounder, and just to humor me, they allowed me to do a little casting around a bridge or jetty on our way out to the flounder grounds. But flounder fishing didn't appeal to me. I had read *Field & Stream* all my life, and *real* ocean fishing was standing waist deep in the surf casting into a storm of breaking fish and diving birds—not sitting in an open skiff on a cold day catching flatties. I had been conditioned to believe that the epitome of fishing was casting lures for gamefish. The stumpy boat rods and fat little reels and flounder spreaders that my friends used depressed me. Flattie fishing just couldn't be what saltwater angling was all about!

"The more I read about striped bass, the more I felt they were it. Everyone wrote about them. Everyone talked about them. And, supposedly, you could even catch them on a lure. But I was getting to the point where I believed nobody ever really caught any—except maybe

---

[2] The common killifish, *Fundulus heteroclitus.*

[384]

in fantastic faraway places like Cuttyhunk and Martha's Vineyard. I read Frank Keating's column in the *Long Island Press*, and he also talked about remote locations like Shinnecock and Montauk. But every so often, he'd say so-and-so made a catch of striped bass at East Rockaway—a place I actually knew! So that weekend, I'd persuade my cousin, Billy, to go out with me to catch striped bass. But, of course, we never did catch one.

"We did have one high point, however, in those early days. My cousin kept a locker at Henning's Bait and Tackle Shop under the Atlantic Beach bridge where he had an old outboard. We'd rent a boat from Henning's and go out fishing. Billy and I were both all of 14 years of age. We were really putting out maximum effort that summer for stripers, and on this particular trip, we went out the inlet— all at my urging, of course—and the engine quit on us. Billy is a mechanical genius—he's an engineer today—and he went to work on the motor and finally got it going. But rather than risk any further breakdowns, we decided to head in while I trolled. I'll never forget the details of that day: I had a Bronson reel, 12-pound test braided nylon line—it was colored black—and a Pflueger Mullet Mustang lure. All of a sudden, my line went slack! I was puzzled, but I started reeling in. 'Maybe I've somehow caught the line in the prop,' I thought. When the line came up tight, I looked down and saw a great big bluefish with my plug in his mouth. I almost went overboard! Billy started scrambling all over the boat looking for a gaff, while I sat there like a dodo staring at this fish that didn't even know it was hooked! This was back in the days when blues weren't so common or big yet, and what we saw would have made us heroes in Keating's column—if we could ever have gotten it in. But we lost it, of course. Billy got real discouraged, but I was more determined than ever to catch a bona fide saltwater gamefish. After all, the incident proved that the mythical bluefish might not be so mythical after all.

"Our next plan of action was night fishing. So many of Keating's articles read: 'They're catching them at night.' So that was it. That phrase became our motto. We whispered it in the corridors at school. 'They're catching 'em at night.' But neither Billy's mother nor mine would let us go out at night. So we had to do the whole thing secretly. Billy would come to our apartment to stay over, and about midnight, my parents would go to sleep. When we heard my father snoring, that was our signal to move out. What an incredible trip! To get to East Rockaway, we had to take a subway, a bus, the Long Island Railroad, and then a taxi. Then, of course, we had to reverse the whole procedure coming home. We used up most of the night just traveling back and forth! Sometimes, when we got to Atlantic Beach, we weren't adequately dressed and about froze to death. After all our trouble, we'd sit there anchored beneath the bridge, shivering so hard we could hardly cast. Naturally, we never caught anything. Yet all this hardship and frustration only increased my determination to catch a striped bass. I was 'true hungry.' "

Al's big break came when a friend of the family, Harry Miller, asked him if he'd like to join the Long Island Surf Fishing Club. This organization started out shortly after World War I as the Jones Beach Rod and Gun Club, then changed its name to the Jones Beach Surf Fishing Club when a majority of members decided that fishing was more important to them than hunting. Finally, when the organization moved its headquarters to Astoria after World War II, it became the Long Island Surf Fishing Club. With nearly 200 members, this angling fraternity was one of the area's largest, most influential, and a frequent leader in the annual Schaefer Beer Fishing Tournaments. Al was just 15 years of age when he joined.

"Club meetings were usually built around a fishing movie of some sort. You know, Zane Grey catching marlin in the South Seas, or Gadabout Gaddis snook fishing in Florida. To show you how fanatical these guys were about fishing, one day our film acquisitions man brought in a pornographic movie called "Bouncing Bluefish," or something like that, which started out with a girl in a blue sweater. Well, as soon as the rest of the fellows saw it wasn't going to be a real fishing film, they started shouting and carrying on and made the projectionist turn the darn thing off!

"The club talk was always exciting, and I think I was a member three years before I could go to sleep after coming home from one of the meetings. Everything that was important to me was discussed there! It was as though I was at the edge of a great world looking in, and sooner or later, I knew I would be invited to participate.

"Meanwhile, I had gotten very active with club business. I started out as the Schaefer Contest Chairman, which is very ironic when you consider our club's association with such tournaments ultimately caused me to resign.[3] And over the years, I served on every one of the

---

[3]In one of those unfortunate encounters between one member's conscience and a majority's desires, Al Reinfelder resigned from the Long Island Surf Fishing Club in October 1963—ten years after he joined. He had decided that competitive

different committees until, not long before I left, I served on the board, and then as chairman of the board.

"However, all this wasn't really helping me to learn the kind of hard-core information I needed to catch striped bass. There were a few fishermen who always seemed to catch fish, but they kept to themselves and were never too specific about where they fished or what they caught their fish on. I knew one thing—or thought I did—I knew how to fish the Atlantic Beach bridge! Then, one day in a casual conversation with Harry Miller, he told me, 'You know, Ed Sens is the greatest bridge fisherman who ever lived.' Wow! I just had to get to know Ed Sens!

"At that time, Sens was in charge of the Angler-Swimmer part of the Schaefer Contest. It's something you see at the New York and Boston sports shows. An angler plays a swimmer in a harness and tries to land him just the way you would a fish. You've got to be careful not to break the swimmer off; you've got to wear him down on 45-pound test line just the way you would a big fish. It may sound a little strange, but this is a very popular event whenever they stage an outdoor recreation show. And there's keen competition between the fishing clubs to see who can land a swimmer in the fastest time.

"When I first volunteered for it, I had no idea what this event was all about. All I knew was that Ed Sens was in charge of it, and that Ed Sens was 'the greatest bridge fisherman who ever lived.' So I just marched up to him at the next club meeting and said, 'I'd like to be in the Angler-Swimmer Contest.' He said, 'All right,' and that was it. To show you how green I was, I had to ask one of the other guys to explain what all the little buttons and switches on a conventional reel were for. I then got a Surfmaster model reel and a surf-casting rod especially for the contest and practiced every weekend with some of the swimmers on a Bronx high school swimming team. When I came home from school, I'd even tie the line to the radiator in my room and learn all I could about the tolerances of my line, the rod and the reel's drag. I learned how to establish drag with my fingers alone, using both hands in a cradlelike vise around the spool. And I got so I could feel within an ounce of when that line would break so I could ease up at just the critical moment to start applying pressure all over again. By

---

fishing was aesthetically, if not morally, wrong, and he refused to contribute any of the fish he caught to the club's total poundage in the Schaefer Tournament. Since the number of fish caught by Al Reinfelder and his partner at the time, Louis Palma, were great, a majority of club members passed a resolution stating that *any* club member *had* to contribute the fish he caught to any contest the club saw fit to enter. Al resigned rather than submit to the new ruling.

the end of those weeks and months of practice, I was the leading angler —except for Ed Sens—in the club, and we were to have the 'swim-off' to see who would represent us in the contest at the New York Coloseum.

"Now, here's an interesting psychological development: By this time, Eddie was a hero and a father-figure to me. And now, I was supposed to compete against him. To complicate things further, he had called me at home just before the competition and asked me to go fishing with him afterwards. I'd have to stay out all night, and he talked quite a while with my mother to persuade her it was all right. Needless to say, that forthcoming adventure was very much on my mind when we both went up to face the swimmers at poolside. To make a long story short, I popped my line. Here I knew the tolerances of those 45 pounds of line strength better than any one up at Ashaway! Yet I popped it. Ed was very, very good. But I just don't think I was prepared yet to see him lose. And I sometimes wonder if I didn't pop the line subconsciously on purpose.

"Now, the date was March 31, 1953. I'll never forget it. All that evening before and after the contest, I kept wondering how there could be any striped bass in New York so early. But then I had absolute faith in Ed. If he had said that we'd catch blue marlin that night in the Harlem River, I would have believed him! When I went over to Ed's place after the swim-off, I found he lived in a veritable tackle shop. His apartment wasn't so spacious or anything like that. It was just very obviously the apartment of a fisherman. For starters, he had about 100 Upperman bucktails made that afternoon drying on all the lampshades. Then around the place were fly- and lure-making equipment, great spools of line, and rods stashed in every corner. I felt like a little kid in a candy store!

"First, he rigged me up. He gave me a light surf rod, a conventional reel with 25- or 30-pound test line. Then he used a monofilament leader about five feet long tied to a light wire leader about 18 inches long attached to a brand-new Upperman bucktail. The wire was to save your fish if it got close to barnacle-encrusted pilings. Eddie was always very fastidious about his connecting links, and he didn't use a swivel between the mono and the wire. But between the wire and the bucktail, he used a snap—one that he had made himself. He used to work in Abercrombie & Fitch tying flies, so you know he had to be good. He was most particular about the bucktail; it had to look as much like a streamer as a jig. Eddie had started out in fresh water, and he

[388]

had formerly been one of New York State's best trout fishermen and guides. But he now preferred salt water and striped bass. And he brought to salt water all the attention to detail and tackle refinement he'd learned in fresh.

"When we got in the car, I asked where we were going and he said: 'You don't ask questions; you keep your mouth shut. Whatever you see, you don't see. Whatever you hear, you don't hear. Got it?' So I sat in the back and didn't murmur a word for the rest of the trip. But then none of us did. Besides Eddie and myself, there was Bob Hutton,[4] Al Covello, Jack Russell, and Glenn Voparil. Bob, Jack, and Glenn were all young fellows like myself. But it was quiet in that car. You'd have thought we were the Mafia off to do someone in.

"I noticed we were driving through the Bronx. And then it began to snow. Incredible! Light stuff—but snow. I'd been watching the papers for news of the first striped bass catches, but I'd seen nothing. Now, with this last snowfall of winter, I just couldn't believe we were really going to catch fish. I even wondered for a moment whether I wasn't the victim of an elaborate joke of some sort—like a piscatorial snipe hunt.

"Still, if Ed said we were going to fish a bridge and catch striped bass, it had to be so. Thus, every bridge we passed over, I held my breath: 'Is this it?' Half the bridges we crossed went over subways or railroads, but then I was beginning to think anything's possible! Finally, we came to the Pelham Bay Bridge, turned around, and parked on the street. We all got out. *This was it!*

"I was so excited I started to whip my rod around, and first thing I know, my bucktail was caught in a tree. I yanked so hard on the branch, the rest heard the commotion. Eddie called out, 'Where are you, kid?'—'I'm hung up in a tree, Eddie.'—'Ah, you stupid kid.'— Eddie came over and yanked the bucktail down. The leader was all twisted, and he started mumbling something about I should have known better than to take a dumb kid fishing. Of course, that kind of talk terrorized me, and I figured I'd screwed the entire deal.

"But then he put on a new leader and started to tell me what to do: 'Street lights on the bridge throw a shadow from the bridge onto the water. The fish wait on the dark side of this shadow with their noses right up against the light. When you get out on the bridge, I want you to make a 45-degree cast to the left. Then a 45-degree cast to the right.

---

[4]Robert Hutton later married Edmund Sen's daughter.

And I want you to look in the water for fish. You must do everything I say. Nothing more and nothing less. Whatever you know, you don't know. You got that? I was so choked with emotion at the thought of actually catching a striped bass that I almost did handsprings. But I figured I had to keep my cool. So, I said 'yes,' and probably shouted the word by mistake.

" 'Okay,' he said. 'You fish the bank with the others. I'll take Hutton out first.' So I went down to the bank and wondered what was going on. After being told about the fish under the lights, it seemed pretty futile to be down on the bank—which it was, since none of us caught anything. But pretty soon Hutton came off the bridge and said to me, 'I lost an 18-pounder.'—'How do you know it weighed 18 pounds?'—'Eddie said so.'—'Oh.'—'He told me to send you up.' So I started up on the bridge. I stumbled every six steps and was completely out of my mind with the thought that I might even see a live striped bass after all these years! When I got there, Eddie asked me to get up on the side of the bridge. You can't lean over the wall of the Pelham Bay structure very well, so the only way you can fish the bridge is to sit up on the edge. I had the jitters so bad I figured I'd probably end up falling in the water some 40 feet below!

"When I got up, Eddie said, 'Okay, there's a 12-pounder right under you.' Well, I didn't see anything, of course, and figured maybe he was saying that to encourage me. He told me to make a 45-degree cast to the left, and I made one without backlashing. A miracle! But Eddie made some insulting remark about the way I held my rod. And I told him I'd hold the rod any way he liked. So he said to get it under my left arm. And I did. And to this day, I fish that way no matter where or what kind of fishing I'm doing—all because of that first instruction. That's the kind of impression Ed Sens made on me.

"The 12-pounder didn't like my offering, so Eddie told me to cast 45-degrees to the right. He then said there was a smaller fish moving after my lure. 'It's a seven-pounder,' he announced. Just then I got a hit. When I set the hook, I had a striper on! After a lot of flurry and hollering, I began to work the fish over to the bank where Al Covello was fishing. Al hauled the striper out for me, and I practically leaped off the bridge to get to where the fish was. Ed said you had to kiss your first bass, and this I did. Then Eddie smashed the fish's head on the corner of the sidewalk and we weighed him: 6¾ pounds. Just like Eddie said. I forgot whether there were any other fish caught that night. All I remember was mine!"

[390]

GWR: Did you go back to the Pelham Bay Bridge later that year?

Reinfelder: Almost every night. I don't think we missed more than a dozen evenings that entire spring! But it was not an easy trip to get there. My parents had moved to Queens by then, and Glenn Voparil (my partner) and I had to take the subway into Manhattan, change trains for uptown and Pelham Bay, and then hike to the bridge from the subway stop. It was a long trip—both ways—and sometimes we'd just get back in time in the morning to clean the fish, change clothes, and be ready for school.

GWR: What did your fellow commuters think of you walking on the subway with a couple of fish?

Reinfelder: They never noticed. You know New Yorkers.

GWR: How many fish did you get that spring?

Reinfelder: I have a diary somewhere that would tell me. We kept records of every outing. Every time we caught a fish, we put down the time we caught him, what direction we'd been casting, the tide, the lure—everything.

GWR: Did this note-taking help you later on? Did you discover any patterns in the way you caught these fish?

Reinfelder: No, nothing. I know some striper fishermen who seem to benefit from such diaries. But over the years, I find my experience with these fish has varied enormously. Feeding seems to depend entirely on the type and availability of bait. And this, of course, depends on distant or uncontrollable variables like offshore upwellings and wind. Moon tides are definitely more productive than any other because the high water creates strong currents, which moves more bait per hour past a given feeding station. But beyond that, I couldn't tell you what lure a striped bass will favor on a given night—or even whether the fish will always be where you expect them. Fishing diaries are fun to look back on years after they're written. But I'm afraid they don't teach me anything I can apply to my fishing next season.

GWR: Did you fish again with Ed Sens?

Reinfelder: Frequently. In fact, he led several of the Pelham Bay expeditions later that spring. But one day in May he startled me by saying, 'All this fishing from the Pelham Bay Bridge has only been practice.'—'Practice for what, Ed?'—'The real fishing out at Jones Beach. That's where the best striped bass fishing in the country is!'— I nearly fell over. Jones Beach?!

But it was true. And for more than a decade, the fishing we had there was unparalleled by anything I've done since at Montauk or Martha's Vineyard. Bridge fishing is different from trolling or surf casting, I know. But I'm talking about sheer action. When a big bass breaks a line at a bridge, the line snaps with a sound like a .22 rifle.

[391]

Maybe the proximity of the span to the water acts as a sounding board that increases the snap's reverberation. Whatever it is, some nights when a bunch of us were working a particularly productive bridge, so many lines were popped on really big fish, it sounded like warfare!

We became so familiar with the fish that over a period of several seasons, you could watch certain age groups grow. One year, small fish would predominate at a given bridge; the next year, the fish would be a few pounds larger, and so on. Conversely, we also watched most of these fish populations diminish. Some of it was due to overfishing as more and more people discovered the bridges. But much of it, too, was due to damming the freshwater feeder streams that once made the Great South Bay a true estuary and provided river herring with access to their breeding ponds. And then, of course, the bulkheading and filling of the marshes to make homesites with a casual attitude by the developers and state officials toward proper sewage disposal killed much of the rest of the bay. A lot of the fellows thought the fact that the bridge fishing was so very good "now" meant that it would always be good. But bridges only concentrate fish; they don't provide areas for the fish to reproduce. You need entire river and coastal systems for that. But most of the guys never appreciated how rare and special our fishing really was. The reason I can talk about this now is that it's just about finished—I'm giving away no secrets. In its heyday, it was too good to share with outsiders. I remember nights when the fish in those little channels were there in such numbers you could throw out anything and have it taken every cast. I remember fishing with partners who would get tired or cold, or were just plain ill, and who would go back to whatever vehicle we had to sleep in. And I would come back with a fish and make a great to-do about putting it in the trunk. I tried to get them up, roused, willing to go on fishing. I used to plead, "You'll never have fishing like this again. It's changing, dying. And you've got to take advantage of it while it's here. Five years, 10 years from now, when there's no place left to fish, when your kids will sit and stare incredulously at your fishing stories that to their generation are impossible dreams because the marshes are gone and the sea is dead, what will your lousy headcold mean to you then? Come on out and fish!" That's the way I felt about it. And I still do. Jones Beach gave me an expertise in bridge fishing that I should be able to apply anywhere in this country on a variety of fishes. Only trouble is, we're losing our best littoral fishing everywhere so fast that knowledge on how to fish the shadow line may soon be obsolete, simply because bridge fishing for striped bass, snook, and sea trout may soon be things of the past. I strongly suspect that our current boom in striper activity may be nothing more than the bloom on a rose—its finest final hour before the flower fades and dies.

[392]

GWR: Can you describe a little more about how the shadow line works? Whether fishing a bridge uptide is better than downtide? Things like that.

Reinfelder: Briefly, the shadow line is where the bridge's shadow falls on the water and creates an edge with that area lit by the bridge's street lights. In reasonably shallow water, the effect of this shadow line extends all the way to bottom, usually at a greater distance from the bridge because the light comes off the structure at an angle. Fish are caught along this line on top or on the bottom. When they're close to the surface, you can see them as perfectly black torpedo-shaped silhouettes. Or, if they're on the downtide side of the bridge—what we call the "back" of the bridge, as the uptide side is its "front"—you'll see most often the fish in the illuminated part with their nose up against the dark side of the shadow line. There're exceptions and variations to these rules depending on individual bridges, types of abutments supporting them, adjacent pilings, holes or rubble formations on the bottom, and so forth. But once you understand that the bridge is like a headquarters where the fish hang out in particular favored locations —where the bridge lights attract food, and the tide sweeps this food to the fish—then you're on your way to being a savvy bridge fisherman.

As for which side is better to fish—the front or the back—I suppose ultimately the back is more attractive because you have to worry less about getting your lure snagged on the pilings since the current is always working the lure away from you. And likewise, when you get a big fish on, the current becomes something of an ally in landing him. But naturally you shouldn't fish a bridge where you're most comfortable; you fish it according to where the fish are.

Bridge fishing can be the greatest show on earth. The night and the lights on the water provide a theatrical setting, and your position overhead looking down on the fish is very much like occupying a box seat at a circus. And some nights that's exactly what it is. The water will be whipped to foam by hundreds of big fish attacking schools of squid, silversides, or even chasing swimming crabs. One of my last nights out was like that. The date was November 28. Most other fishermen had long since quit for the season—either taken up duck hunting or were inside watching television. But that evening my partner and I caught over 150 pounds of bass each, and finally just had to stop. There were so many fish, there was no skill in taking them. But I stood there and watched the water around the pilings churned white by feeding bass. It was sensational!

GWR: Besides giving you a balcony seat, are there any other advantages to fishing a bridge from the bridge than from a boat?

Reinfelder: Very definitely. For one thing, you have great control over the presentation of your lure from a bridge. You can often see the fish and put the lure right across its nose. If the fish doesn't hit, you can experiment by varying the speed, regularity, or angle of retrieve. You learn more this way than by casting blind from a boat.

Another thing, you can make the retrieve of a jig or bait tail[5] more true from a height than on a horizontal plane. With the eye of your hook riding up, you control the swim of the bait tail with greater facility from a bridge than you would from a boat. You can go deep, or swim a steady course just under the surface, or even troll the shadow line far better from the bridge than from a boat.

Finally, there's the noise factor. By and large, bridges are quiet places. There's the hum of traffic overhead, which the fish undoubtedly hear as vibrations through the pilings. But like a car on a road with crows, the birds don't associate it with harm as long as it keeps moving. You may have a surge and slap of water around the abutments on a windy, strong-tide night. But this is still calm stuff compared to what you'll find at the jetties or along the beach. Therefore, fish are definitely more sensitive to noise around bridges, and you've got to think "silence" all the time. Your cast should enter the water with as little splash as possible. And, if you're going to fish from a boat, you should cut your engine well upcurrent of the bridge and drift down to where you want to anchor. If you want to fish the back of the bridge, then up-anchor and drift through. Don't start your engine. Likewise, if you want to move to a new span along the front, up-anchor, drift through, and then run up the main channel through the center span to work your way around to a new location. That way you approximate ordinary boat traffic, and you have half a chance the fish will ignore you. But, of course, all these little moving difficulties are eliminated if you're fishing directly from the bridge in the first place.

However, boats do help in one respect: They stop police harassment.
GWR: Why were they after you?
Reinfelder: It's a long story, but during World War II, the government restricted access to many key links around New York City to protect them from saboteurs. Pelham Bay Bridge was one of these. After the war, instead of abandoning a law that had served its purpose, the government maintained the restrictions, possibly because of the Cold War, or just possibly because government officials enjoy managing people's lives. At Pelham Bay we never had any problems because the bridge attendant there was a sympathetic soul who seemed able to live with fishermen. In any event, he let us fish there even when we weren't supposed to.

But then along came Robert Moses, our most illustrious Parks Com-

---

[5]A lure developed by Al and described in his *Bait Tail Fishing*, published in 1969.

[394]

missioner. He was a super people manager who felt that all pedestrians should be confined to pedestrian areas in New York State parks. And he figured that the bridges along the parkways had been built to serve drivers going to or from the parks, not fishermen who may like the bridges for other purposes. Anyway, he prohibited fishing from these bridges, and the local police, all too eager to have something to do, enforced these laws to the limit. But in a way, Moses' regime was the best thing which ever happened to us. His rules eliminated all the casual fishermen, leaving just us diehards with all those fish. And if you'll pardon a diversion, I'll tell you a famous story about the early days of these prohibitions.

GWR: By all means.

Reinfelder: The fellow who first originated the bridge fishing techniques we used on Long Island was Mike "Stretch" Olinek. He was to Ed Sens what Ed Sens was later to me. And just as Ed and Mike parted company, in a similar way Eddie and I broke up years later. Anyway, Stretch had been fishing the Atlantic Beach Bridge since the days it first stood on wooden pilings. When the highway department built the new bridge, they built it with a high arched span, just about eliminating the best of the old fishing, and most of the old-timers drifted away. But Stretch had fished that area all his life and he just wouldn't give up. There was no place to hide along the top of the new bridge, and the attendant was a very zealous government employee who knew all the rules, and the rules very specifically prohibited fishing. So Stretch was out there fishing one night, and the attendant came out of his little booth on top of the bridge and told Olinek to scram. Stretch told him to mind his own business. Well, this little bridge attendant started jumping up and down and badgering Stretch to the point where Olinek couldn't concentrate on his fishing. Things got so bad that Stretch finally turned around—all six-foot-five of him—and laid the bridge attendant out cold. A passing motorist saw the action and called the cops. In a few minutes, a police car roared up the bridge with sirens wailing and stopped by Stretch and this prone figure on the sidewalk. "What's going on here?" asked one of the policemen.— "Nothing," said Stretch.—"What's this guy doing lying here?" asked the other policeman.—"Oh, him. He tried to keep me from fishing."— Then the police told Stretch he was under arrest, and they started to drag him to the squad car. Well, he apparently fought them all the way and just at the car, he broke free. But he didn't run away. No, he ran back to the rail, picked up his rod, and made one last cast!

GWR: What finally happened to Stretch?

Reinfelder: They locked him up. They said he had a "dangerous disposition." Maybe so. But only if you interfered with his fishing.

[395]

GWR: You mentioned your breakup with Ed Sens. Would you mind talking about that?

Reinfelder: Well, there's an unhappy parallel between what finally happened between Stretch and Ed, and then later between Ed and myself. And I almost passed on the syndrome not long ago.

Stretch met Ed when Sens worked at Abercrombie's. This was back during World War II, and everyone was short of gas and tires, and so there wasn't much fishing beyond what you could catch within range of the subways. Eddie used to guide in the Catskills on weekends, but he was increasingly absorbed by saltwater fishing and wanted to do more of it. Stretch had a car, and Ed offered to share expenses with him.

Stretch was good at bridge fishing, but his real forte were the jetties. As Ed later developed into the best bridge man I've ever known, I suppose we can rank Stretch Olinek as one of the all-time great jetty fishermen. In fact, so many people used to spy on him, that one of the tricks he developed was always to carry a decoy lure on his line when he walked out on a jetty at night and then to put it back on when he walked off the jetty with a fish or two. He never had to lie that way. Everyone saw the lure he was "using" and no one asked any questions. But everyone got faked-out just the same.

One curious habit of Stretch's was that he always carried a cloth with which to polish his tin squids. Every idle moment he had, he would spend rubbing them to the point where they seemed to glow in the dark. The quickest way to get Stretch riled was to make a move as if you were going to touch one of his tins with your bare hand. He'd rear up about seven feet tall and shout, "What are you doing?!" Conversely, the most personal gesture he could make was to let you examine one of the tins. It was like a blessing.

Eddie and Stretch used to fish regularly together until one night, over a very little thing, they parted ways. Stretch had a theory that the system to use in fishing jetties was to go directly to the end, make a long cast to the left, and then a long cast to the right. If you didn't get a hit, you moved on to the next jetty. He had absolute faith in this procedure and insisted that it was the only way to go.

One night, Eddie and Stretch decided to fish the same jetty—only Eddie said he'd stay back and fish the cove where the jetty came ashore. Since Stretch *knew* Eddie couldn't possibly catch any fish there, he was perfectly happy with the plan. Next thing, Olinek heard Eddie calling, "Hey, Mike, come back. There're fish here." And Eddie hauled in a bluefish. The next cast he was into a striper.—"Hey, Mike, the action's all back here"—really pleading for Olinek to join him.

Still, Stretch made his first cast to the left.

Meanwhile, Eddie had hooked a weakfish.

Then Stretch makes a cast to the right.

And Eddie was into another blue. By this time, Sens was going crazy. "The fish are down here, Mike!" he was yelling. "Come on back!"

Then Stretch walked off the jetty to where Eddie was fishing. "Let's go home, wise guy," he said. "I've had it with you." And all the way home, Stretch went on about how "I showed you everything I know, and now you're a smark aleck. This is it, we're through." And they never fished together again.

Many years later, something similar happened between Eddie and myself. By that time, I had quit the Long Island Surf Fishing Club and was fishing mostly with Lou Palma—the fellow with whom I developed the Alou Eel.[6] We both lived in the same apartment house and used to borrow the building superintendent's jeep. The sup used it to haul garbage, but we dubbed it "The Pumpkin" because at midnight we put roof racks on the jeep and a fish box in back and converted it to a professional fishing buggy.

We had learned that with the time difference in tides between the various bridges along Jones Beach, you could get up to nine hours fishing during one outgoing tide. We'd work each different bridge at its peak and then rush on to the next one. And because we were a little more hungry about our fishing than most others, we'd sometimes get to one of the more popular bridges with a boxful of fish and find most of the other fellows just getting started. Naturally this was resented— especially when we'd start adding more fish to what we already had, and these other guys still hadn't caught anything. Eddie started calling me up to tell me how stupid I looked running around on the bridges. And I'd say, "Look, Eddie, if I'm in your way, just say so, and I'll clear out." And all Eddie would reply was, "Ah, kid, you just look so stupid."

Well, one night, by working hard on one of these marathon outings, Louie and I caught 200 pounds of big bass. And I called up Eddie to tell him the wheres and what lures of that trip. We used to trade information all the time. Eddie was out, but I told his wife, Helen. The next night, Eddie called up, and I asked him how he'd done. He said, "Okay, I got 200 pounds of fish, too"—which was surprising since I knew the bridges and I knew that 200 pounds of fish weren't that easy to come by for one man. So I asked him where he'd been fishing, and he wouldn't tell me. I mean, he called up just to make a point of not telling me where he had been fishing. So I told him if that's the way he felt about things, then that was the end of our relationship. Oh, we tried to revive it, but it was no good after that. The spell of 15 years was broken. And I was just sick about it for weeks afterward.

But then, weirdly, I found the same thing beginning to happen in

---

[6]*Alou* is an acronym formed from the names *Al* (Reinfelder) and *Lou* (Palma.)

my relations with Peter Stepanek, one of the young fellows who fishes with me from time to time, and who's known to other Long Island fishermen as "Peter the Hungry." This guy is really great. At the start, he learned just about everything from me. He sort of idolized me. I don't say that boastfully—it's just a part of the teacher-pupil relationship, the same way I idolized Eddie. Well, one night we were together, and he made a crack that, I suppose, was meant to be a joke. But it didn't sound very funny to me. Maybe I was just tired, but I called him a smart ass and almost decided not to take him fishing again. But then I said to myself, "You clown, how many times is this pattern going to repeat itself?" And to get it out of my system, I told Pete the whole story of Olinek and Sens and then Sens and myself. And I haven't felt any similar vanity in my relationships with other fishermen since.

GWR: What other run-ins with the authorities did anglers have besides the scene between Olinek and the Atlantic Beach bridge attendant?

Reinfelder: Oh, there were so many. Some nights the cops seemed to have nothing better to do but cruise the park areas chasing fishermen out. I suppose they considered us a kind of prototype beatnik: We wore sloppy clothes, didn't drive the newest cars, and sometimes hadn't even shaved! In the mid-1950's, things weren't too bad yet. There was very little traffic in the Jones Beach area at night, and some of the guys would park their cars right on the bridges. When they'd see the lights of another vehicle coming, they'd pull in their lines and run like the devil for the car, leap in, and take off. If the approaching vehicle was a police car, the guys would just go surf fishing for the rest of the night. But if it was merely someone out riding, the boys would turn around, park on the bridge again, and go on fishing.

This may sound all right, but it was very hectic. If you were playing a fish, you had to horse it in or pop it off. In the excitement, some guys smashed car windows trying to shove rods through when the windows weren't even down. On top of that, the police started stopping just any car that looked like it had fishermen inside. The cops would ask for your driver's license, what you were up to—the usual roadside routine. Then, sometimes they'd even write up a ticket for some incredible offense like claiming you had no rear-view visibility because of all the junk or clothing on the shelf over the back seat. Of course, the fact that we also had side mirrors didn't seem to matter.

Well, the guys got tired of playing cat-and-mouse with the fuzz, and we figured there had to be a better way. So two different schools of action developed: one along the Meadowbrook Parkway founded by Ed Sens, and the other on the Wautaugh bridges originated by someone I only knew as "Tony."

Eddie's technique was to park the car in the bushes off the road, sometimes sweeping away his car tracks with brush. In the early days, we made roads through the underbrush from snow fences, but they didn't hold up very well. Later, we used timbers to create a kind of track, and many of them are still there. Then, when you were out on the bridge and a car came along, you'd jump over the bridge railing and stand on the little concrete ledge there and duck down out of sight. Usually the cops would never see you.

The Wautaugh technique was to fish near the ends of the bridge and *run off* when a car approached and hide in the bushes. You lost a lot of fishing time this way, and naturally I found the system far less convenient than merely ducking down out of sight on the outside of the bridge railing. The bridges were all built with a pair of wooden posts over each piling. If you got on the outside of the double post and held the railing with a dark-colored shirt on, no one could see you. Even if someone walked by at night, in 9 cases out of 10, they'd never even notice you. Over the years, I found that when I was wearing dark clothes, black sneakers, a black watch cap, and my beard, no one noticed me—not even fishing friends who were sometimes out looking for me at a particular bridge where I told them I'd be.

Well, there was one exception: One night in late summer I was on a bridge playing an 18-pound bass when a guy drove slowly by with his date. I ducked down, but not quick enough. The girl saw me—or rather she saw *something*. They were going slow enough so that I heard her say something to her boyfriend. The car stopped and began to back up. They were curious to find out what she'd seen. Well, here I was with a good-size striper trying to pull me off the bridge! And here, just on the other side of the railing, was an idling car with a couple of people looking my way. Finally, I couldn't stay down any longer. I stood up to get better grips on the bridge and my rod, and I said something like "Good evening" to the girl in the open car window about two feet from my face. The girl about had a stroke! She started screaming, and then there was the mingled screech of tires and the hysterical shrieks of the girl as the car took off. I was really sorry about frightening her like that, but I got the fish.

All our diversionary tactics pretty well foiled the police. They took to cruising the bridges with searchlights, but they spotted very few of us. One night, though, they coordinated an attack on the third Wautaugh bridge with a police boat in the channel, a launching dory, and squad cars on the road. Their timing was a little off, however, and the boat gave their plan away before the squad cars arrived.

What an adventure! Searchlights flashing, red lights blinking, sirens wailing—and about 10 of us scattering in all directions along the shore and through the underbrush! I think the cops finally caught one. Eddie and I made it to his jeep and took off over the dunes on some trails he knew. Then we got back on the highway, went over to the Meadow-brook, and had great fishing all the rest of the night.

Out of self-defense, we finally got involved in counterinsurgency work, and our grandest coup was infiltrating the local force with one of our own boys. During the summer months, the police take on dep-uties to help manage the city crowds running back and forth to Jones Beach. Glenn Voparil volunteered and was soon able to let us know a night or more in advance about one of their proposed Keystone Cop raids. In addition, when competition on the bridges became too great from outsiders—fishermen we'd never seen before—Glenn would ride over to the bridge, get out his bull horn, and tell these other guys they had just five minutes to clear out. About 15 minutes later, our group would pull up, park our cars, and go fishing. Glenn would some-times come back after changing his clothes to join us.

But, ultimately, the advent of outsiders was one of the big factors that finished the Jones Beach fishing. Even the cops in time realized what we had going for ourselves, and some of them began to join the bridge ranks, inviting all their friends. That was worse than all their harassment! Eddie never told anyone outside the club about the bridges. And if there was still good fishing there, I wouldn't be telling you.

Over the years, Al passed through various phases on his way to angling maturity. At first, he coveted all fish and species—although at the precocious age of 10, he was already releasing any fish he did not plan to eat. Then his interest narrowed to striped bass. Once again, he caught all he could, releasing the little ones, keeping the rest, and selling what he and his neighbors could not use.

The next step in this evolution was a compulsive desire for big fish— those over 50 pounds. Night after night, Al went out with visions of record stripers before him. But his best fish from the bridges was just 43 pounds[7]—there being no way he could hold a truly monstrous striper when it decided to run in under the bridge and through the pilings. But about this time, the concept of big catches, tournament body counts, total poundages, and the commercial aspects underlying much of his so-called sport fishing began to trouble Al. He was in his early twenties, just finishing college, and beginning work as a math teacher in a public high school. It was a time of conscience and re-consideration.

One day, an advertisement in *Life* magazine caught his eye and so angered Al that he sat down and dashed off a letter to the banking

---

[7]His largest striper—a 47-pounder—was not taken from a bridge.

[400]

concern that sponsored the page. It showed a man and his son in a row-boat getting ready to go fishing with a large motorboat ("designed to look like an automobile," Al's letter said) racing by in the background and occupied by a family also on their way out fishing. The ad caption read simply: "How do they do *more* with their money than you do with yours?"

Al's angry three-page epistle attacked the cheap appeal of an ad sponsoring the idea that a man and his son in a rowboat could not have as much fun as a family in a flashy cruiser. While Al's commentary ended with the recognition that his letter would probably end up in some junior executive's wastebasket, the very act of writing it focused some of his feelings about what constitutes recreation and sport in fishing. From this point on in his angling life, Al began to concentrate on technique, on presentation of the lure, and the type of lure itself. This was a first step in the development of the Alou Eel.

Probably the very first step in that lure's creation occurred the night Al met Lou Palma. Reinfelder was just coming out of his apartment in Bayside, Queens, on a bass-fishing expedition when he met Palma just en route to a flounder-fishing trip. Since the two saltwater anglers lived on the same landing, it was only natural they should start sharing fishing adventures.

Al introduced Lou to striped bass angling and quickly made a convert of him. Together they concentrated their efforts on the North Shore of Long Island, starting with the Pelham Bay Bridge, and gradually, as that structure faded due to pollution and the filling of the marshes above it, the two anglers switched their allegiance to the Bayville Bridge further out on the Island. There they discovered a maze of tributary creeks and marshland that forced them into the totally different science of bankside and rubber-raft fishing.

"We found some wonderful water in that area stretching from Bayville to Glen Cove. But most of the access was in private hands, and our only option was to sharpen our South Shore skills of trespass and deceit to foil a more sophisticated North Shore police force. Probably our finest hour came when one of the few access roads to West Creek was closed by a paving crew during a prime tide. We got out the maps and hurriedly tried a number of apparent alternate routes that unfortunately ended up in dead ends or some guy's backyard. We were getting desperate and finally went all the way around to the other side of the creek, only to find the road turned into a private driveway, which turned into a garden where a cocktail party was going on. We knew that just on the other side of the garden was a back road that

[401]

would take us down to the creek. So with a rubber boat on top of our 1953 Buick, we drove slowly into the midst of the party, waving at people as though we were the guests of honor. The ruse worked to the point that a waiter hurried over with a tray of drinks and offered them to us through the car window. 'No, thanks,' I said. 'I'll park the car first.' And we made our way around the booze table, a hedge, and down the gardener's path to our little back road. We parked and had a great night of fishing.

"Not long before this, Louie had come in one day with some imitation eels he had found in a novelty store. They looked authentic and they seemed to have good action, so we sat down and began to figure out ways we could rig them for fishing. One of our first ideas was to put them on a bucktail head, and that was the origin of the bait tail lure. In fact, I tested the idea out in one of the creeks soon afterward and took 11 bass the first night!

"Then we wanted to do other things with the artificial eel concept, but we found ourselves limited to the few imitations available on the market. That was the real genesis of our company. We suddenly realized that to get the designs, size, and textures we needed to create really great striper eels, we'd have to build the darn things ourselves. That was in the fall of 1964, and if we knew then what we know now about the problems in store for us, we'd never have begun!

"The work started with us designing the eel on paper. The original drawing was identical to the eel baits we used while fishing the South Shore jetties and beaches. There was a lead head for weight, with both hooks rigged out the belly. It was only an accident when one day we experimented with rigging the rear hook turned up and found we had not only a better flip-flop action in the lure, but we could more readily slide it over the rocks without snagging, just like the Real McCoy.

"We started reading handbooks on metals, mold making, and plastic fabrication, and the first eel I carved myself. But I didn't take into account the matter of shrinkage—that is, each time you make a casting, your product gets smaller. So we ended up with a veritable shoestring we called the 'Little Louie,' and rejected it when it didn't catch anything. Then we overcompensated and came up with a obscenely fat version we called 'Big Al.' But 'Big Al' at least looked more promising than 'Little Louie,' and since it's a lot easier to reduce a casting in size than to build it up, we took it from there.

"Not only were we trying to get a very definite density and texture in our plastic, we wanted to have a finished lure all ready to pop on a snap and catch fish. Previously, anybody who had made an eel had left

[402]

it up to the angler to rig it any way he wanted to catch fish. That's a fine notion, but the point is, most anglers don't have any idea what constitutes a fish-catching eel. So we decided we'd leave nothing to error. We'd even mold in the proper bend for the lead keel and use alloys so the angler *couldn't* change the shape of the keel even if he tried. We knew what caught fish, and we figured if we could put a finished fish-producing product in each and every angler's hands, the lure would sell itself by word of mouth. And that's approximately what happened.

"By February 1965 we had our eel. We were even able to make up a dozen a day. We were cooking up the eels in a stove in the cellar, and occasionally we'd get a small fire. Smoke would start billowing out the cellar door, and while one of us would be putting out the fire, the other would go outside with a stoogie and puff away like mad, and every time anyone walked by, we'd say, 'Man, what a terrific cigar!' But then we suddenly realized that what with tobacco bills, burnt stoves, and only a dozen Alou eels a day, we'd be bankrupt before spring!

"Our first big break came when we sold a batch of eels to Ted Schmidt of Teddy's Tackle Shop in Brooklyn. It was a truly peak experience, and we wanted everything just right when we delivered them. On the way over, we noticed that some of the eels had gotten tangled up. So Louie and I stopped by a pub to use the bar to rearrange them. The bartender was very impressed with our lures and knew right off what they were for: 'These are for eel fishing,' he said. 'An eel sees one on the hooks, and he jumps on, too!'

"After this triumph, we got another stove and jumped production to 48 eels a day. And one afternoon we got another big break: Abercrombie & Fitch ordered 48—a whole day's work. Well, we were naturally tickled, and both of us escorted the order into Manhattan. But when we got back, we found to our horror that the eels we had just sold were made out of an uncured plastic mixture that would tend to develop little hollows which would ruin the weight and action of the lure. So Louie and I stayed up all night making 48 more eels and then, without saying anything to Abercrombie's, took the new batch in and exchanged them—all the while with the salesmen wringing their hands and looking very frantic and saying over and over again, 'What are you doing? What are you doing?' We explained, 'These eels are much better,' and left it at that. But we thankfully made the exchange before one of the defective ones was sold.

"Now, if I went into all the details of those early days—the incidents

[403]

of our being cheated when we went to outside help to get the eels produced in greater numbers, and the few moments of triumph that gave us hope to carry on with our harebrained scheme—you'd have another chapter to write. But probably I can best sum up our progress with three phrases that Louie and I pasted on our workshop wall to smile about whenever things seemed most grim: 'Who Will Buy It?'—'Clam, Clam.'—and 'The Greatest Thing on the Market.'

"Phrase number one: When we first started working on the eel, I went to my uncle Kurt Fischer, a jeweler, for advice about what engraving tools to get and how to use them. I showed him the molds, and he said, 'This is too big for trout.' And I explained, 'But it's not for trout, Uncle Kurt. It's for striped bass.' And he looked at me and said, 'But if trout won't bite it, who will buy it?'

"Phrase number two: When we finally had an eel we were proud of, we took some to Empire Sporting Goods in Flushing to see if they'd buy them. The guy who really ran things there was a likeable fellow by the name of Saul, but with a traditional and somewhat narrow attitude about what constituted a fishing lure. He picked up one of the eels, began to fondle and squeeze it, and then said 'Ugh, Clam! Clam!' and began to pull the thing apart with little plopping snaps of elastic. So much for our first attempt to market the Alou! And so much for Saul!

"Finally, phrase three came into being when Frank Keating devoted an entire column in the Sunday *Long Island Press* to the lure, its development, how to fish it, et cetera. He ended the article with the words: 'In my view, this is the greatest thing on the market today!' So that was it. Frank's column was the first of many that helped carry sales from 1,000 eels a year in 1966, to 2,500 the next year, to 15,000 by 1968, and then to well over 100,000 eels annually by the time we sold our operation to the Garcia Corporation in 1969."

GWR: Al, one final question: With most of the places you used to fish closed now because of pollution, development, or people pressure, where do you fish today?
Reinfelder: You got to be kidding! Not even the CIA has that kind of information![8]

---

[8]In retrospect, my closing question to Al seems frivolous, for while reading galley proof on this chapter, I received word that Al had drowned while canoeing on the Delaware—May 18, 1973. Two days later in *The New York Times*, outdoor editor Nelson Bryant observed that "it is only rarely a man like Al Reinfelder touches our lives, and, although his magic was with us for just a little time, nothing will ever be quite the same."

During his too few years of angling, Al became convinced that the fisherman, who spends day after day, season after season, along a favorite shore or bay, is more sensitive than most people to the aesthetic and social implications of environmental destruction. Hence, anglers could and should form the nuclei of environmental action groups concerned with the welfare of all our estuaries, beaches, and bays.

In 1972 Al participated in the formation of the Striped Bass Fund, Inc., a nonprofit, tax-deductible agency devoted to "the protection, preservation, and enhancement of the striped bass fishery—its spawning grounds, nursery, and habitat." His boundless enthusiasm helped overcome the defeatism of many who said, "Oh, my grief, not *another* conservation group!" Early in 1973, Al became the Fund's president and rapidly extended the influence of the organization by helping a number of agencies already active in the field, such as Save Our Stripers and the Hudson River Fishermen's Association. Al sought to make the hazards confronting the striped bass (wetlands destruction, indiscriminate siting of new power plants, and water pollution) national issues. He hoped to draw attention, not only to the plight of our marine sport fisheries, but to the health of the country as a whole.

Al's loss has been a shock to conservationists everywhere. Yet he would have been the last man to spend time and emotion berating the fates. Instead, he would have wanted to see the Striped Bass Fund continue working toward a time when men will live in harmony and understanding with the resources of the sea. If all sportsmen one day contribute a part of their lives to the attainment of these ideals, it will be the finest memorial Al Reinfelder could ever have.

[405]

PHOTO ALBUM

When Thomas Harriot and artist John White visited the
New World toward the end of the sixteenth century, they
found the Algonkian Indians of the mid-Atlantic coast
well versed in the uses of weir and spear for taking a
variety of fishes.

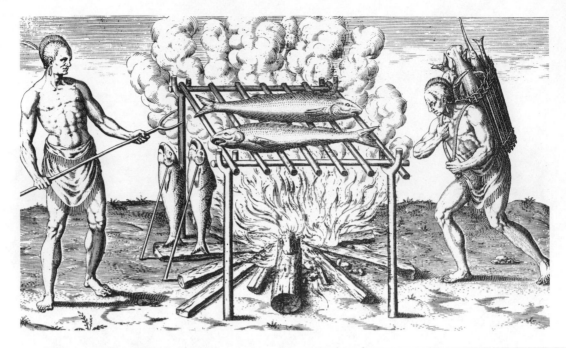

This scene from Harriot's 1590 report on "the new found land of Virginia" shows one Indian broiling fish—does the overshot mouth suggest channel bass?—and another Indian bringing in a load of other fish.

The cod-fishing industry was already 200 years old when this illustration for Moll's Map of North America appeared in 1715. Note the cold-weather dress of the fisherman, his primitive hook and sinker, and the "staging area" where the fish were processed. These were the humble beginnings of an empire—and a sport.

Henry William Herbert, alias Frank Forester, did much as an outdoor writer to create a new respect for the emerging sport of saltwater angling. He also stirred up considerable controversy by insisting that any saltwater fish was "unquestionably" the superior of its freshwater counterpart.
(COURTESY NEW YORK PUBLIC LIBRARY)

Herbert was a fair natural historian and artist, as this engraving demonstrates. While this striped bass was caught in local New Jersey waters, some of the fish Herbert illustrated came from Louis Agassiz's personal collection.
(COURTESY NEW YORK PUBLIC LIBRARY)

Louis Agassiz's second favorite place to work (after the sea itself) was in the classroom, and his influence on the development of American marine science and, by way of association, saltwater angling, was enormous.
(COURTESY MUSEUM OF COMPARATIVE ZOOLOGY LIBRARY, HARVARD UNIVERSITY)

While Agassiz fished to get specimens, Spencer Fullerton Baird fished
for fun—as well as science. First U.S.
Fish Commissioner, Baird most especially enjoyed angling along the
Jersey shore for weakfish, or in the
Potomac above Washington, D.C.,
for striped bass.

(COURTESY LIBRARY OF CONGRESS)

Robert Barnwell Roosevelt was
another devotee of Potomac stripers,
and he especially enjoyed taking
them on a fly rod between sessions
of Congress when he served in the
U.S. House of Representatives.

(COURTESY LIBRARY OF CONGRESS)

Following the Civil War, a new leisure and a new appreciation for saltwater angling emerged in the North. While
only the wealthy could join the exclusive striped bass clubs
of New England, almost anyone with a handline could
spend an afternoon in a cat-boat catching bluefish, as this
Currier & Ives print of 1866 depicts.

(COURTESY LIBRARY OF CONGRESS)

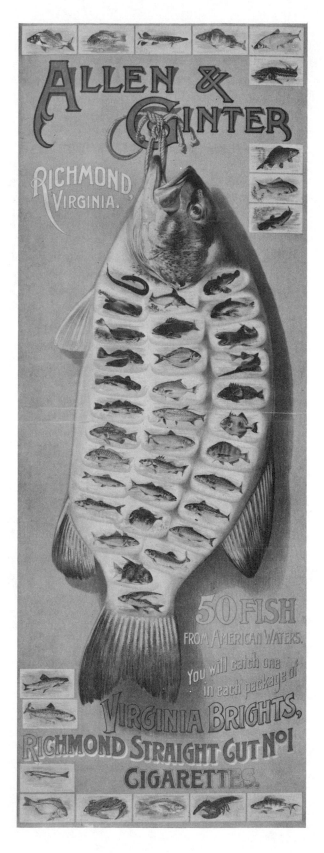

Sea fishing became such a popular pastime after the War Between the States that a majority of the fish cards "you will catch in each package of Virginia Brights" cigarettes, according to this 1870's ad, were saltwater varieties.

This is the island where saltwater sport-fishing rules were initiated. Although the New England striped bass clubs had a variety of customs affecting "a gentleman's conduct" while on the stands fishing, it was not until the advent of the Catalina Tuna Club that a group of men insisted on standardized "sporting tackle" for the taking of particular species of fish.

This is the angler, fish, and guide combination that officially started the sport of big-game angling. Charles Frederick Holder poses with his 183-pound bluefin tuna while his "gaffer," Jim Gardner, looks at the camera.

Later in that first week of June 1898, other distinguished Californians (from the left: H.K. Macomber, E.L. Doran, C.R. Scudder and—far right—Fitch Dewey) caught tuna on "regulation tackle," and C.F. Holder brought his fish out again to pose for the camera. These men then banded together to found the Catalina Tuna Club.

The man who may actually have caught the first large tuna on rod and reel was one Colonel C.P. Morehouse. Although denied this niche in angling history by Charles Holder's more aggressive publicity, Morehouse nonetheless holds a special place with this 251-pound fish caught in 1899, which is still the Catalina record for tuna.

The angler, the guide, the fish, and the device that revolutionized fishing at Catalina. Guide George Farnsworth found that using a kite was the one way to keep a bait away from the boat and in front of feeding tuna. He also found kites worked well for billfish, and in 1913, William C. Boschen caught this 355-pound broadbill swordfish—the first ever taken on rod and reel—on one of Farnsworth's kite-drawn baits.

A typical turn-of-the-century Catalina fishing boat. Note the fighting chair behind the helmsman.

Soon billfish were as popular with Catalinamen as the tuna that had led to the club's founding. Experienced anglers were able to distinguish the rounded dorsal tip of a "finning out" broadbill swordfish (below) from the more angular dorsal of a cruising striped marlin (bottom).

(PHOTOS BY AL TETZLAFF)

Zane Grey pioneered many techniques for broadbill swordfishing; among them, this unusual "baiting tower" from which he presented his bait to finning fish.

Just some of the angling equipment named for Zane Grey: ZG teasers at left; ZG hooks and ZG Ashaway line, right. In the foreground of the teaser shot, note the strip-bait rig with wire "safety pin" used for sailfishing in Florida 50 years ago—and still being used today.

(PHOTOS BY ROMER GREY)

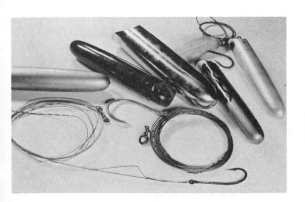

On a trip to Mexican waters in 1929, the "poopdeck gang" pose together for an album shot. From left to right: George Thomas III; D. Scott Chisholm; George Thomas, Jr.; and George Farnsworth.

Farnsworth oiling the log.

Here he gaffs a *cabrilla* in the lower jaw for easy, harmless release.

While the Thomases were in Mexico with Farnsworth, L.P. Streeter, one of the founders of the Aransas Tarpon Club, was keeping up with his duties as a Tuna Club member by taking this 140-pound striped marlin on regulation light tackle off Catalina.

George H. Clark was founder of the Southern California Tuna Club in 1925, but also joined the Catalina Tuna Club in 1930, the year he caught this 166-pound striped marlin. This photo is inscribed to Harlan Major: "Taken on your 'Majormade' rod—Worked like a charm. Best regards, Georgie."

A leaping striped marlin with a remora clinging to its side.
(PHOTO BY AL TETZLAFF)

Zane Grey wandered the Pacific in search of still larger gamefish. He found some of them in New Zealand during his first trip there in 1926. Here he's hooked to a big marlin, with one already aboard strapped in the bow.

He finally found his pot of gold at the end of the rainbow in Tahiti in 1930, where he caught this 1,040-pound blue marlin. Since sharks mutilated the tail at boatside, this record was later disqualified by the International Game Fish Association when the group was created in 1939—the year of ZG's death. However, the achievement of this first 1,000-pound fish can be measured by the fact that another one was not taken again on rod and reel until 1952.

Meanwhile, back at Catalina, following the death of William Boschen, George Farnsworth adopted the George Thomases as his new patrons. Here is Farnsworth at the helm of *Aerial*, with George C. Thomas III manning the tackle.

At the height of the 24-thread versus 39-thread controversy in 1927, George C. Thomas III used the lighter (regulation Tuna Club) line to take this 573-pound broadbill swordfish. Still the West Coast record, the fish was hooked in the corner of the mouth and fought for precisely five hours, five minutes. George Farnsworth was the guide, and a live mackerel was the bait.

The first line manufacturer to specialize in twisted linen for surf casting was Captain Lester Crandall who started supplying the striped bass clubs of New England with Ashaway-brand lines as early as 1842.

A 1948 photo showing three generations of Ashaway's leadership: A.J. Crandall (left) was born in 1864 and managed the company until 1951 when his son Julian (middle) took over. Bob Crandall (right) was to have picked up the reins when Julian retired, but tragically he died in February 1970.

By the 1930s, casting tournaments were all the rage as men—and women—reached for 500 and then 600 feet in their record heaves. Competition was particularly keen between East and West Coast teams, and on at least one occasion, a tournament was held between rival Atlantic and Pacific clubs using the telegraph to pass the results of each cast back and forth across the continent.

(PHOTOS BY HARLAN MAJOR)

However, the 1930s also saw the development of a good many top-notch surfmen with little interest in competition casting. Here's Ollie Rodman on the beach at Wellfleet, Cape Cod, early in the decade. (Note the stubby-style rod.)

Here is Ollie later on with a fine
catch of Cuttyhunk stripers.

Another outstanding thirties-reared surf fisherman is Vlad
Evanoff shown here on a Rockaway, Long Island, jetty about
1955, and later on the beach at Cape Hatteras with the 52-
pound channel bass he caught on special assignment for
the now defunct *Life* magazine.

Otto J. Scheer (pictured here in 1933) was still another great surf fishing pioneer. However, his pioneering was done from a boat specially built for the shallow waters and rocky outcroppings around Montauk Point, Long Island.

(PHOTO BY HARLAN MAJOR)

New Englanders like to believe they were the first to utilize motor vehicles to patrol the beaches for feeding bass. But these Texans of the 1920s obviously knew a beach buggy when they saw one—only difference is their surf bass are of the spotted (channel) variety, not stripers.

Following World War II, an army of veterans took to the beaches to try their hands at surf fishing. One of the most successful was a young fellow by the name of Frank Woolner, shown here with his first "Lucky 13" beach buggy and a 49-pound striper taken from the surf at North Truro, Massachusetts, in 1947.

By the 1950s many beach buggies were equipped with outboards up front and an aluminum boat on top so that the surf fisherman could "reach" just a little further offshore on calm days. Here Frank Woolner (left) and Hal Lyman (right), editor and publisher respectively of *Salt Water Sportsman*, stand amid an assortment of tackle.

One sport fishing community to weather nearly a century of change is Port Aransas, Texas, shown here in the late twenties. The Coast Guard station stands to left; the Tarpon Inn is the long two-tiered structure with balconies looking over the cluster of small white buildings at right.

At one time the principal game fish of the Aransas area were tarpon like this 5½-footer caught by photographer F.A. Gildersleeve of Waco on August 22, 1925.

Don Farley started taking out parties when the third Tarpon Inn opened in 1925. In 1937, he was guide for President Roosevelt—a somewhat disillusioning experience described in Chapter 15.

(PHOTO BY GEORGE REIGER)

Inside the Inn are numerous mementoes of past glories such as these souvenir tarpon scales signed and dated by various members of the Roosevelt party. FDR's fish weighed 77 pounds and is documented at far left.

(PHOTO BY GEORGE REIGER)

Other mementoes include a picture of one of the previous Tarpon Inns showing the cupola from which non-angling guests watched fishing activity offshore. A baby tarpon is mounted above, and an aerial photograph of the inlet is framed below.

(PHOTO BY GEORGE REIGER)

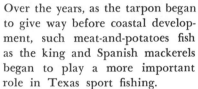

Over the years, as the tarpon began to give way before coastal development, such meat-and-potatoes fish as the king and Spanish mackerels began to play a more important role in Texas sport fishing.

Harlan Major (with pipe and knickers) was still a newcomer to Atlantic Coast fishing when he took this 8-foot 3½-inch record sailfish on a kite-trolled bait and 3/6 tackle. Captain Howard Lance at left.

(PHOTO BY HARLAN MAJOR)

When British angler L. Mitchell-Henry (left) developed a "gear-shift" type brake system for big-game reels, he came to New York in 1932 with the hope that he could develop an American market for his patent. Though unsuccessful in this endeavor, Mitchell-Henry met Harlan Major, and the two men learned much from one another about differing techniques and tackle in the Pacific and on both sides of the Atlantic.

(PHOTO BY HARLAN MAJOR)

In 1934, Englishman W.E.S. Tuker (left, with a 509-pounder) and New Englander George Garey (right, with a 488-pounder) began to take numerous large broadbill swordfish off the coast of Chile where the two men worked for a nitrate company. By the end of 1936, the two men had caught the five largest broadbill ever taken on rod and reel including Garey's 842-pound world record.

Tuker hosted Harlan Major in 1935 in Tocopilla where he took this 674½-pound broadbill.

(PHOTO BY HARLAN MAJOR)

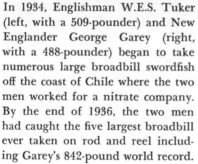

In 1937, Harlan Major flew across the Pacific to publicize the fishing possibilities of the various islands visited by Pan American Airways. He fulfilled his promise that he would take marlin off Guam with this 112-pounder caught on May 10. George Scharf, the owner of the boat he used, stands to the right of the fish.

(PHOTO BY HARLAN MAJOR)

The chief value of Harlan Major's successful campaign to persuade the Long Island Railroad to establish a "Fisherman's Special" express run directly to Montauk Point, New York, was to extend the possibilities of countless city-based sea anglers. The first mobs of fishermen arrived in 1933 to use the sometimes makeshift excursion boats provided for them.

(PHOTOS BY HARLAN MAJOR)

Captain Bill Fagen weighs in a Long Island broadbill. Many prominent guides learned their craft while fishing summers at Montauk.

(PHOTO BY HARLAN MAJOR)

Tommy Gifford on August 25, 1929, with a 300-pound Montauk-caught broadbill brought in by William A. Bonnell.

Captain Charles Thompson—one of the early explorers of Bimini and a man who indirectly led to Ernest Hemingway's own interest in the island—with a tuna at Montauk.

(PHOTO BY HARLAN MAJOR)

Harlan Major (at left) admires a 505-pound broadbill (at that time, the Atlantic sport fishing record) brought in by A. Rex Flinn and Captain Bill Hatch (with bowtie and gaff) in 1932. The Montauk Yacht Clubhouse is in the background.

A sequence of shots showing Captain Bill Fagen swinging a 360-pounder inboard with a davit and then later at the Montauk dock with proud angler Charles L. Lehmann. The date: June 26, 1932. An important pioneer, Lehmann contributed the chapter on "Swordfish" for Eugene V. Connett's *American Big Game Fishing*.

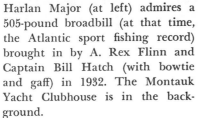

Like most chartermen, Tommy Gifford felt that any fish caught aboard
his boat was *his* fish as much as the
angler's. However, while most guides
go along with the game of pretend-
ing that the fisherman did it all
himself, Tommy made enemies by
frequently talking about the fish
and posing with it to the exclusion
of the angler. Both shots circa 1930.

One of the most important patrons
Gifford ever had was Michael
Lerner, here shown with Tommy
and mate Larry Bagby off Cape
Breton, fighting and landing a
broadbill swordfish from a dory.
(PHOTOS BY HEDLEY DOTY)

One of Gifford's most important contributions to saltwater angling was his development of the outrigger in the early thirties. Here's his *Lady Grace* alongside a 478-pound blue marlin caught by Michael Lerner at Bimini. Note the cumbersome proto-type outriggers and the outlandish flag advertising the catch.

Gifford's favorite fishing boat: the 26-foot *Stormy Petrel*. Note the abbreviated outriggers and, just behind the flying bridge controls, the A-frame with search-light which Tommy insisted was far superior to a gin pole for landing large fish.

Gifford's last boat was the *Caribe Maid*, here shown with Tommy at the helm running into San Juan, Puerto Rico.

In May 1935, Ernest Hemingway became the first angler to bring an unmutilated tuna in to Bimini. The fish weighed 310 pounds and capped three seasons of effort by other fishermen. All other tuna had been hit by sharks before they were boated.

Hemingway met the Lerners on a Bimini trip and became one of their closest friends. Here he congratulates Helen Lerner on a blue marlin catch.

H.L. Woodward was Cuba's great pioneer big-game angler. He took this 372-pound blue marlin off Havana in just 30 minutes on September 1, 1940. However, after three seasons, Ernest Hemingway had surpassed all the older man's angling achievements.

Ernest Hemingway's home at Key
West, Florida, which he used as a
basecamp for angling expeditions
to Cuba and the Bahamas. This
1930s photograph shows the house
before Hemingway added a swimming pool and second-story walk-
way connecting the main building
with the smaller one (his work-
room/study) behind.

(COURTESY LIBRARY OF CONGRESS)

Today a tour of Hemingway's Key
West home reveals such unauthentic
items as a mounted baby tarpon
and a saltwater fly reel which better
reflects contemporary angling taste
than Hemingway habit.

(PHOTO BY DON ZAHNER)

The dean of big-game anglers is Michael Lerner, shown here testing the drag on a reel during a run to the swordfish grounds off Louisburg, Nova Scotia.

While guides Bill Hatch and Eddie Wall prepare the mackerel baits, Lerner sits tense with anticipation during the run offshore.

All the time and preparation bear fruit when the broadbill is finally gaffed and hauled inboard.

This is the fish that initiated Michael Lerner's important relationship with the American Museum of Natural History. Caught off Bimini and mounted by Al Pflueger, Lerner's blue marlin is shown in its original location in the museum in 1934.

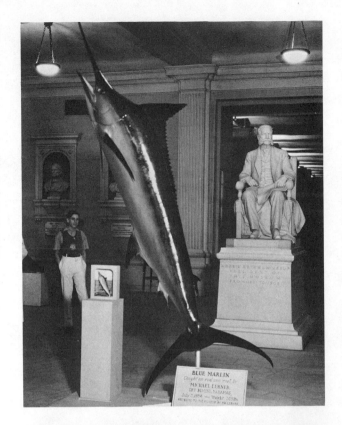

Mike visits a Museum office in 1938 to plan his expedition to Australia and New Zealand with Harry C. Raven (left) and Dr. William King Gregory (center), chairman of the Department of Fishes.

The Lerners fished many of the areas made famous by Zane Grey. Bill Hatch looks on proprietarily (extreme left) while a New Zealand crew boats a striped marlin for Helen Lerner off Mayor Island.

The Lerners' visit to Australia resulted in many fine mounts for the museum, as well as a meeting with Clive Firth (between Dr. Gregory and Mike Lerner) which led to the founding of the International Game Fish Association.

Lerner's quest for giant broadbill took him to Tocopilla, Chile, where unbelievable concentrations of bait attracted birds and predator fishes on a scale rarely seen today in the hard-fished waters of the Pacific.

Native Chileans harpooned some of the broadbill found off the coast, but they barely made a dent in the billfish population with such limited equipment by today's long-line and hunter-aircraft standards.

In the years since Harlan Major had visited with the Tocopilla angling team of W.E.S. Tuker and George Garey, the two men had continued to take large broadbill with their "reels under" tackle. At left (top), Garey working on a 844-pounder which became the world's record before Tuker took it back again. And (bottom), Tuker heads home in the *Copihuie* (named for Chile's national flower) after a successful swordfish outing.

From practically the first day they tried angling off Tocopilla in 1940, the Lerners, too, had action on broadbill.

In a warehouse at Tocopilla, Douglas Osborn, photographer David Douglas Duncan, and Bill Hatch make plaster casts of an especially large broadbill while a crowd of Chileans look on.

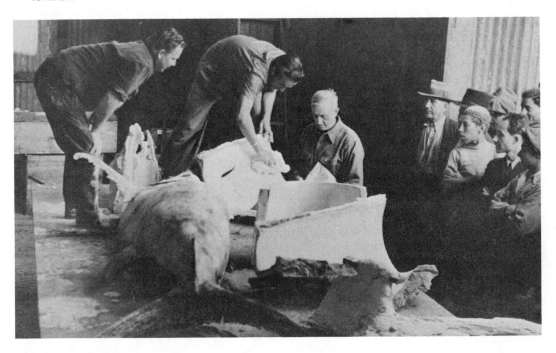

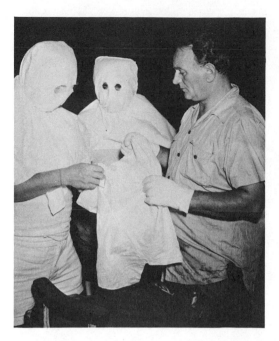

While the Lerners were in Talara, Peru, Mike participated in probably the most unusual fishing any saltwater angler has ever done. Outfitting himself and his crew with pillowcases to protect their faces from jets of ink, they proceeded to do battle with giant squid.

Frequently as they tried to boat one squid, a larger one would attack it, and the men ended up landing two for one.

Douglas Osborn and Michael Lerner unveil after a successful bout with one of the big squid.

Back in Talara, Mike supervises Hatch and Osborn in preparing the head and tentacles of a large squid for a plaster mold for eventual shipment to the American Museum of Natural History.

Not all the Lerners' time in South America was spent big-game fishing. There were also days for beach walking (above), helping Francesca LaMonte identify a string of inshore fishes, and (left) a side trip to the Incan ruins of Machu Picchu.

Following the war, Lerner devoted still more time and money to marine research when he turned over some of his Bimini property to the American Museum of Natural History for its use as a Caribbean field station. Shown above is an aerial view of the Lerners' home, The Anchorage, with docks and fish pens.

(PHOTO BY DADE W. THORNTON)

In 1937 the first Lerner marine laboratory was little more than a canvas tent.

Today, this is just one part of the expanded laboratory facilities.

When Mike officially donated the Lerner Marine Laboratory to the American Museum of Natural History on March 29, 1948, close friend and fellow angler, Philip Wylie, flew over from Florida to participate in the ceremony.

(PHOTO BY FREDDIE MAURA)

New big-game fishing grounds have developed in the past two decades, and among the most popular are the waters around Baja California Sur. A striped marlin takes well to the air when hooked on 6-pound test line!

(PHOTO BY AL TETZLAFF)

A striped marlin is brought alongside for tagging and release. Today more and more anglers are letting their fish go in preference to bringing them in for pictures.

(PHOTO BY AL TETZLAFF)

One of the reasons for the success of Baja's billfishery is the expanded use of live bait. Even boats that don't ordinarily have live wells find ways to carry the bait.

(PHOTO BY GEORGE REIGER)

Here Ray Cannon demonstrates one way to hook a live bait for Gil Kimball, manager of Camino Real's sport fishing fleet at the Cape.

(PHOTO BY GEORGE REIGER)

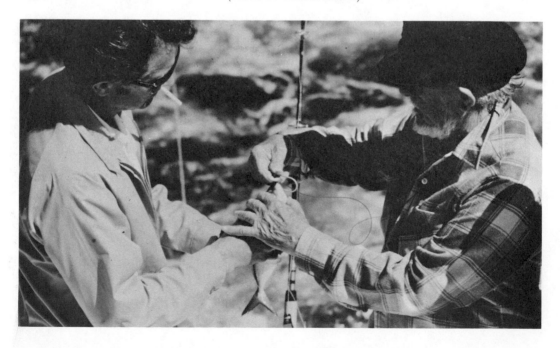

But even in paradise, there are intrusions. When tuna start moving up the coast, the purse seiners move into the Cape, and sport fishing just isn't what it was the day before.

(PHOTO BY GEORGE REIGER)

Sometimes there's revenge. Here's the wreck of the Japanese longliner lured ashore by local fishermen described in Ray Cannon's chapter. Note the Mexicans fishing off the stern where once Japanese fished for Mexican fish.

(PHOTO BY GEORGE REIGER)

Meanwhile, up the Pacific coast in California, Oregon and Washington states, saltwater sport fishing is finding thousands of new adherents yearly. Here a fleet heads out of an Oregon port for a day of salmon fishing.

(PHOTO BY DON HOLM)

When a fog closes down on the salmon fleet off San Francisco, the mood of the fishermen becomes thoughtful as well as patient. However, big fish are never far off, and mere minutes after the photo was taken, the man standing by his equipment had this 22-pound king to show for his vigilance.

(PHOTOS BY GEORGE REIGER)

But albacore fishing is the big news in the Pacific these days—especially off the coast of Oregon where Don Holm has just landed one caught on the traditional Japanese feather lure. Though long known to Pacific sportsmen, the Japanese feather didn't come East until 1926 when John Philip Sousa, Jr. (son of the famous bandmaster) sent a box of them from the Orient to Oliver C. Grinnell for use in his tuna fishing at Montauk.

(PHOTO BY DON HOLM)

While new grounds and an expanding interest in light tackle is the current trend of Pacific angling, a revived interest in fly tackle modified for saltwater use is the passion of many Atlantic coast fishermen. Frank Woolner in New England (above) proves that the fly rod can be an effective tool to take schoolie-sized stripers along the shore, while Lefty Kreh in Florida (below) casting equally well from the right or left hand, concentrates on permit, bonefish, and tarpon.

(PHOTOS BELOW BY GEORGE REIGER)

Who would have guessed that this innocent young eel angler would one day grow up to be the country's best-known bridge fisherman, and its leading manufacturer of artificial eels.

Here is an older Al Reinfelder with partner, Lou Palma, and a haul of midnight stripers.

From bridge or boat, Reinfelder was one of the country's most accomplished striped bass anglers.

APPENDIX A

The outing Frank Forester referred to was documented in the New York *Commercial Advertiser* of July 6, 1827. The fact that the catch was considered newsworthy enough to report and unusual enough for Forester to comment on suggests that such a huge bag was exceptional. However, even half this number of fish over a similar time span multiplied by countless anglers off and on during the season represents a considerable dent in the local king whiting population:

Great Fishing

On Friday last, a gentleman of this city went out from Rockaway, into Jamaica Bay, with his son, a lad of twelve years of age. They commenced fishing at half past seven in the morning, spent half an hour in dining at noon, and quit fishing at half past one; having taken with their rods in the six hours, *four hundred and seventy-two* king-fish. Their guide was Joseph Bannister. None of these fish were taken by him, as he was diligently employed during the whole time in preparing bait. That it may not be said that this was a wanton waste of one of the finest kinds of fish produced in our waters, it is deemed right to add, that a large number of families in the neighborhood were supplied gratuitously with them, and none of this lot of noble fish were wasted.

Mr. Bannister will be found on inquiry at Mrs. Phebe Hicks' boarding house, where the parties were staying. This house is most cheerfully recommended for its delightful situation, great cleanliness, excellent fare and kind and obliging family, as well as for the highly respectable company usually frequenting it.

Mr. Bannister provides a boat and bait, and is the oarsman for the day. His charge is $1.25.

[455]

APPENDIX B

Probably our first record of a bluefish "cycle" goes back to 1794, when Zaccheus Macy published in the Collections of the Massachusetts Historical Society his "Short Journal of the First Settlement of the Island of Nantucket, With Some of the Most Remarkable Things That Had Happened Since, to the Present Time."

Macy describes a pestilence that swept the island's Indian population in 1763, and then adds:

Before this period, and from the first coming of the English to Nantucket, a large fat fish called the Bluefish, thirty of which would fill a barrel, was caught in great plenty all around the island, from the first of the sixth month to the middle of the ninth month. But it is remarkable, that in the year 1764, the very year in which the sickness ended, they all disappeared and that none have ever been taken since. This has been a great loss to us.

One of the earliest references to weakfish "cycles" is a Captain Atwood's testimony before the Rhode Island Legislature in 1871:

In the days of my boyhood, my neighbors often spoke of a fish called "the drummer," which is the same variety that you call the Squeteague, which were so plentiful that they could be taken by the boat-load. But in 1816, when I first went into a fishing boat, they had disappeared, and I did not see a single specimen for many years. Since that time, however, they have commenced returning in considerable numbers.

Squeteague or weakfish are just making another comeback after a similar slump during the 1960's. The reason for these ebbs and flows of certain fish populations is still not understood by marine biologists. Everything from changing water temperatures to the possibility of epizootics has been investigated, but there is still no satisfactory answer.

[456]

BIBLIOGRAPHY

Adams, Leon D. *Striped Bass Fishing in California and Oregon*. Palo Alto, Calif., 1953.

Aflalo, Frederick G. *Sea Fish*. London, 1868.

———— *Sea-Fishing on the English Coast*. London, 1891.

———— *Sunset Playgrounds*. London, 1909.

———— *The Sea and the Rod*. London, 1892.

Agassiz, Louis. "Address Delivered on the Centennial Anniversary of the Birth of Alexander von Humboldt." Boston, Boston Society of Natural History, 1869.

———— *An Essay on Classification*. London, 1859.

———— *Contributions to the Natural History of the United States of America*. Boston, 1857.

———— *Recherches sur Les Poissons Fossiles*. Paris, France, 1844.

Babcock, Louis L. *The Tarpon*. New York, 1936.

Baker, Carlos. *Ernest Hemingway: A Life Story*. New York, 1969.

Bandini, Ralph. *Men, Fish and Tackle*. Bronson, Mich., 1936.

———— *Veiled Horizons*. New York, 1939.

Bay, Kenneth E. *Salt Water Flies*. New York, 1972.

Bayless, Kenneth M. *Low Bridge*. New York, 1950.

Berners, Dame Juliana. *Treatyse of Fysshynge wyth an Angle*. n.p., 1496.

Bickerdyke, John. *Angling in Salt-Water*. London, 1887.

———— *Practical Letters to Sea Fishers*, Second Edition (revised). London, 1902.

Boyle, Robert H. *The Hudson River—a natural and unnatural history*. New York, 1969.

Breder, Charles M., Jr., *Field Book of Marine Fishes of the Atlantic Coast*. New York, 1929.

Brookes, Richard. *Art of Angling: Rock and Sea Fishing*. London, 1801.

Brooks, Joe. *A World of Fishing*. New York, 1964.

———— *Bermuda Fishing*. Harrisburg, Pa., 1957.

———— *Complete Book of Fly Fishing*. New York, 1958.

———— *Salt Water Game Fishing*. New York, 1968.

Brown, John J. *The American Angler's Guide*. New York, 1849.

Bruette, William A., Editor. *Sportsmen's Encyclopedia*, Vols. I and II. New York, 1923.

Burnaby, Andrew. *Travels Through the Middle Settlements in North America, in the Years of 1759 and 1760, with Observations Upon the State of the Colonies*. London, 1775.

"Buzzacott," Francis H. *The Complete American and Canadian Sportsman's Encyclopedia of Valuable Instruction*, Revised Edition. Chicago, 1905.

Caine, Lou S. *Game Fish of the South*. New York, 1935.

————, Editor. *Salt Water Tackle Digest*. Chicago, 1947.

Camp, Raymond R. *Fishing the Surf*. Boston, 1950.

Camp, Samuel G. *Fishing Kits and Equipment*. New York, 1913.

Cannon, Raymond. *How to Fish the Pacific Coast*. Menlo Park, Calif., 1953.

———— *The Sea of Cortez*. Menlo Park, Calif., 1966.

Church, Albert Cook. *American Fishermen*. New York, 1940.

Churchill, E. G. S.- *Tarpon Fishing in Mexico and Florida*. London, 1907.

Clark, John. *Fish & Man*. Highlands, New Jersey, 1967.

Connett, Eugene V., Editor. *American Big Game Fishing*. London, 1935.

Cooper, Eric. *Sea Fishing from Bass to Tunny*. London, 1937.

Cooper, Lane. *Louis Agassiz as a Teacher*. Ithaca, N. Y., 1945.

Dahne, Robert A. *Salt-Water Fishing*. New York, 1950.

Davis, J. Charles II. *California Salt Water Fishing*. New York, 1949.

———— *Salt Water Fishing on the Pacific Coast*. New York, 1964.

DeKay, James Ellsworth. *Zoology of New York, or the New-York Fauna*. New York, 1842.

Dimock, A. W. *The Book of the Tarpon*. New York, 1911.

Elliott, William. *Carolina Sports By Land and Water, Including Incidents of Devil-Fishing &c*. Charleston, S. C., 1846.

Endicott, Wendell. *Adventures with Rod and Harpoon Along the Florida Keys*. New York, 1925.

Evanoff, Vlad. *1001 Fishing Tips and Tricks*. New York, 1970.

———— *Another 1001 Fishing Tips and Tricks*. New York, 1970.

———— *Fishing Secrets of the Experts*. New York, 1962.

———— *Natural Baits for Fishermen*. New York, 1952.

———— *Natural Salt Water Fishing Baits*. New York, 1953.

———— *Surf Fishing*. New York, 1948.

Farrington, Chisie. *Women Can Fish*. New York, 1951.

Farrington, S. Kip, Jr. *A Book of Fishes*. Philadelphia, 1946.

———— *Atlantic Game Fishing*. New York, 1937.

———— *Bill, The Broadbill Swordfish*. New York, 1942.

———— *Fishing the Atlantic Offshore and On*. New York, 1949.

———— *Fishing the Pacific Offshore and On*. New York, 1953.

—————— *Fishing with Hemingway and Glassell*. New York, 1971.

—————— *Pacific Game Fishing*. New York, 1942.

—————— *Sport Fishing Boats*. New York, 1949.

Foree, Aylesa. *Louis Agassiz; Pied Piper of Science*. New York, 1958.

Francis, Phil. *Florida Fish and Fishing*. New York, 1955.

Gabrielson, Ira N., and Francesca LaMonte. *The New Fisherman's Encyclopedia*. Harrisburg, Pa., 1950.

Gaddis, R. V. "Gadabout." *The Flying Fisherman*. New York, 1967.

Gifford, Tommy. *Anglers and Muscleheads*. New York, 1960.

Gingrich, Arnold. *The Well-Tempered Angler*. New York, 1966.

Goadby, Peter. *Big Fish and Blue Water*. New York, 1972.

Goode, George Brown. *American Fishes: A Popular Treatise upon the Game and Food Fishes of North America*. New York, 1888.

Goodspeed, Charles Eliot. *Angling in America, Its Early History and Literature*. Boston, 1939.

Goulding, F. R. *The Young Marooners on the Florida Coast*. New York, 1887.

Gregg, W. H. *Where, When and How to Catch Fish on the East Coast of Florida*. New York, 1902.

Grey, Romer Carl. *Adventures of a Deep-Sea Angler*. New York, 1930.

Grey, Zane. *An American Angler in Australia*. New York, 1937.

—————— *Tales of Fishes*. New York, 1919.

—————— *Tales of Fishing Virgin Seas*. New York, 1925.

—————— *Tales of Southern Rivers*. New York, 1924.

—————— *Tales of Swordfish and Tuna*. New York, 1927.

—————— *Tales of Tahitian Waters*. New York, 1931.

—————— *Tales of the Angler's Eldorado New Zealand*. New York, 1926.

Gruber, Frank. *Zane Grey: A Biography*. New York, 1969.

Gwathney, John H. *Fly-Fishing in the South*. Richmond, Va., 1942.

Hallock, Charles. *Camp Life in Florida: A Handbook for Sportsmen and Settlers*. New York, 1876.

—————— *The Fishing Tourist*. New York, 1873.

—————— *The Sportsman's Gazetteer and General Guide*. New York, 1878.

Harris, William C. *The Angler's Guide Book and Tourist's Gazetteer of the Fishing Waters of the United States and Canada*. New York, 1885.

—————— *The Fishes That Are Caught on Hook and Line*. New York, 1892.

Harris, William C. and Tarleton H. Bean. *The Basses, Fresh-water and Marine*. New York, 1905.

Hedges, F. A. Mitchell. *Battles with Giant Fish*. New York, 1928.

Heilner, Van Campen. *Adventures in Angling*. Cincinnati, Ohio, 1922.

[459]

———— *Beneath the Southern Cross.* Boston, 1930.

———— *Salt Water Fishing.* Philadelphia, 1937.

———— *Salt Water Fishing.* New York, 1953.

Heilner, Van Campen, and Frank Stick. *The Call of the Surf.* New York, 1920.

Hemingway, Ernest. *Islands in the Stream.* New York, 1970.

———— *The Old Man and the Sea.* New York, 1952.

Henshall, James A. *Bass, Pike, Perch and Other Game Fishes of America.* New York, 1903.

———— *Camping and Cruising in Florida.* Cincinnati, Ohio, 1884.

———— *Favorite Fish and Fishing.* New York, 1908.

———— *Notes on Fishes Collected in Florida in 1892.* Washington, D. C., 1895.

Herbert, Henry William. *Fishing with Hook and Line: A Manual for Amateur Anglers.* New York, n.d.

———— *Frank Forester's Fish and Fishing of the United States and British Provinces of North America.* London, 1849.

———— *Supplement to Frank Forester's Fish and Fishing of the United States and British Provinces of North America.* New York, 1850.

Holder, Charles Frederick. *All About Pasadena and Its Vicinity.* New York, 1889.

———— *Along the Florida Reef.* New York, 1892.

———— *An Isle of Summer.* n.p., 1901.

———— *Big Game at Sea.* London, 1908.

———— *Big Game Fishes of the United States.* New York, 1903.

———— *Life in the Open: Sport with Rod, Gun, Horse and Hound in Southern California.* New York, 1906.

———— *Louis Agassiz: His Life and Work.* New York, 1893.

———— *Recreations of a Sportsman on the Pacific Coast.* New York, 1910.

———— *Salt Water Game Fishing.* New York, 1914.

———— *The Boy Anglers.* New York, 1904.

———— *The Channel Islands of California.* Chicago, 1910.

———— *The Fishes of the Pacific Coast.* New York, 1912.

———— *The Game Fishes of the World.* New York, 1913.

———— *The Holders of Holderness.* Pasadena, Calif., 1902.

———— *The Log of a Sea Angler.* Boston, 1906.

Holder, Charles Frederick, and J. B. Holder. *Elements of Zoology.* New York, 1884.

Holder, Charles Frederick, and Dr. David Starr Jordan. *Fish Stories, Alleged and Experienced, with a Little History Natural and Unnatural.* New York, 1909.

Holm, Donald Raymond. *101 Best Fishing Trips in Oregon.* Caldwell, Idaho, 1970.

———— *Fishing the Pacific*. New York, 1972.

———— *Pacific North! Adventures in Sportfishing*. Caldwell, Idaho, 1969.

Hosaka, Edward Y. *Sport Fishing in Hawaii*. Honolulu, 1944.

Hudson, Frank. *Sea-Fishing For Amateurs*. London, 1887.

Hulit, Leonard. *In Fishing with a Boy: The Tale of a Rejuvenation*. Cincinnati, Ohio, 1921.

———— *The Salt Water Angler*. New York, 1924.

Hunt, William Southworth. *Frank Forester: A Tragedy in Exile*. Newark, N. J., 1933.

Ichthyosarus. *Hints and Wrinkles on Sea Fishing*. London, n.d.

Jansen, Jerry. *Successful Surf Fishing*. New York, 1959.

Jensen, Albert C. *The Cod*. New York, 1972.

Jordan, David Starr. *The Days of a Man*. Vols. I and II. Yonkers-on-Hudson, N. Y., 1922.

———— *A Guide to the Study of Fishes*, Vols. I and II. New York, 1905.

———— *Science Sketches*. Chicago, 1887.

Jordan, David Starr, and Barton Warren Evermann. *American Food & Game Fishes*. New York, 1902.

Kaplan, Moise N. *Big Game Anglers' Paradise*. New York, 1937.

Kilbourne, S. A. and George Brown Goode. *Game Fishes of the United States*. New York, 1878.

Kipling, Rudyard. *"Captains Courageous," a Story of the Grand Banks*. New York, 1897.

————*From Sea to Sea, and Other Sketches*. Vol. I and II. London, 1914.

Koller, Larry. *The Complete Book of Salt Water Fishing*. New York, 1954.

Kreh, Lefty, and Mark Sosin. *Practical Fishing Knots*. New York, 1972.

Kushin, Nathan. *Florida Fishing and Other Stories*. New York, 1952.

LaMonte, Francesca. *Marine Game Fishes of the World*. New York, 1952.

———— *North American Game Fishes*. New York, 1946.

Lankford, John, Editor. *Captain John Smith's America. Selections from His Writings*. New York, 1967.

Low, Francis H. *Fishing Is for Me*. New York, 1963.

Lurie, Edward. *Louis Agassiz, A Life in Science*. Chicago, 1960.

Lyman, Henry. *Blue Fishing*. New York, 1955.

Lyman, Henry, and Frank Woolner. *Tackle Talk*. South Brunswick, N. J., 1971.

———— *The Complete Book of Striped Bass Fishing*. New York, 1954.

———— *The Complete Book of Weakfishing*. New York, 1959.

Lyons, Nick, Editor. *Fisherman's Bounty*. New York, 1970.

McClane, A. J., Editor. *McClane's Standard Fishing Encyclopedia.* New York, 1965.

———— *Spinning for Fresh and Salt Water Fish of North America.* New York, 1952.

McDonald, John Dennis. *The Complete Fly Fisherman, The Notes and Letters of Theodore Gordon.* New York, 1947.

———— *The Origins of Angling.* Garden City, N. Y., 1963.

Macrate, Arthur N., Jr. *History of the Tuna Club.* Catalina, Calif., 1948.

Major, Harlan. *Basic Fishing.* New York, 1947.

———— *Fishing Behind the Eight Ball.* Harrisburg, Pa., 1952.

———— *Norwegian Holiday.* New York, 1950.

———— *Salt Water Fishing Tackle.* New York, 1939.

———— *Sure You Can Fish.* New York, 1942.

Marron, Eugenie. *Albacora.* New York, 1957.

Mather, Fred. *Men I Have Fished With.* New York, 1897.

———— *My Angling Friends.* New York, 1901.

Miller, Stewart. *Fishing in and Around the Bahamas.* Miami, Fla., 1938.

———— *Florida Fishing.* New York, 1931.

Mitchell-Henry, L. *Tunny Fishing—At Home and Abroad.* London, 1934.

Montgomery, Constance Coppel. *Hemingway in Michigan.* New York, 1966.

Moss, Frank. *Successful Ocean Game Fishing.* Camden, Maine, 1971.

Muller, J. W., and Arthur Knowlson. *Fishing Around New York.* New York, 1909.

Mundus, Capt. Frank, and Bill Wisner. *Sportfishing For Sharks.* New York, 1971.

Norris, Thaddeus. *The American Angler's Book*, Memorial Edition. Philadelphia, 1877.

Peare, Catherine Owens. *A Scientist of Two Worlds.* Philadelphia, 1958.

Pearson, Anthony. *Successful Shore Fishing.* London, 1967.

Perlmutter, Alfred. *Guide to Marine Fishes.* New York, 1961.

Pinchot, Gifford. *Just Fishing Talk.* Milford, Pa., 1936.

Pollard, Jack, Editor. *Australian and New Zealand Fishing.* Sydney, 1969.

Pond, Frederick Eugene, Editor. *Life and Adventures of "Ned Buntline" (pseud.) with Ned Buntline's Anecdote of Frank Forester (pseud.)* New York, 1919.

Reiger, George, Editor. *Zane Grey: Outdoorsman.* Englewood Cliffs, N. J., 1972.

[462]

Reiger, John F., Editor. *The Passing of the Great West, Selected Papers of George Bird Grinnell*. New York, 1972.

Reinfelder, Al. *Bait Tail Fishing*. New York, 1969.

Rhead, Louis. *The Book of Fish and Fishing*. New York, 1920.

Rodman, Oliver H. P. *A Handbook of Salt-Water Fishing*. New York, 1940.

———— *Saltwater Fisherman's Favorite Four*. New York, 1948.

———— *Striped Bass, Where, When and How to Catch Them*. New York, 1944.

Rodman, Oliver H. P., and Edward C. Janes. *The Boy's Complete Book of Fresh and Salt Water Fishing*. Boston, 1949.

Roman, Erl. *Fishing for Fun in Salty Waters*. Philadelphia, 1940.

Roosevelt, Robert Barnwell. *Game Fish of the Northern States of America and British Provinces*. New York, 1862.

———— *Superior Fishing*. New York, 1865.

Sand, George X. *Salt-Water Fly Fishing*. New York, 1970.

Scharff, Robert. *Standard Handbook of Salt-Water Fishing*. New York, 1966.

Scott, Genio C. *Fishing in American Waters*. New York, 1869.

Shapiro, Sidney, Editor. *Our Changing Fisheries*. Washington, D. C., 1971.

Shields, George O., Editor. *American Game Fishes: Their Habits, Habitat, and Peculiarities: How, When, and Where to Angle for Them*. Chicago and New York, 1892.

Smith, Jerome V. C. *Natural History of the Fishes of Massachusetts*. Boston, 1833.

Smith, John. *Description of New England*. London, 1616.

Sosin, Mark, and John Clark. *Through the Fish's Eye*. New York, 1973.

Spangler, A. M. *"Near By" Fresh and Salt Water Fishing*. Philadelphia, 1889.

Stilwell, Hart. *Fishing in Mexico*. New York, 1948.

———— *Hunting and Fishing in Texas*. New York, 1946.

Sylvester, Jerry. *Salt Water Fishing Is Easy*. Harrisburg, Pa., 1956.

Teller, James David. *Louis Agassiz, Scientist and Teacher*. Columbus, Ohio, 1947.

Thomas, George C., Jr., and George C. Thomas III. *Game Fish of the Pacific, Southern California and Mexico*. Philadelphia, 1930.

Thompson, Leslie P. *Fishing in New England*. London, 1955.

Turner-Turner, J. *The Giant Fish of Florida*. London, 1902.

Ulrich, Heinz. *America's Best Bay, Surf, and Shoreline Fishing*. New York, 1960.

———— *America's Best Deep-Sea Fishing*. New York, 1963.

———— *How the Experts Catch Trophy Fish*. Cranbury, N. J., 1969.

[463]

Vesey-Fitzgerald, Brian, and Francesca LaMonte. *Game Fish of the World*. London, 1949.

Walton, Izaak. *The Compleat Angler, or the Contemplative Man's Recreation*, Fifth Edition. London, 1676.

Ward, Rowland. *The English Angler in Florida*. London, 1898.

Waterman, Charles F. *Modern Fresh and Salt Water Fly Fishing*. New York, 1972.

Watson, Hy S., and Captain Paul A. Curtis, Jr., Editors. *The Outdoorsman's Handbook*, Sixth Edition. Cincinnati, Ohio, 1920.

Wells, A. Laurence. *The Observer's Book of Sea Fishes*. London, 1959.

Westman, Dr. James R. *A Biological Survey of the Salt Waters of Long Island*. Albany N. Y., 1938.

White, Luke Mathews. *Henry William Herbert and the American Publishing Scene*. Newark, N. J., 1943.

Whitehead, Charles E. *The Camp-Fires of the Everglades, or Wild Sports in the South*. Edinburgh, 1891.

Wilcocks, J. C. *The Sea-Fisherman, or Fishing Pilotage*. Guernsey, Great Britain, 1865.

"Wildfowler." *Shooting Adventures, Canine Lore, and Sea-Fishing Trips*, Vols. I and II. London, 1879.

Wisner, Bill. *How to Catch Salt Water Fish*. New York, 1955.

Woolner, Frank. *Modern Salt-Water Sport Fishing*. New York, 1972.

Wylie, Philip. *Crunch and Des: Stories of Florida Fishing*. New York, 1948.

———— *Denizens of the Deep, True Tales of Deep-Sea Fishing*. New York, 1953.

———— *Fish and Tin Fish*. New York, 1944.

———— *Salt Water Daffy*. New York, 1941.

———— *The Best of Crunch and Des*. New York, 1954.

———— *The Big Ones Get Away!* New York, 1954.

———— *Treasure Cruise, and Other Crunch and Des Stories*. New York, 1956.

Yale, Leroy M., and others. *The Out-Of-Door Library: Angling*. New York, 1897.

INDEX

ABOUT THE AUTHOR

Saltwater angling editor for *Field & Stream* and Washington (D.C.) editor for *National Wildlife* and *International Wildlife* magazines, George Reiger has fished throughout North and Central Americas, Europe, and the Pacific Islands as far west as the Fijis. Born in New York City, Mr. Reiger graduated with honors from the Lawrenceville School and Princeton University. He studied law at the University of Virginia, took a master's degree at Columbia, and taught English literature at the U.S. Naval Academy. He served as a Naval Lieutenant in the Vietnam War, receiving the Navy Commendation Medal, Purple Heart, and the Vietnamese Armed Forces Medal of Honor, among other decorations. He also worked as a project team leader with the RAND Corporation and served as an interpreter/translator at the Paris Peace Talks.

Mr. Reiger combines his interests in political and natural history through regular contributions to popular and professional journals in both fields. His first love, however, is outdoor and conservation history, and he was the editor of the highly successful *Zane Grey: Outdoorsman*.